M000087198

Pandas 1.x Cookbook

Second Edition

Practical recipes for scientific computing, time series analysis, and exploratory data analysis using Python

Matt Harrison
Theodore Petrou

BIRMINGHAM - MUMBAI

Pandas 1.x Cookbook
Second Edition

Copyright © 2020 Packt Publishing

All rights reserved. No part of this book may be reproduced, stored in a retrieval system, or transmitted in any form or by any means, without the prior written permission of the publisher, except in the case of brief quotations embedded in critical articles or reviews.

Every effort has been made in the preparation of this book to ensure the accuracy of the information presented. However, the information contained in this book is sold without warranty, either express or implied. Neither the authors, nor Packt Publishing or its dealers and distributors, will be held liable for any damages caused or alleged to have been caused directly or indirectly by this book.

Packt Publishing has endeavored to provide trademark information about all of the companies and products mentioned in this book by the appropriate use of capitals. However, Packt Publishing cannot guarantee the accuracy of this information.

Producer: Tushar Gupta
Acquisition Editor – Peer Reviews: Suresh Jain
Content Development Editor: Kate Blackham
Technical Editor: Gaurav Gavas
Project Editor: Kishor Rit
Proofreader: Safis Editing
Indexer: Pratik Shirodkar
Presentation Designer: Sandip Tadge

First published: October 2017
Second edition: February 2020

Production reference: 1260220

Published by Packt Publishing Ltd.
Livery Place
35 Livery Street
Birmingham B3 2PB, UK.

ISBN 978-1-83921-310-6

www.packt.com

`Packt.com`

Subscribe to our online digital library for full access to over 7,000 books and videos, as well as industry leading tools to help you plan your personal development and advance your career. For more information, please visit our website.

Why subscribe?

- ▶ Spend less time learning and more time coding with practical eBooks and Videos from over 4,000 industry professionals
- ▶ Learn better with Skill Plans built especially for you
- ▶ Get a free eBook or video every month
- ▶ Fully searchable for easy access to vital information
- ▶ Copy and paste, print, and bookmark content

Did you know that Packt offers eBook versions of every book published, with PDF and ePub files available? You can upgrade to the eBook version at `www.Packt.com` and as a print book customer, you are entitled to a discount on the eBook copy. Get in touch with us at `customercare@packtpub.com` for more details.

At `www.Packt.com`, you can also read a collection of free technical articles, sign up for a range of free newsletters, and receive exclusive discounts and offers on Packt books and eBooks.

Contributors

About the authors

Matt Harrison has been using Python since 2000. He runs MetaSnake, which provides corporate training for Python and Data Science.

He is the author of *Machine Learning Pocket Reference*, the best-selling *Illustrated Guide to Python 3*, and *Learning the Pandas Library*, as well as other books.

Theodore Petrou is a data scientist and the founder of Dunder Data, a professional educational company focusing on exploratory data analysis. He is also the head of Houston Data Science, a meetup group with more than 2,000 members that has the primary goal of getting local data enthusiasts together in the same room to practice data science. Before founding Dunder Data, Ted was a data scientist at Schlumberger, a large oil services company, where he spent the vast majority of his time exploring data.

Some of his projects included using targeted sentiment analysis to discover the root cause of part failure from engineer text, developing customized client/server dashboarding applications, and real-time web services to avoid the mispricing of sales items. Ted received his masters degree in statistics from Rice University, and used his analytical skills to play poker professionally and teach math before becoming a data scientist. Ted is a strong supporter of learning through practice and can often be found answering questions about pandas on Stack Overflow.

About the reviewer

Simon Hawkins holds a master's degree in aeronautical engineering from Imperial College London. During the early part of his career, he worked exclusively in the defense and nuclear sectors as a technology analyst focusing on various modelling capabilities and simulation techniques for high-integrity equipment. He then transitioned into the world of e-commerce and the focus shifted toward data analysis. Today, he is interested in all things data science and is a member of the pandas core development team.

Table of Contents

Preface

pandas is a library for creating and manipulating structured data with Python. What do I mean by structured? I mean tabular data in rows and columns like what you would find in a spreadsheet or database. Data scientists, analysts, programmers, engineers, and more are leveraging it to mold their data.

pandas is limited to "small data" (data that can fit in memory on a single machine). However, the syntax and operations have been adopted or inspired other projects: PySpark, Dask, Modin, cuDF, Baloo, Dexplo, Tabel, StaticFrame, among others. These projects have different goals, but some of them will scale out to big data. So there is a value in understanding how pandas works as the features are becoming the defacto API for interacting with structured data.

I, Matt Harrison, run a company, MetaSnake, that does corporate training. My bread and butter is training large companies that want to level up on Python and data skills. As such, I've taught thousands of Python and pandas users over the years. My goal in producing the second version of this book is to highlight and help with the aspects that many find confusing when coming to pandas. For all of its benefits, there are some rough edges or confusing aspects of pandas. I intend to navigate you to these and then guide you through them, so you will be able to deal with them in the real world.

If your company is interested in such live training, feel free to reach out (`matt@metasnake.com`).

Who this book is for

This book contains nearly 100 recipes, ranging from very simple to advanced. All recipes strive to be written in clear, concise, and modern idiomatic pandas code. The *How it works...* sections contain extremely detailed descriptions of the intricacies of each step of the recipe. Often, in the *There's more...* section, you will get what may seem like an entirely new recipe. This book is densely packed with an extraordinary amount of pandas code.

As a generalization, the recipes in the first seven chapters tend to be simpler and more focused on the fundamental and essential operations of pandas than the later chapters, which focus on more advanced operations and are more project-driven. Due to the wide range of complexity, this book can be useful to both novice and everyday users alike. It has been my experience that even those who use pandas regularly will not master it without being exposed to idiomatic pandas code. This is somewhat fostered by the breadth that pandas offers. There are almost always multiple ways of completing the same operation, which can have users get the result they want but in a very inefficient manner. It is not uncommon to see an order of magnitude or more in performance difference between two sets of pandas solutions to the same problem.

The only real prerequisite for this book is a fundamental knowledge of Python. It is assumed that the reader is familiar with all the common built-in data containers in Python, such as lists, sets, dictionaries, and tuples.

What this book covers

Chapter 1, Pandas Foundations, covers the anatomy and vocabulary used to identify the components of the two main pandas data structures, the Series and the DataFrame. Each column must have exactly one type of data, and each of these data types is covered. You will learn how to unleash the power of the Series and the DataFrame by calling and chaining together their methods.

Chapter 2, Essential DataFrame Operations, focuses on the most crucial and typical operations that you will perform during data analysis.

Chapter 3, Creating and Persisting DataFrames, discusses the various ways to ingest data and create DataFrames.

Chapter 4, Beginning Data Analysis, helps you develop a routine to get started after reading in your data.

Chapter 5, Exploratory Data Analysis, covers basic analysis techniques for comparing numeric and categorical data. This chapter will also demonstrate common visualization techniques.

Chapter 6, Selecting Subsets of Data, covers the many varied and potentially confusing ways of selecting different subsets of data.

Chapter 7, Filtering Rows, covers the process of querying your data to select subsets of it based on Boolean conditions.

Chapter 8, Index Alignment, targets the very important and often misunderstood index object. Misuse of the Index is responsible for lots of erroneous results, and these recipes show you how to use it correctly to deliver powerful results.

Chapter 9, Grouping for Aggregation, Filtration, and Transformation, covers the powerful grouping capabilities that are almost always necessary during data analysis. You will build customized functions to apply to your groups.

Chapter 10, Restructuring Data into a Tidy Form, explains what tidy data is and why it's so important, and then it shows you how to transform many different forms of messy datasets into tidy ones.

Chapter 11, Combining Pandas Objects, covers the many available methods to combine DataFrames and Series vertically or horizontally. We will also do some web-scraping and connect to a SQL relational database.

Chapter 12, Time Series Analysis, covers advanced and powerful time series capabilities to dissect by any dimension of time possible.

Chapter 13, Visualization with Matplotlib, Pandas, and Seaborn, introduces the matplotlib library, which is responsible for all of the plotting in pandas. We will then shift focus to the pandas plot method and, finally, to the seaborn library, which is capable of producing aesthetically pleasing visualizations not directly available in pandas.

Chapter 14, Debugging and Testing Pandas, explores mechanisms of testing our DataFrames and pandas code. If you are planning on deploying pandas in production, this chapter will help you have confidence in your code.

To get the most out of this book

There are a couple of things you can do to get the most out of this book. First, and most importantly, you should download all the code, which is stored in Jupyter Notebooks. While reading through each recipe, run each step of code in the notebook. Make sure you explore on your own as you run through the code. Second, have the pandas official documentation open (`http://pandas.pydata.org/pandas-docs/stable/`) in one of your browser tabs. The pandas documentation is an excellent resource containing over 1,000 pages of material. There are examples for most of the pandas operations in the documentation, and they will often be directly linked from the *See also* section. While it covers the basics of most operations, it does so with trivial examples and fake data that don't reflect situations that you are likely to encounter when analyzing datasets from the real world.

What you need for this book

pandas is a third-party package for the Python programming language and, as of the printing of this book, is on version 1.0.1. Currently, Python is at version 3.8. The examples in this book should work fine in versions 3.6 and above.

There are a wide variety of ways in which you can install pandas and the rest of the libraries mentioned on your computer, but an easy method is to install the Anaconda distribution. Created by Anaconda, it packages together all the popular libraries for scientific computing in a single downloadable file available on Windows, macOS, and Linux. Visit the download page to get the Anaconda distribution (`https://www.anaconda.com/distribution`).

In addition to all the scientific computing libraries, the Anaconda distribution comes with Jupyter Notebook, which is a browser-based program for developing in Python, among many other languages. All of the recipes for this book were developed inside of a Jupyter Notebook and all of the individual notebooks for each chapter will be available for you to use.

It is possible to install all the necessary libraries for this book without the use of the Anaconda distribution. For those that are interested, visit the pandas installation page (`http://pandas.pydata.org/pandas-docs/stable/install.html`).

Download the example code files

You can download the example code files for this book from your account at `www.packt.com`. If you purchased this book elsewhere, you can visit `www.packtpub.com/support/errata` and register to have the files emailed directly to you.

You can download the code files by following these steps:

1. Log in or register at `www.packt.com`.
2. Select the **Support** tab.
3. Click on **Code Downloads**.
4. Enter the name of the book in the **Search** box and follow the on-screen instructions.

Once the file is downloaded, please make sure that you unzip or extract the folder using the latest version of:

- WinRAR / 7-Zip for Windows
- Zipeg / iZip / UnRarX for Mac
- 7-Zip / PeaZip for Linux

The code bundle for the book is also hosted on GitHub at `https://github.com/PacktPublishing/Pandas-Cookbook-Second-Edition`. In case there's an update to the code, it will be updated on the existing GitHub repository.

We also have other code bundles from our rich catalog of books and videos available at `https://github.com/PacktPublishing/`. Check them out!

Running a Jupyter Notebook

The suggested method to work through the content of this book is to have a Jupyter Notebook up and running so that you can run the code while reading through the recipes. Following along on your computer allows you to go off exploring on your own and gain a deeper understanding than by just reading the book alone.

Assuming that you have installed the Anaconda distribution on your machine, you have two options available to start the Jupyter Notebook, from the Anaconda GUI or the command line. I highly encourage you to use the command line. If you are going to be doing much with Python, you will need to feel comfortable from there.

After installing Anaconda, open a command prompt (type `cmd` at the search bar on Windows, or open a Terminal on Mac or Linux) and type:

```
$ jupyter-notebook
```

It is not necessary to run this command from your home directory. You can run it from any location, and the contents in the browser will reflect that location.

Although we have now started the Jupyter Notebook program, we haven't actually launched a single individual notebook where we can start developing in Python. To do so, you can click on the New button on the right-hand side of the page, which will drop down a list of all the possible kernels available for you to use. If you just downloaded Anaconda, then you will only have a single kernel available to you (Python 3). After selecting the Python 3 kernel, a new tab will open in the browser, where you can start writing Python code.

You can, of course, open previously created notebooks instead of beginning a new one. To do so, navigate through the filesystem provided in the Jupyter Notebook browser home page and select the notebook you want to open. All Jupyter Notebook files end in `.ipynb`.

Alternatively, you may use cloud providers for a notebook environment. Both Google and Microsoft provide free notebook environments that come preloaded with pandas.

Download the color images

We also provide a PDF file that has color images of the screenshots/diagrams used in this book. You can download it here: `https://static.packt-cdn.com/downloads/9781839213106_ColorImages.pdf`.

Conventions

There are a number of text conventions used throughout this book.

`CodeInText`: Indicates code words in text, database table names, folder names, filenames, file extensions, pathnames, dummy URLs, user input, and Twitter handles. Here is an example: "You may need to install `xlwt` or `openpyxl` to write XLS or XLSX files respectively."

A block of code is set as follows:

```
import pandas as pd
import numpy as np
movies = pd.read_csv("data/movie.csv")
movies
```

When we wish to draw your attention to a particular part of a code block, the relevant lines or items are set in bold:

```
import pandas as pd
import numpy as np
movies = pd.read_csv("data/movie.csv")
movies
```

Any command-line input or output is written as follows:

```
>>> employee = pd.read_csv('data/employee.csv')
>>> max_dept_salary = employee.groupby('DEPARTMENT')['BASE_SALARY'].max()
```

Bold: Indicates a new term, an important word, or words that you see on the screen, for example, in menus or dialog boxes, also appear in the text like this. Here is an example: "Select **System info** from the **Administration** panel."

Warnings or important notes appear like this.

Tips and tricks appear like this.

Assumptions for every recipe

It should be assumed that at the beginning of each recipe pandas, NumPy, and matplotlib are imported into the namespace. For plots to be embedded directly within the notebook, you must also run the magic command `%matplotlib inline`. Also, all data is stored in the `data` directory and is most commonly stored as a CSV file, which can be read directly with the `read_csv` function:

```
>>> %matplotlib inline
>>> import numpy as np
>>> import matplotlib.pyplot as plt
>>> import pandas as pd
>>> my_dataframe = pd.read_csv('data/dataset_name.csv')
```

Dataset descriptions

There are about two dozen datasets that are used throughout this book. It can be very helpful to have background information on each dataset as you complete the steps in the recipes. A detailed description of each dataset may be found in the `dataset_descriptions` Jupyter Notebook found at `https://github.com/PacktPublishing/Pandas-Cookbook-Second-Edition`. For each dataset, there will be a list of the columns, information about each column and notes on how the data was procured.

Sections

In this book, you will find several headings that appear frequently.

To give clear instructions on how to complete a recipe, we use these sections as follows:

How to do it...

This section contains the steps required to follow the recipe.

How it works...

This section usually consists of a detailed explanation of what happened in the previous section.

There's more...

This section consists of additional information about the recipe in order to make the reader more knowledgeable about the recipe.

Get in touch

Feedback from our readers is always welcome.

General feedback: If you have questions about any aspect of this book, mention the book title in the subject of your message and email us at customercare@packtpub.com.

Errata: Although we have taken every care to ensure the accuracy of our content, mistakes do happen. If you have found a mistake in this book we would be grateful if you would report this to us. Please visit, www.packtpub.com/support/errata, selecting your book, clicking on the Errata Submission Form link, and entering the details.

Piracy: If you come across any illegal copies of our works in any form on the Internet, we would be grateful if you would provide us with the location address or website name. Please contact us at copyright@packt.com with a link to the material.

If you are interested in becoming an author: If there is a topic that you have expertise in and you are interested in either writing or contributing to a book, please visit authors.packtpub.com.

Reviews

Please leave a review. Once you have read and used this book, why not leave a review on the site that you purchased it from? Potential readers can then see and use your unbiased opinion to make purchase decisions, we at Packt can understand what you think about our products, and our authors can see your feedback on their book. Thank you!

For more information about Packt, please visit packt.com.

1
Pandas Foundations

Most users of the pandas library will use an import alias so they can refer to it as pd. In general in this book, we will not show the pandas and NumPy imports, but they look like this:

```
>>> import pandas as pd
>>> import numpy as np
```

Introduction

The goal of this chapter is to introduce a foundation of pandas by thoroughly inspecting the Series and DataFrame data structures. It is important for pandas users to know the difference between a Series and a DataFrame.

The pandas library is useful for dealing with *structured data*. What is structured data? Data that is stored in tables, such as CSV files, Excel spreadsheets, or database tables, is all structured. Unstructured data consists of free form text, images, sound, or video. If you find yourself dealing with structured data, pandas will be of great utility to you.

In this chapter, you will learn how to select a single column of data from a DataFrame (a two-dimensional dataset), which is returned as a Series (a one-dimensional dataset). Working with this one-dimensional object makes it easy to show how different methods and operators work. Many Series methods return another Series as output. This leads to the possibility of calling further methods in succession, which is known as *method chaining*.

The Index component of the Series and DataFrame is what separates pandas from most other data analysis libraries and is the key to understanding how many operations work. We will get a glimpse of this powerful object when we use it as a meaningful label for Series values. The final two recipes contain tasks that frequently occur during a data analysis.

The pandas DataFrame

Before diving deep into pandas, it is worth knowing the components of the DataFrame. Visually, the outputted display of a pandas DataFrame (in a Jupyter Notebook) appears to be nothing more than an ordinary table of data consisting of rows and columns. Hiding beneath the surface are the three components—the *index*, *columns*, and *data* that you must be aware of to maximize the DataFrame's full potential.

This recipe reads in the movie dataset into a pandas DataFrame and provides a labeled diagram of all its major components.

```
>>> movies = pd.read_csv("data/movie.csv")
>>> movies
```

	color	direc/_name	...	aspec/ratio	movie/likes
0	Color	James Cameron	...	1.78	33000
1	Color	Gore Verbinski	...	2.35	0
2	Color	Sam Mendes	...	2.35	85000
3	Color	Christopher Nolan	...	2.35	164000
4	NaN	Doug Walker	...	NaN	0
...	...	...	...	...	...
4911	Color	Scott Smith	...	NaN	84
4912	Color	NaN	...	16.00	32000
4913	Color	Benjamin Roberds	...	NaN	16
4914	Color	Daniel Hsia	...	2.35	660
4915	Color	Jon Gunn	...	1.85	456

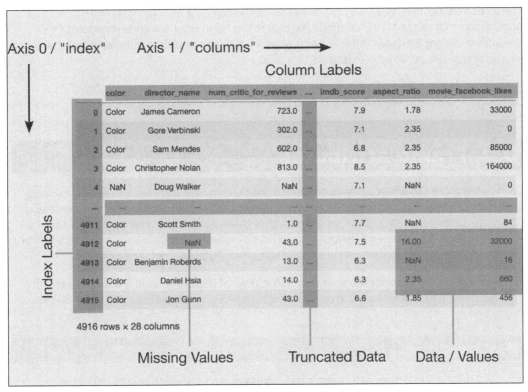

DataFrame anatomy

How it works...

pandas first reads the data from disk into memory and into a DataFrame using the `read_csv` function. By convention, the terms *index label* and *column name* refer to the individual members of the index and columns, respectively. The term *index* refers to all the index labels as a whole, just as the term *columns* refers to all the column names as a whole.

The labels in index and column names allow for pulling out data based on the index and column name. We will show that later. The index is also used for *alignment*. When multiple Series or DataFrames are combined, the indexes align first before any calculation occurs. A later recipe will show this as well.

Collectively, the columns and the index are known as the *axes*. More specifically, the index is axis 0, and the columns are axis 1.

pandas uses **NaN** (**not a number**) to represent missing values. Notice that even though the color column has string values, it uses `NaN` to represent a missing value.

The three consecutive dots, . . . , in the middle of the columns indicate that there is at least one column that exists but is not displayed due to the number of columns exceeding the predefined display limits. By default, pandas shows 60 rows and 20 columns, but we have limited that in the book, so the data fits in a page.

The .head method accepts an optional parameter, n, which controls the number of rows displayed. The default value for n is 5. Similarly, the .tail method returns the last n rows.

DataFrame attributes

Each of the three DataFrame components–the index, columns, and data–may be accessed from a DataFrame. You might want to perform operations on the individual components and not on the DataFrame as a whole. In general, though we can pull out the data into a NumPy array, unless all the columns are numeric, we usually leave it in a DataFrame. DataFrames are ideal for managing heterogenous columns of data, NumPy arrays not so much.

This recipe pulls out the index, columns, and the data of the DataFrame into their own variables, and then shows how the columns and index are inherited from the same object.

How to do it...

1. Use the DataFrame attributes index, columns, and values to assign the index, columns, and data to their own variables:

```
>>> movies = pd.read_csv("data/movie.csv")
>>> columns = movies.columns
>>> index = movies.index
>>> data = movies.to_numpy()
```

2. Display each component's values:

```
>>> columns
Index(['color', 'director_name', 'num_critic_for_reviews',
'duration',
       'director_facebook_likes', 'actor_3_facebook_likes',
'actor_2_name',
       'actor_1_facebook_likes', 'gross', 'genres', 'actor_1_
name',
       'movie_title', 'num_voted_users', 'cast_total_facebook_
likes',
       'actor_3_name', 'facenumber_in_poster', 'plot_keywords',
       'movie_imdb_link', 'num_user_for_reviews', 'language',
'country',
       'content_rating', 'budget', 'title_year', 'actor_2_
```

```
facebook_likes',
        'imdb_score', 'aspect_ratio', 'movie_facebook_likes'],
      dtype='object')
>>> index
RangeIndex(start=0, stop=4916, step=1)
>>> data
array([['Color', 'James Cameron', 723.0, ..., 7.9, 1.78, 33000],
        ['Color', 'Gore Verbinski', 302.0, ..., 7.1, 2.35, 0],
        ['Color', 'Sam Mendes', 602.0, ..., 6.8, 2.35, 85000],
        ...,
        ['Color', 'Benjamin Roberds', 13.0, ..., 6.3, nan, 16],
        ['Color', 'Daniel Hsia', 14.0, ..., 6.3, 2.35, 660],
        ['Color', 'Jon Gunn', 43.0, ..., 6.6, 1.85, 456]],
dtype=object)
```

3. Output the Python type of each DataFrame component (the word following the last dot of the output):

```
>>> type(index)
<class 'pandas.core.indexes.range.RangeIndex'>
>>> type(columns)
<class 'pandas.core.indexes.base.Index'>
>>> type(data)
<class 'numpy.ndarray'>
```

4. The index and the columns are closely related. Both of them are subclasses of `Index`. This allows you to perform similar operations on both the index and the columns:

```
>>> issubclass(pd.RangeIndex, pd.Index)
True
>>> issubclass(columns.__class__, pd.Index)
True
```

How it works...

The index and the columns represent the same thing but along different axes. They are occasionally referred to as the *row index* and *column index*.

There are many types of index objects in pandas. If you do not specify the index, pandas will use a `RangeIndex`. A `RangeIndex` is a subclass of an `Index` that is analogous to Python's `range` object. Its entire sequence of values is not loaded into memory until it is necessary to do so, thereby saving memory. It is completely defined by its start, stop, and step values.

There's more...

When possible, `Index` objects are implemented using hash tables that allow for very fast selection and data alignment. They are similar to Python sets in that they support operations such as intersection and union, but are dissimilar because they are ordered and can have duplicate entries.

Notice how the `.values` DataFrame attribute returned a NumPy n-dimensional array, or `ndarray`. Most of pandas relies heavily on the `ndarray`. Beneath the index, columns, and data are NumPy `ndarrays`. They could be considered the base object for pandas that many other objects are built upon. To see this, we can look at the values of the index and columns:

```
>>> index.to_numpy()
array([   0,    1,    2, ..., 4913, 4914, 4915], dtype=int64))
>>> columns.to_numpy()
array(['color', 'director_name', 'num_critic_for_reviews', 'duration',
'director_facebook_likes', 'actor_3_facebook_likes',
'actor_2_name', 'actor_1_facebook_likes', 'gross', 'genres',
'actor_1_name', 'movie_title', 'num_voted_users',
'cast_total_facebook_likes', 'actor_3_name',
'facenumber_in_poster', 'plot_keywords', 'movie_imdb_link',
'num_user_for_reviews', 'language', 'country', 'content_rating',
'budget', 'title_year', 'actor_2_facebook_likes', 'imdb_score',
'aspect_ratio', 'movie_facebook_likes'], dtype=object)
```

Having said all of that, we usually do not access the underlying NumPy objects. We tend to leave the objects as pandas objects and use pandas operations. However, we regularly apply NumPy functions to pandas objects.

Understanding data types

In very broad terms, data may be classified as either continuous or categorical. Continuous data is always numeric and represents some kind of measurements, such as height, wage, or salary. Continuous data can take on an infinite number of possibilities. Categorical data, on the other hand, represents discrete, finite amounts of values such as car color, type of poker hand, or brand of cereal.

pandas does not broadly classify data as either continuous or categorical. Instead, it has precise technical definitions for many distinct data types. The following describes common pandas data types:

- ▶ float – The NumPy float type, which supports missing values
- ▶ int – The NumPy integer type, which does not support missing values
- ▶ 'Int64' – pandas nullable integer type
- ▶ object – The NumPy type for storing strings (and mixed types)
- ▶ 'category' – pandas categorical type, which does support missing values
- ▶ bool – The NumPy Boolean type, which does not support missing values (None becomes False, np.nan becomes True)
- ▶ 'boolean' – pandas nullable Boolean type
- ▶ datetime64[ns] – The NumPy date type, which does support missing values (NaT)

In this recipe, we display the data type of each column in a DataFrame. After you ingest data, it is crucial to know the type of data held in each column as it fundamentally changes the kind of operations that are possible with it.

How to do it...

1. Use the .dtypes attribute to display each column name along with its data type:

```
>>> movies = pd.read_csv("data/movie.csv")
>>> movies.dtypes
color                          object
director_name                  object
num_critic_for_reviews        float64
duration                      float64
director_facebook_likes       float64
                                ...
title_year                    float64
actor_2_facebook_likes        float64
imdb_score                    float64
aspect_ratio                  float64
movie_facebook_likes            int64
Length: 28, dtype: object
```

2. Use the `.value_counts` method to return the counts of each data type:

```
>>> movies.dtypes.value_counts()
float64    13
int64       3
object     12
dtype: int64
```

3. Look at the `.info` method:

```
>>> movies.info()
<class 'pandas.core.frame.DataFrame'>
RangeIndex: 4916 entries, 0 to 4915
Data columns (total 28 columns):
color                       4897 non-null object
director_name               4814 non-null object
num_critic_for_reviews      4867 non-null float64
duration                    4901 non-null float64
director_facebook_likes     4814 non-null float64
actor_3_facebook_likes      4893 non-null float64
actor_2_name                4903 non-null object
actor_1_facebook_likes      4909 non-null float64
gross                       4054 non-null float64
genres                      4916 non-null object
actor_1_name                4909 non-null object
movie_title                 4916 non-null object
num_voted_users             4916 non-null int64
cast_total_facebook_likes   4916 non-null int64
actor_3_name                4893 non-null object
facenumber_in_poster        4903 non-null float64
plot_keywords               4764 non-null object
movie_imdb_link             4916 non-null object
num_user_for_reviews        4895 non-null float64
language                    4904 non-null object
country                     4911 non-null object
content_rating              4616 non-null object
budget                      4432 non-null float64
title_year                  4810 non-null float64
```

```
actor_2_facebook_likes          4903 non-null float64
imdb_score                      4916 non-null float64
aspect_ratio                    4590 non-null float64
movie_facebook_likes            4916 non-null int64
dtypes: float64(13), int64(3), object(12)
memory usage: 1.1+ MB
```

How it works...

Each DataFrame column lists one type. For instance, every value in the column `aspect_ratio` is a 64-bit float, and every value in `movie_facebook_likes` is a 64-bit integer. pandas defaults its core numeric types, integers, and floats to 64 bits regardless of the size necessary for all data to fit in memory. Even if a column consists entirely of the integer value 0, the data type will still be int64.

The `.value_counts` method returns the count of all the data types in the DataFrame when called on the `.dtypes` attribute.

The `object` data type is the one data type that is unlike the others. A column that is of the `object` data type may contain values that are of any valid Python object. Typically, when a column is of the `object` data type, it signals that the entire column is strings. When you load CSV files and string columns are missing values, pandas will stick in a NaN (float) for that cell. So the column might have both object and float (missing) values in it. The `.dtypes` attribute will show the column as an `object` (or O on the series). It will not show it as a mixed type column (that contains both strings and floats):

```
>>> pd.Series(["Paul", np.nan, "George"]).dtype
dtype('O')
```

The `.info` method prints the data type information in addition to the count of non-null values. It also lists the amount of memory used by the DataFrame. This is useful information, but is printed on the screen. The `.dtypes` attribute returns a pandas Series if you needed to use the data.

There's more...

Almost all of pandas data types are built from NumPy. This tight integration makes it easier for users to integrate pandas and NumPy operations. As pandas grew larger and more popular, the object data type proved to be too generic for all columns with string values. pandas created its own categorical data type to handle columns of strings (or numbers) with a fixed number of possible values.

Selecting a column

Selected a single column from a DataFrame returns a Series (that has the same index as the DataFrame). It is a single dimension of data, composed of just an index and the data. You can also create a Series by itself without a DataFrame, but it is more common to pull them off of a DataFrame.

This recipe examines two different syntaxes to select a single column of data, a Series. One syntax uses the *index operator* and the other uses *attribute access* (or dot notation).

How to do it...

1. Pass a column name as a string to the indexing operator to select a Series of data:

```
>>> movies = pd.read_csv("data/movie.csv")
>>> movies["director_name"]
0              James Cameron
1             Gore Verbinski
2                 Sam Mendes
3          Christopher Nolan
4                Doug Walker
                 ...
4911             Scott Smith
4912                     NaN
4913         Benjamin Roberds
4914             Daniel Hsia
4915                Jon Gunn
Name: director_name, Length: 4916, dtype: object
```

2. Alternatively, you may use attribute access to accomplish the same task:

```
>>> movies.director_name
0              James Cameron
1             Gore Verbinski
2                 Sam Mendes
3          Christopher Nolan
4                Doug Walker
                 ...
4911             Scott Smith
4912                     NaN
```

```
4913        Benjamin Roberds
4914           Daniel Hsia
4915             Jon Gunn
Name: director_name, Length: 4916, dtype: object
```

3. We can also index off of the `.loc` and `.iloc` attributes to pull out a Series. The former allows us to pull out by column name, while the latter by position. These are referred to as *label-based* and *positional-based* in the pandas documentation.

   The usage of `.loc` specifies a selector for both rows and columns separated by a comma. The row selector is a slice with no start or end name (`:`) which means select all of the rows. The column selector will just pull out the column named *director_name*.

   The `.iloc` index operation also specifies both row and column selectors. The row selector is the slice with no start or end index (`:`) that selects all of the rows. The column selector, `1`, pulls off the second column (remember that Python is zero-based):

```
>>> movies.loc[:, "director_name"]
0          James Cameron
1          Gore Verbinski
2            Sam Mendes
3        Christopher Nolan
4            Doug Walker
              ...
4911          Scott Smith
4912               NaN
4913      Benjamin Roberds
4914          Daniel Hsia
4915            Jon Gunn
Name: director_name, Length: 4916, dtype: object
```

```
>>> movies.iloc[:, 1]
0          James Cameron
1          Gore Verbinski
2            Sam Mendes
3        Christopher Nolan
4            Doug Walker
              ...
4911          Scott Smith
```

```
4912                          NaN
4913          Benjamin Roberds
4914             Daniel Hsia
4915               Jon Gunn
Name: director_name, Length: 4916, dtype: object
```

4. Jupyter shows the series in a monospace font, and shows the index, type, length, and name of the series. It will also truncate data according to the pandas configuration settings. See the image for a description of these.

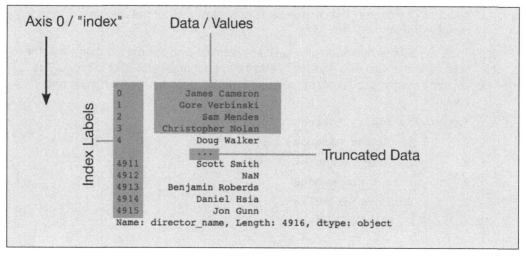

Series anatomy

You can also view the index, type, length, and name of the series with the appropriate attributes:

```
>>> movies["director_name"].index
RangeIndex(start=0, stop=4916, step=1)


>>> movies["director_name"].dtype
dtype('O')


>>> movies["director_name"].size
4196


>>> movies["director_name"].name
'director_name'
```

5. Verify that the output is a Series:

```
>>> type(movies["director_name"])
<class 'pandas.core.series.Series'>
```

6. Note that even though the type is reported as `object`, because there are missing values, the Series has both floats and strings in it. We can use the `.apply` method with the `type` function to get back a Series that has the type of every member. Rather than looking at the whole Series result, we will *chain* the `.unique` method onto the result, to look at just the unique types that are found in the `director_name` column:

```
>>> movies["director_name"].apply(type).unique()
array([<class 'str'>, <class 'float'>], dtype=object)
```

How it works...

A pandas DataFrame typically has multiple columns (though it may also have only one column). Each of these columns can be pulled out and treated as a Series.

There are many mechanisms to pull out a column from a DataFrame. Typically the easiest is to try and access it as an attribute. Attribute access is done with the dot operator (`.notation`). There are good things about this:

▶ Least amount of typing

▶ Jupyter will provide completion on the name

▶ Jupyter will provide completion on the Series attributes

There are some downsides as well:

▶ Only works with columns that have names that are valid Python attributes and do not conflict with existing DataFrame attributes

▶ Cannot create a new column, can only update existing ones

What is a valid Python attribute? A sequence of alphanumerics that starts with a character and includes underscores. Typically these are in lowercase to follow standard Python naming conventions. This means that column names with spaces or special characters will not work with an attribute.

Selecting column names using the index operator (`[`) will work with any column name. You can also create and update columns with this operator. Jupyter will provide completion on the column name when you use the index operator, but sadly, will not complete on subsequent Series attributes.

I often find myself using attribute access because getting completion on the Series attribute is very handy. But, I also make sure that the column names are valid Python attribute names that don't conflict with existing DataFrame attributes. I also try not to update using either attribute or index assignment, but rather using the `.assign` method. You will see many examples of using `.assign` in this book.

There's more...

To get completion in Jupyter an press the *Tab* key following a dot, or after starting a string in an index access. Jupyter will pop up a list of completions, and you can use the up and down arrow keys to highlight one, and hit *Enter* to complete it.

Calling Series methods

A typical workflow in pandas will have you going back and forth between executing statements on Series and DataFrames. Calling Series methods is the primary way to use the abilities that the Series offers.

Both Series and DataFrames have a tremendous amount of power. We can use the built-in `dir` function to uncover all the attributes and methods of a Series. In the following code, we also show the number of attributes and methods common to both Series and DataFrames. Both of these objects share the vast majority of attribute and method names:

```
>>> s_attr_methods = set(dir(pd.Series))
>>> len(s_attr_methods)
471
>>> df_attr_methods = set(dir(pd.DataFrame))
>>> len(df_attr_methods)
458
>>> len(s_attr_methods & df_attr_methods)
400
```

As you can see there is a lot of functionality on both of these objects. Don't be overwhelmed by this. Most pandas users only use a subset of the functionality and get along just fine.

This recipe covers the most common and powerful Series methods and attributes. Many of the methods are nearly equivalent for DataFrames.

How to do it...

1. After reading in the movies dataset, select two Series with different data types. The `director_name` column contains strings (pandas calls this an *object* or *O* data type), and the column `actor_1_facebook_likes` contains numerical data (formally `float64`):

```
>>> movies = pd.read_csv("data/movie.csv")
>>> director = movies["director_name"]
>>> fb_likes = movies["actor_1_facebook_likes"]


>>> director.dtype
dtype('O')


>>> fb_likes.dtype
dtype('float64')
```

2. The `.head` method lists the first five entries of a Series. You may provide an optional argument to change the number of entries returned. Another option is to use the `.sample` method to view some of the data. Depending on your dataset, this might provide better insight into your data as the first rows might be very different from subsequent rows:

```
>>> director.head()
0            James Cameron
1           Gore Verbinski
2               Sam Mendes
3        Christopher Nolan
4              Doug Walker
Name: director_name, dtype: object


>>> director.sample(n=5, random_state=42)
2347        Brian Percival
4687           Lucio Fulci
691          Phillip Noyce
3911         Sam Peckinpah
2488       Rowdy Herrington
Name: director_name, dtype: object


>>> fb_likes.head()
```

```
0        1000.0
1       40000.0
2       11000.0
3       27000.0
4         131.0
Name: actor_1_facebook_likes, dtype: float64
```

3. The data type of the Series usually determines which of the methods will be the most useful. For instance, one of the most useful methods for the `object` data type Series is `.value_counts`, which calculates the frequencies:

```
>>> director.value_counts()
Steven Spielberg     26
Woody Allen          22
Clint Eastwood       20
Martin Scorsese      20
Ridley Scott         16
                     ..
Eric England          1
Moustapha Akkad       1
Jay Oliva             1
Scott Speer           1
Leon Ford             1
Name: director_name, Length: 2397, dtype: int64
```

4. The `.value_counts` method is typically more useful for Series with `object` data types but can occasionally provide insight into numeric Series as well. Used with `fb_likes`, it appears that higher numbers have been rounded to the nearest thousand as it is unlikely that so many movies received exactly 1,000 likes:

```
>>> fb_likes.value_counts()
1000.0      436
11000.0     206
2000.0      189
3000.0      150
12000.0     131
            ...
362.0         1
216.0         1
859.0         1
```

```
225.0          1
334.0          1
Name: actor_1_facebook_likes, Length: 877, dtype: int64
```

5. Counting the number of elements in the Series may be done with the `.size` or `.shape` attribute or the built-in `len` function. The `.unique` method will return a NumPy array with the unique values:

```
>>> director.size
4916
>>> director.shape
(4916,)
>>> len(director)
4916
>>> director.unique()
array(['James Cameron', 'Gore Verbinski', 'Sam Mendes', ...,
        'Scott Smith', 'Benjamin Roberds', 'Daniel Hsia'],
dtype=object)
```

6. Additionally, there is the `.count` method, which doesn't return the count of items, but the number of non-missing values:

```
>>> director.count()
4814

>>> fb_likes.count()
4909
```

7. Basic summary statistics are provided with `.min`, `.max`, `.mean`, `.median`, and `.std`:

```
>>> fb_likes.min()
0.0

>>> fb_likes.max()
640000.0

>>> fb_likes.mean()
6494.488490527602

>>> fb_likes.median()
982.0
```

```
>>> fb_likes.std()
15106.986883848309
```

8. To simplify *step 7*, you may use the `.describe` method to return both the summary statistics and a few of the quantiles at once. When `.describe` is used with an `object` data type column, a completely different output is returned:

```
>>> fb_likes.describe()
count        4909.000000
mean         6494.488491
std         15106.986884
min             0.000000
25%           607.000000
50%           982.000000
75%         11000.000000
max        640000.000000
Name: actor_1_facebook_likes, dtype: float64


>>> director.describe()
count                 4814
unique                2397
top       Steven Spielberg
freq                    26
Name: director_name, dtype: object
```

9. The `.quantile` method calculates the quantile of numeric data. Note that if you pass in a scaler, you will get scalar output, but if you pass in a list, the output is a pandas Series:

```
>>> fb_likes.quantile(0.2)
510.0
>>> fb_likes.quantile(
...     [0.1, 0.2, 0.3, 0.4, 0.5, 0.6, 0.7, 0.8, 0.9]
... )
0.1     240.0
0.2     510.0
0.3     694.0
0.4     854.0
0.5     982.0
0.6    1000.0
```

```
0.7      8000.0
0.8      13000.0
0.9      18000.0
Name: actor_1_facebook_likes, dtype: float64
```

10. Since the `.count` method in *step 6* returned a value less than the total number of Series elements found in *step 5*, we know that there are missing values in each Series. The `.isna` method can be used to determine whether each individual value is missing or not. The result is a Series. You may see this referred to as a *Boolean array* (a Series with Boolean values that has the same index and length as the original Series):

```
>>> director.isna()
0           False
1           False
2           False
3           False
4           False
            ...
4911        False
4912        True
4913        False
4914        False
4915        False
Name: director_name, Length: 4916, dtype: bool
```

11. It is possible to replace all missing values within a Series with the `.fillna` method:

```
>>> fb_likes_filled = fb_likes.fillna(0)
>>> fb_likes_filled.count()
4916
```

12. To remove the entries in Series elements with missing values, use the `.dropna` method:

```
>>> fb_likes_dropped = fb_likes.dropna()
>>> fb_likes_dropped.size
4909
```

How it works...

The methods used in this recipe were chosen because of how frequently they are used in data analysis.

The steps in this recipe return different types of objects.

The result from the .head method in *step 1* is another Series. The .value_counts method also produces a Series but has the unique values from the original Series as the index and the count as its values. In *step 5*, the .size property and .count method return scalar values, but the .shape property returns a one-item tuple. This is a convention borrowed from NumPy, which allows for arrays of arbitrary dimensions.

In *step 7*, each individual method returns a scalar value.

In *step 8*, the .describe method returns a Series with all the summary statistic names as the index and the statistic as the values.

In *step 9*, the .quantile method is flexible and returns a scalar value when passed a single value but returns a Series when given a list.

In *steps 10, 11*, and *12*, .isna, .fillna, and .dropna all return a Series.

There's more...

The .value_counts method is one of the most informative Series methods and heavily used during exploratory analysis, especially with categorical columns. It defaults to returning the counts, but by setting the normalize parameter to True, the relative frequencies are returned instead, which provides another view of the distribution:

```
>>> director.value_counts(normalize=True)
Steven Spielberg      0.005401
Woody Allen           0.004570
Clint Eastwood        0.004155
Martin Scorsese       0.004155
Ridley Scott          0.003324
                        ...
Eric England          0.000208
Moustapha Akkad       0.000208
Jay Oliva             0.000208
Scott Speer           0.000208
Leon Ford             0.000208
Name: director_name, Length: 2397, dtype: float64
```

In this recipe, we determined that there were missing values in the Series by observing that the result from the `.count` method did not match the `.size` attribute. A more direct approach is to inspect the `.hasnans` attribute:

```
>>> director.hasnans
True
```

There exists a complement of `.isna`; the `.notna` method, which returns `True` for all the non-missing values:

```
>>> director.notna()
0          True
1          True
2          True
3          True
4          True
          ...
4911       True
4912       False
4913       True
4914       True
4915       True
Name: director_name, Length: 4916, dtype: bool
```

There is also a `.isnull` method, which is an alias for `.isna`. I'm lazy so if I can type less while still being explicit about my intentions, then I'm all for it. Because pandas uses NaN all over the place, I prefer the spelling of `.isna` to `.isnull`. We don't ever see NULL anywhere in the pandas or Python world.

Series operations

There exist a vast number of operators in Python for manipulating objects. For instance, when the plus operator is placed between two integers, Python will add them together:

```
>>> 5 + 9   # plus operator example. Adds 5 and 9
14
```

Series and DataFrames support many of the Python operators. Typically, a new Series or DataFrame is returned when using an operator.

In this recipe, a variety of operators will be applied to different Series objects to produce a new Series with completely different values.

How to do it...

1. Select the `imdb_score` column as a Series:

    ```
    >>> movies = pd.read_csv("data/movie.csv")
    >>> imdb_score = movies["imdb_score"]
    >>> imdb_score
    0        7.9
    1        7.1
    2        6.8
    3        8.5
    4        7.1
             ...
    4911     7.7
    4912     7.5
    4913     6.3
    4914     6.3
    4915     6.6
    Name: imdb_score, Length: 4916, dtype: float64
    ```

2. Use the plus operator to add one to each Series element:

    ```
    >>> imdb_score + 1
    0        8.9
    1        8.1
    2        7.8
    3        9.5
    4        8.1
             ...
    4911     8.7
    4912     8.5
    4913     7.3
    4914     7.3
    4915     7.6
    Name: imdb_score, Length: 4916, dtype: float64
    ```

3. The other basic arithmetic operators, minus (-), multiplication (*), division (/), and exponentiation (**) work similarly with scalar values. In this step, we will multiply the series by 2.5:

    ```
    >>> imdb_score * 2.5
    ```

```
0            19.75
1            17.75
2            17.00
3            21.25
4            17.75
             ...
4911         19.25
4912         18.75
4913         15.75
4914         15.75
4915         16.50
Name: imdb_score, Length: 4916, dtype: float64
```

4. Python uses a double slash (//) for floor division. The floor division operator truncates the result of the division. The percent sign (%) is the modulus operator, which returns the remainder after a division. The Series instances also support these operations:

```
>>> imdb_score // 7
0            1.0
1            1.0
2            0.0
3            1.0
4            1.0
             ...
4911         1.0
4912         1.0
4913         0.0
4914         0.0
4915         0.0
Name: imdb_score, Length: 4916, dtype: float64
```

5. There exist six comparison operators, greater than (>), less than (<), greater than or equal to (>=), less than or equal to (<=), equal to (==), and not equal to (!=). Each comparison operator turns each value in the Series to True or False based on the outcome of the condition. The result is a Boolean array, which we will see is very useful for filtering in later recipes:

```
>>> imdb_score > 7
0            True
```

```
1          True
2          False
3          True
4          True
           . . .
4911       True
4912       True
4913       False
4914       False
4915       False
Name: imdb_score, Length: 4916, dtype: bool
>>> director = movies["director_name"]
>>> director == "James Cameron"
0          True
1          False
2          False
3          False
4          False
           . . .
4911       False
4912       False
4913       False
4914       False
4915       False
Name: director_name, Length: 4916, dtype: bool
```

How it works...

All the operators used in this recipe apply the same operation to each element in the Series. In native Python, this would require a for loop to iterate through each of the items in the sequence before applying the operation. pandas relies heavily on the NumPy library, which allows for vectorized computations, or the ability to operate on entire sequences of data without the explicit writing of for loops. Each operation returns a new Series with the same index, but with the new values.

There's more...

All of the operators used in this recipe have method equivalents that produce the exact same result. For instance, in *step 1*, `imdb_score + 1` can be reproduced with the `.add` method.

Using the method rather than the operator can be useful when we chain methods together.

Here are a few examples:

```
>>> imdb_score.add(1)   # imdb_score + 1
0        8.9
1        8.1
2        7.8
3        9.5
4        8.1
         ...
4911     8.7
4912     8.5
4913     7.3
4914     7.3
4915     7.6
Name: imdb_score, Length: 4916, dtype: float64
```

```
>>> imdb_score.gt(7)   # imdb_score > 7
0        True
1        True
2        False
3        True
4        True
         ...
4911     True
4912     True
4913     False
4914     False
4915     False
Name: imdb_score, Length: 4916, dtype: bool
```

Why does pandas offer a method equivalent to these operators? By its nature, an operator only operates in exactly one manner. Methods, on the other hand, can have parameters that allow you to alter their default functionality.

Other recipes will dive into this further, but here is a small example. The `.sub` method performs subtraction on a Series. When you do subtraction with the `-` operator, missing values are ignored. However, the `.sub` method allows you to specify a `fill_value` parameter to use in place of missing values:

```
>>> money = pd.Series([100, 20, None])
>>> money - 15
0    85.0
1     5.0
2     NaN
dtype: float64


>>> money.sub(15, fill_value=0)
0    85.0
1     5.0
2   -15.0
dtype: float64
```

Following is a table of operators and the corresponding methods:

Operator group	Operator	Series method name
Arithmetic	+,-,*,/,//,%,**	.add, .sub, .mul, .div, .floordiv, .mod, .pow
Comparison	<,>,<=,>=,==,!=	.lt, .gt, .le, .ge, .eq, .ne

You may be curious as to how a Python Series object, or any object for that matter, knows what to do when it encounters an operator. For example, how does the expression `imdb_score * 2.5` know to multiply each element in the Series by 2.5? Python has a built-in, standardized way for objects to communicate with operators using *special methods*.

Special methods are what objects call internally whenever they encounter an operator. Special methods always begin and end with two underscores. Because of this, they are also called *dunder* methods as the method that implements the operator is surrounded by double underscores (dunder being a lazy geeky programmer way of saying "double underscores"). For instance, the special method `.__mul__` is called whenever the multiplication operator is used. Python interprets the `imdb_score * 2.5` expression as `imdb_score.__mul__(2.5)`.

There is no difference between using the special method and using an operator as they are doing the exact same thing. The operator is just syntactic sugar for the special method. However, calling the `.mul` method is different than calling the `.__mul__` method.

Chaining Series methods

In Python, every variable points to an object, and many attributes and methods return new objects. This allows sequential invocation of methods using attribute access. This is called *method chaining or flow programming*. pandas is a library that lends itself well to method chaining, as many Series and DataFrame methods return more Series and DataFrames, upon which more methods can be called.

To motivate method chaining, let's take an English sentence and translate the chain of events into a chain of methods. Consider the sentence: *A person drives to the store to buy food, then drives home and prepares, cooks, serves, and eats the food before cleaning the dishes.*

A Python version of this sentence might take the following form:

```
(person.drive('store')
.buy('food')
.drive('home')
.prepare('food')
.cook('food')
.serve('food')
.eat('food')
.cleanup('dishes')
)
```

In the preceding code, the `person` is the object (or instance of a class) that calls a method. Each method returns another instance that allows the chain of calls to happen. The parameter passed to each of the methods specifies how the method operates.

Although it is possible to write the entire method chain in a single unbroken line, it is far more palatable to write a single method per line. Since Python does not normally allow a single expression to be written on multiple lines, we have a couple of options. My preferred style is to wrap everything in parentheses. Alternatively, you may end each line with a backslash (\) to indicate that the line continues on the next line. To improve readability even more, you can align the method calls vertically.

This recipe shows a similar method chaining using a pandas Series.

How to do it...

1. Load in the movie dataset, and pull two columns out of it:

```
>>> movies = pd.read_csv("data/movie.csv")
>>> fb_likes = movies["actor_1_facebook_likes"]
>>> director = movies["director_name"]
```

2. Two of the most common methods to append to the end of a chain are the `.head` or the `.sample` method. This suppresses long output. If the resultant DataFrame is very wide, I like to transpose the results using the `.T` property. (For shorter chains, there isn't as great a need to place each method on a different line):

```
>>> director.value_counts().head(3)
Steven Spielberg     26
Woody Allen          22
Clint Eastwood       20
Name: director_name, dtype: int64
```

3. A common way to count the number of missing values is to chain the `.sum` method after a call to `.isna`:

```
>>> fb_likes.isna().sum()
7
```

4. All the non-missing values of `fb_likes` should be integers as it is impossible to have a partial Facebook like. In most pandas versions, any numeric columns with missing values must have their data type as `float` (pandas 0.24 introduced the `Int64` type, which supports missing values but is not used by default). If we fill missing values from `fb_likes` with zeros, we can then convert it to an integer with the `.astype` method:

```
>>> fb_likes.dtype
dtype('float64')
>>> (fb_likes.fillna(0).astype(int).head())
0     1000
1    40000
2    11000
3    27000
4      131
Name: actor_1_facebook_likes, dtype: int64
```

How it works...

Step 2 first uses the `.value_counts` method to return a Series and then chains the `.head` method to select the first three elements. The final returned object is a Series, which could also have had more methods chained on it.

In *step 3*, the `.isna` method creates a Boolean array. pandas treats `False` and `True` as `0` and `1`, so the `.sum` method returns the number of missing values.

Each of the three chained methods in *step 4* returns a Series. It may not seem intuitive, but the `.astype` method returns an entirely new Series with a different data type.

There's more...

One potential downside of chaining is that debugging becomes difficult. Because none of the intermediate objects created during the method calls is stored in a variable, it can be hard to trace the exact location in the chain where it occurred.

One of the nice aspects of putting each call on its own line is that it enables debugging of more complicated commands. I typically build up these chains one method at a time, but occasionally I need to come back to previous code or tweak it slightly.

To debug this code, I start by commenting out all of the commands except the first. Then I uncomment the first chain, make sure it works, and move on to the next.

If I were debugging the previous code, I would comment out the last two method calls and make sure I knew what `.fillna` was doing:

```
>>> (
...      fb_likes.fillna(0)
...      # .astype(int)
...      # .head()
... )
0         1000.0
1        40000.0
2        11000.0
3        27000.0
4          131.0
           ...
4911       637.0
4912       841.0
4913         0.0
```

```
4914        946.0
4915         86.0
Name: actor_1_facebook_likes, Length: 4916, dtype: float64
```

Then I would uncomment the next method and ensure that it was working correctly:

```
>>> (
...       fb_likes.fillna(0).astype(int)
...       #  .head()
... )
0          1000
1         40000
2         11000
3         27000
4           131
           ...
4911        637
4912        841
4913          0
4914        946
4915         86
Name: actor_1_facebook_likes, Length: 4916, dtype: int64
```

Another option for debugging chains is to call the `.pipe` method to show an intermediate value. The `.pipe` method on a Series needs to be passed a function that accepts a Series as input and can return anything (but we want to return a Series if we want to use it in a method chain).

This function, `debug_ser`, will print out the value of the intermediate result:

```
>>> def debug_ser(ser):
...       print("BEFORE")
...       print(ser)
...       print("AFTER")
...       return ser

>>> (fb_likes.fillna(0).pipe(debug_ser).astype(int).head())
BEFORE
0          1000.0
1         40000.0
```

```
2          11000.0
3          27000.0
4            131.0

              ...
4911         637.0
4912         841.0
4913           0.0
4914         946.0
4915          86.0
Name: actor_1_facebook_likes, Length: 4916, dtype: float64
AFTER
0      1000
1     40000
2     11000
3     27000
4       131
Name: actor_1_facebook_likes, dtype: int64
```

If you want to create a global variable to store an intermediate value you can also use `.pipe`:

```
>>> intermediate = None
>>> def get_intermediate(ser):
...     global intermediate
...     intermediate = ser
...     return ser

>>> res = (
...     fb_likes.fillna(0)
...     .pipe(get_intermediate)
...     .astype(int)
...     .head()
... )

>>> intermediate
0      1000.0
1     40000.0
2     11000.0
```

```
3        27000.0
4          131.0

          . . .
4911       637.0
4912       841.0
4913         0.0
4914       946.0
4915        86.0
Name: actor_1_facebook_likes, Length: 4916, dtype: float64
```

As was mentioned at the beginning of the recipe, it is possible to use backslashes for multi line code. *Step 4* may be rewritten this way:

```
>>> fb_likes.fillna(0)\
...     .astype(int)\
...     .head()
0     1000
1    40000
2    11000
3    27000
4      131
Name: actor_1_facebook_likes, dtype: int64
```

I prefer wrapping the chain with parentheses. Having to continually add trailing backslashes when you add a method to the chain is annoying.

Renaming column names

One of the most common operations on a DataFrame is to rename the column names. I like to rename my columns so that they are also valid Python attribute names. This means that they do not start with numbers and are lowercased alphanumerics with underscores. Good column names should also be descriptive, brief, and not clash with existing DataFrame or Series attributes.

In this recipe, the column names are renamed. The motivation for renaming is to make your code easier to understand, and also let your environment assist you. Recall that Jupyter will allow you to complete Series methods if you accessed the Series using dot notation (but will not allow method completion on index access).

How to do it...

1. Read in the movie dataset, and make the index meaningful by setting it as the movie title:

```
>>> movies = pd.read_csv("data/movie.csv")
```

2. The renamed DataFrame method accepts dictionaries that map the old value to the new value. Let's create one for the columns:

```
>>> col_map = {
...        "director_name": "director",
...        "num_critic_for_reviews": "critic_reviews",
... }
```

3. Pass the dictionaries to the rename method, and assign the result to a new variable:

```
>>> movies.rename(columns=col_map).head()
       color          director  ...  aspec/ratio  movie/likes
0      Color     James Cameron  ...         1.78        33000
1      Color     Gore Verbinski ...         2.35            0
2      Color       Sam Mendes   ...         2.35        85000
3      Color Christopher Nolan  ...         2.35       164000
4        NaN       Doug Walker  ...          NaN            0
```

How it works...

The `.rename` method on a DataFrame allows for column labels to be renamed. We can rename the columns by assigning to the columns attribute. But we cannot chain on an assignment. As I keep saying, I prefer chaining because it makes our code easier to read. The next section shows an example of renaming via assignment to the `.column` attribute:

There's more...

In this recipe, we changed the names of the columns. You can also rename the index using the `.rename` method if you want to. This makes more sense if the columns are string values. So we will set the index to the `movie_title` column and then map those values to new ones:

```
>>> idx_map = {
...        "Avatar": "Ratava",
...        "Spectre": "Ertceps",
...        "Pirates of the Caribbean: At World's End": "POC",
```

```
... }
>>> col_map = {
...     "aspect_ratio": "aspect",
...     "movie_facebook_likes": "fblikes",
... }
>>> (
...     movies.set_index("movie_title")
...     .rename(index=idx_map, columns=col_map)
...     .head(3)
... )
             color    director_name  ...   aspect   fblikes
movie_title                          ...
Ratava       Color    James Cameron  ...   1.78     33000
POC          Color    Gore Verbinski ...   2.35         0
Ertceps      Color        Sam Mendes ...   2.35     85000
```

There are multiple ways to rename row and column labels. It is possible to reassign the index and column attributes to a Python list. This assignment works when the list has the same number of elements as the row and column labels.

The following code shows an example. We will read the data from the CSV file, and use the `index_col` parameter to tell pandas to use the `movie_title` column as the index. Then we use the `.tolist` method on each Index object to create a Python list of labels. We then modify three values in each of the lists and reassign them to the `.index` and `.column` attributes:

```
>>> movies = pd.read_csv(
...     "data/movie.csv", index_col="movie_title"
... )
>>> ids = movies.index.to_list()
>>> columns = movies.columns.to_list()
# rename the row and column labels with list assignments
>>> ids[0] = "Ratava"
>>> ids[1] = "POC"
>>> ids[2] = "Ertceps"
>>> columns[1] = "director"
>>> columns[-2] = "aspect"
>>> columns[-1] = "fblikes"
>>> movies.index = ids
```

```
>>> movies.columns = columns
>>> movies.head(3)
          color          director   ...  aspect  fblikes
Ratava    Color    James Cameron    ...    1.78    33000
POC       Color   Gore Verbinski    ...    2.35        0
Ertceps   Color      Sam Mendes     ...    2.35    85000
```

Another option is to pass a function into the `.rename` method. The function takes a column name and returns a new name. Assuming there are spaces and uppercases in the columns, this code will clean them up:

```
>>> def to_clean(val):
...      return val.strip().lower().replace(" ", "_")

>>> movies.rename(columns=to_clean).head(3)
          color          director   ...  aspect  fblikes
Ratava    Color    James Cameron    ...    1.78    33000
POC       Color   Gore Verbinski    ...    2.35        0
Ertceps   Color      Sam Mendes     ...    2.35    85000
```

In pandas code in the wild, you will also see list comprehensions used to clean up the column names. With the new cleaned up list, you can reassign the result back to the `.columns` attribute. Assuming there are spaces and uppercases in the columns, this code will clean them up:

```
>>> cols = [
...      col.strip().lower().replace(" ", "_")
...      for col in movies.columns
... ]
>>> movies.columns = cols
>>> movies.head(3)
          color          director   ...  aspect  fblikes
Ratava    Color    James Cameron    ...    1.78    33000
POC       Color   Gore Verbinski    ...    2.35        0
Ertceps   Color      Sam Mendes     ...    2.35    85000
```

Because this code mutates the original DataFrame, consider using the `.rename` method.

Creating and deleting columns

During data analysis, it is likely that you will need to create new columns to represent new variables. Commonly, these new columns will be created from previous columns already in the dataset. pandas has a few different ways to add new columns to a DataFrame.

In this recipe, we create new columns in the movie dataset by using the `.assign` method and then delete columns with the `.drop` method.

How to do it...

1. One way to create a new column is to do an index assignment. Note that this will not return a new DataFrame but *mutate* the existing DataFrame. If you assign the column to a scalar value, it will use that value for every cell in the column. Let's create the `has_seen` column in the movie dataset to indicate whether or not we have seen the movie. We will assign zero for every value. By default, new columns are appended to the end:

    ```
    >>> movies = pd.read_csv("data/movie.csv")
    >>> movies["has_seen"] = 0
    ```

2. While this method works and is common, as I find myself chaining methods very often, I prefer to use the `.assign` method instead. This will return a new DataFrame with the new column. Because it uses the parameter name as the column name, the column name must be a valid parameter name:

    ```
    >>> movies = pd.read_csv("data/movie.csv")
    >>> idx_map = {
    ...     "Avatar": "Ratava",
    ...     "Spectre": "Ertceps",
    ...     "Pirates of the Caribbean: At World's End": "POC",
    ... }
    >>> col_map = {
    ...     "aspect_ratio": "aspect",
    ...     "movie_facebook_likes": "fblikes",
    ... }
    >>> (
    ...     movies.rename(
    ...         index=idx_map, columns=col_map
    ...     ).assign(has_seen=0)
    ... )
    ```

	color	director_name	...	fblikes	has_seen
0	Color	James Cameron	...	33000	0
1	Color	Gore Verbinski	...	0	0
2	Color	Sam Mendes	...	85000	0
3	Color	Christopher Nolan	...	164000	0
4	NaN	Doug Walker	...	0	0
...	...	...	...	...	...
4911	Color	Scott Smith	...	84	0
4912	Color	NaN	...	32000	0
4913	Color	Benjamin Roberds	...	16	0
4914	Color	Daniel Hsia	...	660	0
4915	Color	Jon Gunn	...	456	0

3. There are several columns that contain data on the number of Facebook likes. Let's add up all actor and director Facebook like columns and assign them to the `total_likes` column. We can do this in a couple of ways.

We can add each of the columns:

```
>>> total = (
...     movies["actor_1_facebook_likes"]
...     + movies["actor_2_facebook_likes"]
...     + movies["actor_3_facebook_likes"]
...     + movies["director_facebook_likes"]
... )
```

```
>>> total.head(5)
0     2791.0
1    46563.0
2    11554.0
3    95000.0
4        NaN
dtype: float64
```

My preference is to use methods that we can chain, so I prefer calling `.sum` here. I will pass in a list of columns to select to `.loc` to pull out just those columns that I want to sum:

```
>>> cols = [
...     "actor_1_facebook_likes",
```

```
...         "actor_2_facebook_likes",
...         "actor_3_facebook_likes",
...         "director_facebook_likes",
... ]
>>> sum_col = movies.loc[:, cols].sum(axis="columns")
>>> sum_col.head(5)
0      2791.0
1     46563.0
2     11554.0
3     95000.0
4       274.0
dtype: float64
```

Then we can assign this Series to the new column. Note that when we called the + operator, the result had missing numbers (NaN), but the `.sum` method ignores missing numbers by default, so we get a different result:

```
>>> movies.assign(total_likes=sum_col).head(5)
    color       direc/_name  ...  movie/likes  total/likes
0   Color     James Cameron  ...        33000       2791.0
1   Color     Gore Verbinski ...            0      46563.0
2   Color       Sam Mendes   ...        85000      11554.0
3   Color  Christopher Nolan ...       164000      95000.0
4   NaN         Doug Walker  ...            0        274.0
```

Another option is to pass in a function as the value of the parameter in the call to the `.assign` method. This function accepts a DataFrame as input and should return a Series:

```
>>> def sum_likes(df):
...     return df[
...         [
...             c
...             for c in df.columns
...             if "like" in c
...             and ("actor" in c or "director" in c)
...         ]
...     ].sum(axis=1)
```

```
>>> movies.assign(total_likes=sum_likes).head(5)
```

	color	direc/_name	...	movie/likes	total/likes
0	Color	James Cameron	...	33000	2791.0
1	Color	Gore Verbinski	...	0	46563.0
2	Color	Sam Mendes	...	85000	11554.0
3	Color	Christopher Nolan	...	164000	95000.0
4	NaN	Doug Walker	...	0	274.0

4. From the *Calling Series methods* recipe in this chapter, we know that this dataset contains missing values. When numeric columns are added to one another as in the preceding step using the plus operator, the result is NaN if there is any value missing. However, with the `.sum` method it converts NaN to zero.

   Let's check if there are missing values in our new column using both methods:

```
>>> (
...      movies.assign(total_likes=sum_col)["total_likes"]
...      .isna()
...      .sum()
... )
0
```

```
>>> (
...      movies.assign(total_likes=total)["total_likes"]
...      .isna()
...      .sum()
... )
122
```

We could fill in the missing values with zero as well:

```
>>> (
...      movies.assign(total_likes=total.fillna(0))[
...          "total_likes"
...      ]
...      .isna()
...      .sum()
... )
0
```

5. There is another column in the dataset named `cast_total_facebook_likes`. It would be interesting to see what percentage of this column comes from our newly created column, `total_likes`. Before we create our percentage column, let's do some basic data validation. We will ensure that `cast_total_facebook_likes` is greater than or equal to `total_likes`:

```
>>> def cast_like_gt_actor(df):
...        return (
...            df["cast_total_facebook_likes"]
...            >= df["total_likes"]
...        )


>>> df2 = movies.assign(
...        total_likes=total,
...        is_cast_likes_more=cast_like_gt_actor,
... )
```

6. `is_cast_likes_more` is now a column from a Boolean array. We can check whether all the values of this column are `True` using the `.all` method:

```
>>> df2["is_cast_likes_more"].all()
False
```

7. It turns out that there is at least one movie with more `total_likes` than `cast_total_facebook_likes`. It could be that director Facebook likes are not part of the cast total likes. Let's backtrack and delete the `total_likes` column. We can use the `.drop` method with the `columns` parameter to do that:

```
>>> df2 = df2.drop(columns="total_likes")
```

8. Let's recreate a Series of just the total actor likes:

```
>>> actor_sum = movies[
...        [
...            c
...            for c in movies.columns
...            if "actor_" in c and "_likes" in c
...        ]
... ].sum(axis="columns")


>>> actor_sum.head(5)
0      2791.0
1     46000.0
```

```
2       11554.0
3       73000.0
4         143.0
dtype: float64
```

9. Check again whether all the values in `cast_total_facebook_likes` are greater than `actor_sum`. We can do this with the `>=` operator or the `.ge` method:

```
>>> movies["cast_total_facebook_likes"] >= actor_sum
0          True
1          True
2          True
3          True
4          True
           ...
4911       True
4912       True
4913       True
4914       True
4915       True
Length: 4916, dtype: bool


>>> movies["cast_total_facebook_likes"].ge(actor_sum)
0          True
1          True
2          True
3          True
4          True
           ...
4911       True
4912       True
4913       True
4914       True
4915       True
Length: 4916, dtype: bool


>>> movies["cast_total_facebook_likes"].ge(actor_sum).all()
True
```

10. Finally, let's calculate the percentage of the `cast_total_facebook_likes` that come from `actor_sum`:

```
>>> pct_like = actor_sum.div(
...     movies["cast_total_facebook_likes"]
... ).mul(100)
```

11. Let's validate that the minimum and maximum of this Series fall between 0 and 1:

```
>>> pct_like.describe()
count    4883.000000
mean       83.327889
std        14.056578
min        30.076696
25%        73.528368
50%        86.928884
75%        95.477440
max       100.000000
dtype: float64
```

12. We can then create a Series using the `movie_title` column as the index. The Series constructor lets us pass in both the values and an index:

```
>>> pd.Series(
...     pct_like.to_numpy(), index=movies["movie_title"]
... ).head()
movie_title
Avatar                                         57.736864
Pirates of the Caribbean: At World's End       95.139607
Spectre                                        98.752137
The Dark Knight Rises                          68.378310
Star Wars: Episode VII - The Force Awakens    100.000000
dtype: float64
```

How it works...

Many pandas operations are flexible, and column creation is one of them. This recipe assigns both a scalar value, as seen in *step 1*, and a Series, as seen in *step 2*, to create a new column.

Step 3 adds four different Series together with the plus operator and the `.sum` method. *Step 4* uses method chaining to find and fill missing values. *Step 5* uses the greater than or equal comparison operator to return a Boolean Series, which is then evaluated with the `.all` method in *step 6* to check whether every single value is `True` or not.

The `.drop` method accepts the name of the row or column to delete. It defaults to dropping rows by the index names. To drop columns, you must set the `axis` parameter to either `1` or `'columns'`. The default value for axis is `0` or `'index'`.

Steps 8 and *9* redo the work of *step 3* to *step 6* without the `total_likes` column. *Step 10* finally calculates the desired column we wanted since *step 4*. *Step 11* validates that the percentages are between 0 and 100.

There's more...

It is possible to insert a new column into a specific location in a DataFrame with the `.insert` method. The `.insert` method takes the integer position of the new column as its first argument, the name of the new column as its second, and the values as its third. You will need to use the `.get_loc` Index method to find the integer location of the column name.

The `.insert` method modifies the calling DataFrame in-place, so there won't be an assignment statement. It also returns `None`. For this reason, I prefer the `.assign` method to create new columns. If I need them in order, I can pass in an ordered list of columns into the index operator (or to `.loc`).

The profit of each movie is calculated by subtracting budget from gross and inserting it after `gross` with the following:

```
>>> profit_index = movies.columns.get_loc("gross") + 1
>>> profit_index
9
>>> movies.insert(
...     loc=profit_index,
...     column="profit",
...     value=movies["gross"] - movies["budget"],
... )
```

An alternative to deleting columns with the `.drop` method is to use the `del` statement. This also does not return a new DataFrame, so favor `.drop` over this:

```
>>> del movies["director_name"]
```

2
Essential DataFrame Operations

Introduction

Introduction

This chapter covers many fundamental operations of the DataFrame. Many of the recipes will be similar to those in *Chapter 1*, *Pandas Foundations*, which primarily covered operations on a Series.

Selecting multiple DataFrame columns

We can select a single column by passing the column name to the index operator of a DataFrame. This was covered in the *Selecting a column* recipe in *Chapter 1*, *Pandas Foundations*. It is often necessary to focus on a subset of the current working dataset, which is accomplished by selecting multiple columns.

In this recipe, all the *actor* and *director* columns will be selected from the movie dataset.

How to do it...

1. Read in the movie dataset, and pass in a list of the desired columns to the indexing operator:

```
>>> import pandas as pd
>>> import numpy as np
```

```
>>> movies = pd.read_csv("data/movie.csv")
>>> movie_actor_director = movies[
...     [
...         "actor_1_name",
...         "actor_2_name",
...         "actor_3_name",
...         "director_name",
...     ]
... ]
>>> movie_actor_director.head()
  actor_1_name actor_2_name actor_3_name director_name
0   CCH Pounder   Joel Dav...    Wes Studi   James Ca...
1   Johnny Depp   Orlando ...   Jack Dav...   Gore Ver...
2   Christop...   Rory Kin...   Stephani...   Sam Mendes
3    Tom Hardy   Christia...   Joseph G...   Christop...
4   Doug Walker   Rob Walker          NaN   Doug Walker
```

2. There are instances when one column of a DataFrame needs to be selected. Using the index operation can return either a Series or a DataFrame. If we pass in a list with a single item, we will get back a DataFrame. If we pass in just a string with the column name, we will get a Series back:

```
>>> type(movies[["director_name"]])
<class 'pandas.core.frame.DataFrame'>


>>> type(movies["director_name"])
<class 'pandas.core.series.Series'>
```

3. We can also use `.loc` to pull out a column by name. Because this index operation requires that we pass in a row selector first, we will use a colon (`:`) to indicate a slice that selects all of the rows. This can also return either a DataFrame or a Series:

```
>>> type(movies.loc[:, ["director_name"]])
<class 'pandas.core.frame.DataFrame'>


>>> type(movies.loc[:, "director_name"])
<class 'pandas.core.series.Series'>
```

How it works...

The DataFrame index operator is very flexible and capable of accepting a number of different objects. If a string is passed, it will return a single-dimensional Series. If a list is passed to the indexing operator, it returns a DataFrame of all the columns in the list in the specified order.

Step 2 shows how to select a single column as a DataFrame and as a Series. Usually, a single column is selected with a string, resulting in a Series. When a DataFrame is desired, put the column name in a single-element list.

Step 3 shows how to use the `loc` attribute to pull out a Series or a DataFrame.

There's more...

Passing a long list inside the indexing operator might cause readability issues. To help with this, you may save all your column names to a list variable first. The following code achieves the same result as step 1:

```
>>> cols = [
...      "actor_1_name",
...      "actor_2_name",
...      "actor_3_name",
...      "director_name",
... ]
>>> movie_actor_director = movies[cols]
```

One of the most common exceptions raised when working with pandas is `KeyError`. This error is mainly due to mistyping of a column or index name. This same error is raised whenever a multiple column selection is attempted without the use of a list:

```
>>> movies[
...      "actor_1_name",
...      "actor_2_name",
...      "actor_3_name",
...      "director_name",
... ]
Traceback (most recent call last):
   ...
KeyError: ('actor_1_name', 'actor_2_name', 'actor_3_name', 'director_
name')
```

Selecting columns with methods

Although column selection is usually done with the indexing operator, there are some DataFrame methods that facilitate their selection in an alternative manner. The `.select_dtypes` and `.filter` methods are two useful methods to do this.

If you want to select by type, you need to be familiar with pandas data types. The *Understanding data types* recipe in *Chapter 1, Pandas Foundations*, explains the types.

How to do it...

1. Read in the movie dataset. Shorten the column names for display. Use the `.get_dtype_counts` method to output the number of columns with each specific data type:

    ```
    >>> movies = pd.read_csv("data/movie.csv")
    >>> def shorten(col):
    ...     return (
    ...         str(col)
    ...         .replace("facebook_likes", "fb")
    ...         .replace("_for_reviews", "")
    ...     )
    >>> movies = movies.rename(columns=shorten)
    >>> movies.dtypes.value_counts()
    float64    13
    int64       3
    object     12
    dtype: int64
    ```

2. Use the `.select_dtypes` method to select only the integer columns:

    ```
    >>> movies.select_dtypes(include="int").head()
       num_voted_users  cast_total_fb  movie_fb
    0           886204           4834     33000
    1           471220          48350         0
    2           275868          11700     85000
    3          1144337         106759    164000
    4                8            143         0
    ```

3. If you would like to select all the numeric columns, you may pass the string `number` to the `include` parameter:

```
>>> movies.select_dtypes(include="number").head()
   num_critics  duration  ...  aspect_ratio  movie_fb
0        723.0     178.0  ...          1.78     33000
1        302.0     169.0  ...          2.35         0
2        602.0     148.0  ...          2.35     85000
3        813.0     164.0  ...          2.35    164000
4          NaN       NaN  ...           NaN         0
```

4. If we wanted integer and string columns we could do the following:

```
>>> movies.select_dtypes(include=["int", "object"]).head()
   color         direc/_name  ...  conte/ating  movie_fb
0  Color       James Cameron  ...        PG-13     33000
1  Color      Gore Verbinski  ...        PG-13         0
2  Color         Sam Mendes   ...        PG-13     85000
3  Color   Christopher Nolan  ...        PG-13    164000
4    NaN         Doug Walker  ...          NaN         0
```

5. To exclude only floating-point columns, do the following:

```
>>> movies.select_dtypes(exclude="float").head()
   color  director_name  ...  content_rating  movie_fb
0  Color      James Ca...  ...          PG-13     33000
1  Color      Gore Ver...  ...          PG-13         0
2  Color      Sam Mendes   ...          PG-13     85000
3  Color      Christop...  ...          PG-13    164000
4    NaN     Doug Walker   ...            NaN         0
```

6. An alternative method to select columns is with the `.filter` method. This method is flexible and searches column names (or index labels) based on which parameter is used. Here, we use the `like` parameter to search for all the Facebook columns or the names that contain the exact string, `fb`. The `like` parameter is checking for substrings in column names:

```
>>> movies.filter(like="fb").head()
   director_fb  actor_3_fb  ...  actor_2_fb  movie_fb
0          0.0       855.0  ...       936.0     33000
1        563.0      1000.0  ...      5000.0         0
2          0.0       161.0  ...       393.0     85000
3      22000.0     23000.0  ...     23000.0    164000
4        131.0         NaN  ...        12.0         0
```

7. The `.filter` method has more tricks (or parameters) up its sleeve. If you use the `items` parameters, you can pass in a list of column names:

```
>>> cols = [
...        "actor_1_name",
...        "actor_2_name",
...        "actor_3_name",
...        "director_name",
... ]
>>> movies.filter(items=cols).head()
        actor_1_name   ...        director_name
0        CCH Pounder   ...        James Cameron
1        Johnny Depp   ...        Gore Verbinski
2     Christoph Waltz  ...          Sam Mendes
3          Tom Hardy   ...     Christopher Nolan
4         Doug Walker  ...          Doug Walker
```

8. The `.filter` method allows columns to be searched with *regular expressions* using the `regex` parameter. Here, we search for all columns that have a digit somewhere in their name:

```
>>> movies.filter(regex=r"\d").head()
     actor_3_fb actor_2_name  ...   actor_3_name actor_2_fb
0        855.0   Joel Dav...  ...     Wes Studi      936.0
1       1000.0   Orlando ...  ...     Jack Dav...   5000.0
2        161.0   Rory Kin...  ...     Stephani...    393.0
3      23000.0   Christia...  ...     Joseph G...  23000.0
4          NaN   Rob Walker   ...           NaN      12.0
```

How it works...

Step 1 lists the frequencies of all the different data types. Alternatively, you may use the `.dtypes` attribute to get the exact data type for each column. The `.select_dtypes` method accepts either a list or single data type in its `include` or `exclude` parameters and returns a DataFrame with columns of just those given data types (or not those types if excluding columns). The list values may be either the string name of the data type or the actual Python object.

The `.filter` method selects columns by only inspecting the column names and not the actual data values. It has three mutually exclusive parameters: `items`, `like`, and `regex`, only one of which can be used at a time.

The `like` parameter takes a string and attempts to find all the column names that contain that exact string somewhere in the name. To gain more flexibility, you may use the `regex` parameter instead to select column names through a regular expression. This particular regular expression, `r'\d'`, represents all digits from zero to nine and matches any string with at least a single digit in it.

The filter method comes with another parameter, `items`, which takes a list of exact column names. This is nearly an exact duplication of the index operation, except that a `KeyError` will not be raised if one of the strings does not match a column name. For instance, `movies.filter(items=['actor_1_name', 'asdf'])` runs without error and returns a single column DataFrame.

There's more...

One confusing aspect of `.select_dtypes` is its flexibility to take both strings and Python objects. The following list should clarify all the possible ways to select the many different column data types. There is no standard or preferred method of referring to data types in pandas, so it's good to be aware of both ways:

- `np.number`, `'number'` – Selects both integers and floats regardless of size
- `np.float64`, `np.float_`, `float`, `'float64'`, `'float_'`, `'float'` – Selects only 64-bit floats
- `np.float16`, `np.float32`, `np.float128`, `'float16'`, `'float32'`, `'float128'` – Respectively selects exactly 16, 32, and 128-bit floats
- `np.floating`, `'floating'` – Selects all floats regardless of size
- `np.int0`, `np.int64`, `np.int_`, `int`, `'int0'`, `'int64'`, `'int_'`, `'int'` – Selects only 64-bit integers
- `np.int8`, `np.int16`, `np.int32`, `'int8'`, `'int16'`, `'int32'` – Respectively selects exactly 8, 16, and 32-bit integers
- `np.integer`, `'integer'` – Selects all integers regardless of size
- `'Int64'` – Selects nullable integer; no NumPy equivalent
- `np.object`, `'object'`, `'O'` – Select all object data types
- `np.datetime64`, `'datetime64'`, `'datetime'` – All datetimes are 64 bits
- `np.timedelta64`, `'timedelta64'`, `'timedelta'` – All timedeltas are 64 bits
- `pd.Categorical`, `'category'` – Unique to pandas; no NumPy equivalent

Because all integers and floats default to 64 bits, you may select them by using the string `'int'` or `'float'` as you can see from the preceding bullet list. If you want to select all integers and floats regardless of their specific size, use the string `'number'`.

Ordering column names

One of the first tasks to consider after initially importing a dataset as a DataFrame is to analyze the order of the columns. As humans we are used to reading languages from left to right, which impacts our interpretations of the data. It's far easier to find and interpret information when column order is given consideration.

There are no standardized set of rules that dictate how columns should be organized within a dataset. However, it is good practice to develop a set of guidelines that you consistently follow. This is especially true if you work with a group of analysts who share lots of datasets.

The following is a guideline to order columns:

▶ Classify each column as either categorical or continuous

▶ Group common columns within the categorical and continuous columns

▶ Place the most important groups of columns first with categorical columns before continuous ones

This recipe shows you how to order the columns with this guideline. There are many possible orderings that are sensible.

How to do it...

1. Read in the movie dataset, and scan the data:

```
>>> movies = pd.read_csv("data/movie.csv")
>>> def shorten(col):
...     return col.replace("facebook_likes", "fb").replace(
...         "_for_reviews", ""
...     )
>>> movies = movies.rename(columns=shorten)
```

2. Output all the column names and scan for similar categorical and continuous columns:

```
>>> movies.columns
Index(['color', 'director_name', 'num_critic', 'duration',
'director_fb',
       'actor_3_fb', 'actor_2_name', 'actor_1_fb', 'gross',
'genres',
       'actor_1_name', 'movie_title', 'num_voted_users', 'cast_
total_fb',
       'actor_3_name', 'facenumber_in_poster', 'plot_keywords',
```

```
        'movie_imdb_link', 'num_user', 'language', 'country',
    'content_rating',
        'budget', 'title_year', 'actor_2_fb', 'imdb_score',
    'aspect_ratio',
        'movie_fb'],
      dtype='object')
```

3. The columns don't appear to have any logical ordering to them. Organize the names sensibly into lists so that the guideline from the previous section is followed:

```
>>> cat_core = [
...        "movie_title",
...        "title_year",
...        "content_rating",
...        "genres",
... ]
>>> cat_people = [
...        "director_name",
...        "actor_1_name",
...        "actor_2_name",
...        "actor_3_name",
... ]
>>> cat_other = [
...        "color",
...        "country",
...        "language",
...        "plot_keywords",
...        "movie_imdb_link",
... ]
>>> cont_fb = [
...        "director_fb",
...        "actor_1_fb",
...        "actor_2_fb",
...        "actor_3_fb",
...        "cast_total_fb",
...        "movie_fb",
... ]
>>> cont_finance = ["budget", "gross"]
```

```
>>> cont_num_reviews = [
...     "num_voted_users",
...     "num_user",
...     "num_critic",
... ]
>>> cont_other = [
...     "imdb_score",
...     "duration",
...     "aspect_ratio",
...     "facenumber_in_poster",
... ]
```

4. Concatenate all the lists together to get the final column order. Also, ensure that this list contains all the columns from the original:

```
>>> new_col_order = (
...     cat_core
...     + cat_people
...     + cat_other
...     + cont_fb
...     + cont_finance
...     + cont_num_reviews
...     + cont_other
... )
>>> set(movies.columns) == set(new_col_order)
True
```

5. Pass the list with the new column order to the indexing operator of the DataFrame to reorder the columns:

```
>>> movies[new_col_order].head()
    movie_title  title_year  ...  aspect_ratio  facenumber_in_poster
0        Avatar      2009.0  ...          1.78                   0.0
1   Pirates ...      2007.0  ...          2.35                   0.0
2       Spectre      2015.0  ...          2.35                   1.0
3    The Dark...      2012.0  ...          2.35                   0.0
4    Star War...         NaN  ...           NaN                   0.0
```

How it works...

You can select a subset of columns from a DataFrame, with a list of specific column names. For instance, `movies[['movie_title', 'director_name']]` creates a new DataFrame with only the `movie_title` and `director_name` columns. Selecting columns by name is the default behavior of the index operator for a pandas DataFrame.

Step 3 neatly organizes all of the column names into separate lists based on their type (categorical or continuous) and by how similar their data is. The most important columns, such as the title of the movie, are placed first.

Step 4 concatenates all of the lists of column names and validates that this new list contains the same exact values as the original column names. Python sets are unordered and the equality statement checks whether each member of one set is a member of the other. Manually ordering columns in this recipe is susceptible to human error as it's easy to mistakenly forget a column in the new column list.

Step 5 completes the reordering by passing the new column order as a list to the indexing operator. This new order is now much more sensible than the original.

There's more...

There are alternative guidelines for ordering columns besides the suggestion mentioned earlier. Hadley Wickham's seminal paper on *Tidy Data* suggests placing the fixed variables first, followed by measured variables. As this data does not come from a controlled experiment, there is some flexibility in determining which variables are fixed and which ones are measured. Good candidates for measured variables are those that we would like to predict, such as *gross*, the *budget*, or the *imdb_score*. For instance, in this ordering, we can mix categorical and continuous variables. It might make more sense to place the column for the number of Facebook likes directly after the name of that actor. You can, of course, come up with your own guidelines for column order as the computational parts are unaffected by it.

Summarizing a DataFrame

In the *Calling Series methods* recipe in *Chapter 1, Pandas Foundations*, a variety of methods operated on a single column or Series of data. Many of these were *aggregation* or *reducing* methods that returned a single scalar value. When these same methods are called from a DataFrame, they perform that operation for each column at once and reduce the results for each column in the DataFrame. They return a Series with the column names in the index and the summary for each column as the value.

In this recipe, we explore a variety of the most common DataFrame attributes and methods with the movie dataset.

How to do it...

1. Read in the movie dataset, and examine the basic descriptive properties, `.shape`, `.size`, and `.ndim`, along with running the `len` function:

```
>>> movies = pd.read_csv("data/movie.csv")
>>> movies.shape
(4916, 28)
>>> movies.size
137648
>>> movies.ndim
2
>>> len(movies)
4916
```

2. The `.count` method shows the number of non-missing values for each column. It is an aggregation method as it summarizes every column in a single value. The output is a Series that has the original column names as its index:

```
>>> movies.count()
color                       4897
director_name               4814
num_critic_for_reviews      4867
duration                    4901
director_facebook_likes     4814
                            ...
title_year                  4810
actor_2_facebook_likes      4903
imdb_score                  4916
aspect_ratio                4590
movie_facebook_likes        4916
Length: 28, dtype: int64
```

3. The other methods that compute summary statistics, `.min`, `.max`, `.mean`, `.median`, and `.std`, return Series that have the column names of the numeric columns in the index and their aggregations as the values:

```
>>> movies.min()
num_critic_for_reviews         1.00
duration                       7.00
director_facebook_likes        0.00
```

```
actor_3_facebook_likes          0.00
actor_1_facebook_likes          0.00

                                 ...
title_year                   1916.00
actor_2_facebook_likes          0.00
imdb_score                      1.60
aspect_ratio                    1.18
movie_facebook_likes            0.00
Length: 16, dtype: float64
```

4. The `.describe` method is very powerful and calculates all the descriptive statistics and quartiles at once. The end result is a DataFrame with the descriptive statistics names as its index. I like to transpose the results using `.T` as I can usually fit more information on the screen that way:

```
>>> movies.describe().T
                count         mean    ...         75%         max
num_criti...   4867.0   137.988905   ...      191.00       813.0
duration       4901.0   107.090798   ...      118.00       511.0
director_...   4814.0   691.014541   ...      189.75     23000.0
actor_3_f...   4893.0   631.276313   ...      633.00     23000.0
actor_1_f...   4909.0  6494.488491   ...    11000.00    640000.0
...                ...          ...   ...         ...         ...
title_year     4810.0  2002.447609   ...     2011.00      2016.0
actor_2_f...   4903.0  1621.923516   ...      912.00    137000.0
imdb_score     4916.0     6.437429   ...        7.20         9.5
aspect_ratio   4590.0     2.222349   ...        2.35        16.0
movie_fac...   4916.0  7348.294142   ...     2000.00    349000.0
```

5. It is possible to specify exact quantiles in the `.describe` method using the `percentiles` parameter:

```
>>> movies.describe(percentiles=[0.01, 0.3, 0.99]).T
                count         mean    ...         99%         max
num_criti...   4867.0   137.988905   ...      546.68       813.0
duration       4901.0   107.090798   ...      189.00       511.0
director_...   4814.0   691.014541   ...    16000.00     23000.0
actor_3_f...   4893.0   631.276313   ...    11000.00     23000.0
actor_1_f...   4909.0  6494.488491   ...    44920.00    640000.0
...                ...          ...   ...         ...         ...
```

title_year	4810.0	2002.447609	...	2016.00	2016.0
actor_2_f...	4903.0	1621.923516	...	17000.00	137000.0
imdb_score	4916.0	6.437429	...	8.50	9.5
aspect_ratio	4590.0	2.222349	...	4.00	16.0
movie_fac...	4916.0	7348.294142	...	93850.00	349000.0

How it works...

Step 1 gives basic information on the size of the dataset. The `.shape` attribute returns a tuple with the number of rows and columns. The `.size` attribute returns the total number of elements in the DataFrame, which is just the product of the number of rows and columns. The `.ndim` attribute returns the number of dimensions, which is two for all DataFrames. When a DataFrame is passed to the built-in `len` function, it returns the number of rows.

The methods in *step 2* and *step 3* aggregate each column down to a single number. Each column name is now the index label in a Series with its aggregated result as the corresponding value.

If you look closely, you will notice that the output from *step 3* is missing all the object columns from *step 2*. This method ignores string columns by default.

Note that numeric columns have missing values but have a result returned by `.describe`. By default, pandas handles missing values in numeric columns by skipping them. It is possible to change this behavior by setting the `skipna` parameter to `False`. This will cause pandas to return NaN for all these aggregation methods if there exists at least a single missing value.

The `.describe` method displays the summary statistics of the numeric columns. You can expand its summary to include more quantiles by passing a list of numbers between 0 and 1 to the `percentiles` parameter. See the *Developing a data analysis routine* recipe for more on the `.describe` method.

There's more...

To see how the `.skipna` parameter affects the outcome, we can set its value to `False` and rerun *step 3* from the preceding recipe. Only numeric columns without missing values will calculate a result:

```
>>> movies.min(skipna=False)
num_critic_for_reviews      NaN
duration                    NaN
director_facebook_likes     NaN
actor_3_facebook_likes      NaN
```

```
actor_1_facebook_likes       NaN
                             . . .
title_year                   NaN
actor_2_facebook_likes       NaN
imdb_score                   1.6
aspect_ratio                 NaN
movie_facebook_likes         0.0
Length: 16, dtype: float64
```

Chaining DataFrame methods

The *Chaining Series methods* recipe in *Chapter 1*, *Pandas Foundations*, showcased several examples of chaining Series methods together. All the method chains in this chapter will begin from a DataFrame. One of the keys to method chaining is to know the exact object being returned during each step of the chain. In pandas, this will nearly always be a DataFrame, Series, or scalar value.

In this recipe, we count all the missing values in each column of the movie dataset.

How to do it...

1. We will use the `.isnull` method to get a count of the missing values. This method will change every value to a Boolean, indicating whether it is missing:

    ```
    >>> movies = pd.read_csv("data/movie.csv")
    >>> def shorten(col):
    ...       return col.replace("facebook_likes", "fb").replace(
    ...           "_for_reviews", ""
    ...       )
    >>> movies = movies.rename(columns=shorten)
    >>> movies.isnull().head()
        color  director_name  ...  aspect_ratio  movie_fb
    0   False          False  ...         False     False
    1   False          False  ...         False     False
    2   False          False  ...         False     False
    3   False          False  ...         False     False
    4    True          False  ...          True     False
    ```

2. We will chain the `.sum` method that interprets `True` and `False` as `1` and `0`, respectively. Because this is a reduction method, it aggregates the results into a Series:

```
>>> (movies.isnull().sum().head())
color                19
director_name       102
num_critic           49
duration             15
director_fb         102
dtype: int64
```

3. We can go one step further and take the sum of this Series and return the count of the total number of missing values in the entire DataFrame as a scalar value:

```
>>> movies.isnull().sum().sum()
2654
```

4. A way to determine whether there are any missing values in the DataFrame is to use the `.any` method twice in succession:

```
>>> movies.isnull().any().any()
True
```

How it works...

The `.isnull` method returns a DataFrame the same size as the calling DataFrame but with all values transformed to Booleans. See the counts of the following data types to verify this:

```
>>> movies.isnull().dtypes.value_counts()
bool     28
dtype: int64
```

In Python, Booleans evaluate to 0 and 1, and this makes it possible to sum them by column, as done in *step 2*. The resulting Series itself also has a `.sum` method, which gets us the grand total of missing values in the DataFrame.

In *step 4*, the `.any` method on a DataFrame returns a Series of Booleans indicating if there exists at least one `True` for each column. The `.any` method is chained again on this resulting Series of Booleans to determine if any of the columns have missing values. If *step 4* evaluates as `True`, then there is at least one missing value in the entire DataFrame.

There's more...

Most of the columns in the movie dataset with the `object` data type contain missing values. By default, aggregation methods (`.min`, `.max`, and `.sum`), do not return anything for `object` columns. as seen in the following code snippet, which selects three `object` columns and attempts to find the maximum value of each one:

```
>>> movies[["color", "movie_title", "color"]].max()
Series([], dtype: float64)
```

To force pandas to return something for each column, we must fill in the missing values. Here, we choose an empty string:

```
>>> movies.select_dtypes(["object"]).fillna("").max()
color                           Color
director_name           Étienne Faure
actor_2_name            Zubaida Sahar
genres                        Western
actor_1_name            Óscar Jaenada
                          ...
plot_keywords     zombie|zombie spoof
movie_imdb_link      http://www.imdb....
language                        Zulu
country                West Germany
content_rating                    X
Length: 12, dtype: object
```

For purposes of readability, method chains are often written as one method call per line surrounded by parentheses. This makes it easier to read and insert comments on what is returned at each step of the chain, or comment out lines to debug what is happening:

```
>>> (movies.select_dtypes(["object"]).fillna("").max())
color                           Color
director_name           Étienne Faure
actor_2_name            Zubaida Sahar
genres                        Western
actor_1_name            Óscar Jaenada
                          ...
plot_keywords     zombie|zombie spoof
movie_imdb_link      http://www.imdb....
language                        Zulu
```

```
country                West Germany
content_rating                    X
Length: 12, dtype: object
```

DataFrame operations

A primer on operators was given in the *Series operations* recipe from *Chapter 1, Pandas Foundations*, which will be helpful here. The Python arithmetic and comparison operators work with DataFrames, as they do with Series.

When an arithmetic or comparison operator is used with a DataFrame, each value of each column gets the operation applied to it. Typically, when an operator is used with a DataFrame, the columns are either all numeric or all object (usually strings). If the DataFrame does not contain homogeneous data, then the operation is likely to fail. Let's see an example of this failure with the college dataset, which contains both numeric and object data types. Attempting to add 5 to each value of the DataFrame raises a `TypeError` as integers cannot be added to strings:

```
>>> colleges = pd.read_csv("data/college.csv")
>>> colleges + 5
Traceback (most recent call last):
  ...
TypeError: can only concatenate str (not "int") to str
```

To successfully use an operator with a DataFrame, first select homogeneous data. For this recipe, we will select all the columns that begin with `'UGDS_'`. These columns represent the fraction of undergraduate students by race. To get started, we import the data and use the institution name as the label for our index, and then select the columns we desire with the `.filter` method:

```
>>> colleges = pd.read_csv(
...     "data/college.csv", index_col="INSTNM"
... )
>>> college_ugds = colleges.filter(like="UGDS_")
>>> college_ugds.head()
```

	UGDS_WHITE	UGDS_BLACK	...	UGDS_NRA	UGDS_UNKN
INSTNM			...		
Alabama A...	0.0333	0.9353	...	0.0059	0.0138
Universit...	0.5922	0.2600	...	0.0179	0.0100
Amridge U...	0.2990	0.4192	...	0.0000	0.2715
Universit...	0.6988	0.1255	...	0.0332	0.0350
Alabama S...	0.0158	0.9208	...	0.0243	0.0137

This recipe uses multiple operators with a DataFrame to round the undergraduate columns to the nearest hundredth. We will then see how this result is equivalent to the .round method.

How to do it...

1. pandas does *bankers* rounding, numbers that are exactly halfway between either side to the even side. Look at what happens to the UGDS_BLACK row of this series when we round it to two decimal places:

```
>>> name = "Northwest-Shoals Community College"
>>> college_ugds.loc[name]
UGDS_WHITE      0.7912
UGDS_BLACK      0.1250
UGDS_HISP       0.0339
UGDS_ASIAN      0.0036
UGDS_AIAN       0.0088
UGDS_NHPI       0.0006
UGDS_2MOR       0.0012
UGDS_NRA        0.0033
UGDS_UNKN       0.0324
Name: Northwest-Shoals Community College, dtype: float64
```

```
>>> college_ugds.loc[name].round(2)
UGDS_WHITE      0.79
UGDS_BLACK      0.12
UGDS_HISP       0.03
UGDS_ASIAN      0.00
UGDS_AIAN       0.01
UGDS_NHPI       0.00
UGDS_2MOR       0.00
UGDS_NRA        0.00
UGDS_UNKN       0.03
Name: Northwest-Shoals Community College, dtype: float64
```

If we add .0001 before rounding, it changes to rounding up:

```
>>> (college_ugds.loc[name] + 0.0001).round(2)
UGDS_WHITE      0.79
UGDS_BLACK      0.13
```

```
        UGDS_HISP     0.03
        UGDS_ASIAN    0.00
        UGDS_AIAN     0.01
        UGDS_NHPI     0.00
        UGDS_2MOR     0.00
        UGDS_NRA      0.00
        UGDS_UNKN     0.03
        Name: Northwest-Shoals Community College, dtype: float64
```

2. Let's do this to the DataFrame. To begin our rounding adventure with operators, we will first add `.00501` to each value of `college_ugds`:

```
>>> college_ugds + 0.00501
                   UGDS_WHITE   UGDS_BLACK   ...   UGDS_NRA   UGDS_UNKN
INSTNM                                       ...
Alabama A...       0.03831      0.94031      ...   0.01091    0.01881
Universit...       0.59721      0.26501      ...   0.02291    0.01501
Amridge U...       0.30401      0.42421      ...   0.00501    0.27651
Universit...       0.70381      0.13051      ...   0.03821    0.04001
Alabama S...       0.02081      0.92581      ...   0.02931    0.01871
...                ...          ...     ...  ...   ...        ...
SAE Insti...       NaN          NaN          ...   NaN        NaN
Rasmussen...       NaN          NaN          ...   NaN        NaN
National ...       NaN          NaN          ...   NaN        NaN
Bay Area ...       NaN          NaN          ...   NaN        NaN
Excel Lea...       NaN          NaN          ...   NaN        NaN
```

3. Use the floor division operator, `//`, to round down to the nearest whole number percentage:

```
>>> (college_ugds + 0.00501) // 0.01
                   UGDS_WHITE   UGDS_BLACK   ...   UGDS_NRA   UGDS_UNKN
INSTNM                                       ...
Alabama A...       3.0          94.0         ...   1.0        1.0
Universit...       59.0         26.0         ...   2.0        1.0
Amridge U...       30.0         42.0         ...   0.0        27.0
Universit...       70.0         13.0         ...   3.0        4.0
Alabama S...       2.0          92.0         ...   2.0        1.0
...                ...          ...     ...  ...   ...        ...
```

	UGDS_WHITE	UGDS_BLACK	...	UGDS_NRA	UGDS_UNKN
SAE Insti...	NaN	NaN	...	NaN	NaN
Rasmussen...	NaN	NaN	...	NaN	NaN
National ...	NaN	NaN	...	NaN	NaN
Bay Area ...	NaN	NaN	...	NaN	NaN
Excel Lea...	NaN	NaN	...	NaN	NaN

4. To complete the rounding exercise, divide by `100`:

```
>>> college_ugds_op_round = (
...     (college_ugds + 0.00501) // 0.01 / 100
... )
>>> college_ugds_op_round.head()
```

	UGDS_WHITE	UGDS_BLACK	...	UGDS_NRA	UGDS_UNKN
INSTNM			...		
Alabama A...	0.03	0.94	...	0.01	0.01
Universit...	0.59	0.26	...	0.02	0.01
Amridge U...	0.30	0.42	...	0.00	0.27
Universit...	0.70	0.13	...	0.03	0.04
Alabama S...	0.02	0.92	...	0.02	0.01

5. Now use the round DataFrame method to do the rounding automatically for us. Due to bankers rounding, we add a small fraction before rounding:

```
>>> college_ugds_round = (college_ugds + 0.00001).round(2)
>>> college_ugds_round
```

	UGDS_WHITE	UGDS_BLACK	...	UGDS_NRA	UGDS_UNKN
INSTNM			...		
Alabama A...	0.03	0.94	...	0.01	0.01
Universit...	0.59	0.26	...	0.02	0.01
Amridge U...	0.30	0.42	...	0.00	0.27
Universit...	0.70	0.13	...	0.03	0.04
Alabama S...	0.02	0.92	...	0.02	0.01
...	...	...	...	...	....
SAE Insti...	NaN	NaN	...	NaN	NaN
Rasmussen...	NaN	NaN	...	NaN	NaN
National ...	NaN	NaN	...	NaN	NaN
Bay Area ...	NaN	NaN	...	NaN	NaN
Excel Lea...	NaN	NaN	...	NaN	NaN

6. Use the equals DataFrame method to test the equality of two DataFrames:

```
>>> college_ugds_op_round.equals(college_ugds_round)
True
```

How it works...

Steps 1 and *2* use the plus operator, which attempts to add a scalar value to each value of each column of the DataFrame. As the columns are all numeric, this operation works as expected. There are some missing values in each of the columns but they stay missing after the operation.

Mathematically, adding `.005` should be enough so that the floor division in the next step correctly rounds to the nearest whole percentage. The trouble appears because of the inexactness of floating-point numbers:

```
>>> 0.045 + 0.005
0.04999999999999996
```

There is an extra `.00001` added to each number to ensure that the floating-point representation has the first four digits the same as the actual value. This works because the maximum precision of all the points in the dataset is four decimal places.

Step 3 applies the floor division operator, `//`, to all the values in the DataFrame. As we are dividing by a fraction, in essence, it is multiplying each value by `100` and truncating any decimals. Parentheses are needed around the first part of the expression, as floor division has higher precedence than addition. *Step 4* uses the division operator to return the decimal to the correct position.

In *step 5*, we reproduce the previous steps with the round method. Before we can do this, we must again add an extra `.00001` to each DataFrame value for a different reason from *step 2*. NumPy and Python 3 round numbers that are exactly halfway between either side to the even number. The bankers rounding (or *ties to even* `http://bit.ly/2x3V5TU`) technique is not usually what is formally taught in schools. It does not consistently bias numbers to the higher side (`http://bit.ly/2zhsPy8`).

It is necessary here to round up so that both DataFrame values are equal. The `.equals` method determines if all the elements and indexes between two DataFrames are exactly the same and returns a Boolean.

There's more...

Just as with Series, DataFrames have method equivalents of the operators. You may replace the operators with their method equivalents:

```
>>> college2 = (
...     college_ugds.add(0.00501).floordiv(0.01).div(100)
... )
>>> college2.equals(college_ugds_op_round)
True
```

Comparing missing values

pandas uses the NumPy NaN (np.nan) object to represent a missing value. This is an unusual object and has interesting mathematical properties. For instance, it is not equal to itself. Even Python's None object evaluates as True when compared to itself:

```
>>> np.nan == np.nan
False
>>> None == None
True
```

All other comparisons against np.nan also return False, except not equal to (!=):

```
>>> np.nan > 5
False
>>> 5 > np.nan
False
>>> np.nan != 5
True
```

Getting ready

Series and DataFrames use the equals operator, ==, to make element-by-element comparisons. The result is an object with the same dimensions. This recipe shows you how to use the equals operator, which is very different from the .equals method.

As in the previous recipe, the columns representing the fraction of each race of undergraduate students from the college dataset will be used:

```
>>> college = pd.read_csv(
...     "data/college.csv", index_col="INSTNM"
... )
>>> college_ugds = college.filter(like="UGDS_")
```

How to do it...

1. To get an idea of how the equals operator works, let's compare each element to a scalar value:

```
>>> college_ugds == 0.0019
```

	UGDS_WHITE	UGDS_BLACK	...	UGDS_NRA	UGDS_UNKN
INSTNM			...		
Alabama A...	False	False	...	False	False
Universit...	False	False	...	False	False
Amridge U...	False	False	...	False	False
Universit...	False	False	...	False	False
Alabama S...	False	False	...	False	False
...	...	...	...	...	...
SAE Insti...	False	False	...	False	False
Rasmussen...	False	False	...	False	False
National ...	False	False	...	False	False
Bay Area ...	False	False	...	False	False
Excel Lea...	False	False	...	False	False

2. This works as expected but becomes problematic whenever you attempt to compare DataFrames with missing values. You may be tempted to use the equals operator to compare two DataFrames with one another on an element-by-element basis. Take, for instance, `college_ugds` compared against itself, as follows:

```
>>> college_self_compare = college_ugds == college_ugds
>>> college_self_compare.head()
```

	UGDS_WHITE	UGDS_BLACK	...	UGDS_NRA	UGDS_UNKN
INSTNM			...		
Alabama A...	True	True	...	True	True
Universit...	True	True	...	True	True
Amridge U...	True	True	...	True	True
Universit...	True	True	...	True	True
Alabama S...	True	True	...	True	True

3. At first glance, all the values appear to be equal, as you would expect. However, using the `.all` method to determine if each column contains only `True` values yields an unexpected result:

```
>>> college_self_compare.all()
UGDS_WHITE    False
UGDS_BLACK    False
```

```
UGDS_HISP     False
UGDS_ASIAN    False
UGDS_AIAN     False
UGDS_NHPI     False
UGDS_2MOR     False
UGDS_NRA      False
UGDS_UNKN     False
dtype: bool
```

4. This happens because missing values do not compare equally with one another. If you tried to count missing values using the equal operator and summing up the Boolean columns, you would get zero for each one:

```
>>> (college_ugds == np.nan).sum()
UGDS_WHITE    0
UGDS_BLACK    0
UGDS_HISP     0
UGDS_ASIAN    0
UGDS_AIAN     0
UGDS_NHPI     0
UGDS_2MOR     0
UGDS_NRA      0
UGDS_UNKN     0
dtype: int64
```

5. Instead of using == to find missing numbers, use the .isna method:

```
>>> college_ugds.isna().sum()
UGDS_WHITE    661
UGDS_BLACK    661
UGDS_HISP     661
UGDS_ASIAN    661
UGDS_AIAN     661
UGDS_NHPI     661
UGDS_2MOR     661
UGDS_NRA      661
UGDS_UNKN     661
dtype: int64
```

6. The correct way to compare two entire DataFrames with one another is not with the equals operator (==) but with the `.equals` method. This method treats NaNs that are in the same location as equal (note that the `.eq` method is the equivalent of ==):

```
>>> college_ugds.equals(college_ugds)
True
```

How it works...

Step 1 compares a DataFrame to a scalar value while *step 2* compares a DataFrame with another DataFrame. Both operations appear to be quite simple and intuitive at first glance. The second operation is checking whether the DataFrames have identically labeled indexes and thus the same number of elements. The operation will fail if this isn't the case.

Step 3 verifies that none of the columns in the DataFrames are equivalent to each other. *Step 4* further shows the non-equivalence of `np.nan` and itself. *Step 5* verifies that there are indeed missing values in the DataFrame. Finally, *step 6* shows the correct way to compare DataFrames with the `.equals` method, which always returns a Boolean scalar value.

There's more...

All the comparison operators have method counterparts that allow for more functionality. Somewhat confusingly, the `.eq` DataFrame method does element-by-element comparison, just like the equals (==) operator. The `.eq` method is not at all the same as the `.equals` method. The following code duplicates *step 1*:

```
>>> college_ugds.eq(0.0019)   # same as college_ugds == .0019
```

INSTNM	UGDS_WHITE	UGDS_BLACK	...	UGDS_NRA	UGDS_UNKN
Alabama A...	False	False	...	False	False
Universit...	False	False	...	False	False
Amridge U...	False	False	...	False	False
Universit...	False	False	...	False	False
Alabama S...	False	False	...	False	False
...	...	...	...	...	...
SAE Insti...	False	False	...	False	False
Rasmussen...	False	False	...	False	False
National ...	False	False	...	False	False
Bay Area ...	False	False	...	False	False
Excel Lea...	False	False	...	False	False

Inside the `pandas.testing` sub-package, a function exists that developers should use when creating unit tests. The `assert_frame_equal` function raises an `AssertionError` if two DataFrames are not equal. It returns `None` if the two DataFrames are equal:

```
>>> from pandas.testing import assert_frame_equal
>>> assert_frame_equal(college_ugds, college_ugds) is None
True
```

Unit tests are a very important part of software development and ensure that the code is running correctly. pandas contains many thousands of unit tests that help ensure that it is running properly. To read more on how pandas runs its unit tests, see the *Contributing to pandas* section in the documentation (`http://bit.ly/2vmCSU6`).

Transposing the direction of a DataFrame operation

Many DataFrame methods have an `axis` parameter. This parameter controls the direction in which the operation takes place. Axis parameters can be `'index'` (or 0) or `'columns'` (or 1). I prefer the string versions are they are more explicit and tend to make the code easier to read.

Nearly all DataFrame methods default the axis parameter to 0, which applies to operations along the index. This recipe shows you how to invoke the same method along both axes.

How to do it...

1. Read in the college dataset; the columns that begin with UGDS represent the percentage of the undergraduate students of a particular race. Use the filter method to select these columns:

```
>>> college = pd.read_csv(
...     "data/college.csv", index_col="INSTNM"
... )
>>> college_ugds = college.filter(like="UGDS_")
>>> college_ugds.head()
```

	UGDS_WHITE	UGDS_BLACK	...	UGDS_NRA	UGDS_UNKN
INSTNM			...		
Alabama A...	0.0333	0.9353	...	0.0059	0.0138
Universit...	0.5922	0.2600	...	0.0179	0.0100
Amridge U...	0.2990	0.4192	...	0.0000	0.2715

```
Universit...       0.6988      0.1255   ...      0.0332      0.0350
Alabama S...       0.0158      0.9208   ...      0.0243      0.0137
```

2. Now that the DataFrame contains homogenous column data, operations can be sensibly done both vertically and horizontally. The `.count` method returns the number of non-missing values. By default, its `axis` parameter is set to `0`:

```
>>> college_ugds.count()
UGDS_WHITE     6874
UGDS_BLACK     6874
UGDS_HISP      6874
UGDS_ASIAN     6874
UGDS_AIAN      6874
UGDS_NHPI      6874
UGDS_2MOR      6874
UGDS_NRA       6874
UGDS_UNKN      6874
dtype: int64
```

The `axis` parameter is almost always set to `0`. So, *step 2* is equivalent to both `college_ugds.count(axis=0)` and `college_ugds.count(axis='index')`.

3. Changing the axis parameter to `'columns'` changes the direction of the operation so that we get back a count of non-missing items in each row:

```
>>> college_ugds.count(axis="columns").head()
INSTNM
Alabama A & M University                9
University of Alabama at Birmingham     9
Amridge University                      9
University of Alabama in Huntsville     9
Alabama State University                9
dtype: int64
```

4. Instead of counting non-missing values, we can sum all the values in each row. Each row of percentages should add up to 1. The `.sum` method may be used to verify this:

```
>>> college_ugds.sum(axis="columns").head()
INSTNM
Alabama A & M University                1.0000
University of Alabama at Birmingham     0.9999
Amridge University                      1.0000
University of Alabama in Huntsville     1.0000
```

```
    Alabama State University                    1.0000
    dtype: float64
```

5. To get an idea of the distribution of each column, the `.median` method can be used:

```
>>> college_ugds.median(axis="index")
UGDS_WHITE    0.55570
UGDS_BLACK    0.10005
UGDS_HISP     0.07140
UGDS_ASIAN    0.01290
UGDS_AIAN     0.00260
UGDS_NHPI     0.00000
UGDS_2MOR     0.01750
UGDS_NRA      0.00000
UGDS_UNKN     0.01430
dtype: float64
```

How it works...

The direction of operation on the axis is one of the more confusing aspects of pandas. Many pandas users have difficulty remembering the meaning of the axis parameter. I remember them by reminding myself that a Series only has one axis, the index (or 0). A DataFrame also has an index (axis 0) and columns (axis 1).

There's more...

The `.cumsum` method with `axis=1` accumulates the race percentages across each row. It gives a slightly different view of the data. For example, it is very easy to see the exact percentage of white and black students for each school:

```
>>> college_ugds_cumsum = college_ugds.cumsum(axis=1)
>>> college_ugds_cumsum.head()
```

	UGDS_WHITE	UGDS_BLACK	...	UGDS_NRA	UGDS_UNKN
INSTNM			...		
Alabama A...	0.0333	0.9686	...	0.9862	1.0000
Universit...	0.5922	0.8522	...	0.9899	0.9999
Amridge U...	0.2990	0.7182	...	0.7285	1.0000
Universit...	0.6988	0.8243	...	0.9650	1.0000
Alabama S...	0.0158	0.9366	...	0.9863	1.0000

Determining college campus diversity

Many articles are written every year on the different aspects and impacts of diversity on college campuses. Various organizations have developed metrics attempting to measure diversity. *US News* is a leader in providing rankings for many different categories of colleges, with diversity being one of them. Their top 10 diverse colleges with Diversity Index are given as follows:

```
>>> pd.read_csv(
...     "data/college_diversity.csv", index_col="School"
... )
```

	Diversity Index
School	
Rutgers University--Newark Newark, NJ	0.76
Andrews University Berrien Springs, MI	0.74
Stanford University Stanford, CA	0.74
University of Houston Houston, TX	0.74
University of Nevada--Las Vegas Las Vegas, NV	0.74
University of San Francisco San Francisco, CA	0.74
San Francisco State University San Francisco, CA	0.73
University of Illinois--Chicago Chicago, IL	0.73
New Jersey Institute of Technology Newark, NJ	0.72
Texas Woman's University Denton, TX	0.72

Our college dataset classifies race into nine different categories. When trying to quantify something without an obvious definition, such as diversity, it helps to start with something simple. In this recipe, our diversity metric will equal the count of the number of races having greater than 15% of the student population.

How to do it...

1. Read in the college dataset, and filter for just the undergraduate race columns:

```
>>> college = pd.read_csv(
...     "data/college.csv", index_col="INSTNM"
... )
>>> college_ugds = college.filter(like="UGDS_")
```

2. Many of these colleges have missing values for all their race columns. We can count all the missing values for each row and sort the resulting Series from the highest to lowest. This will reveal the colleges that have missing values:

```
>>> (
...        college_ugds.isnull()
...        .sum(axis="columns")
...        .sort_values(ascending=False)
...        .head()
... )
INSTNM
Excel Learning Center-San Antonio South          9
Philadelphia College of Osteopathic Medicine     9
Assemblies of God Theological Seminary            9
Episcopal Divinity School                         9
Phillips Graduate Institute                       9
dtype: int64
```

3. Now that we have seen the colleges that are missing all their race columns, we can use the .dropna method to drop all rows that have all nine race percentages missing. We can then count the remaining missing values:

```
>>> college_ugds = college_ugds.dropna(how="all")
>>> college_ugds.isnull().sum()
UGDS_WHITE    0
UGDS_BLACK    0
UGDS_HISP     0
UGDS_ASIAN    0
UGDS_AIAN     0
UGDS_NHPI     0
UGDS_2MOR     0
UGDS_NRA      0
UGDS_UNKN     0
dtype: int64
```

4. There are no missing values left in the dataset. We can now calculate our diversity metric. To get started, we will use the greater than or equal DataFrame method, .ge, to return a DataFrame with a Boolean value for each cell:

```
>>> college_ugds.ge(0.15)
           UGDS_WHITE   UGDS_BLACK   ...   UGDS_NRA   UGDS_UNKN
```

INSTNM			...		
Alabama A...	False	True	...	False	False
Universit...	True	True	...	False	False
Amridge U...	True	True	...	False	True
Universit...	True	False	...	False	False
Alabama S...	False	True	...	False	False
...	...	...	...	...	...
Hollywood...	True	True	...	False	False
Hollywood...	False	True	...	False	False
Coachella...	True	False	...	False	False
Dewey Uni...	False	False	...	False	False
Coastal P...	True	True	...	False	False

5. From here, we can use the `.sum` method to count the `True` values for each college. Notice that a Series is returned:

```
>>> diversity_metric = college_ugds.ge(0.15).sum(
...     axis="columns"
... )
>>> diversity_metric.head()
INSTNM
Alabama A & M University                1
University of Alabama at Birmingham     2
Amridge University                      3
University of Alabama in Huntsville     1
Alabama State University                1
dtype: int64
```

6. To get an idea of the distribution, we will use the `.value_counts` method on this Series:

```
>>> diversity_metric.value_counts()
1    3042
2    2884
3     876
4      63
0       7
5       2
dtype: int64
```

7. Amazingly, two schools have more than 15% in five different race categories. Let's sort the `diversity_metric` Series to find out which ones they are:

```
>>> diversity_metric.sort_values(ascending=False).head()
INSTNM
Regency Beauty Institute-Austin         5
Central Texas Beauty College-Temple     5
Sullivan and Cogliano Training Center   4
Ambria College of Nursing               4
Berkeley College-New York               4
dtype: int64
```

8. It seems a little suspicious that schools can be that diverse. Let's look at the raw percentages from these top two schools. We will use `.loc` to select rows based on the index label:

```
>>> college_ugds.loc[
...     [
...         "Regency Beauty Institute-Austin",
...         "Central Texas Beauty College-Temple",
...     ]
... ]
```

	UGDS_WHITE	UGDS_BLACK	...	UGDS_NRA	UGDS_UNKN
INSTNM			...		
Regency B...	0.1867	0.2133	...	0.0	0.2667
Central T...	0.1616	0.2323	...	0.0	0.1515

9. It appears that several categories were aggregated into the unknown and two or more races column. Regardless of this, they both appear to be quite diverse. We can see how the top five US News schools fared with this basic diversity metric:

```
>>> us_news_top = [
...     "Rutgers University-Newark",
...     "Andrews University",
...     "Stanford University",
...     "University of Houston",
...     "University of Nevada-Las Vegas",
... ]
>>> diversity_metric.loc[us_news_top]
INSTNM
Rutgers University-Newark               4
```

```
Andrews University                    3
Stanford University                   3
University of Houston                 3
University of Nevada-Las Vegas        3
dtype: int64
```

How it works...

Step 2 counts and then displays the schools with the highest number of missing values. As there are nine columns in the DataFrame, the maximum number of missing values per school is nine. Many schools are missing values for each column. *Step 3* removes rows that have all their values missing. The .dropna method in *step 3* has the how parameter, which defaults to the string 'any', but may also be changed to 'all'. When set to 'any', it drops rows that contain one or more missing values. When set to 'all', it only drops rows where all values are missing.

In this case, we conservatively drop rows that are missing all values. This is because it's possible that some missing values represent 0 percent. This did not happen to be the case here, as there were no missing values after the dropna method was performed. If there were still missing values, we could have run the .fillna(0) method to fill all the remaining values with 0.

Step 5 begins our diversity metric calculation using the greater than or equal to method, .ge. This results in a DataFrame of all Booleans, which is summed horizontally by setting axis='columns'.

The .value_counts method is used in *step 6* to produce a distribution of our diversity metric. It is quite rare for schools to have three races with 15% or more of the undergraduate student population. *Step 7* and *step 8* find two schools that are the most diverse based on our metric. Although they are diverse, it appears that many of the races are not fully accounted for and are defaulted into the unknown and two or more categories.

Step 9 selects the top five schools from the *US News* article. It then selects their diversity metric from our newly created Series. It turns out that these schools also score highly with our simple ranking system.

There's more...

Alternatively, we can find the schools that are least diverse by ordering them by their maximum race percentage:

```
>>> (
...     college_ugds.max(axis=1)
```

```
...         .sort_values(ascending=False)
...         .head(10)
... )
INSTNM
Dewey University-Manati                                     1.0
Yeshiva and Kollel Harbotzas Torah                          1.0
Mr Leon's School of Hair Design-Lewiston                    1.0
Dewey University-Bayamon                                    1.0
Shepherds Theological Seminary                              1.0
Yeshiva Gedolah Kesser Torah                                1.0
Monteclaro Escuela de Hoteleria y Artes Culinarias          1.0
Yeshiva Shaar Hatorah                                       1.0
Bais Medrash Elyon                                          1.0
Yeshiva of Nitra Rabbinical College                        1.0
dtype: float64
```

We can also determine if any school has all nine race categories exceeding 1%:

```
>>> (college_ugds > 0.01).all(axis=1).any()
True
```

3

Creating and Persisting DataFrames

Introduction

There are many ways to create a DataFrame. This chapter will cover some of the most common ones. It will also show how to persist them.

Creating DataFrames from scratch

Usually, we create a DataFrame from an existing file or a database, but we can also create one from scratch. We can create a DataFrame from parallel lists of data.

How to do it...

1. Create parallel lists with your data in them. Each of these lists will be a column in the DataFrame, so they should have the same type:

```
>>> import pandas as pd
>>> import numpy as np
>>> fname = ["Paul", "John", "Richard", "George"]
>>> lname = ["McCartney", "Lennon", "Starkey", "Harrison"]
>>> birth = [1942, 1940, 1940, 1943]
```

2. Create a dictionary from the lists, mapping the column name to the list:

```
>>> people = {"first": fname, "last": lname, "birth": birth}
```

3. Create a DataFrame from the dictionary:

```
>>> beatles = pd.DataFrame(people)
>>> beatles
        first       last  birth
0        Paul  McCartney   1942
1        John     Lennon   1940
2     Richard    Starkey   1940
3      George   Harrison   1943
```

How it works...

By default, pandas will create a `RangeIndex` for our DataFrame when we call the constructor:

```
>>> beatles.index
RangeIndex(start=0, stop=4, step=1)
```

We can specify another index for the DataFrame if we desire:

```
>>> pd.DataFrame(people, index=["a", "b", "c", "d"])
      first       last  birth
a      Paul  McCartney   1942
b      John     Lennon   1940
c   Richard    Starkey   1940
d    George   Harrison   1943
```

There's more...

You can also create a DataFrame from a list of dictionaries:

```
>>> pd.DataFrame(
...     [
...         {
...             "first": "Paul",
...             "last": "McCartney",
...             "birth": 1942,
...         },
```

```
...         {
...             "first": "John",
...             "last": "Lennon",
...             "birth": 1940,
...         },
...         {
...             "first": "Richard",
...             "last": "Starkey",
...             "birth": 1940,
...         },
...         {
...             "first": "George",
...             "last": "Harrison",
...             "birth": 1943,
...         },
...     ]
... )
     birth    first        last
0    1942     Paul     McCartney
1    1940     John       Lennon
2    1940  Richard      Starkey
3    1943   George     Harrison
```

Note that the columns are ordered by the alphabetic ordering of the keys when you use rows of dictionaries. You can use the `columns` parameter to specify the column order if that is important to you:

```
>>> pd.DataFrame(
...     [
...         {
...             "first": "Paul",
...             "last": "McCartney",
...             "birth": 1942,
...         },
...         {
...             "first": "John",
...             "last": "Lennon",
...             "birth": 1940,
```

```
...            },
...            {
...                "first": "Richard",
...                "last": "Starkey",
...                "birth": 1940,
...            },
...            {
...                "first": "George",
...                "last": "Harrison",
...                "birth": 1943,
...            },
...        ],
...        columns=["last", "first", "birth"],
... )
         last     first  birth
0   McCartney      Paul   1942
1     Lennon       John   1940
2     Starkey   Richard   1940
3    Harrison    George   1943
```

Writing CSV

For better or worse, there are a lot of CSV files in the world. Like most technologies, there are good and bad parts to CSV files. On the plus side, they are human-readable, can be opened in any text editor, and most spreadsheet software can load them. On the downside, there is no standard for CSV files, so encoding may be weird, there is no way to enforce types, and they can be large because they are text-based (though they can be compressed).

In this recipe, we will show how to create a CSV file from a pandas DataFrame.

There are a few methods on the DataFrame that start with `to_`. These are methods that export DataFrames. We are going to use the `.to_csv` method. We will write out to a string buffer in the examples, but you will usually use a filename instead.

How to do it...

1. Write the DataFrame to a CSV file:

```
>>> beatles
```

```
          first      last  birth
     0      Paul  McCartney  1942
     1      John    Lennon   1940
     2   Richard   Starkey   1940
     3    George   Harrison  1943


>>> from io import StringIO
>>> fout = StringIO()
>>> beatles.to_csv(fout)  # use a filename instead of fout
```

2. Look at the file contents:

```
>>> print(fout.getvalue())
,first,last,birth
0,Paul,McCartney,1942
1,John,Lennon,1940
2,Richard,Starkey,1940
3,George,Harrison,1943
```

There's more...

The `.to_csv` method has a few options. You will notice that it included the index in the output but did not give the index a column name. If you were to read this CSV file into a DataFrame using the `read_csv` function, it would not use this as the index by default. Instead, you will get a column named *Unnamed: 0* in addition to an index. These columns are redundant:

```
>>> _ = fout.seek(0)
>>> pd.read_csv(fout)
   Unnamed: 0    first      last  birth
0           0     Paul  McCartney  1942
1           1     John    Lennon   1940
2           2  Richard   Starkey   1940
3           3   George   Harrison  1943
```

The `read_csv` function has an `index_col` parameter that you can use to specify the location of the index:

```
>>> _ = fout.seek(0)
>>> pd.read_csv(fout, index_col=0)
```

```
       first        last  birth
0       Paul   McCartney   1942
1       John     Lennon    1940
2    Richard    Starkey    1940
3     George   Harrison    1943
```

Alternatively, if we didn't want to include the index when writing the CSV file, we can set the index parameter to `False`:

```
>>> fout = StringIO()
>>> beatles.to_csv(fout, index=False)
>>> print(fout.getvalue())
first,last,birth
Paul,McCartney,1942
John,Lennon,1940
Richard,Starkey,1940
George,Harrison,1943
```

Reading large CSV files

The pandas library is an *in-memory* tool. You need to be able to fit your data in memory to use pandas with it. If you come across a large CSV file that you want to process, you have a few options. If you can process portions of it at a time, you can read it into chunks and process each chunk. Alternatively, if you know that you should have enough memory to load the file, there are a few hints to help pare down the file size.

Note that in general, you should have three to ten times the amount of memory as the size of the DataFrame that you want to manipulate. Extra memory should give you enough extra space to perform many of the common operations.

How to do it...

In this section, we will look at the *diamonds* dataset. This dataset easily fits into the memory of my 2015 MacBook, but let's pretend that the file is a lot bigger than it is, or that the memory of my machine is limited such that when pandas tries to load it with the `read_csv` function, I get a memory error.

1. Determine how much memory the whole file will take up. We will use the `nrows` parameter of `read_csv` to limit how much data we load to a small sample:

   ```
   >>> diamonds = pd.read_csv("data/diamonds.csv", nrows=1000)
   ```

```
>>> diamonds
        carat      cut color clarity  ...  price     x     y     z
0        0.23    Ideal     E     SI2  ...    326  3.95  3.98  2.43
1        0.21  Premium     E     SI1  ...    326  3.89  3.84  2.31
2        0.23     Good     E     VS1  ...    327  4.05  4.07  2.31
3        0.29  Premium     I     VS2  ...    334  4.20  4.23  2.63
4        0.31     Good     J     SI2  ...    335  4.34  4.35  2.75
..        ...      ...   ...     ...  ...    ...   ...   ...   ...
995      0.54    Ideal     D    VVS2  ...   2897  5.30  5.34  3.26
996      0.72    Ideal     E     SI1  ...   2897  5.69  5.74  3.57
997      0.72     Good     F     VS1  ...   2897  5.82  5.89  3.48
998      0.74  Premium     D     VS2  ...   2897  5.81  5.77  3.58
999      1.12  Premium     J     SI2  ...   2898  6.68  6.61  4.03
```

2. Use the `.info` method to see how much memory the sample of data uses:

```
>>> diamonds.info()
<class 'pandas.core.frame.DataFrame'>
RangeIndex: 1000 entries, 0 to 999
Data columns (total 10 columns):
carat       1000 non-null float64
cut         1000 non-null object
color       1000 non-null object
clarity     1000 non-null object
depth       1000 non-null float64
table       1000 non-null float64
price       1000 non-null int64
x           1000 non-null float64
y           1000 non-null float64
z           1000 non-null float64
dtypes: float64(6), int64(1), object(3)
memory usage: 78.2+ KB
```

We can see that 1,000 rows use about 78.2 KB of memory. If we had 1 billion rows, that would take about 78 GB of memory. It turns out that it is possible to rent machines in the cloud that have that much memory but let's see if we can take it down a little.

3. Use the `dtype` parameter to `read_csv` to tell it to use the correct (or smaller) numeric types:

```
>>> diamonds2 = pd.read_csv(
...     "data/diamonds.csv",
...     nrows=1000,
...     dtype={
...         "carat": np.float32,
...         "depth": np.float32,
...         "table": np.float32,
...         "x": np.float32,
...         "y": np.float32,
...         "z": np.float32,
...         "price": np.int16,
...     },
... )
```

```
>>> diamonds2.info()
<class 'pandas.core.frame.DataFrame'>
RangeIndex: 1000 entries, 0 to 999
Data columns (total 10 columns):
carat      1000 non-null float32
cut        1000 non-null object
color      1000 non-null object
clarity    1000 non-null object
depth      1000 non-null float32
table      1000 non-null float32
price      1000 non-null int16
x          1000 non-null float32
y          1000 non-null float32
z          1000 non-null float32
dtypes: float32(6), int16(1), object(3)
memory usage: 49.0+ KB
```

Make sure that summary statistics are similar with our new dataset to the original:

```
>>> diamonds.describe()
              carat          depth   ...            y            z
count   1000.000000    1000.000000   ...   1000.000000   1000.000000
```

mean	0.689280	61.722800	...	5.599180	3.457530
std	0.195291	1.758879	...	0.611974	0.389819
min	0.200000	53.000000	...	3.750000	2.270000
25%	0.700000	60.900000	...	5.630000	3.450000
50%	0.710000	61.800000	...	5.760000	3.550000
75%	0.790000	62.600000	...	5.910000	3.640000
max	1.270000	69.500000	...	7.050000	4.330000

```
>>> diamonds2.describe()
```

	carat	depth	...	y	z
count	1000.000000	1000.000000	...	1000.000000	1000.000000
mean	0.689453	61.718750	...	5.601562	3.457031
std	0.195312	1.759766	...	0.611816	0.389648
min	0.199951	53.000000	...	3.750000	2.269531
25%	0.700195	60.906250	...	5.628906	3.449219
50%	0.709961	61.812500	...	5.761719	3.550781
75%	0.790039	62.593750	...	5.910156	3.640625
max	1.269531	69.500000	...	7.050781	4.328125

By changing the numeric types, we use about 62% of the memory. Note that we lose some precision, which may or may not be acceptable.

4. Use the `dtype` parameter to use change object types to categoricals. First, inspect the `.value_counts` method of the object columns. If they are low cardinality, you can convert them to categorical columns to save even more memory:

```
>>> diamonds2.cut.value_counts()
Ideal        333
Premium      290
Very Good    226
Good          89
Fair          62
Name: cut, dtype: int64
```

```
>>> diamonds2.color.value_counts()
E    240
F    226
```

```
G      139
D      129
H      125
I       95
J       46
Name: color, dtype: int64


>>> diamonds2.clarity.value_counts()
SI1     306
VS2     218
VS1     159
SI2     154
VVS2     62
VVS1     58
I1       29
IF       14
Name: clarity, dtype: int64
```

Because these are of low cardinality, we can convert them to categoricals and use around 37% of the original size:

```
>>> diamonds3 = pd.read_csv(
...     "data/diamonds.csv",
...     nrows=1000,
...     dtype={
...         "carat": np.float32,
...         "depth": np.float32,
...         "table": np.float32,
...         "x": np.float32,
...         "y": np.float32,
...         "z": np.float32,
...         "price": np.int16,
...         "cut": "category",
...         "color": "category",
...         "clarity": "category",
...     },
... )
```

```
>>> diamonds3.info()
<class 'pandas.core.frame.DataFrame'>
RangeIndex: 1000 entries, 0 to 999
Data columns (total 10 columns):
carat       1000 non-null float32
cut         1000 non-null category
color       1000 non-null category
clarity     1000 non-null category
depth       1000 non-null float32
table       1000 non-null float32
price       1000 non-null int16
x           1000 non-null float32
y           1000 non-null float32
z           1000 non-null float32
dtypes: category(3), float32(6), int16(1)
memory usage: 29.4 KB
```

5. If there are columns that we know we can ignore, we can use the `usecols`
    parameter to specify the columns we want to load. Here, we will ignore columns *x*, *y*,
    and *z*:

```
>>> cols = [
...     "carat",
...     "cut",
...     "color",
...     "clarity",
...     "depth",
...     "table",
...     "price",
... ]
>>> diamonds4 = pd.read_csv(
...     "data/diamonds.csv",
...     nrows=1000,
...     dtype={
...         "carat": np.float32,
...         "depth": np.float32,
...         "table": np.float32,
...         "price": np.int16,
```

```
...           "cut": "category",
...           "color": "category",
...           "clarity": "category",
...       },
...       usecols=cols,
... )
```

```
>>> diamonds4.info()
<class 'pandas.core.frame.DataFrame'>
RangeIndex: 1000 entries, 0 to 999
Data columns (total 7 columns):
carat      1000 non-null float32
cut        1000 non-null category
color      1000 non-null category
clarity    1000 non-null category
depth      1000 non-null float32
table      1000 non-null float32
price      1000 non-null int16
dtypes: category(3), float32(3), int16(1)
memory usage: 17.7 KB
```

We are now at 21% of the original size.

6. If the preceding steps are not sufficient to create a small enough DataFrame, you might still be in luck. If you can process chunks of the data at a time and do not need all of it in memory, you can use the `chunksize` parameter:

```
>>> cols = [
...       "carat",
...       "cut",
...       "color",
...       "clarity",
...       "depth",
...       "table",
...       "price",
... ]
>>> diamonds_iter = pd.read_csv(
...       "data/diamonds.csv",
```

```
...         nrows=1000,
...         dtype={
...             "carat": np.float32,
...             "depth": np.float32,
...             "table": np.float32,
...             "price": np.int16,
...             "cut": "category",
...             "color": "category",
...             "clarity": "category",
...         },
...         usecols=cols,
...         chunksize=200,
... )

>>> def process(df):
...         return f"processed {df.size} items"

>>> for chunk in diamonds_iter:
...         process(chunk)
```

How it works...

Because CSV files contain no information about type, pandas tries to infer the types of the columns. If all of the values of a column are whole numbers and none of them are missing, then it uses the `int64` type. If the column is numeric but not whole numbers, or if there are missing values, it uses `float64`. These data types may store more information that you need. For example, if your numbers are all below 200, you could use a smaller type, like `np.int16` (or `np.int8` if they are all positive).

As of pandas 0.24, there is a new type `'Int64'` (note the capitalization) that supports integer types with missing numbers. You will need to specify it with the `dtype` parameter if you want to use this type, as pandas will convert integers that have missing numbers to `float64`.

If the column turns out to be non-numeric, pandas will convert it to an `object` column, and treat the values as strings. String values in pandas take up a bunch of memory as each value is stored as a Python string. If we convert these to categoricals, pandas will use much less memory as it only stores the string once, rather than creating new strings (even if they repeat) for every row.

The pandas library can also read CSV files found on the internet. You can point the `read_csv` function to the URL directly.

There's more...

If we use `int8` for the price, we will lose information. You can use the NumPy `iinfo` function to list limits for NumPy integer types:

```
>>> np.iinfo(np.int8)
iinfo(min=-128, max=127, dtype=int8)
```

You can use the `finfo` function for information about floating-point numbers:

```
>>> np.finfo(np.float16)
finfo(resolution=0.001, min=-6.55040e+04,
      max=6.55040e+04, dtype=float16)
```

You can also ask a DataFrame or Series how many bytes it is using with the `.memory_usage` method. Note that this also includes the memory requirements of the index. Also, you need to pass `deep=True` to get the usage of Series with object types:

```
>>> diamonds.price.memory_usage()
8080
```

```
>>> diamonds.price.memory_usage(index=False)
8000
```

```
>>> diamonds.cut.memory_usage()
8080
```

```
>>> diamonds.cut.memory_usage(deep=True)
63413
```

Once you have your data in a format you like, you can save it in a binary format that tracks types, such as the Feather format (pandas leverages the `pyarrow` library to do this). This format is meant to enable in-memory transfer of structured data between languages and optimized so that data can be used as is without internal conversion. Reading from this format is much quicker and easy once you have the types defined:

```
>>> diamonds4.to_feather("d.arr")
>>> diamonds5 = pd.read_feather("d.arr")
```

Another binary option is the Parquet format. Whereas Feather optimizes the binary data for the in-memory structure, Parquet optimizes for the on-disk format. Parquet is used by many big data products. The pandas library has support for **Parquet** as well.

```
>>> diamonds4.to_parquet("/tmp/d.pqt")
```

Right now there is some conversion required for pandas to load data from both Parquet and Feather. But both are quicker than CSV and persist types.

Using Excel files

While CSV files are common, it seems that the world is ruled by Excel. I've been surprised in my consulting work to see how many companies are using Excel as a critical if not the critical tool for making decisions.

In this recipe, we will show how to create and read Excel files. You may need to install `xlwt` or `openpyxl` to write XLS or XLSX files, respectively.

How to do it...

1. Create an Excel file using the `.to_excel` method. You can write either `xls` files or `xlsx` files:

```
>>> beatles.to_excel("beat.xls")
```
```
>>> beatles.to_excel("beat.xlsx")
```

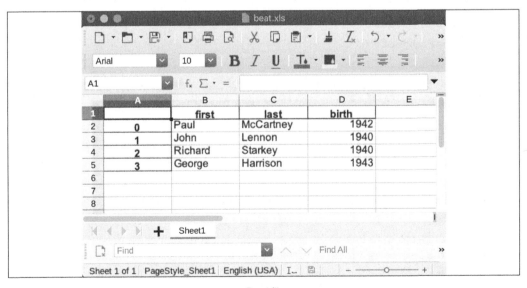

Excel file

2. Read the Excel file with the `read_excel` function:

```
>>> beat2 = pd.read_excel("/tmp/beat.xls")
>>> beat2
   Unnamed: 0    first        last  birth
0           0     Paul   McCartney   1942
1           1     John      Lennon   1940
2           2  Richard     Starkey   1940
3           3   George    Harrison   1943
```

3. Because this file had an index column included, you can specify that with the `index_col` parameter:

```
>>> beat2 = pd.read_excel("/tmp/beat.xls", index_col=0)
>>> beat2
     first        last  birth
0     Paul   McCartney   1942
1     John      Lennon   1940
2  Richard     Starkey   1940
3   George    Harrison   1943
```

4. Inspect data types of the file to check that Excel preserved the types:

```
>>> beat2.dtypes
first     object
last      object
birth      int64
dtype: object
```

How it works...

The Python ecosystem has many packages, which include the ability to read and write to Excel. This functionality has been integrated into pandas, you just need to make sure that you have the appropriate libraries for reading and writing to Excel.

There's more...

We can use pandas to write to a sheet of a spreadsheet. You can pass a `sheet_name` parameter to the `.to_excel` method to tell it the name of the sheet to create:

```
>>> xl_writer = pd.ExcelWriter("beat2.xlsx")
```

```
>>> beatles.to_excel(xl_writer, sheet_name="All")
>>> beatles[beatles.birth < 1941].to_excel(
...     xl_writer, sheet_name="1940"
... )
>>> xl_writer.save()
```

This file will have two sheets, one labeled All that has the whole DataFrame, and another labeled 1940 that is filtered to births before 1941.

Working with ZIP files

As was mentioned previously, CSV files are very common for sharing data. Because they are plain text files, they can get big. One solution for managing the size of CSV files is to compress them. In this recipe, we will look at loading files from ZIP files.

We will load a CSV file that is compressed as the only thing in the ZIP file. This is the behavior that you get if you were to right-click on a file in the **Finder** on Mac and click **Compress beatles.csv**. We will also look at reading a CSV file from a ZIP file with multiple files in it.

The first file is from the fueleconomy.gov website. It is a list of all car makes that have been available in the US market from 1984-2018.

The second file is a survey of users of the Kaggle website. It was intended to get information about the users, their background, and the tools that they prefer.

How to do it...

1. If the CSV file is the only file in the ZIP file, you can just call the read_csv function on it:

```
>>> autos = pd.read_csv("data/vehicles.csv.zip")
>>> autos
       barrels08  barrelsA08  ...  phevHwy  phevComb
0      15.695714         0.0  ...        0         0
1      29.964545         0.0  ...        0         0
2      12.207778         0.0  ...        0         0
3      29.964545         0.0  ...        0         0
4      17.347895         0.0  ...        0         0
...          ...         ...  ...      ...       ...
41139  14.982273         0.0  ...        0         0
41140  14.330870         0.0  ...        0         0
```

```
41141   15.695714         0.0  ...        0          0
41142   15.695714         0.0  ...        0          0
41143   18.311667         0.0  ...        0          0
```

```
>>> autos.modifiedOn.dtype
dtype('O')
```

2. One thing to be aware of is that if you have date columns in the CSV file, they will be left as strings. You have two options to convert them. You can use the `parse_dates` parameter from `read_csv` and convert them when loading the file. Alternatively, you can use the more powerful `to_datetime` function after loading:

```
>>> autos.modifiedOn
0          Tue Jan 01 00:00:00 EST 2013
1          Tue Jan 01 00:00:00 EST 2013
2          Tue Jan 01 00:00:00 EST 2013
3          Tue Jan 01 00:00:00 EST 2013
4          Tue Jan 01 00:00:00 EST 2013
                        ...
39096      Tue Jan 01 00:00:00 EST 2013
39097      Tue Jan 01 00:00:00 EST 2013
39098      Tue Jan 01 00:00:00 EST 2013
39099      Tue Jan 01 00:00:00 EST 2013
39100      Tue Jan 01 00:00:00 EST 2013
Name: modifiedOn, Length: 39101, dtype: object
```

```
>>> pd.to_datetime(autos.modifiedOn)
0          2013-01-01
1          2013-01-01
2          2013-01-01
3          2013-01-01
4          2013-01-01
                ...
39096      2013-01-01
39097      2013-01-01
39098      2013-01-01
39099      2013-01-01
39100      2013-01-01
```

```
Name: modifiedOn, Length: 39101, dtype: datetime64[ns]
```

Here's the code to convert during load time:

```
>>> autos = pd.read_csv(
...         "data/vehicles.csv.zip", parse_dates=["modifiedOn"]
... )
>>> autos.modifiedOn
0          2013-01-0...
1          2013-01-0...
2          2013-01-0...
3          2013-01-0...
4          2013-01-0...
             ...
41139      2013-01-0...
41140      2013-01-0...
41141      2013-01-0...
41142      2013-01-0...
41143      2013-01-0...
Name: modifiedOn, Length: 41144, dtype: datetime64[ns, tzlocal()]
```

3. If the ZIP file has many files it in, reading a CSV file from it is a little more involved. The `read_csv` function does not have the ability to specify a file inside a ZIP file. Instead, we will use the `zipfile` module from the Python standard library.

   I like to print out the names of the files in the zip file; that makes it easy to see what filename to choose. Note that this file has a long question in the second row (this first row is a question identifier, which I'm keeping for the column names). I'm pulling out the second row as `kag_questions`. The responses are stored in the `survey` variable:

```
>>> import zipfile

>>> with zipfile.ZipFile(
...         "data/kaggle-survey-2018.zip"
... ) as z:
...         print("\n".join(z.namelist()))
...         kag = pd.read_csv(
...             z.open("multipleChoiceResponses.csv")
...         )
...         kag_questions = kag.iloc[0]
```

```
...       survey = kag.iloc[1:]
multipleChoiceResponses.csv
freeFormResponses.csv
SurveySchema.csv

>>> survey.head(2).T
1               2
Time from...        710         434
Q1             Female       Male
Q1_OTHER_...          -1          -1
Q2              45-49       30-34
Q3         United S...   Indonesia
...                ...         ...
Q50_Part_5          NaN         NaN
Q50_Part_6          NaN         NaN
Q50_Part_7          NaN         NaN
Q50_Part_8          NaN         NaN
Q50_OTHER...          -1          -1
```

How it works...

ZIP files with only a single file can be read directly with the `read_csv` function. If the ZIP file contains multiple files, you will need to resort to another mechanism to read the data. The standard library includes the `zipfile` module that can pull a file out of a ZIP file.

Sadly, the `zipfile` module will not work with URLs (unlike the `read_csv` function). So, if your ZIP file is in a URL, you will need to download it first.

There's more...

The `read_csv` function will work with other compression types as well. If you have GZIP, BZ2, or XZ files, pandas can handle those as long as they are just compressing a CSV file and not a directory.

Working with databases

We mentioned that pandas is useful for tabular or structured data. Many organizations use databases to store tabular data. In this recipe, we will work with databases to insert and read data.

Note that this example uses the SQLite database, which is included with Python. However, Python has the ability to connect with most SQL databases and pandas, in turn, can leverage that.

How to do it...

1. Create a SQLite database to store the Beatles information:

```
>>> import sqlite3
>>> con = sqlite3.connect("data/beat.db")
>>> with con:
...     cur = con.cursor()
...     cur.execute("""DROP TABLE Band""")
...     cur.execute(
...         """CREATE TABLE Band(id INTEGER PRIMARY KEY,
...         fname TEXT, lname TEXT, birthyear INT)"""
...     )
...     cur.execute(
...         """INSERT INTO Band VALUES(
...         0, 'Paul', 'McCartney', 1942)"""
...     )
...     cur.execute(
...         """INSERT INTO Band VALUES(
...         1, 'John', 'Lennon', 1940)"""
...     )
...     _ = con.commit()
```

2. Read the table from the database into a DataFrame. Note that if we are reading a table, we need to use a SQLAlchemy connection. SQLAlchemy is a library that abstracts databases for us:

```
>>> import sqlalchemy as sa
>>> engine = sa.create_engine(
...     "sqlite:///data/beat.db", echo=True
```

```
... )
>>> sa_connection = engine.connect()

>>> beat = pd.read_sql(
...     "Band", sa_connection, index_col="id"
... )
>>> beat
     fname        lname   birthyear
id
0    Paul   McCartney       1942
1    John      Lennon       1940
```

3. Read from the table using a SQL query. This can use a SQLite connection or a SQLAlchemy connection:

```
>>> sql = """SELECT fname, birthyear from Band"""
>>> fnames = pd.read_sql(sql, con)
>>> fnames
   fname   birthyear
0   Paul        1942
1   John        1940
```

How it works...

The pandas library leverages the SQLAlchemy library, which can talk to most SQL databases. This lets you create DataFrames from tables, or you can run a SQL select query and create the DataFrame from the query.

Reading JSON

JavaScript Object Notation (**JSON**) is a common format used for transferring data over the internet. Contrary to the name, it does not require JavaScript to read or create. The Python standard library ships with the json library that will encode and decode from JSON:

```
>>> import json
>>> encoded = json.dumps(people)
>>> encoded
'{"first": ["Paul", "John", "Richard", "George"], "last": ["McCartney",
"Lennon", "Starkey", "Harrison"], "birth": [1942, 1940, 1940, 1943]}'
```

```
>>> json.loads(encoded)
{'first': ['Paul', 'John', 'Richard', 'George'], 'last': ['McCartney',
'Lennon', 'Starkey', 'Harrison'], 'birth': [1942, 1940, 1940, 1943]}
```

How to do it...

1. Read the data using the `read_json` function. If your JSON is of the form where it is a dictionary mapping to lists of columns, you can ingest it without much fanfare. This orientation is called *columns* in pandas:

```
>>> beatles = pd.read_json(encoded)
>>> beatles
        first       last  birth
0        Paul  McCartney   1942
1        John     Lennon   1940
2     Richard    Starkey   1940
3      George   Harrison   1943
```

2. One thing to be aware of when reading JSON is that it needs to be in a specific format for pandas to load it. However, pandas supports data oriented in a few styles. They are:

   ❏ `columns` – (default) A mapping of column names to a list of values in the columns.

   ❏ `records` – A list of rows. Each row is a dictionary mapping a column to a value.

   ❏ `split` – A mapping of `columns` to column names, `index` to index values, and `data` to a list of each row of data (each row is a list as well).

   ❏ `index` – A mapping of index value to a row. A row is a dictionary mapping a column to a value.

   ❏ `values` – A list of each row of data (each row is a list as well). This does not include column or index values.

   ❏ `table` – A mapping of `schema` to the DataFrame schema, and `data` to a list of dictionaries.

   Following are examples of these styles. The `columns` style was the example shown previously:

```
>>> records = beatles.to_json(orient="records")
>>> records
'[{"first":"Paul","last":"McCartney","birth":1942},{"first":"John"
```

```
,"last":"Lennon","birth":1940},{"first":"Richard","last":"Starkey"
,"birth":1940},{"first":"George","last":"Harrison","birth":1943}]'
```

```
>>> pd.read_json(records, orient="records")
   birth    first        last
0   1942     Paul   McCartney
1   1940     John      Lennon
2   1940  Richard     Starkey
3   1943   George    Harrison
```

```
>>> split = beatles.to_json(orient="split")
>>> split
'{"columns":["first","last","birth"],"index":[0,1,2,3],"data":[["P
aul","McCartney",1942],["John","Lennon",1940],["Richard","Starkey"
,1940],["George","Harrison",1943]]}'
```

```
>>> pd.read_json(split, orient="split")
     first        last  birth
0     Paul   McCartney   1942
1     John      Lennon   1940
2  Richard     Starkey   1940
3   George    Harrison   1943
```

```
>>> index = beatles.to_json(orient="index")
>>> index
'{"0":{"first":"Paul","last":"McCartney","birth":1942},"1":{"first
":"John","last":"Lennon","birth":1940},"2":{"first":"Richard","las
t":"Starkey","birth":1940},"3":{"first":"George","last":"Harrison"
,"birth":1943}}'
>>> pd.read_json(index, orient="index")
   birth    first        last
0   1942     Paul   McCartney
1   1940     John      Lennon
2   1940  Richard     Starkey
3   1943   George    Harrison
```

```
>>> values = beatles.to_json(orient="values")
```

```
>>> values
'[["Paul","McCartney",1942],["John","Lennon",1940],["Richard","Sta
rkey",1940],["George","Harrison",1943]]'
>>> pd.read_json(values, orient="values")
         0         1     2
0     Paul  McCartney  1942
1     John     Lennon  1940
2  Richard    Starkey  1940
3   George   Harrison  1943

>>> (
...     pd.read_json(values, orient="values").rename(
...         columns=dict(
...             enumerate(["first", "last", "birth"])
...         )
...     )
... )
     first       last  birth
0     Paul  McCartney   1942
1     John     Lennon   1940
2  Richard    Starkey   1940
3   George   Harrison   1943

>>> table = beatles.to_json(orient="table")
>>> table
'{"schema": {"fields":[{"name":"index","type":"integer"},{"name
":"first","type":"string"},{"name":"last","type":"string"},{"n
ame":"birth","type":"integer"}],"primaryKey":["index"],"pandas_
version":"0.20.0"}, "data": [{"index":0,"first":"Paul","last":"M
cCartney","birth":1942},{"index":1,"first":"John","last":"Lennon
","birth":1940},{"index":2,"first":"Richard","last":"Starkey","
birth":1940},{"index":3,"first":"George","last":"Harrison","bir
th":1943}]}'
>>> pd.read_json(table, orient="table")
     first       last  birth
0     Paul  McCartney   1942
1     John     Lennon   1940
2  Richard    Starkey   1940
3   George   Harrison   1943
```

How it works...

JSON can be formatted in many ways. Preferably, the JSON you need to consume comes in a supported orientation. If it does not, I find it easier to use standard Python to create data in a dictionary that maps column names to values and pass this into the `DataFrame` constructor.

If you need to generate JSON (say you are creating a web service), I would suggest the *columns* or *records* orientation.

There's more...

If you are working on a web service and need to add additional data to the JSON, just use the `.to_dict` method to generate dictionaries. You can add your new data to the dictionary, and then convert that dictionary to JSON:

```
>>> output = beat.to_dict()

>>> output

{'fname': {0: 'Paul', 1: 'John'}, 'lname': {0: 'McCartney', 1: 'Lennon'},
'birthyear': {0: 1942, 1: 1940}}


>>> output["version"] = "0.4.1"

>>> json.dumps(output)

'{"fname": {"0": "Paul", "1": "John"}, "lname": {"0": "McCartney", "1":
"Lennon"}, "birthyear": {"0": 1942, "1": 1940}, "version": "0.4.1"}'
```

Reading HTML tables

You can use pandas to read HTML tables from websites. This makes it easy to ingest tables such as those found on Wikipedia or other websites.

In this recipe, we will scrape tables from the Wikipedia entry for *The Beatles Discography*. In particular, we want to scrape the table in the image that was in Wikipedia during 2019:

		Peak chart positions							
Title	Release	UK [1][2]	AUS [3]	CAN [4]	FRA [5]	GER [6]	NOR [7]	US [8][9]	Certifications
Please Please Me ‡	• Released: 22 March 1963 • Label: Parlophone (UK)	1	—	—	5	5	—	—	• BPI: Gold[10] • ARIA: Gold[11] • MC: Gold[12] • RIAA: Platinum[13]
With the Beatles[B] ‡	• Released: 22 November 1963 • Label: Parlophone (UK), Capitol (CAN), Odeon (FRA)	1	—	—	5	1	—	—	• BPI: Gold[10] • ARIA: Gold[11] • BVMI: Gold[15] • MC: Gold[12] • RIAA: Gold[13]

List of studio albums,[A] with selected chart positions and certifications

Wikipedia table for studio albums

How to do it...

1. Use the `read_html` function to load all of the tables from `https://en.wikipedia.org/wiki/The_Beatles_discography`:

   ```
   >>> url = https://en.wikipedia.org/wiki/The_Beatles_discography
   >>> dfs = pd.read_html(url)
   >>> len(dfs)
   51
   ```

2. Inspect the first DataFrame:

   ```
   >>> dfs[0]
      The Beatles discography The Beatles discography.1
   0  The Beat...               The Beat...
   1  Studio a...                        23
   2  Live albums                         5
   3  Compilat...                        53
   4  Video al...                        15
   5  Music vi...                        64
   6          EPs                        21
   7      Singles                        63
   8     Mash-ups                         2
   9     Box sets                        15
   ```

3. The preceding table is a summary of the count of studio albums, live albums, compilation albums, and so on. This is not the table we wanted. We could loop through each of the tables that `read_html` created, or we could give it a hint to find a specific table.

The function has the `match` parameter, which can be a string or a regular expression. It also has an `attrs` parameter, that allows you to pass in an HTML tag attribute key and value (in a dictionary) and will use that to identify the table.

I used the Chrome browser to inspect the HTML to see if there is an attribute on the `table` element or a unique string in the table to use.

Here is a portion of the HTML:

```
<table class="wikitable plainrowheaders" style="text-
align:center;">
  <caption>List of studio albums,<sup id="cite_ref-1"
class="reference"><a href="#cite_note-1">[A]</a></sup> with
selected chart positions and certifications
  </caption>
  <tbody>
    <tr>
      <th scope="col" rowspan="2" style="width:20em;">Title
      </th>
      <th scope="col" rowspan="2" style="width:20em;">Release
        . . .
```

There are no attributes on the table, but we can use the string, `List of studio albums`, to match the table. I'm also going to stick in a value for `na_values` that I copied from the Wikipedia page:

```
>>> url = https://en.wikipedia.org/wiki/The_Beatles_discography
>>> dfs = pd.read_html(
...     url, match="List of studio albums", na_values="—"
... )
>>> len(dfs)
1

>>> dfs[0].columns
Int64Index([0, 1, 2, 3, 4, 5, 6, 7, 8, 9], dtype='int64')
```

4. The columns are messed up. We can try and use the first two rows for the columns, but they are still messed up:

```
>>> url = https://en.wikipedia.org/wiki/The_Beatles_discography
>>> dfs = pd.read_html(
...     url,
```

```
...       match="List of studio albums",
...       na_values="—",
...       header=[0, 1],
... )
>>> len(dfs)
1

>>> dfs[0]
          Title        Release   ... Peak chart positions
Certifications
          Title        Release   ...            US[8][9]
Certifications
0    Please P...  Released... ...            NaN         BPI:
Gol...
1    With the...  Released... ...            NaN         BPI:
Gol...
2    Introduc...  Released... ...              2         RIAA:
Pl...
3    Meet the...  Released... ...              1         MC:
Plat...
4    Twist an...  Released... ...            NaN         MC: 3×
P...
..          ...          ... ...            ...
...
22   The Beat...  Released... ...              1         BPI: 2×
...
23   Yellow S...  Released... ...              2         BPI:
Gol...
24    Abbey Road  Released... ...              1         BPI: 2×
...
25     Let It Be  Released... ...              1         BPI:
Gol...
26   "—" deno...  "—" deno... ...   "—" deno...            "—"
deno...


>>> dfs[0].columns
MultiIndex(levels=[['Certifications', 'Peak chart positions',
'Release', 'Title'], ['AUS[3]', 'CAN[4]', 'Certifications',
'FRA[5]', 'GER[6]', 'NOR[7]', 'Release', 'Title', 'UK[1][2]',
```

```
'US[8][9]']],
  codes=[[3, 2, 1, 1, 1, 1, 1, 1, 1, 0], [7, 6, 8, 0, 1, 3, 4, 5,
9, 2]])
```

This is not something that is easy to fix programmatically. In this case, the easiest solution is to update the columns manually:

```
>>> df = dfs[0]
>>> df.columns = [
...       "Title",
...       "Release",
...       "UK",
...       "AUS",
...       "CAN",
...       "FRA",
...       "GER",
...       "NOR",
...       "US",
...       "Certifications",
... ]
>>> df
```

	Title	Release	...		US	Certifications
0	Please P...	Released...	...		NaN	BPI: Gol...
1	With the...	Released...	...		NaN	BPI: Gol...
2	Introduc...	Released...	...		2	RIAA: Pl...
3	Meet the...	Released...	...		1	MC: Plat...
4	Twist an...	Released...	...		NaN	MC: 3x P...
..	...	...	...		...	...
22	The Beat...	Released...	...		1	BPI: 2x ...
23	Yellow S...	Released...	...		2	BPI: Gol...
24	Abbey Road	Released...	...		1	BPI: 2x ...
25	Let It Be	Released...	...		1	BPI: Gol...
26	"–" deno...	"–" deno...	...	"–" deno...	"–" deno...

5. There is more cleanup that we should do to the data. Any row where the title starts with `Released` is another release of the previous row. pandas does not have the ability to parse rows that have a rowspan more than 1 (which the "release" rows have). In the Wikipedia page, these rows look like this:

```
<th scope="row" rowspan="2">
```

```
    <i><a href="/wiki/A_Hard_Day%27s_Night_(album)" title="A Hard
Day's Night (album)">A Hard Day's Night</a></i>
    <img alt="double-dagger" src="//upload.wikimedia.org/wikipedia/
commons/f/f9/Double-dagger-14-plain.png" decoding="async"
width="9" height="14" data-file-width="9" data-file-height="14">
</th>
```

We will skip these rows. They confuse pandas, and the data pandas puts in these
rows is not correct. We will split the release column into two columns, `release_date` and `label`:

```
>>> res = (
...     df.pipe(
...         lambda df_: df_[
...             ~df_.Title.str.startswith("Released")
...         ]
...     )
...     .assign(
...         release_date=lambda df_: pd.to_datetime(
...             df_.Release.str.extract(
...                 r"Released: (.*) Label"
...             )[0].str.replace(r"\[E\]", "")
...         ),
...         label=lambda df_: df_.Release.str.extract(
...             r"Label: (.*)"
...         ),
...     )
...     .loc[
...         :,
...         [
...             "Title",
...             "UK",
...             "AUS",
...             "CAN",
...             "FRA",
...             "GER",
...             "NOR",
...             "US",
...             "release_date",
```

```
...                 "label",
...             ],
...         ]
... )
>>> res
          Title    UK  ...  release_date       label
0    Please P...     1  ...    1963-03-22  Parlopho...
1    With the...     1  ...    1963-11-22  Parlopho...
2    Introduc...   NaN  ...    1964-01-10  Vee-Jay ...
3    Meet the...   NaN  ...    1964-01-20  Capitol ...
4    Twist an...   NaN  ...    1964-02-03  Capitol ...
..          ...   ...  ...           ...         ...
21   Magical ...    31  ...    1967-11-27  Parlopho...
22   The Beat...     1  ...    1968-11-22       Apple
23   Yellow S...     3  ...    1969-01-13  Apple (U...
24   Abbey Road      1  ...    1969-09-26       Apple
25   Let It Be       1  ...    1970-05-08       Apple
```

How it works...

The `read_html` function looks through the HTML for `table` tags and parses the contents into DataFrames. This can ease the scraping of websites. Unfortunately, as the example shows, sometimes data in HTML tables may be hard to parse. Rowspans and multiline headers may confuse pandas. You will want to make sure that you perform a sanity check on the result.

Sometimes, the table in HTML is simple such that pandas can ingest it with no problems. For the table we looked at, we needed to chain a few operations onto the output to clean it up.

There's more...

You can also use the `attrs` parameter to select a table from the page. Next, I select read data from GitHub's view of a CSV file. Note that I am not reading this from the raw CSV data but from GitHub's online file viewer. I have inspected the table and noticed that it has a class attribute with the value `csv-data`. We will use that to limit the table selected:

```
>>> url = https://github.com/mattharrison/datasets/blob/master/data/
anscombes.csv
>>> dfs = pd.read_html(url, attrs={"class": "csv-data"})
```

```
>>> len(dfs)
1
>>> dfs[0]
```

	Unnamed: 0	quadrant	x	y
0	NaN	I	10.0	8.04
1	NaN	I	14.0	9.96
2	NaN	I	6.0	7.24
3	NaN	I	9.0	8.81
4	NaN	I	4.0	4.26
..	...	...	...	...
39	NaN	IV	8.0	6.58
40	NaN	IV	8.0	7.91
41	NaN	IV	8.0	8.47
42	NaN	IV	8.0	5.25
43	NaN	IV	8.0	6.89

Note that GitHub hijacks a `td` element to show the line number, hence the `Unnamed: 0` column. It appears to be using JavaScript to dynamically add line numbers to the web page, so while the web page shows line numbers, the source code has empty cells, hence the `NaN` values in that column. You would want to drop that column as it is useless.

One thing to be aware of is that websites can change. Do not count on your data being there (or being the same) next week. My recommendation is to save the data after retrieving it.

Sometimes you need to use a different tool. If the `read_html` function is not able to get your data from a website, you may need to resort to screen scraping. Luckily, Python has tools for that too. Simple scraping can be done with the requests library. The **Beautiful Soup** library is another tool that makes going through the HTML content easier.

4
Beginning Data Analysis

Introduction

It is important to consider the steps that you, as an analyst, take when you first encounter a dataset after importing it into your workspace as a DataFrame. Is there a set of tasks that you usually undertake to examine the data? Are you aware of all the possible data types? This chapter begins by covering the tasks you might want to undertake when first encountering a new dataset. The chapter proceeds by answering common questions about things that are not that simple to do in pandas.

Developing a data analysis routine

Although there is no standard approach when beginning a data analysis, it is typically a good idea to develop a routine for yourself when first examining a dataset. Similar to everyday routines that we have for waking up, showering, going to work, eating, and so on, a data analysis routine helps you to quickly get acquainted with a new dataset. This routine can manifest itself as a dynamic checklist of tasks that evolves as your familiarity with pandas and data analysis expands.

Exploratory Data Analysis (**EDA**) is a term used to describe the process of analyzing datasets. Typically it does not involve model creation, but summarizing the characteristics of the data and visualizing them. This is not new and was promoted by John Tukey in his book *Exploratory Data Analysis* in 1977.

Many of these same processes are still applicable and useful to understand a dataset. Indeed, they can also help with creating machine learning models later.

This recipe covers a small but fundamental part of EDA: the collection of *metadata* and *descriptive statistics* in a routine and systematic way. It outlines a standard set of tasks that can be undertaken when first importing any dataset as a pandas DataFrame. This recipe may help form the basis of the routine that you can implement when first examining a dataset.

Metadata describes the dataset or, more aptly, data about the data. Examples of metadata include the number of columns/rows, column names, data types of each column, the source of the dataset, the date of collection, the acceptable values for different columns, and so on. Univariate descriptive statistics are summary statistics about variables (columns) of the dataset, independent of all other variables.

How to do it...

First, some metadata on the college dataset will be collected, followed by basic summary statistics of each column:

1. Read in the dataset, and view a sample of rows with the `.sample` method:

```
>>> import pandas as pd
>>> import numpy as np
>>> college = pd.read_csv("data/college.csv")
>>> college.sample(random_state=42)
          INSTNM          CITY  ... MD_EARN_WNE_P10  GRAD_DEBT_
MDN_SUPP
3649  Career P...  San Antonio  ...           20700            14977
```

2. Get the dimensions of the DataFrame with the `.shape` attribute:

```
>>> college.shape
(7535, 27)
```

3. List the data type of each column, the number of non-missing values, and memory usage with the `.info` method:

```
>>> college.info()
<class 'pandas.core.frame.DataFrame'>
RangeIndex: 7535 entries, 0 to 7534
Data columns (total 27 columns):
 #   Column              Non-Null Count   Dtype
---  ------              --------------   -----
 0   INSTNM              7535 non-null    object
```

1	CITY	7535 non-null	object
2	STABBR	7535 non-null	object
3	HBCU	7164 non-null	float64
4	MENONLY	7164 non-null	float64
5	WOMENONLY	7164 non-null	float64
6	RELAFFIL	7535 non-null	int64
7	SATVRMID	1185 non-null	float64
8	SATMTMID	1196 non-null	float64
9	DISTANCEONLY	7164 non-null	float64
10	UGDS	6874 non-null	float64
11	UGDS_WHITE	6874 non-null	float64
12	UGDS_BLACK	6874 non-null	float64
13	UGDS_HISP	6874 non-null	float64
14	UGDS_ASIAN	6874 non-null	float64
15	UGDS_AIAN	6874 non-null	float64
16	UGDS_NHPI	6874 non-null	float64
17	UGDS_2MOR	6874 non-null	float64
18	UGDS_NRA	6874 non-null	float64
19	UGDS_UNKN	6874 non-null	float64
20	PPTUG_EF	6853 non-null	float64
21	CURROPER	7535 non-null	int64
22	PCTPELL	6849 non-null	float64
23	PCTFLOAN	6849 non-null	float64
24	UG25ABV	6718 non-null	float64
25	MD_EARN_WNE_P10	6413 non-null	object
26	GRAD_DEBT_MDN_SUPP	7503 non-null	object

```
dtypes: float64(20), int64(2), object(5)
memory usage: 1.6+ MB
```

4. Get summary statistics for the numerical columns and transpose the DataFrame for more readable output:

```
>>> college.describe(include=[np.number]).T
```

	count	mean	...	75%	max
HBCU	7164.0	0.014238	...	0.000000	1.0
MENONLY	7164.0	0.009213	...	0.000000	1.0
WOMENONLY	7164.0	0.005304	...	0.000000	1.0
RELAFFIL	7535.0	0.190975	...	0.000000	1.0

SATVRMID	1185.0	522.819409	...	555.000000	765.0
...	...	...	...	...	...
PPTUG_EF	6853.0	0.226639	...	0.376900	1.0
CURROPER	7535.0	0.923291	...	1.000000	1.0
PCTPELL	6849.0	0.530643	...	0.712900	1.0
PCTFLOAN	6849.0	0.522211	...	0.745000	1.0
UG25ABV	6718.0	0.410021	...	0.572275	1.0

5. Get summary statistics for the object (string) columns:

```
>>> college.describe(include=[np.object]).T
```

	count	unique	top	freq
INSTNM	7535	7535	Academy ...	1
CITY	7535	2514	New York	87
STABBR	7535	59	CA	773
MD_EARN_W...	6413	598	PrivacyS...	822
GRAD_DEBT...	7503	2038	PrivacyS...	1510

How it works...

After importing your dataset, a common task is to print out a sample of rows of the DataFrame for manual inspection with the `.sample` method. The `.shape` attribute returns some metadata; a tuple containing the number of rows and columns.

A method to get more metadata at once is the `.info` method. It provides each column name, the number of non-missing values, the data type of each column, and the approximate memory usage of the DataFrame. Usually, a column in pandas has a single type (however, it is possible to have a column that has mixed types, and it will be reported as `object`). DataFrames, as a whole, might be composed of columns with different data types.

Step 4 and *step 5* produce descriptive statistics on different types of columns. By default, `.describe` outputs a summary for all the numeric columns and silently drops any non-numeric columns. You can pass in other options to the `include` parameter to include counts and frequencies for a column with non-numeric data types. Technically, the data types are part of a hierarchy where `np.number` resides above integers and floats.

We can classify data as being either continuous or categorical. Continuous data is always numeric and can usually take on an infinite number of possibilities, such as height, weight, and salary. Categorical data represent discrete values that take on a finite number of possibilities, such as ethnicity, employment status, and car color. Categorical data can be represented numerically or with characters.

Categorical columns are usually going to be either of the type `np.object` or `pd.Categorical`. *Step 5* ensures that both of these types are represented. In both *step 4* and *step 5*, the output DataFrame is transposed with the `.T` property. This may ease readability for DataFrames with many columns as it typically allows more data to fit on the screen without scrolling.

There's more...

It is possible to specify the exact quantiles returned from the `.describe` method when used with numeric columns:

```
>>> college.describe(
...     include=[np.number],
...     percentiles=[
...         0.01,
...         0.05,
...         0.10,
...         0.25,
...         0.5,
...         0.75,
...         0.9,
...         0.95,
...         0.99,
...     ],
... ).T
```

	count	mean	...	99%	max
HBCU	7164.0	0.014238	...	1.000000	1.0
MENONLY	7164.0	0.009213	...	0.000000	1.0
WOMENONLY	7164.0	0.005304	...	0.000000	1.0
RELAFFIL	7535.0	0.190975	...	1.000000	1.0
SATVRMID	1185.0	522.819409	...	730.000000	765.0
...	...	...	...	...	...
PPTUG_EF	6853.0	0.226639	...	0.946724	1.0
CURROPER	7535.0	0.923291	...	1.000000	1.0
PCTPELL	6849.0	0.530643	...	0.993908	1.0
PCTFLOAN	6849.0	0.522211	...	0.986368	1.0
UG25ABV	6718.0	0.410021	...	0.917383	1.0

Data dictionaries

A crucial part of data analysis involves creating and maintaining a data dictionary. A data dictionary is a table of metadata and notes on each column of data. One of the primary purposes of a data dictionary is to explain the meaning of the column names. The college dataset uses a lot of abbreviations that are likely to be unfamiliar to an analyst who is inspecting it for the first time.

A data dictionary for the college dataset is provided in the following `college_data_dictionary.csv` file:

```
>>> pd.read_csv("data/college_data_dictionary.csv")
     column_name  description
0         INSTNM  Institut...
1           CITY  City Loc...
2         STABBR  State Ab...
3           HBCU  Historic...
4        MENONLY  0/1 Men ...
..          ...          ...
22       PCTPELL  Percent ...
23      PCTFLOAN  Percent ...
24       UG25ABV  Percent ...
25     MD_EARN_... Median E...
26     GRAD_DEB... Median d...
```

As you can see, it is immensely helpful in deciphering the abbreviated column names. DataFrames are not the best place to store data dictionaries. A platform such as Excel or Google Sheets with easy ability to edit values and append columns is a better choice. Alternatively, they can be described in a Markdown cell in Jupyter. A data dictionary is one of the first things that you can share as an analyst with collaborators.

It will often be the case that the dataset you are working with originated from a database whose administrators you will have to contact to get more information. Databases have representations of their data, called schemas. If possible, attempt to investigate your dataset with a **Subject Matter Expert** (**SME** – people who have expert knowledge of the data).

Reducing memory by changing data types

pandas has precise technical definitions for many data types. However, when you load data from type-less formats such as CSV, pandas has to infer the type.

This recipe changes the data type of one of the object columns from the college dataset to the special pandas categorical data type to drastically reduce its memory usage.

How to do it...

1. After reading in our college dataset, we select a few columns of different data types that will clearly show how much memory may be saved:

```
>>> college = pd.read_csv("data/college.csv")
>>> different_cols = [
...        "RELAFFIL",
...        "SATMTMID",
...        "CURROPER",
...        "INSTNM",
...        "STABBR",
... ]
>>> col2 = college.loc[:, different_cols]
>>> col2.head()
   RELAFFIL  SATMTMID  ...       INSTNM STABBR
0         0     420.0  ...  Alabama ...     AL
1         0     565.0  ...  Universi...     AL
2         1       NaN  ...  Amridge ...     AL
3         0     590.0  ...  Universi...     AL
4         0     430.0  ...  Alabama ...     AL
```

2. Inspect the data types of each column:

```
>>> col2.dtypes
RELAFFIL        int64
SATMTMID      float64
CURROPER        int64
INSTNM         object
STABBR         object
dtype: object
```

3. Find the memory usage of each column with the `.memory_usage` method:

```
>>> original_mem = col2.memory_usage(deep=True)
>>> original_mem
Index            128
```

RELAFFIL	60280
SATMTMID	60280
CURROPER	60280
INSTNM	660240
STABBR	444565

dtype: int64

4. There is no need to use 64 bits for the RELAFFIL column as it contains only 0 or 1. Let's convert this column to an 8-bit (1 byte) integer with the .astype method:

```
>>> col2["RELAFFIL"] = col2["RELAFFIL"].astype(np.int8)
```

5. Use the .dtypes attribute to confirm the data type change:

```
>>> col2.dtypes
```

RELAFFIL	int8
SATMTMID	float64
CURROPER	int64
INSTNM	object
STABBR	object

dtype: object

6. Find the memory usage of each column again and note the large reduction:

```
>>> col2.memory_usage(deep=True)
```

Index	128
RELAFFIL	7535
SATMTMID	60280
CURROPER	60280
INSTNM	660240
STABBR	444565

dtype: int64

7. To save even more memory, you will want to consider changing object data types to categorical if they have a reasonably low cardinality (number of unique values). Let's first check the number of unique values for both the object columns:

```
>>> col2.select_dtypes(include=["object"]).nunique()
```

INSTNM	7535
STABBR	59

dtype: int64

8. The `STABBR` column is a good candidate to convert to categorical as less than one percent of its values are unique:

```
>>> col2["STABBR"] = col2["STABBR"].astype("category")
>>> col2.dtypes
RELAFFIL          int8
SATMTMID       float64
CURROPER         int64
INSTNM          object
STABBR        category
dtype: object
```

9. Compute the memory usage again:

```
>>> new_mem = col2.memory_usage(deep=True)
>>> new_mem
Index           128
RELAFFIL       7535
SATMTMID      60280
CURROPER      60280
INSTNM       660699
STABBR        13576
dtype: int64
```

10. Finally, let's compare the original memory usage with our updated memory usage. The `RELAFFIL` column is, as expected, an eighth of its original size, while the `STABBR` column has shrunk to just three percent of its original size:

```
>>> new_mem / original_mem
Index        1.000000
RELAFFIL     0.125000
SATMTMID     1.000000
CURROPER     1.000000
INSTNM       1.000695
STABBR       0.030538
dtype: float64
```

How it works...

pandas defaults `integer` and `float` data types to 64 bits regardless of the maximum necessary size for the particular DataFrame. Integers, floats, and even Booleans may be coerced to a different data type with the `.astype` method and passing it the exact type, either as a string or specific object, as done in *step 4*.

The `RELAFFIL` column is a good choice to cast to a smaller integer type as the data dictionary explains that its values must be 0 or 1. The memory for `RELAFFIL` is now an eighth of `CURROPER`, which remains as its former type.

Columns that have an `object` data type, such as `INSTNM`, are not like the other pandas data types. For all the other pandas data types, each value in that column is the same data type. For instance, when a column has the `int64` type, every column value is also `int64`. This is not true for columns that have the `object` data type. Each column value can be of any type. They can have a mix of strings, numerics, datetimes, or even other Python objects such as lists or tuples. For this reason, the `object` data type is sometimes referred to as a catch-all for a column of data that doesn't match any of the other data types. The vast majority of the time, though, `object` data type columns will all be strings.

Therefore, the memory of each value in an `object` data type column is inconsistent. There is no predefined amount of memory for each value like the other data types. For pandas to extract the exact amount of memory of an `object` data type column, the `deep` parameter must be set to `True` in the `.memory_usage` method.

Object columns are targets for the largest memory savings. pandas has an additional categorical data type that is not available in NumPy. When converting to category, pandas internally creates a mapping from integers to each unique string value. Thus, each string only needs to be kept a single time in memory. As you can see, this change of data type reduced memory usage by 97%.

You might also have noticed that the index uses an extremely low amount of memory. If no index is specified during DataFrame creation, as is the case in this recipe, pandas defaults the index to a `RangeIndex`. The `RangeIndex` is very similar to the built-in `range` function. It produces values on demand and only stores the minimum amount of information needed to create an index.

There's more...

To get a better idea of how object data type columns differ from integers and floats, a single value from each one of these columns can be modified and the resulting memory usage displayed. The `CURROPER` and `INSTNM` columns are of `int64` and `object` types, respectively:

```
>>> college.loc[0, "CURROPER"] = 10000000
```

```
>>> college.loc[0, "INSTNM"] = (
...     college.loc[0, "INSTNM"] + "a"
... )
>>> college[["CURROPER", "INSTNM"]].memory_usage(deep=True)
Index             80
CURROPER       60280
INSTNM        660804
dtype: int64
```

Memory usage for CURROPER remained the same since a 64-bit integer is more than enough space for the larger number. On the other hand, the memory usage for INSTNM increased by 105 bytes by just adding a single letter to one value.

Python 3 uses *Unicode*, a standardized character representation intended to encode all the world's writing systems. How much memory Unicode strings take on your machine depends on how Python was built. On this machine, it uses up to 4 bytes per character. pandas has some overhead (100 bytes) when making the first modification to a character value. Afterward, increments of 5 bytes per character are sustained.

Not all columns can be coerced to the desired type. Take a look at the MENONLY column, which, from the data dictionary, appears to contain only 0s or 1s. The actual data type of this column upon import unexpectedly turns out to be float64. The reason for this is that there happen to be missing values, denoted by np.nan. There is no integer representation for missing values for the int64 type (note that the Int64 type found in pandas 0.24+ does support missing values, but it is not used by default). Any numeric column with even a single missing value will be turned into a float column. Furthermore, any column of an integer data type will automatically be coerced to a float if one of the values becomes missing:

```
>>> college["MENONLY"].dtype
dtype('float64')
>>> college["MENONLY"].astype(np.int8)
Traceback (most recent call last):
  ...
ValueError: Cannot convert non-finite values (NA or inf) to integer
```

Additionally, it is possible to substitute string names in place of Python objects when referring to data types. For instance, when using the include parameter in the .describe DataFrame method, it is possible to pass a list of either the NumPy or pandas objects or their equivalent string representation. For instance, each of the following produces the same result:

```
college.describe(include=['int64', 'float64']).T
```

```
college.describe(include=[np.int64, np.float64]).T


college.describe(include=['int', 'float']).T


college.describe(include=['number']).T
```

The type strings can also be used in combination with the `.astype` method:

```
>>> college.assign(
...       MENONLY=college["MENONLY"].astype("float16"),
...       RELAFFIL=college["RELAFFIL"].astype("int8"),
... )
```

	INSTNM	CITY	...	MD_EARN_WNE_P10	GRAD_DEBT_MDN_SUPP
0	Alabama ...	Normal	...	30300	33888
1	Universi...	Birmingham	...	39700	21941.5
2	Amridge ...	Montgomery	...	40100	23370
3	Universi...	Huntsville	...	45500	24097
4	Alabama ...	Montgomery	...	26600	33118.5
...	...	...	...	...	...
7530	SAE Inst...	Emeryville	...	NaN	9500
7531	Rasmusse...	Overland...	...	NaN	21163
7532	National...	Highland...	...	NaN	6333
7533	Bay Area...	San Jose	...	NaN	PrivacyS...
7534	Excel Le...	San Antonio	...	NaN	12125

Lastly, it is possible to see the enormous memory difference between the minimal `RangeIndex` and `Int64Index`, which stores every row index in memory:

```
>>> college.index = pd.Int64Index(college.index)
>>> college.index.memory_usage()  # previously was just 80
60280
```

Selecting the smallest of the largest

This recipe can be used to create catchy news headlines such as *Out of the Top 100 Universities, These 5 have the Lowest Tuition*, or *From the Top 50 Cities to Live, these 10 are the Most Affordable.*

During analysis, it is possible that you will first need to find a grouping of data that contains the top n values in a single column and, from this subset, find the bottom m values based on a different column.

In this recipe, we find the five lowest budget movies from the top 100 scoring movies by taking advantage of the convenience methods: `.nlargest` and `.nsmallest`.

How to do it...

1. Read in the movie dataset, and select the columns: `movie_title`, `imdb_score`, and `budget`:

```
>>> movie = pd.read_csv("data/movie.csv")
>>> movie2 = movie[["movie_title", "imdb_score", "budget"]]
>>> movie2.head()
   movie_title  imdb_score        budget
0       Avatar         7.9   237000000.0
1   Pirates ...         7.1   300000000.0
2      Spectre         6.8   245000000.0
3   The Dark...         8.5   250000000.0
4   Star War...         7.1           NaN
```

2. Use the `.nlargest` method to select the top 100 movies by `imdb_score`:

```
>>> movie2.nlargest(100, "imdb_score").head()
                    movie_title  imdb_score        budget
2725           Towering Inferno         9.5           NaN
1920   The Shawshank Redemption         9.3   25000000.0
3402              The Godfather         9.2    6000000.0
2779                     Dekalog         9.1           NaN
4312        Kickboxer: Vengeance         9.1   17000000.0
```

3. Chain the `.nsmallest` method to return the five lowest budget films among those with a top 100 score:

```
>>> (
...       movie2.nlargest(100, "imdb_score").nsmallest(
...           5, "budget"
...       )
... )
                    movie_title  imdb_score        budget
```

4804	Butterfly Girl	8.7	180000.0
4801	Children of Heaven	8.5	180000.0
4706	12 Angry Men	8.9	350000.0
4550	A Separation	8.4	500000.0
4636	The Other Dream Team	8.4	500000.0

How it works...

The first parameter of the `.nlargest` method, n, must be an integer and selects the number of rows to be returned. The second parameter, `columns`, takes a column name as a string. *Step 2* returns the 100 highest-scoring movies. We could have saved this intermediate result as its own variable but instead, we chain the `.nsmallest` method to it in *step 3*, which returns exactly five rows, sorted by budget.

There's more...

It is possible to pass a list of column names to the `columns` parameter of the `.nlargest` and `.nsmallest` methods. This would only be useful to break ties in the event that there were duplicate values sharing the *n*th ranked spot in the first column in the list.

Selecting the largest of each group by sorting

One of the most basic and common operations to perform during data analysis is to select rows containing the largest value of some column within a group. For instance, this would be like finding the highest-rated film of each year or the highest-grossing film by content rating. To accomplish this task, we need to sort the groups as well as the column used to rank each member of the group, and then extract the highest member of each group.

In this recipe, we will find the highest-rated film of each year.

How to do it...

1. Read in the movie dataset and slim it down to just the three columns we care about: `movie_title`, `title_year`, and `imdb_score`:

```
>>> movie = pd.read_csv("data/movie.csv")
>>> movie[["movie_title", "title_year", "imdb_score"]]
                                          movie_title  ...
```

```
0                                        Avatar  ...

1        Pirates of the Caribbean: At World's End  ...

2                                       Spectre  ...

3                         The Dark Knight Rises  ...

4        Star Wars: Episode VII - The Force Awakens  ...

...                                           ...  ...

4911                      Signed Sealed Delivered  ...

4912                              The Following  ...

4913                      A Plague So Pleasant  ...

4914                           Shanghai Calling  ...

4915                         My Date with Drew  ...
```

2. Use the `.sort_values` method to sort the DataFrame by `title_year`. The default behavior sorts from the smallest to the largest. Use the `ascending=True` parameter to invert this behavior:

```
>>> (
...     movie[
...         ["movie_title", "title_year", "imdb_score"]
...     ].sort_values("title_year", ascending=True)
... )
                                            movie_title  ...
4695  Intolerance: Love's Struggle Throughout the Ages  ...
4833                    Over the Hill to the Poorhouse  ...
4767                                  The Big Parade  ...
2694                                       Metropolis  ...
4697                             The Broadway Melody  ...
...                                               ...  ...
4683                                          Heroes  ...
4688                                     Home Movies  ...
4704                                      Revolution  ...
4752                                    Happy Valley  ...
4912                                   The Following  ...
```

3. Notice how only the year was sorted. To sort multiple columns at once, use a list. Let's look at how to sort both year and score:

```
>>> (
...     movie[
...         ["movie_title", "title_year", "imdb_score"]
```

```
...         ].sort_values(
...             ["title_year", "imdb_score"], ascending=False
...         )
... )
```

	movie_title	title_year	imdb_score
4312	Kickboxer: Vengeance	2016.0	9.1
4277	A Beginner's Guide to Snuff	2016.0	8.7
3798	Airlift	2016.0	8.5
27	Captain America: Civil War	2016.0	8.2
98	Godzilla Resurgence	2016.0	8.2
...	...	...	...
1391	Rush Hour	NaN	5.8
4031	Creature	NaN	5.0
2165	Meet the Browns	NaN	3.5
3246	The Bold and the Beautiful	NaN	3.5
2119	The Bachelor	NaN	2.9

4. Now, we use the `.drop_duplicates` method to keep only the first row of every year:

```
>>> (
...     movie[["movie_title", "title_year", "imdb_score"]]
...     .sort_values(
...         ["title_year", "imdb_score"], ascending=False
...     )
...     .drop_duplicates(subset="title_year")
... )
```

	movie_title	title_year	imdb_score
4312	Kickboxe...	2016.0	9.1
3745	Running ...	2015.0	8.6
4369	Queen of...	2014.0	8.7
3935	Batman: ...	2013.0	8.4
3	The Dark...	2012.0	8.5
...	...	...	...
2694	Metropolis	1927.0	8.3
4767	The Big ...	1925.0	8.3
4833	Over the...	1920.0	4.8

```
4695   Intolera...        1916.0        8.0
2725   Towering...         NaN          9.5
```

How it works...

This example shows how I use chaining to build up and test a sequence of pandas operations. In *step 1*, we slim the dataset down to concentrate on only the columns of importance. This recipe would work the same with the entire DataFrame. *Step 2* shows how to sort a DataFrame by a single column, which is not exactly what we wanted. *Step 3* sorts multiple columns at the same time. It works by first sorting all of `title_year` and then, within each value of `title_year`, sorts by `imdb_score`.

The default behavior of the `.drop_duplicates` method is to keep the first occurrence of each unique row, which would not drop any rows as each row is unique. However, the `subset` parameter alters it to only consider the column (or list of columns) given to it. In this example, only one row for each year will be returned. As we sorted by year and score in the last step, the highest-scoring movie for each year is what we get.

There's more...

As in most things pandas, there is more than one way to do this. If you find yourself comfortable with grouping operations, you can use the `.groupby` method to do this as well:

```python
>>> (
...      movie[["movie_title", "title_year", "imdb_score"]]
...      .groupby("title_year", as_index=False)
...      .apply(
...          lambda df: df.sort_values(
...              "imdb_score", ascending=False
...          ).head(1)
...      )
...      .droplevel(0)
...      .sort_values("title_year", ascending=False)
... )
        movie_title   title_year   imdb_score
90 4312  Kickboxe...      2016.0          9.1
89 3745  Running ...      2015.0          8.6
88 4369  Queen of...      2014.0          8.7
87 3935  Batman: ...      2013.0          8.4
```

```
86  3      The Dark...      2012.0        8.5

...                ...          ...           ...

4   4555   Pandora'...      1929.0        8.0

3   2694    Metropolis      1927.0        8.3

2   4767   The Big ...      1925.0        8.3

1   4833   Over the...      1920.0        4.8

0   4695   Intolera...      1916.0        8.0
```

It is possible to sort one column in ascending order while simultaneously sorting another column in descending order. To accomplish this, pass in a list of Booleans to the `ascending` parameter that corresponds to how you would like each column sorted. The following sorts `title_year` and `content_rating` in descending order and `budget` in ascending order. It then finds the lowest budget film for each year and content rating group:

```python
>>> (
...     movie[
...         [
...             "movie_title",
...             "title_year",
...             "content_rating",
...             "budget",
...         ]
...     ]
...     .sort_values(
...         ["title_year", "content_rating", "budget"],
...         ascending=[False, False, True],
...     )
...     .drop_duplicates(
...         subset=["title_year", "content_rating"]
...     )
... )
      movie_title  title_year content_rating       budget
4026    Compadres      2016.0              R    3000000.0
4658  Fight to...      2016.0          PG-13     150000.0
4661    Rodeo Girl      2016.0             PG     500000.0
3252  The Wailing      2016.0      Not Rated          NaN
4659  Alleluia...      2016.0            NaN     500000.0
...           ...         ...            ...          ...
```

2558	Lilyhammer	NaN	TV-MA	34000000.0
807	Sabrina,...	NaN	TV-G	3000000.0
848	Stargate...	NaN	TV-14	1400000.0
2436	Carlos	NaN	Not Rated	NaN
2119	The Bach...	NaN	NaN	3000000.0

By default, `.drop_duplicates` keeps the very first appearance of a value, but this behavior may be modified by passing `keep='last'` to select the last row of each group or `keep=False` to drop all duplicates entirely.

Replicating nlargest with sort_values

The previous two recipes work similarly by sorting values in slightly different manners. Finding the top *n* values of a column of data is equivalent to sorting the entire column in descending order and taking the first *n* values. pandas has many operations that are capable of doing this in a variety of ways.

In this recipe, we will replicate the *Selecting the smallest of the largest recipe* with the `.sort_values` method and explore the differences between the two.

How to do it...

1. Let's recreate the result from the final step of the *Selecting the smallest of the largest* recipe:

```
>>> movie = pd.read_csv("data/movie.csv")
>>> (
...     movie[["movie_title", "imdb_score", "budget"]]
...     .nlargest(100, "imdb_score")
...     .nsmallest(5, "budget")
... )
             movie_title  imdb_score    budget
4804      Butterfly Girl         8.7  180000.0
4801   Children of Heaven         8.5  180000.0
4706         12 Angry Men         8.9  350000.0
4550          A Separation         8.4  500000.0
4636   The Other Dream Team         8.4  500000.0
```

2. Use `.sort_values` to replicate the first part of the expression and grab the first 100 rows with the `.head` method:

```
>>> (
...        movie[["movie_title", "imdb_score", "budget"]]
...        .sort_values("imdb_score", ascending=False)
...        .head(100)
... )
```

	movie_title	imdb_score	budget
2725	Towering...	9.5	NaN
1920	The Shaw...	9.3	25000000.0
3402	The Godf...	9.2	6000000.0
2779	Dekalog	9.1	NaN
4312	Kickboxe...	9.1	17000000.0
...	...	...	...
3799	Anne of ...	8.4	NaN
3777	Requiem ...	8.4	4500000.0
3935	Batman: ...	8.4	3500000.0
4636	The Othe...	8.4	500000.0
2455	Aliens	8.4	18500000.0

3. Now that we have the top 100 scoring movies, we can use `.sort_values` with `.head` again to grab the lowest five by budget:

```
>>> (
...        movie[["movie_title", "imdb_score", "budget"]]
...        .sort_values("imdb_score", ascending=False)
...        .head(100)
...        .sort_values("budget")
...        .head(5)
... )
```

	movie_title	imdb_score	budget
4815	A Charlie Brown Christmas	8.4	150000.0
4801	Children of Heaven	8.5	180000.0
4804	Butterfly Girl	8.7	180000.0
4706	12 Angry Men	8.9	350000.0
4636	The Other Dream Team	8.4	500000.0

How it works...

The `.sort_values` method can nearly replicate `.nlargest` by chaining the `.head` method after the operation, as seen in *step 2*. *Step 3* replicates `.nsmallest` by chaining another `.sort_values` method and completes the query by taking just the first five rows with the `.head` method.

Take a look at the output from the first DataFrame from *step 1* and compare it with the output from *step 3*. Are they the same? No! What happened? To understand why the two results are not equivalent, let's look at the tail of the intermediate steps of each recipe:

```
>>> (
...     movie[["movie_title", "imdb_score", "budget"]]
...     .nlargest(100, "imdb_score")
...     .tail()
... )
```

	movie_title	imdb_score	budget
4023	Oldboy	8.4	3000000.0
4163	To Kill a Mockingbird	8.4	2000000.0
4395	Reservoir Dogs	8.4	1200000.0
4550	A Separation	8.4	500000.0
4636	The Other Dream Team	8.4	500000.0

```
>>> (
...     movie[["movie_title", "imdb_score", "budget"]]
...     .sort_values("imdb_score", ascending=False)
...     .head(100)
...     .tail()
... )
```

	movie_title	imdb_score	budget
3799	Anne of ...	8.4	NaN
3777	Requiem ...	8.4	4500000.0
3935	Batman: ...	8.4	3500000.0
4636	The Othe...	8.4	500000.0
2455	Aliens	8.4	18500000.0

The issue arises because more than 100 movies exist with a rating of at least 8.4. Each of the methods, `.nlargest` and `.sort_values`, breaks ties differently, which results in a slightly different 100-row DataFrame. If you pass in `kind='mergsort'` to the `.sort_values` method, you will get the same result as `.nlargest`.

Calculating a trailing stop order price

There are many strategies to trade stocks. One basic type of trade that many investors employ is the *stop order*. A stop order is an order placed by an investor to buy or sell a stock that executes whenever the market price reaches a certain point. Stop orders are useful to both prevent huge losses and protect gains.

For this recipe, we will only be examining stop orders used to sell currently owned stocks. In a typical stop order, the price does not change throughout the lifetime of the order. For instance, if you purchased a stock for $100 per share, you might want to set a stop order at $90 per share to limit your downside to 10%.

A more advanced strategy would be to continually modify the sale price of the stop order to track the value of the stock if it increases in value. This is called a *trailing stop order*. Concretely, if the same $100 stock increases to $120, then a trailing stop order 10% below the current market value would move the sale price to $108.

The trailing stop order never moves down and is always tied to the maximum value since the time of purchase. If the stock fell from $120 to $110, the stop order would still remain at $108. It would only increase if the price moved above $120.

This recipe requires the use of the third-party package `pandas-datareader`, which fetches stock market prices online. It does not come pre-installed with pandas. To install this package, use the command line and run `conda install pandas-datareader` or `pip install pandas-datareader`. You may need to install the `requests_cache` library as well.

This recipe determines the trailing stop order price given an initial purchase price for any stock.

How to do it...

1. To get started, we will work with Tesla Motors (TSLA) stock and presume a purchase on the first trading day of 2017:

```
>>> import datetime
>>> import pandas_datareader.data as web
>>> import requests_cache
>>> session = requests_cache.CachedSession(
...        cache_name="cache",
...        backend="sqlite",
...        expire_after=datetime.timedelta(days=90),
... )
```

```
>>> tsla = web.DataReader(
...     "tsla",
...     data_source="yahoo",
...     start="2017-1-1",
...     session=session,
... )
>>> tsla.head(8)
                  High           Low  ...     Volume   Adj Close
Date                                  ...
2017-01-03  220.330002    210.960007  ...    5923300  216.990005
2017-01-04  228.000000    214.309998  ...   11213500  226.990005
2017-01-05  227.479996    221.949997  ...    5911700  226.750000
2017-01-06  230.309998    225.449997  ...    5527900  229.009995
2017-01-09  231.919998    228.000000  ...    3979500  231.279999
2017-01-10  232.000000    226.889999  ...    3660000  229.869995
2017-01-11  229.979996    226.679993  ...    3650800  229.729996
2017-01-12  230.699997    225.580002  ...    3790200  229.589996
```

2. For simplicity, we will work with the closing price of each trading day:

```
>>> tsla_close = tsla["Close"]
```

3. Use the .cummax method to track the highest closing price until the current date:

```
>>> tsla_cummax = tsla_close.cummax()
>>> tsla_cummax.head()
Date
2017-01-03      216.990005
2017-01-04      226.990005
2017-01-05      226.990005
2017-01-06      229.009995
2017-01-09      231.279999
Name: Close, dtype: float64
```

4. To limit the downside to 10%, we multiply the result by 0.9. This creates the trailing stop order. We will chain all of the steps together:

```
>>> (tsla["Close"].cummax().mul(0.9).head())
Date
2017-01-03      195.291005
2017-01-04      204.291005
```

```
2017-01-05     204.291005
2017-01-06     206.108995
2017-01-09     208.151999
Name: Close, dtype: float64
```

How it works...

The `.cummax` method works by retaining the maximum value encountered up to and including the current value. Multiplying this series by 0.9, or whatever cushion you would like to use, creates the trailing stop order. In this particular example, TSLA increased in value, and thus, its trailing stop has also increased.

There's more...

This recipe gives just a taste of how useful pandas may be used to trade securities and stops short of calculating a return for if and when the stop order triggers.

A very similar strategy may be used during a weight-loss program. You can set a warning any time you have strayed too far away from your minimum weight. pandas provides you with the `cummin` method to track the minimum value. If you keep track of your daily weight in a series, the following code provides a trailing weight loss of 5% above your lowest recorded weight to date:

```
weight.cummin() * 1.05
```

5

Exploratory
Data Analysis

In this chapter, we will dive more into **Exploratory Data Analysis (EDA)**. This is the process of sifting through the data and trying to make sense of the individual columns and the relationships between them.

This activity can be time-consuming, but can also have big payoffs. The better you understand the data, the more you can take advantage of it. If you intend to make machine learning models, having insight into the data can lead to more performant models and understanding why predications are made.

We are going to use a dataset from `www.fueleconomy.gov` that provides information about makes and models of cars from 1984 through 2018. Using EDA we will explore many of the columns and relationships found in this data.

Summary statistics

Summary statistics include the mean, quartiles, and standard deviation. The `.describe` method will calculate these measures on all of the numeric columns in a DataFrame.

How to do it...

1. Load the dataset:

```
>>> import pandas as pd
>>> import numpy as np
>>> fueleco = pd.read_csv("data/vehicles.csv.zip")
>>> fueleco
```

	barrels08	barrelsA08	...	phevHwy	phevComb
0	15.695714	0.0	...	0	0
1	29.964545	0.0	...	0	0
2	12.207778	0.0	...	0	0
3	29.964545	0.0	...	0	0
4	17.347895	0.0	...	0	0
...	...	...	...	...	...
39096	14.982273	0.0	...	0	0
39097	14.330870	0.0	...	0	0
39098	15.695714	0.0	...	0	0
39099	15.695714	0.0	...	0	0
39100	18.311667	0.0	...	0	0

2. Call individual summary statistics methods such as `.mean`, `.std`, and `.quantile`:

```
>>> fueleco.mean()
barrels08              17.442712
barrelsA08              0.219276
charge120               0.000000
charge240               0.029630
city08                 18.077799
                         ...
youSaveSpend        -3459.572645
charge240b              0.005869
phevCity                0.094703
phevHwy                 0.094269
phevComb                0.094141
Length: 60, dtype: float64

>>> fueleco.std()
barrels08               4.580230
```

```
barrelsA08          1.143837
charge120           0.000000
charge240           0.487408
city08              6.970672

                       ...

youSaveSpend     3010.284617
charge240b          0.165399
phevCity            2.279478
phevHwy             2.191115
phevComb            2.226500
Length: 60, dtype: float64


>>> fueleco.quantile(
...     [0, 0.25, 0.5, 0.75, 1]
... )
        barrels08  barrelsA08  ...  phevHwy  phevComb
0.00     0.060000    0.000000  ...      0.0       0.0
0.25    14.330870    0.000000  ...      0.0       0.0
0.50    17.347895    0.000000  ...      0.0       0.0
0.75    20.115000    0.000000  ...      0.0       0.0
1.00    47.087143   18.311667  ...     81.0      88.0
```

3. Call the `.describe` method:

```
>>> fueleco.describe()
         barrels08   barrelsA08  ...      phevHwy     phevComb
count  39101.00...  39101.00...  ...  39101.00...  39101.00...
mean     17.442712     0.219276  ...     0.094269     0.094141
std       4.580230     1.143837  ...     2.191115     2.226500
min       0.060000     0.000000  ...     0.000000     0.000000
25%      14.330870     0.000000  ...     0.000000     0.000000
50%      17.347895     0.000000  ...     0.000000     0.000000
75%      20.115000     0.000000  ...     0.000000     0.000000
max      47.087143    18.311667  ...    81.000000    88.000000
```

4. To get summary statistics on the object columns, use the `.include` parameter:

```
>>> fueleco.describe(include=object)
               drive eng_dscr  ...    modifiedOn startStop
```

count	37912	23431	...	39101	7405
unique	7	545	...	68	2
top	Front-Wh...	(FFS)	...	Tue Jan ...	N
freq	13653	8827	...	29438	5176

How it works...

I've done data analysis trainings where the client literally slapped their head after teaching them about the .describe method. When I asked what the problem was, they replied that they had spent the last couple of weeks implementing that behavior for their database.

By default, .describe will calculate summary statistics on the numeric columns. You can pass the include parameter to tell the method to include non-numeric data types. Note that this will show the count of unique values, the most frequent value (top), and its frequency counts for the object columns.

There's more...

One tip that often makes more data appear on the screen is transposing a DataFrame. I find that this is useful for the output of the .describe method:

```
>>> fueleco.describe().T
```

	count	mean	...	75%	max
barrels08	39101.0	17.442712	...	20.115	47.087143
barrelsA08	39101.0	0.219276	...	0.000	18.311667
charge120	39101.0	0.000000	...	0.000	0.000000
charge240	39101.0	0.029630	...	0.000	12.000000
city08	39101.0	18.077799	...	20.000	150.000000
...	...	...	...	...	...
youSaveSpend	39101.0	-3459.572645	...	-1500.000	5250.000000
charge240b	39101.0	0.005869	...	0.000	7.000000
phevCity	39101.0	0.094703	...	0.000	97.000000
phevHwy	39101.0	0.094269	...	0.000	81.000000
phevComb	39101.0	0.094141	...	0.000	88.000000

Column types

You can glean information about the data in pandas simply by looking at the types of the columns. In this recipe, we will explore the column types.

How to do it...

1. Inspect the `.dtypes` attribute:

```
>>> fueleco.dtypes
barrels08      float64
barrelsA08     float64
charge120      float64
charge240      float64
city08           int64
                 ...
modifiedOn      object
startStop       object
phevCity         int64
phevHwy          int64
phevComb         int64
Length: 83, dtype: object
```

2. Summarize the types of columns:

```
>>> fueleco.dtypes.value_counts()
float64     32
int64       27
object      23
bool         1
dtype: int64
```

How it works...

When you read a CSV file in pandas, it has to infer the types of the columns. The process looks something like this:

> ► If all of the values in a column look like whole numeric values, convert them to integers and give the column the type `int64`

▶ If the values are float-like, give them the type `float64`

▶ If the values are numeric, float-like, or integer-like, but missing values, assign them to the type `float64` because the value typically used for missing values, `np.nan`, is a floating-point type

▶ If the values have `false` or `true` in them, assign them to Booleans

▶ Otherwise, leave the column as strings and give it the `object` type (these can be missing values with the `float64` type)

Note that if you use the `parse_dates`, parameter, it is possible that some of the columns were converted to datetimes. *Chapters 12* and *13* show examples of parsing dates.

By just looking at the output of `.dtypes` I can divine more about the data than just the data types. I can see if something is a string or missing values. Object types may be strings or categorical data, but they could also be numeric-like values that need to be nudged a little so that they are numeric. I typically leave integer columns alone. I tend to treat them as continuous values. If the values are float values, this indicates that the column could be:

▶ All floating-point values with no missing values

▶ Floating-point values with missing values

▶ Integer values that were missing some values and hence converted to floats

There's more...

When pandas converts columns to floats or integers, it uses the 64-bit versions of those types. If you know that your integers fall into a certain range (or you are willing to sacrifice some precision on floats), you can save some memory by converting these columns to columns that use less memory.

```
>>> fueleco.select_dtypes("int64").describe().T
                 count          mean   ...      75%     max
city08         39101.0     18.077799   ...     20.0   150.0
cityA08        39101.0      0.569883   ...      0.0   145.0
co2            39101.0     72.538989   ...     -1.0   847.0
co2A           39101.0      5.543950   ...     -1.0   713.0
comb08         39101.0     20.323828   ...     23.0   136.0
...                ...           ...   ...      ...     ...
year           39101.0   2000.635406   ...   2010.0  2018.0
youSaveSpend   39101.0  -3459.572645   ...  -1500.0  5250.0
phevCity       39101.0      0.094703   ...      0.0    97.0
phevHwy        39101.0      0.094269   ...      0.0    81.0
phevComb       39101.0      0.094141   ...      0.0    88.0
```

We can see that the `city08` and `comb08` columns don't go above 150. The `iinfo` function in NumPy will show us the limits for integer types. We can see that we would not want to use an `int8` for this column, but we can use an `int16`. By converting to that type, the column will use 25% of the memory:

```
>>> np.iinfo(np.int8)
iinfo(min=-128, max=127, dtype=int8)
>>> np.iinfo(np.int16)
iinfo(min=-32768, max=32767, dtype=int16)


>>> fueleco[["city08", "comb08"]].info(memory_usage="deep")
<class 'pandas.core.frame.DataFrame'>
RangeIndex: 39101 entries, 0 to 39100
Data columns (total 2 columns):
 #   Column  Non-Null Count  Dtype
---  ------  --------------  -----
 0   city08  39101 non-null  int64
 1   comb08  39101 non-null  int64
dtypes: int64(2)
memory usage: 611.1 KB


>>> (
...     fueleco[["city08", "comb08"]]
...     .assign(
...         city08=fueleco.city08.astype(np.int16),
...         comb08=fueleco.comb08.astype(np.int16),
...     )
...     .info(memory_usage="deep")
... )
<class 'pandas.core.frame.DataFrame'>
RangeIndex: 39101 entries, 0 to 39100
Data columns (total 2 columns):
 #   Column  Non-Null Count  Dtype
---  ------  --------------  -----
 0   city08  39101 non-null  int16
 1   comb08  39101 non-null  int16
dtypes: int16(2)
memory usage: 152.9 KB
```

Note that there is an analogous `finfo` function in NumPy for retrieving float information.

An option for conserving memory for string columns is to convert them to categories. If each value for a string column is unique, this will slow down pandas and use more memory, but if you have low cardinality, you can save a lot of memory. The `make` column has low cardinality, but the `model` column has a higher cardinality, and there is less memory saving for that column.

Below, we will show pulling out just these two columns. But instead of getting a Series, we will index with a list with just that column name in it. This will gives us back a DataFrame with a single column. We will update the column type to categorical and look at the memory usage. Remember to pass in `memory_usage='deep'` to get the memory usage for object columns:

```
>>> fueleco.make.nunique()
134
>>> fueleco.model.nunique()
3816


>>> fueleco[["make"]].info(memory_usage="deep")
<class 'pandas.core.frame.DataFrame'>
RangeIndex: 39101 entries, 0 to 39100
Data columns (total 1 columns):
 #   Column  Non-Null Count  Dtype
---  ------  --------------  -----
 0   make    39101 non-null  object
dtypes: object(1)
memory usage: 2.4 MB


>>> (
...      fueleco[["make"]]
...      .assign(make=fueleco.make.astype("category"))
...      .info(memory_usage="deep")
... )
<class 'pandas.core.frame.DataFrame'>
RangeIndex: 39101 entries, 0 to 39100
Data columns (total 1 columns):
 #   Column  Non-Null Count  Dtype
---  ------  --------------  -----
 0   make    39101 non-null  category
dtypes: category(1)
```

```
memory usage: 90.4 KB


>>> fueleco[["model"]].info(memory_usage="deep")
<class 'pandas.core.frame.DataFrame'>
RangeIndex: 39101 entries, 0 to 39100
Data columns (total 1 columns):
 #   Column   Non-Null Count   Dtype
---  ------   --------------   -----
 0   model    39101 non-null   object
dtypes: object(1)
memory usage: 2.5 MB


>>> (
...       fueleco[["model"]]
...       .assign(model=fueleco.model.astype("category"))
...       .info(memory_usage="deep")
... )
<class 'pandas.core.frame.DataFrame'>
RangeIndex: 39101 entries, 0 to 39100
Data columns (total 1 columns):
 #   Column   Non-Null Count   Dtype
---  ------   --------------   -----
 0   model    39101 non-null   category
dtypes: category(1)
memory usage: 496.7 KB
```

Categorical data

I broadly classify data into dates, continuous values, and categorical values. In this section, we will explore quantifying and visualizing categorical data.

How to do it...

1. Pick out the columns with data types that are object:

   ```
   >>> fueleco.select_dtypes(object).columns
   Index(['drive', 'eng_dscr', 'fuelType', 'fuelType1', 'make',
   'model',
   ```

```
         'mpgData', 'trany', 'VClass', 'guzzler', 'trans_dscr',
'tCharger',
         'sCharger', 'atvType', 'fuelType2', 'rangeA', 'evMotor',
'mfrCode',
         'c240Dscr', 'c240bDscr', 'createdOn', 'modifiedOn',
'startStop'],
      dtype='object')
```

2. Use `.nunique` to determine the cardinality:

    ```
    >>> fueleco.drive.nunique()
    7
    ```

3. Use `.sample` to see some of the values:

    ```
    >>> fueleco.drive.sample(5, random_state=42)
    4217      4-Wheel ...
    1736      4-Wheel ...
    36029     Rear-Whe...
    37631     Front-Wh...
    1668      Rear-Whe...
    Name: drive, dtype: object
    ```

4. Determine the number and percent of missing values:

    ```
    >>> fueleco.drive.isna().sum()
    1189
    ```

    ```
    >>> fueleco.drive.isna().mean() * 100
    3.0408429451932175
    ```

5. Use the `.value_counts` method to summarize a column:

    ```
    >>> fueleco.drive.value_counts()
    Front-Wheel Drive              13653
    Rear-Wheel Drive               13284
    4-Wheel or All-Wheel Drive      6648
    All-Wheel Drive                 2401
    4-Wheel Drive                   1221
    2-Wheel Drive                    507
    Part-time 4-Wheel Drive          198
    Name: drive, dtype: int64
    ```

6. If there are too many values in the summary, you might want to look at the top 6 and collapse the remaining values:

```
>>> top_n = fueleco.make.value_counts().index[:6]
>>> (
...     fueleco.assign(
...         make=fueleco.make.where(
...             fueleco.make.isin(top_n), "Other"
...         )
...     ).make.value_counts()
... )
Other        23211
Chevrolet     3900
Ford          3208
Dodge         2557
GMC           2442
Toyota        1976
BMW           1807
Name: make, dtype: int64
```

7. Use pandas to plot the counts and visualize them:

```
>>> import matplotlib.pyplot as plt
>>> fig, ax = plt.subplots(figsize=(10, 8))
>>> top_n = fueleco.make.value_counts().index[:6]
>>> (
...     fueleco.assign(
...         make=fueleco.make.where(
...             fueleco.make.isin(top_n), "Other"
...         )
...     )
...     .make.value_counts()
...     .plot.bar(ax=ax)
... )
>>> fig.savefig("c5-catpan.png", dpi=300)
```

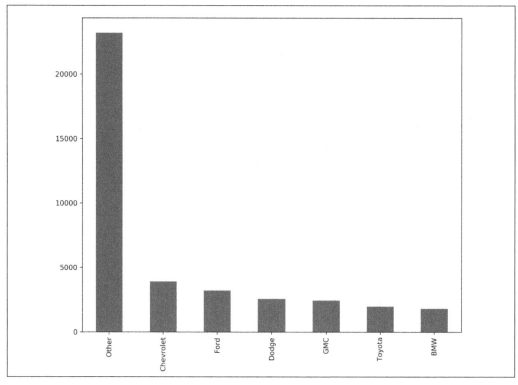

pandas categorical

8. Use `seaborn` to plot the counts and visualize them:

```
>>> import seaborn as sns
>>> fig, ax = plt.subplots(figsize=(10, 8))
>>> top_n = fueleco.make.value_counts().index[:6]
>>> sns.countplot(
...     y="make",
...     data=(
...         fueleco.assign(
...             make=fueleco.make.where(
...                 fueleco.make.isin(top_n), "Other"
...             )
...         )
...     ),
... )
>>> fig.savefig("c5-catsns.png", dpi=300)
```

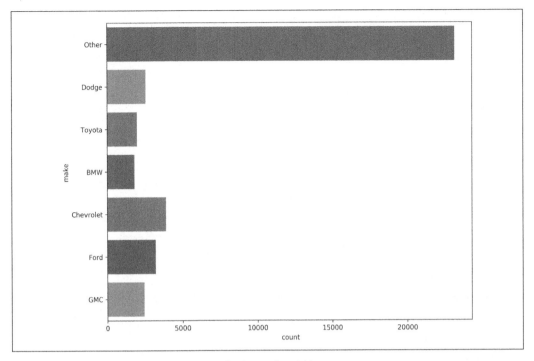

Seaborn categorical

How it works...

When we are examining a categorical variable, we want to know how many unique values there are. If this is a large value, the column might not be categorical, but either free text or a numeric column that pandas didn't know how to store as numeric because it came across a non-valid number.

The `.sample` method lets us look at a few of the values. With most columns, it is important to determine how many are missing. It looks like there are over 1,000 rows, or about 3% of the values, that are missing. Typically, we need to talk to an SME to determine why these values are missing and whether we need to impute them or drop them.

Here is some code to look at the rows where the *drive* is missing:

```
>>> fueleco[fueleco.drive.isna()]
       barrels08   barrelsA08   ...   phevHwy   phevComb
7138    0.240000          0.0   ...         0          0
8144    0.312000          0.0   ...         0          0
8147    0.270000          0.0   ...         0          0
```

18215	15.695714	0.0	...	0	0
18216	14.982273	0.0	...	0	0
...	...	...	...	...	...
23023	0.240000	0.0	...	0	0
23024	0.546000	0.0	...	0	0
23026	0.426000	0.0	...	0	0
23031	0.426000	0.0	...	0	0
23034	0.204000	0.0	...	0	0

My favorite method for inspecting categorical columns is the `.value_counts` method. This is my goto method and I usually start with it, as I can divine answers to many of the other questions with the output of this method. By default, it does not show missing values, but you can use the `dropna` parameter to fix that:

```
>>> fueleco.drive.value_counts(dropna=False)
Front-Wheel Drive                13653
Rear-Wheel Drive                 13284
4-Wheel or All-Wheel Drive        6648
All-Wheel Drive                   2401
4-Wheel Drive                     1221
NaN                               1189
2-Wheel Drive                      507
Part-time 4-Wheel Drive            198
Name: drive, dtype: int64
```

Finally, you can visualize this output using pandas or seaborn. A bar plot is an appropriate plot to do this. However, if this is a higher cardinality column, you might have too many bars for an effective plot. You can limit the number of columns as we do in *step 6,* or use the `order` parameter for `countplot` to limit them with seaborn.

I use pandas for quick and dirty plotting because it is typically a method call away. However, the seaborn library has various tricks up its sleeve that we will see in later recipes that are not easy to do in pandas.

There's more...

Some columns report `object` data types, but they are not really categorical. In this dataset, the `rangeA` column has an `object` data type. However, if we use my favorite categorical method, `.value_counts`, to examine it, we see that it is not really categorical, but a numeric column posing as a category.

This is because, as seen in the output of `.value_counts`, there are slashes (/) and dashes (-) in some of the entries and pandas did not know how to convert those values to numbers, so it left the whole column as a string column.

```
>>> fueleco.rangeA.value_counts()
290          74
270          56
280          53
310          41
277          38
             ..
328           1
250/370       1
362/537       1
310/370       1
340-350       1
Name: rangeA, Length: 216, dtype: int64
```

Another way to find offending characters is to use the `.str.extract` method with a regular expression:

```
>>> (
...      fueleco.rangeA.str.extract(r"([^0-9.])")
...      .dropna()
...      .apply(lambda row: "".join(row), axis=1)
...      .value_counts()
... )
/     280
-      71
Name: rangeA, dtype: int64
```

This is actually a column that has two types: float and string. The data type is reported as `object` because that type can hold heterogenous typed columns. The missing values are stored as NaN and the non-missing values are strings:

```
>>> set(fueleco.rangeA.apply(type))
{<class 'str'>, <class 'float'>}
```

Here is the count of missing values:

```
>>> fueleco.rangeA.isna().sum()
37616
```

According to the `fueleconomy.gov` website, the `rangeA` value represents the range for the second fuel type of dual fuel vehicles (E85, electricity, CNG, and LPG). Using pandas, we can replace the missing values with zero, replace dashes with slashes, then split and take the mean value of each row (in the case of a dash/slash):

```
>>> (
...         fueleco.rangeA.fillna("0")
...         .str.replace("-", "/")
...         .str.split("/", expand=True)
...         .astype(float)
...         .mean(axis=1)
... )
0          0.0
1          0.0
2          0.0
3          0.0
4          0.0
          ...
39096      0.0
39097      0.0
39098      0.0
39099      0.0
39100      0.0
Length: 39101, dtype: float64
```

We can also treat numeric columns as categories by binning them. There are two powerful functions in pandas to aid binning, `cut` and `qcut`. We can use `cut` to cut into equal-width bins, or bin widths that we specify. For the `rangeA` column, most of the values were empty and we replaced them with 0, so 10 equal-width bins look like this:

```
>>> (
...         fueleco.rangeA.fillna("0")
...         .str.replace("-", "/")
...         .str.split("/", expand=True)
...         .astype(float)
...         .mean(axis=1)
...         .pipe(lambda ser_: pd.cut(ser_, 10))
...         .value_counts()
... )
```

```
(-0.45, 44.95]        37688
(269.7, 314.65]         559
(314.65, 359.6]         352
(359.6, 404.55]         205
(224.75, 269.7]         181
(404.55, 449.5]          82
(89.9, 134.85]           12
(179.8, 224.75]           9
(44.95, 89.9]             8
(134.85, 179.8]           5
dtype: int64
```

Alternatively, `qcut` (quantile cut) will cut the entries into bins with the same size. Because the `rangeA` column is heavily skewed, and most of the entries are 0, we can't quantize 0 into multiple bins, so it fails. But it does (somewhat) work with `city08`. I say somewhat because the values for `city08` are whole numbers and so they don't evenly bin into 10 buckets, but the sizes are close:

```
>>> (
...        fueleco.rangeA.fillna("0")
...        .str.replace("-", "/")
...        .str.split("/", expand=True)
...        .astype(float)
...        .mean(axis=1)
...        .pipe(lambda ser_: pd.qcut(ser_, 10))
...        .value_counts()
... )
Traceback (most recent call last):
   ...
ValueError: Bin edges must be unique: array([  0. ,     0. ,     0. ,     0. ,
0. ,    0. ,    0. ,    0. ,    0. ,
       0. , 449.5]).


>>> (
...        fueleco.city08.pipe(
...            lambda ser: pd.qcut(ser, q=10)
...        ).value_counts()
... )
```

```
(5.999, 13.0]      5939
(19.0, 21.0]       4477
(14.0, 15.0]       4381
(17.0, 18.0]       3912
(16.0, 17.0]       3881
(15.0, 16.0]       3855
(21.0, 24.0]       3676
(24.0, 150.0]      3235
(13.0, 14.0]       2898
(18.0, 19.0]       2847
Name: city08, dtype: int64
```

Continuous data

My broad definition of continuous data is data that is stored as a number, either an integer or a float. There is some gray area between categorical and continuous data. For example, the grade level could be represented as a number (ignoring Kindergarten, or using 0 to represent it). A grade column, in this case, could be both categorical and continuous, so the techniques in this section and the previous section could both apply to it.

We will examine a continuous column from the fuel economy dataset in this section. The `city08` column lists the miles per gallon that are expected when driving a car at the lower speeds found in a city.

How to do it...

1. Pick out the columns that are numeric (typically `int64` or `float64`):

    ```
    >>> fueleco.select_dtypes("number")
            barrels08  barrelsA08  ...  phevHwy  phevComb
    0       15.695714        0.0   ...        0         0
    1       29.964545        0.0   ...        0         0
    2       12.207778        0.0   ...        0         0
    3       29.964545        0.0   ...        0         0
    4       17.347895        0.0   ...        0         0
    ...           ...        ...   ...      ...       ...
    39096   14.982273        0.0   ...        0         0
    39097   14.330870        0.0   ...        0         0
    ```

39098	15.695714	0.0	...	0	0
39099	15.695714	0.0	...	0	0
39100	18.311667	0.0	...	0	0

2. Use `.sample` to see some of the values:

```
>>> fueleco.city08.sample(5, random_state=42)
4217     11
1736     21
36029    16
37631    16
1668     17
Name: city08, dtype: int64
```

3. Determine the number and percent of missing values:

```
>>> fueleco.city08.isna().sum()
0

>>> fueleco.city08.isna().mean() * 100
0.0
```

4. Get the summary statistics:

```
>>> fueleco.city08.describe()
count    39101.000000
mean        18.077799
std          6.970672
min          6.000000
25%         15.000000
50%         17.000000
75%         20.000000
max        150.000000
Name: city08, dtype: float64
```

5. Use pandas to plot a histogram:

```
>>> import matplotlib.pyplot as plt
>>> fig, ax = plt.subplots(figsize=(10, 8))
>>> fueleco.city08.hist(ax=ax)
>>> fig.savefig(
...     "c5-conthistpan.png", dpi=300
... )
```

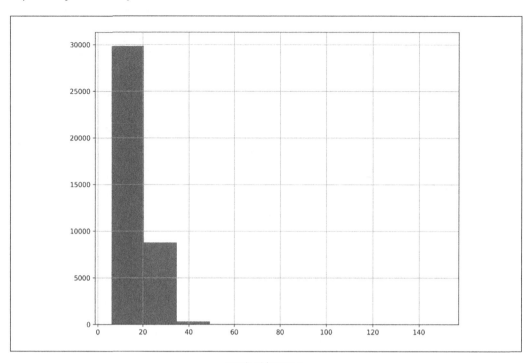

pandas histogram

6. This plot looks very skewed, so we will increase the number of bins in the histogram to see if the skew is hiding behaviors (as skew makes bins wider):

```
>>> import matplotlib.pyplot as plt
>>> fig, ax = plt.subplots(figsize=(10, 8))
>>> fueleco.city08.hist(ax=ax, bins=30)
>>> fig.savefig(
...     "c5-conthistpanbins.png", dpi=300
... )
```

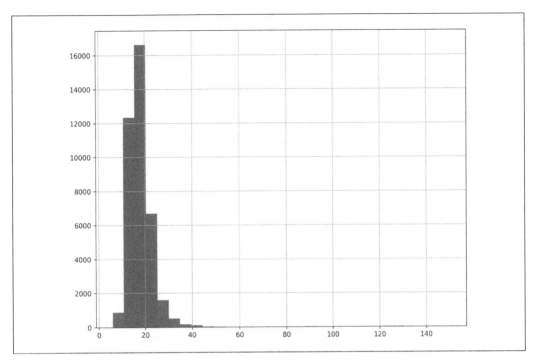

pandas histogram

7. Use seaborn to create a distribution plot, which includes a histogram, a **kernel density estimation** (**KDE**), and a rug plot:

```
>>> fig, ax = plt.subplots(figsize=(10, 8))
>>> sns.distplot(fueleco.city08, rug=True, ax=ax)
>>> fig.savefig(
...     "c5-conthistsns.png", dpi=300
... )
```

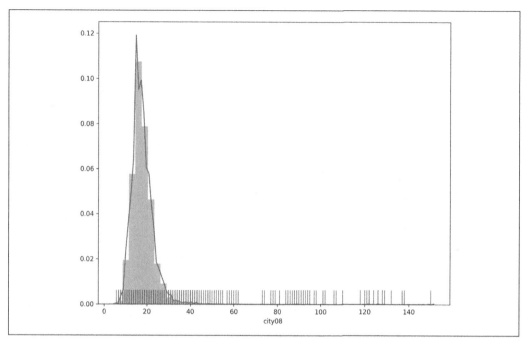

Seaborn histogram

How it works...

It is good to get a feel for how numbers behave. Looking at a sample of the data will let you know what some of the values are. We also want to know whether values are missing. Recall that pandas will ignore missing values when we perform operations on columns.

The summary statistics provided by .describe are very useful. This is probably my favorite method for inspecting continuous values. I like to make sure I check the minimum and maximum values to make sure that they make sense. It would be strange if there was a negative value as a minimum for the miles per gallon column. The quartiles also give us an indication of how skewed the data is. Because the quartiles are reliable indicators of the tendencies of the data, they are not affected by outliers.

Another thing to be aware of is infinite values, either positive or negative. This column does not have infinite values, but these can cause some math operations or plots to fail. If you have infinite values, you need to determine how to handle them. Clipping and removing them are common options that are easy with pandas.

I'm a huge fan of plotting, and both pandas and seaborn make it easy to visualize the distribution of continuous data. Take advantage of plots because, as the cliché goes, a picture tells a thousand words. I've found that platitude to be true in my adventures with data.

There's more...

The seaborn library has many options for summarizing continuous data. In addition to the `distplot` function, there are functions for creating box plots, boxen plots, and violin plots.

A boxen plot is an enhanced box plot. The R folks created a plot called a *letter value* plot, and when the seaborn author replicated it, the name was changed to boxen. The median value is the black line. It steps half of the way from the median 50 to 0 and 100. So the tallest block shows the range from 25-75 quantiles. The next box on the low end goes from 25 to half of that value (or 12.5), so the 12.5-25 quantile. This pattern repeats, so the next box is the 6.25-12.5 quantile, and so on.

A violin plot is basically a histogram that has a copy flipped over on the other side. If you have a bi-model histogram, it tends to look like a violin, hence the name:

```
>>> fig, axs = plt.subplots(nrows=3, figsize=(10, 8))
>>> sns.boxplot(fueleco.city08, ax=axs[0])
>>> sns.violinplot(fueleco.city08, ax=axs[1])
>>> sns.boxenplot(fueleco.city08, ax=axs[2])
>>> fig.savefig("c5-contothersns.png", dpi=300)
```

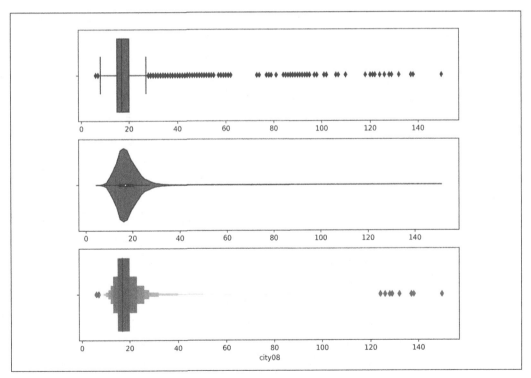

A boxplot, violin plot, and boxen plot created with seaborn

If you are concerned with whether the data is normal, you can quantify this with numbers and visualizations using the SciPy library.

The Kolmogorov-Smirnov test can evaluate whether a distribution is normal. It provides us with a p-value. If this value is significant (< 0.05), then the data is not normal:

```
>>> from scipy import stats
>>> stats.kstest(fueleco.city08, cdf="norm")
KstestResult(statistic=0.9999999990134123, pvalue=0.0)
```

We can plot a probability plot to see whether the values are normal. If the samples track the line, then the data is normal:

```
>>> from scipy import stats
>>> fig, ax = plt.subplots(figsize=(10, 8))
>>> stats.probplot(fueleco.city08, plot=ax)
>>> fig.savefig("c5-conprob.png", dpi=300)
```

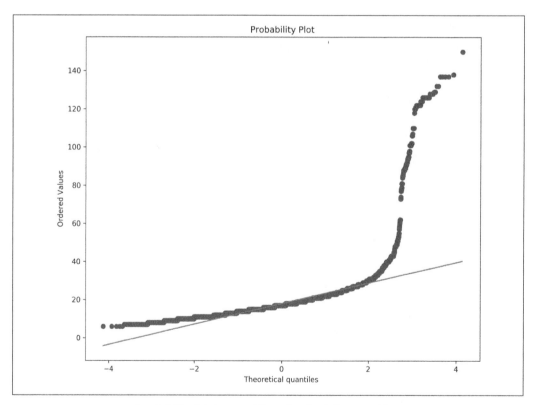

A probability plot shows us if the values track the normal line

Comparing continuous values across categories

The previous sections discussed looking at a single column. This section will show how to compare continuous variables in different categories. We will look at mileage numbers in different brands: Ford, Honda, Tesla, and BMW.

How to do it...

1. Make a mask for the brands we want and then use a group by operation to look at the mean and standard deviation for the `city08` column for each group of cars:

```
>>> mask = fueleco.make.isin(
...     ["Ford", "Honda", "Tesla", "BMW"]
... )
>>> fueleco[mask].groupby("make").city08.agg(
...     ["mean", "std"]
... )
            mean        std
make
BMW     17.817377   7.372907
Ford    16.853803   6.701029
Honda   24.372973   9.154064
Tesla   92.826087   5.538970
```

2. Visualize the `city08` values for each make with seaborn:

```
>>> g = sns.catplot(
...     x="make", y="city08", data=fueleco[mask], kind="box"
... )
>>> g.ax.figure.savefig("c5-catbox.png", dpi=300)
```

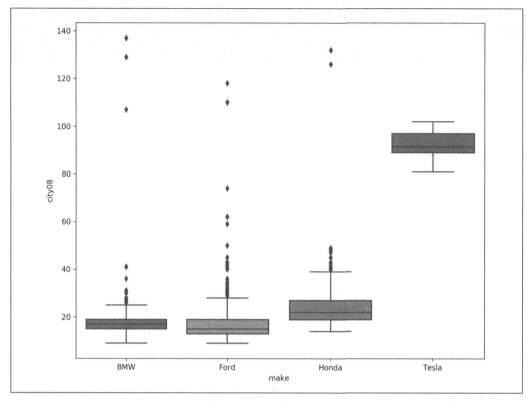

Box plots for each make

How it works...

If the summary statistics change for the different makes, that is a strong indicator that the makes have different characteristics. The central tendency (mean or median) and the variance (or standard deviation) are good measures to compare. We can see that Honda gets better city mileage than both BMW and Ford but has more variance, while Tesla is better than all of them and has the tightest variance.

Using a visualization library like seaborn lets us quickly see the differences in the categories. The difference between the four car makes is drastic, but you can see that there are outliers for the non-Tesla makes that appear to have better mileage than Tesla.

There's more...

One drawback of a boxplot is that while it indicates the spread of the data, it does not reveal how many samples are in each make. You might naively think that each boxplot has the same number of samples. We can quantify that this is not the case with pandas:

```
>>> mask = fueleco.make.isin(
...      ["Ford", "Honda", "Tesla", "BMW"]
... )
>>> (fueleco[mask].groupby("make").city08.count())
make
BMW       1807
Ford      3208
Honda      925
Tesla       46
Name: city08, dtype: int64
```

Another option is to do a swarm plot on top of the box plots:

```
>>> g = sns.catplot(
...      x="make", y="city08", data=fueleco[mask], kind="box"
... )
>>> sns.swarmplot(
...      x="make",
...      y="city08",
...      data=fueleco[mask],
...      color="k",
...      size=1,
...      ax=g.ax,
... )
>>> g.ax.figure.savefig(
...      "c5-catbox2.png", dpi=300
... )
```

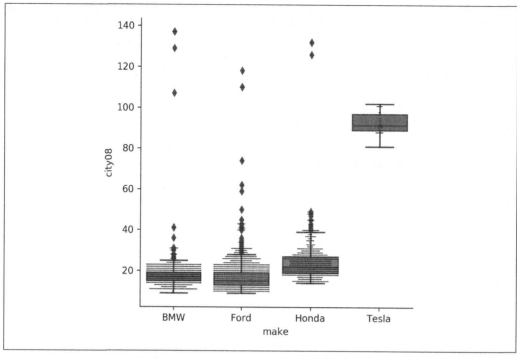

A seaborn boxplot with a swarm plot layered on top

Additionally, the `catplot` function has many more tricks up its sleeves. We are showing two dimensions right now, city mileage and make. We can add more dimensions to the plot.

You can facet the grid by another feature. You can break each of these new plots into its own graph by using the `col` parameter:

```
>>> g = sns.catplot(
...      x="make",
...      y="city08",
...      data=fueleco[mask],
...      kind="box",
...      col="year",
...      col_order=[2012, 2014, 2016, 2018],
...      col_wrap=2,
... )
>>> g.axes[0].figure.savefig(
...      "c5-catboxcol.png", dpi=300
... )
```

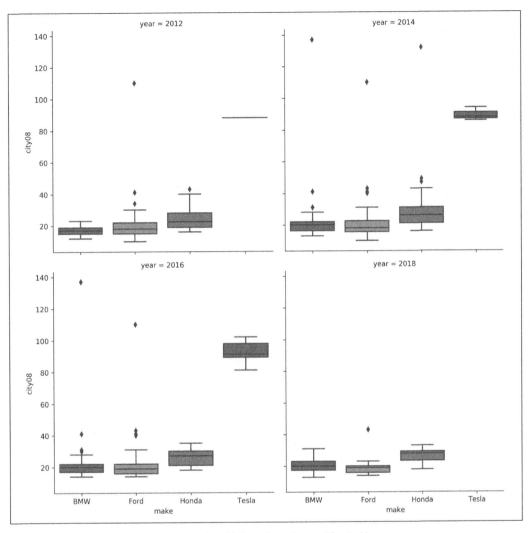

A seaborn boxplot with hues for makes and faceted by year

Alternatively, you can embed the new dimension in the same plot by using the `hue` parameter:

```
>>> g = sns.catplot(
...     x="make",
...     y="city08",
...     data=fueleco[mask],
...     kind="box",
...     hue="year",
...     hue_order=[2012, 2014, 2016, 2018],
```

```
... )
>>> g.ax.figure.savefig(
...        "c5-catboxhue.png", dpi=300
... )
```

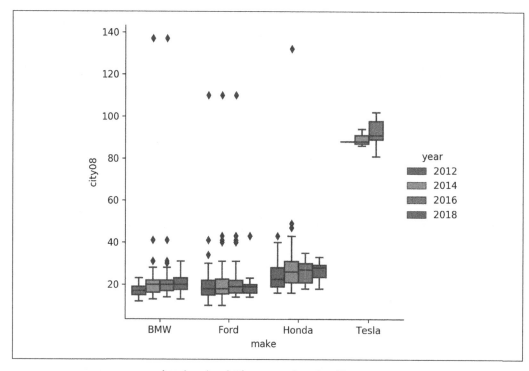

A seaborn boxplot for every make colored by year

If you are in Jupyter, you can style the output of the groupby call to highlight the values at the extremes. Use the .style.background_gradient method to do this:

```
>>> mask = fueleco.make.isin(
...        ["Ford", "Honda", "Tesla", "BMW"]
... )
>>> (
...        fueleco[mask]
...        .groupby("make")
...        .city08.agg(["mean", "std"])
...        .style.background_gradient(cmap="RdBu", axis=0)
... )
```

Out[58]:

make	mean	std
BMW	17.8174	7.37291
Ford	16.8538	6.70103
Honda	24.373	9.15406
Tesla	92.8261	5.53897

Using the pandas style functionality to highlight minimum and maximum values from the mean and standard deviation

Comparing two continuous columns

Evaluating how two continuous columns relate to one another is the essence of regression. But it goes beyond that. If you have two columns with a high correlation to one another, often, you may drop one of them as a redundant column. In this section, we will look at EDA for pairs of continuous columns.

How to do it...

1. Look at the covariance of the two numbers if they are on the same scale:

```
>>> fueleco.city08.cov(fueleco.highway08)
46.33326023673625
```

```
>>> fueleco.city08.cov(fueleco.comb08)
47.41994667819079
```

```
>>> fueleco.city08.cov(fueleco.cylinders)
-5.931560263764761
```

2. Look at the Pearson correlation between the two numbers:

```
>>> fueleco.city08.corr(fueleco.highway08)
0.932494506228495
```

```
>>> fueleco.city08.corr(fueleco.cylinders)
-0.701654842382788
```

3. Visualize the correlations in a heatmap:

```
>>> import seaborn as sns
>>> fig, ax = plt.subplots(figsize=(8, 8))
>>> corr = fueleco[
...     ["city08", "highway08", "cylinders"]
... ].corr()
>>> mask = np.zeros_like(corr, dtype=np.bool)
>>> mask[np.triu_indices_from(mask)] = True
>>> sns.heatmap(
...     corr,
...     mask=mask,
...     fmt=".2f",
...     annot=True,
...     ax=ax,
...     cmap="RdBu",
...     vmin=-1,
...     vmax=1,
...     square=True,
... )
>>> fig.savefig(
...     "c5-heatmap.png", dpi=300, bbox_inches="tight"
... )
```

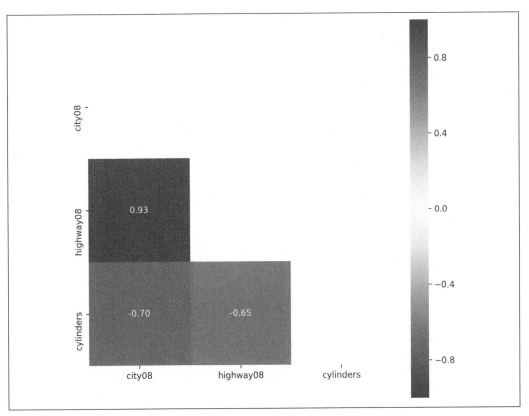

A seaborn heatmap

4. Use pandas to scatter plot the relationships:

```
>>> fig, ax = plt.subplots(figsize=(8, 8))
>>> fueleco.plot.scatter(
...     x="city08", y="highway08", alpha=0.1, ax=ax
... )
>>> fig.savefig(
...     "c5-scatpan.png", dpi=300, bbox_inches="tight"
... )
```

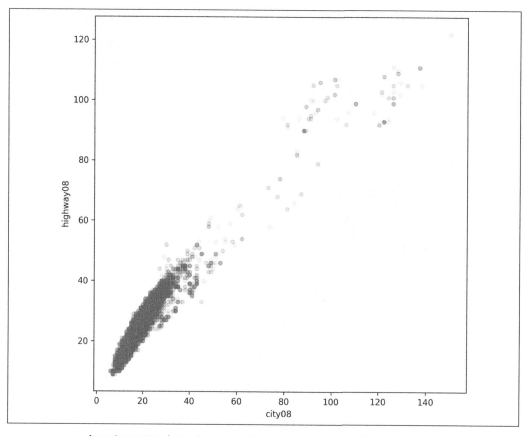

A pandas scatter plot to view the relationships between city and highway mileage

```
>>> fig, ax = plt.subplots(figsize=(8, 8))
>>> fueleco.plot.scatter(
...     x="city08", y="cylinders", alpha=0.1, ax=ax
... )
>>> fig.savefig(
...     "c5-scatpan-cyl.png", dpi=300, bbox_inches="tight"
... )
```

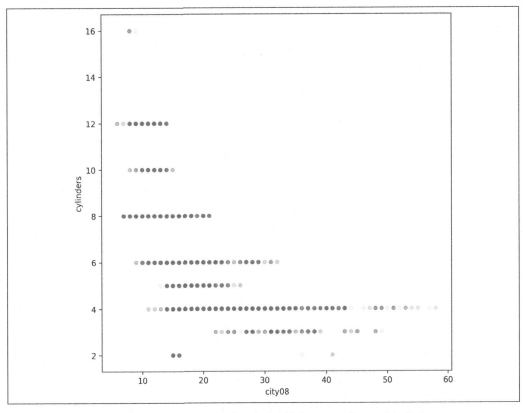

Another pandas scatter to view the relationship between mileage and cylinders

5. Fill in some missing values. From the cylinder plot, we can see that some of the high-end values for mileage are missing. This is because these cars tend to be electric and not have cylinders. We will fix that by filling those values in with 0:

```
>>> fueleco.cylinders.isna().sum()
145
```

```
>>> fig, ax = plt.subplots(figsize=(8, 8))
>>> (
...     fueleco.assign(
...         cylinders=fueleco.cylinders.fillna(0)
...     ).plot.scatter(
...         x="city08", y="cylinders", alpha=0.1, ax=ax
...     )
... )
>>> fig.savefig(
```

```
...        "c5-scatpan-cyl0.png", dpi=300, bbox_inches="tight"
...    )
```

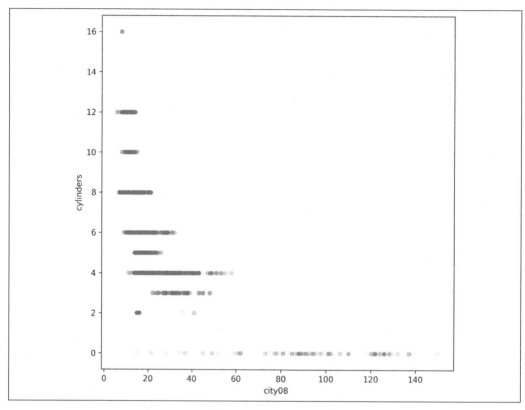

Another pandas scatter to view the relationship between mileage and cylinders,
with missing numbers for cylinders filled in with 0

6. Use seaborn to add a regression line to the relationships:

```
>>> res = sns.lmplot(
...        x="city08", y="highway08", data=fueleco
...    )
>>> res.fig.savefig(
...        "c5-lmplot.png", dpi=300, bbox_inches="tight"
...    )
```

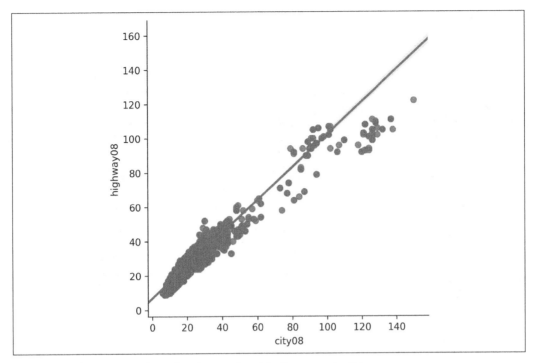

A seaborn scatter plot with a regression line

How it works...

Pearson correlation tells us how one value impacts another. It is between -1 and 1. In this case, we can see that there is a strong correlation between city mileage and highway mileage. As you get better city mileage, you tend to get better highway mileage.

Covariance lets us know how these values vary together. Covariance is useful for comparing multiple continuous columns that have similar correlations. For example, correlation is scale-invariant, but covariance is not. If we compare `city08` to two times `highway08`, they have the same correlation, but the covariance changes.

```
>>> fueleco.city08.corr(fueleco.highway08 * 2)
0.932494506228495


>>> fueleco.city08.cov(fueleco.highway08 * 2)
92.6665204734725
```

A heatmap is a great way to look at correlations in aggregate. We can look for the most blue and most red cells to find the strongest correlations. Make sure you set the `vmin` and `vmax` parameters to -1 and 1, respectively, so that the coloring is correct.

Scatter plots are another way to visualize the relationships between continuous variables. It lets us see the trends that pop out. One tip that I like to give students is to make sure you set the `alpha` parameter to a value less than or equal to .5. This makes the points transparent and tells a different story than scatter plots with markers that are completely opaque.

There's more...

If we have more variables that we want to compare, we can use seaborn to add more dimensions to a scatter plot. Using the `relplot` function, we can color the dots by year and size them by the number of barrels the vehicle consumes. We have gone from two dimensions to four!

```
>>> res = sns.relplot(
...     x="city08",
...     y="highway08",
...     data=fueleco.assign(
...         cylinders=fueleco.cylinders.fillna(0)
...     ),
...     hue="year",
...     size="barrels08",
...     alpha=0.5,
...     height=8,
... )
>>> res.fig.savefig(
...     "c5-relplot2.png", dpi=300, bbox_inches="tight"
... )
```

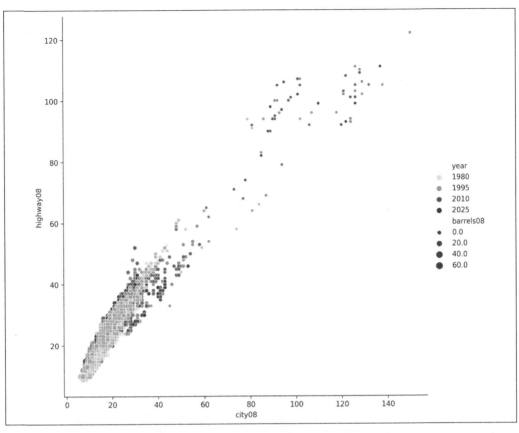

A seaborn scatter plot showing the mileage relationships colored by year
and sized by the number of barrels of gas a car uses

Note that we can also add in categorical dimensions as well for `hue`. We can also facet by
column for categorical values:

```
>>> res = sns.relplot(
...     x="city08",
...     y="highway08",
...     data=fueleco.assign(
...         cylinders=fueleco.cylinders.fillna(0)
...     ),
...     hue="year",
...     size="barrels08",
...     alpha=0.5,
...     height=8,
...     col="make",
```

```
...        col_order=["Ford", "Tesla"],
... )
>>> res.fig.savefig(
...        "c5-relplot3.png", dpi=300, bbox_inches="tight"
... )
```

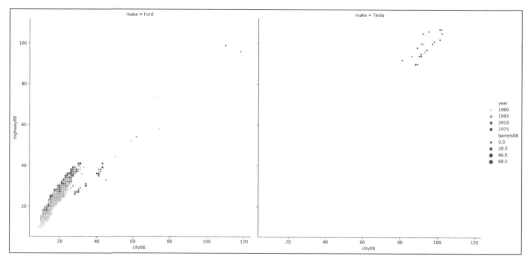

A seaborn scatter plot showing the mileage relationships colored by year,
sized by the number of barrels of gas a car uses, and faceted by make

Pearson correlation is intended to show the strength of a linear relationship. If the two
continuous columns do not have a linear relationship, another option is to use *Spearman
correlation*. This number also varies from -1 to 1. It measures whether the relationship is
monotonic (and doesn't presume that it is linear). It uses the rank of each number rather than
the number. If you are not sure whether there is a linear relationship between your columns,
this is a better metric to use.

```
>>> fueleco.city08.corr(
...        fueleco.barrels08, method="spearman"
... )
-0.9743658646193255
```

Comparing categorical values with categorical values

In this section, we will focus on dealing with multiple categorical values. One thing to keep in
mind is that continuous columns can be converted into categorical columns by binning the
values.

In this section, we will look at makes and vehicle class.

How to do it...

1. Lower the cardinality. Limit the `VClass` column to six values, in a simple class column, `SClass`. Only use Ford, Tesla, BMW, and Toyota:

```
>>> def generalize(ser, match_name, default):
...      seen = None
...      for match, name in match_name:
...          mask = ser.str.contains(match)
...          if seen is None:
...              seen = mask
...          else:
...              seen |= mask
...          ser = ser.where(~mask, name)
...      ser = ser.where(seen, default)
...      return ser

>>> makes = ["Ford", "Tesla", "BMW", "Toyota"]
>>> data = fueleco[fueleco.make.isin(makes)].assign(
...      SClass=lambda df_: generalize(
...          df_.VClass,
...          [
...              ("Seaters", "Car"),
...              ("Car", "Car"),
...              ("Utility", "SUV"),
...              ("Truck", "Truck"),
...              ("Van", "Van"),
...              ("van", "Van"),
...              ("Wagon", "Wagon"),
...          ],
...          "other",
...      )
... )
```

2. Summarize the counts of vehicle classes for each make:

```
>>> data.groupby(["make", "SClass"]).size().unstack()
SClass       Car     SUV   ...   Wagon   other
make                        ...
BMW       1557.0   158.0   ...    92.0     NaN
Ford      1075.0   372.0   ...   155.0   234.0
Tesla       36.0    10.0   ...     NaN     NaN
Toyota     773.0   376.0   ...   132.0   123.0
```

3. Use the `crosstab` function instead of the chain of pandas commands:

```
>>> pd.crosstab(data.make, data.SClass)
SClass     Car   SUV   ...   Wagon   other
make                     ...
BMW       1557   158   ...      92       0
Ford      1075   372   ...     155     234
Tesla       36    10   ...       0       0
Toyota     773   376   ...     132     123
```

4. Add more dimensions:

```
>>> pd.crosstab(
...       [data.year, data.make], [data.SClass, data.VClass]
... )
SClass                           Car                 ...
other
VClass          Compact Cars Large Cars  ...  Special Purpose Vehicle
4WD
year make                                ...
1984 BMW                 6          0    ...            0
     Ford               33          3    ...           21
     Toyota             13          0    ...            3
1985 BMW                 7          0    ...            0
     Ford               31          2    ...            9
...                     ...        ...   ...           ...
2017 Tesla               0          8    ...            0
     Toyota              3          0    ...            0
2018 BMW                37         12    ...            0
     Ford                0          0    ...            0
     Toyota              4          0    ...            0
```

5. Use Cramér's V measure (`https://stackoverflow.com/questions/46498455/categorical-features-correlation/46498792#46498792`) to indicate the categorical correlation:

```
>>> import scipy.stats as ss
>>> import numpy as np
>>> def cramers_v(x, y):
...     confusion_matrix = pd.crosstab(x, y)
...     chi2 = ss.chi2_contingency(confusion_matrix)[0]
...     n = confusion_matrix.sum().sum()
...     phi2 = chi2 / n
...     r, k = confusion_matrix.shape
...     phi2corr = max(
...         0, phi2 - ((k - 1) * (r - 1)) / (n - 1)
...     )
...     rcorr = r - ((r - 1) ** 2) / (n - 1)
...     kcorr = k - ((k - 1) ** 2) / (n - 1)
...     return np.sqrt(
...         phi2corr / min((kcorr - 1), (rcorr - 1))
...     )

>>> cramers_v(data.make, data.SClass)
0.2859720982171866
```

The `.corr` method accepts a callable as well, so an alternative way to invoke this is the following:

```
>>> data.make.corr(data.SClass, cramers_v)
0.2859720982171866
```

6. Visualize the cross tabulation as a bar plot:

```
>>> fig, ax = plt.subplots(figsize=(10, 8))
>>> (
...     data.pipe(
...         lambda df_: pd.crosstab(df_.make, df_.SClass)
...     ).plot.bar(ax=ax)
... )
>>> fig.savefig("c5-bar.png", dpi=300, bbox_inches="tight")
```

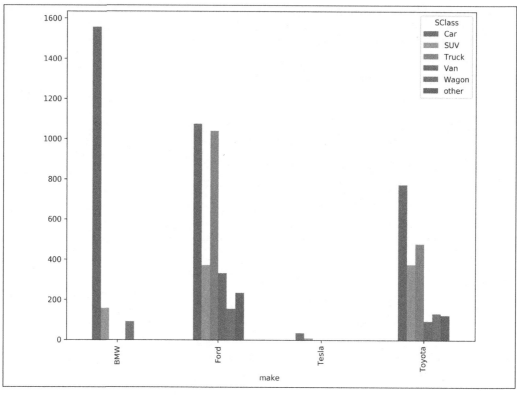

A pandas bar plot

7. Visualize the cross tabulation as a bar chart using seaborn:

```
>>> res = sns.catplot(
...     kind="count", x="make", hue="SClass", data=data
... )
>>> res.fig.savefig(
...     "c5-barsns.png", dpi=300, bbox_inches="tight"
... )
```

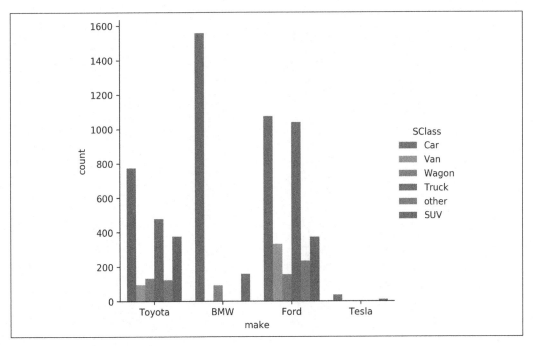

A seaborn bar plot

8. Visualize the relative sizes of the groups by normalizing the cross tabulation and making a stacked bar chart:

```
>>> fig, ax = plt.subplots(figsize=(10, 8))
>>> (
...     data.pipe(
...         lambda df_: pd.crosstab(df_.make, df_.SClass)
...     )
...     .pipe(lambda df_: df_.div(df_.sum(axis=1), axis=0))
...     .plot.bar(stacked=True, ax=ax)
... )
>>> fig.savefig(
...     "c5-barstacked.png", dpi=300, bbox_inches="tight"
... )
```

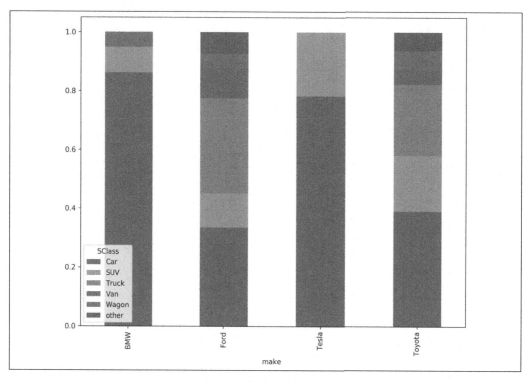

pandas bar plot

How it works...

I reduced the cardinality of the VClass column by using the generalize function that I created. I did this because bar plots need spacing; they need to breathe. I typically will limit the number of bars to fewer than 30. The generalize function is useful for cleaning up data, and you might want to refer back to it in your own data analyses.

We can summarize the counts of categorical columns by creating a cross-tabulation. You can build this up using group by semantics and unstacking the result, or take advantage of the built-in function in pandas, crosstab. Note that crosstab fills in missing numbers with 0 and converts the types to integers. This is because the .unstack method potentially creates sparsity (missing values), and integers (the int64 type) don't support missing values, so the types are converted to floats.

You can add arbitrary depths to the index or columns to create hierarchies in the cross-tabulation.

There exists a number, Cramér's V, for quantifying the relationship between two categorical columns. It ranges from 0 to 1. If it is 0, the values do not hold their value relative to the other column. If it is 1, the values change with respect to each other.

For example, if we compare the `make` column to the `trany` column, this value comes out larger:

```
>>> cramers_v(data.make, data.trany)
```

```
0.6335899102918267
```

What that tells us is that as the `make` changes from Ford to Toyota, the `trany` column should change as well. Compare this to the value for the `make` versus the `model`. Here, the value is very close to 1. Intuitively, that should make sense, as model could be derived from make.

```
>>> cramers_v(data.make, data.model)
```

```
0.9542350243671587
```

Finally, we can use various bar plots to view the counts or the relative sizes of the counts. Note that if you use seaborn, you can add multiple dimensions by setting `hue` or `col`.

Using the pandas profiling library

There is a third-party library, pandas Profiling (`https://pandas-profiling.github.io/pandas-profiling/docs/`), that creates reports for each column. These reports are similar to the output of the `.describe` method, but include plots and other descriptive statistics.

In this section, we will use the pandas Profiling library on the fuel economy data. Use `pip install pandas-profiling` to install the library.

How to do it...

1. Run the `profile_report` function to create an HTML report:

   ```
   >>> import pandas_profiling as pp
   >>> pp.ProfileReport(fueleco)
   ```

Overview

Dataset info

Number of variables	83
Number of observations	39101
Total Missing (%)	13.5%
Total size in memory	24.5 MiB
Average record size in memory	657.0 B

Variables types

Numeric	23
Categorical	23
Boolean	1
Date	0
Text (Unique)	0
Rejected	36
Unsupported	0

Warnings

- `barrelsA08` has 37611 / 96.2% zeros `Zeros`
- `charge120` has constant value 0 `Rejected`
- `charge240` has 38903 / 99.5% zeros `Zeros`
- `city08U` has 29662 / 75.9% zeros `Zeros`
- `cityA08` has 37611 / 96.2% zeros `Zeros`
- `cityA08U` is highly correlated with `cityA08` ($\rho = 0.94672$) `Rejected`
- `cityCD` is highly skewed ($\gamma 1 = 107.76$) `Skewed`
- `cityCD` has 39080 / 99.9% zeros `Zeros`
- `cityE` has 38880 / 99.4% zeros `Zeros`
- `cityUF` is highly skewed ($\gamma 1 = 25.742$) `Skewed`
- `cityUF` has 39022 / 99.8% zeros `Zeros`

pandas profiling summary

city08
Numeric

Distinct count	93
Unique (%)	0.2%
Missing (%)	0.0%
Missing (n)	0
Infinite (%)	0.0%
Infinite (n)	0

Mean	18.078
Minimum	6
Maximum	150
Zeros (%)	0.0%

Statistics   Histogram   Common Values   Extreme Values

Quantile statistics

Minimum	6
5-th percentile	11
Q1	15
Median	17
Q3	20
95-th percentile	27
Maximum	150
Range	144
Interquartile range	5

Descriptive statistics

Standard deviation	6.9707
Coef of variation	0.38559
Kurtosis	96.71
Mean	18.078
MAD	3.8648
Skewness	7.4099
Sum	706860
Variance	48.59
Memory size	305.6 KiB

pandas profiling details

How it works...

The pandas Profiling library generates an HTML report. If you are using Jupyter, it will create it inline. If you want to save this report to a file (or if you are not using Jupyter), you can use the `.to_file` method:

```
>>> report = pp.ProfileReport(fueleco)
>>> report.to_file("fuel.html")
```

This is a great library for EDA. Just make sure that you go through the process of understanding the data. Because this can overwhelm you with the sheer amount of output, it can be tempting to skim over it, rather than to dig into it. Even though this library is excellent for starting EDA, it doesn't do intra-column comparisons (other than correlation), as some of the examples in this chapter have shown.

6

Selecting
Subsets of Data

Introduction

Every dimension of data in a Series or DataFrame is labeled in the Index object. It is this Index that separates pandas data structures from NumPy's *n*-dimensional array. Indexes provide meaningful labels for each row and column of data, and pandas users can select data through the use of these labels. Additionally, pandas allows its users to select data according to the position of the rows and columns. This dual selection capability, one using names and the other using the position, makes for powerful yet confusing syntax to select subsets of data.

Selecting data by label or position is not unique to pandas. Python dictionaries and lists are built-in data structures that select their data in exactly one of these ways. Both dictionaries and lists have precise instructions and limited use cases for what you can index with. A dictionary's key (its label) must be an immutable object, such as a string, integer, or tuple. Lists must either use integers (the position) or slice objects for selection. Dictionaries can only select one object at a time by passing the key to the indexing operator. In this way, pandas is combining the ability to select data using integers, as with lists, and labels, as with dictionaries.

Selecting Series data

Series and DataFrames are complex data containers that have multiple attributes that use an index operation to select data in different ways. In addition to the index operator itself, the `.iloc` and `.loc` attributes are available and use the index operator in their own unique ways.

Series and DataFrames allow selection by position (like Python lists) and by label (like Python dictionaries). When we index off of the .iloc attribute, pandas selects only by position and works similarly to Python lists. The .loc attribute selects only by index label, which is similar to how Python dictionaries work.

The .loc and .iloc attributes are available on both Series and DataFrames. This recipe shows how to select Series data by position with .iloc and by label with .loc. These indexers accept scalar values, lists, and slices.

The terminology can get confusing. An index operation is when you put brackets, [], following a variable. For instance, given a Series s, you can select data in the following ways: s[item] and s.loc[item]. The first performs the index operation directly on the Series. The second performs the index operation on the .loc attribute.

How to do it...

1. Read in the college dataset with the institution name as the index, and select a single column as a Series using an index operation:

```
>>> import pandas as pd
>>> import numpy as np
>>> college = pd.read_csv(
...       "data/college.csv", index_col="INSTNM"
... )
>>> city = college["CITY"]
>>> city
INSTNM
Alabama A & M University
Normal
University of Alabama at Birmingham
Birmingham
Amridge University
Montgomery
University of Alabama in Huntsville
Huntsville
Alabama State University
Montgomery

...

SAE Institute of Technology   San Francisco
Emeryville
Rasmussen College - Overland Park
Overland...
```

```
National Personal Training Institute of Cleveland
Highland...
Bay Area Medical Academy - San Jose Satellite Location
San Jose
Excel Learning Center-San Antonio South
San Antonio
Name: CITY, Length: 7535, dtype: object
```

2. Pull out a scalar value from the Series directly:

```
>>> city["Alabama A & M University"]
'Normal'
```

3. Pull out a scalar value using the `.loc` attribute by name:

```
>>> city.loc["Alabama A & M University"]
'Normal'
```

4. Pull out a scalar value using the `.iloc` attribute by position:

```
>>> city.iloc[0]
'Normal'
```

5. Pull out several values by indexing. Note that if we pass in a list to the index operation, pandas will now return a Series instead of a scalar:

```
>>> city[
...     [
...         "Alabama A & M University",
...         "Alabama State University",
...     ]
... ]
INSTNM
Alabama A & M University      Normal
Alabama State University      Montgomery
Name: CITY, dtype: object
```

6. Repeat the above using `.loc`:

```
>>> city.loc[
...     [
...         "Alabama A & M University",
...         "Alabama State University",
...     ]
... ]
```

```
INSTNM
Alabama A & M University            Normal
Alabama State University      Montgomery
Name: CITY, dtype: object
```

7. Repeat the above using `.iloc`:

```
>>> city.iloc[[0, 4]]
INSTNM
Alabama A & M University            Normal
Alabama State University      Montgomery
Name: CITY, dtype: object
```

8. Use a slice to pull out many values:

```
>>> city[
...     "Alabama A & M University":"Alabama State University"
... ]
INSTNM
Alabama A & M University                  Normal
University of Alabama at Birmingham    Birmingham
Amridge University                     Montgomery
University of Alabama in Huntsville     Huntsville
Alabama State University               Montgomery
Name: CITY, dtype: object
```

9. Use a slice to pull out many values by position:

```
>>> city[0:5]
INSTNM
Alabama A & M University                  Normal
University of Alabama at Birmingham    Birmingham
Amridge University                     Montgomery
University of Alabama in Huntsville     Huntsville
Alabama State University               Montgomery
Name: CITY, dtype: object
```

10. Use a slice to pull out many values with `.loc`:

```
>>> city.loc[
...     "Alabama A & M University":"Alabama State University"
... ]
```

```
INSTNM
Alabama A & M University                          Normal
University of Alabama at Birmingham       Birmingham
Amridge University                            Montgomery
University of Alabama in Huntsville        Huntsville
Alabama State University                      Montgomery
Name: CITY, dtype: object
```

11. Use a slice to pull out many values with `.iloc`:

```
>>> city.iloc[0:5]
INSTNM
Alabama A & M University                          Normal
University of Alabama at Birmingham       Birmingham
Amridge University                            Montgomery
University of Alabama in Huntsville        Huntsville
Alabama State University                      Montgomery
Name: CITY, dtype: object
```

12. Use a Boolean array to pull out certain values:

```
>>> alabama_mask = city.isin(["Birmingham", "Montgomery"])
>>> city[alabama_mask]
INSTNM
University of Alabama at Birmingham       Birmingham
Amridge University                            Montgomery
Alabama State University                      Montgomery
Auburn University at Montgomery           Montgomery
Birmingham Southern College               Birmingham
                                                   ...
Fortis Institute-Birmingham               Birmingham
Hair Academy                                  Montgomery
Brown Mackie College-Birmingham           Birmingham
Nunation School of Cosmetology            Birmingham
Troy University-Montgomery Campus         Montgomery
Name: CITY, Length: 26, dtype: object
```

How it works...

If you have a Series, you can pull out the data using index operations. Depending on what you index with, you might get different types as output. If you index with a scalar on a Series, you will get back a scalar value. If you index with a list or a slice, you will get back a Series.

Looking at the examples, it appears that indexing directly off of the Series provides the best of both worlds: you can index by position or label. I would caution against using it at all. Remember, the Zen of Python states, "Explicit is better than implicit." Both `.iloc` and `.loc` are explicit, but indexing directly off of the Series is not explicit; it requires us to think about what we are indexing with and what type of index we have.

Consider this toy Series that uses integer values for the index:

```
>>> s = pd.Series([10, 20, 35, 28], index=[5, 2, 3, 1])
>>> s
5     10
2     20
3     35
1     28
dtype: int64
```

```
>>> s[0:4]
5     10
2     20
3     35
1     28
dtype: int64
```

```
>>> s[5]
10
>>> s[1]
28
```

When you index with a slice directly on a Series, it uses position, but otherwise it goes by label. This is confusing to the future you and future readers of your code. Remember, optimizing for readability is better than optimizing for easy-to-write code. The takeaway is to use the `.iloc` and `.loc` indexers.

Remember that when you slice by position, pandas uses the *half-open interval*. This interval is probably something you learned back in high school and promptly forgot. The half-open interval includes the first index, but not the end index. However, when you slice by label, pandas uses the *closed interval* and includes both the start and end index. This behavior is inconsistent with Python in general, but is practical for labels.

There's more...

All of the examples in this section could be performed directly on the original DataFrame by using .loc or .iloc. We can pass in a tuple (without parentheses) of row and column labels or positions, respectively:

```
>>> college.loc["Alabama A & M University", "CITY"]
'Normal'

>>> college.iloc[0, 0]
'Normal'

>>> college.loc[
...     [
...         "Alabama A & M University",
...         "Alabama State University",
...     ],
...     "CITY",
... ]
INSTNM
Alabama A & M University         Normal
Alabama State University     Montgomery
Name: CITY, dtype: object

>>> college.iloc[[0, 4], 0]
INSTNM
Alabama A & M University         Normal
Alabama State University     Montgomery
Name: CITY, dtype: object

>>> college.loc[
```

```
...        "Alabama A & M University":"Alabama State University",
...        "CITY",
... ]
INSTNM
Alabama A & M University                 Normal
University of Alabama at Birmingham      Birmingham
Amridge University                       Montgomery
University of Alabama in Huntsville      Huntsville
Alabama State University                 Montgomery
Name: CITY, dtype: object


>>> college.iloc[0:5, 0]
INSTNM
Alabama A & M University                 Normal
University of Alabama at Birmingham      Birmingham
Amridge University                       Montgomery
University of Alabama in Huntsville      Huntsville
Alabama State University                 Montgomery
Name: CITY, dtype: object
```

Care needs to be taken when using slicing off of `.loc`. If the start index appears after the stop index, then an empty Series is returned without an exception:

```
>>> city.loc[
...        "Reid State Technical College":"Alabama State University"
... ]
Series([], Name: CITY, dtype: object)
```

Selecting DataFrame rows

The most explicit and preferred way to select DataFrame rows is with `.iloc` and `.loc`. They are both capable of selecting by rows or by rows and columns.

This recipe shows you how to select rows from a DataFrame using the `.iloc` and `.loc` indexers:

1. Read in the college dataset, and set the index as the institution name:

    ```
    >>> college = pd.read_csv(
    ...        "data/college.csv", index_col="INSTNM"
    ```

```
... )
>>> college.sample(5, random_state=42)
                        CITY STABBR  ...  MD_EARN_WNE_P10  GRAD_DEBT_
MDN_SUPP
INSTNM                               ...
Career Po...  San Antonio    TX  ...            20700
14977
Ner Israe...    Baltimore    MD  ...        PrivacyS...
PrivacyS...
Reflectio...      Decatur    IL  ...              NaN
PrivacyS...
Capital A...  Baton Rouge    LA  ...            26400
PrivacyS...
West Virg...   Montgomery    WV  ...            43400
23969
<BLANKLINE>
[5 rows x 26 columns]
```

2. To select an entire row at that position, pass an integer to `.iloc`:

```
>>> college.iloc[60]
CITY                Anchorage
STABBR                     AK
HBCU                        0
MENONLY                     0
WOMENONLY                   0
                      ...
PCTPELL                0.2385
PCTFLOAN               0.2647
UG25ABV                0.4386
MD_EARN_WNE_P10         42500
GRAD_DEBT_MDN_SUPP    19449.5
Name: University of Alaska Anchorage, Length: 26, dtype: object
```

Because Python is zero-based, this is actually the 61st row. Note that pandas represents this row as a Series.

3. To get the same row as the preceding step, pass the index label to `.loc`:

```
>>> college.loc["University of Alaska Anchorage"]
CITY                Anchorage
STABBR                     AK
```

```
HBCU                            0

MENONLY                         0

WOMENONLY                       0

                              ...

PCTPELL                    0.2385

PCTFLOAN                   0.2647

UG25ABV                    0.4386

MD_EARN_WNE_P10             42500

GRAD_DEBT_MDN_SUPP        19449.5

Name: University of Alaska Anchorage, Length: 26, dtype: object
```

4. To select a disjointed set of rows as a DataFrame, pass a list of integers to .iloc:

```
>>> college.iloc[[60, 99, 3]]
                    CITY STABBR  ...  MD_EARN_WNE_P10  GRAD_DEBT_
MDN_SUPP
INSTNM                           ...
Universit...   Anchorage     AK  ...            42500        19449.5
Internati...       Tempe     AZ  ...            22200          10556
Universit...  Huntsville     AL  ...            45500          24097
<BLANKLINE>
[3 rows x 26 columns]
```

Because we passed in a list of row positions, this returns a DataFrame.

5. The same DataFrame from *step 4* may be reproduced with .loc by passing it a list of the institution names:

```
>>> labels = [
...      "University of Alaska Anchorage",
...      "International Academy of Hair Design",
...      "University of Alabama in Huntsville",
... ]
>>> college.loc[labels]
                    CITY STABBR  ...  MD_EARN_WNE_P10  GRAD_DEBT_
MDN_SUPP
INSTNM                           ...
Universit...   Anchorage     AK  ...            42500        19449.5
Internati...       Tempe     AZ  ...            22200          10556
Universit...  Huntsville     AL  ...            45500          24097
<BLANKLINE>
[3 rows x 26 columns]
```

6. Use slice notation with `.iloc` to select contiguous rows of the data:

```
>>> college.iloc[99:102]
                     CITY STABBR  ...  MD_EARN_WNE_P10  GRAD_DEBT_MDN_
SUPP
INSTNM                           ...
Internati...    Tempe     AZ  ...         22200           10556
GateWay C...  Phoenix     AZ  ...         29800            7283
Mesa Comm...     Mesa     AZ  ...         35200            8000
<BLANKLINE>
[3 rows x 26 columns]
```

7. Slice notation also works with `.loc` and is a *closed interval* (it includes both the start label and the stop label):

```
>>> start = "International Academy of Hair Design"
>>> stop = "Mesa Community College"
>>> college.loc[start:stop]
                     CITY STABBR  ...  MD_EARN_WNE_P10  GRAD_DEBT_MDN_
SUPP
INSTNM                           ...
Internati...    Tempe     AZ  ...         22200           10556
GateWay C...  Phoenix     AZ  ...         29800            7283
Mesa Comm...     Mesa     AZ  ...         35200            8000
<BLANKLINE>
[3 rows x 26 columns]
```

How it works...

When we pass a scalar value, a list of scalars, or a slice to `.iloc` or `.loc`, this causes pandas to scan the index for the appropriate rows and return them. If a single scalar value is passed, a Series is returned. If a list or slice is passed, then a DataFrame is returned.

There's more...

In *step 5*, the list of index labels can be selected directly from the DataFrame returned in *step 4* without the need for copying and pasting:

```
>>> college.iloc[[60, 99, 3]].index.tolist()
['University of Alaska Anchorage', 'International Academy of Hair
Design', 'University of Alabama in Huntsville']
```

Selecting DataFrame rows and columns simultaneously

There are many ways to select rows and columns. The easiest method to select one or more columns from a DataFrame is to index off of the DataFrame. However, this approach has a limitation. Indexing directly on a DataFrame does not allow you to select both rows and columns simultaneously. To select rows and columns, you will need to pass both valid row and column selections separated by a comma to either .iloc or .loc.

The generic form to select rows and columns will look like the following code:

```
df.iloc[row_idxs, column_idxs]
df.loc[row_names, column_names]
```

Where row_idxs and column_idxs can be scalar integers, lists of integers, or integer slices. While row_names and column_names can be the scalar names, lists of names, or names slices, row_names can also be a Boolean array.

In this recipe, each step shows a simultaneous row and column selection using both .iloc and .loc.

How to do it...

1. Read in the college dataset, and set the index as the institution name. Select the first three rows and the first four columns with slice notation:

```
>>> college = pd.read_csv(
...     "data/college.csv", index_col="INSTNM"
... )
>>> college.iloc[:3, :4]
                   CITY  STABBR  HBCU  MENONLY
INSTNM
Alabama A...      Normal     AL   1.0      0.0
Universit...  Birmingham     AL   0.0      0.0
Amridge U...  Montgomery     AL   0.0      0.0

>>> college.loc[:"Amridge University", :"MENONLY"]
                   CITY  STABBR  HBCU  MENONLY
INSTNM
Alabama A...      Normal     AL   1.0      0.0
Universit...  Birmingham     AL   0.0      0.0
Amridge U...  Montgomery     AL   0.0      0.0
```

2. Select all the rows of two different columns:

```
>>> college.iloc[:, [4, 6]].head()
```

	WOMENONLY	SATVRMID
INSTNM		
Alabama A & M University	0.0	424.0
University of Alabama at Birmingham	0.0	570.0
Amridge University	0.0	NaN
University of Alabama in Huntsville	0.0	595.0
Alabama State University	0.0	425.0

```
>>> college.loc[:, ["WOMENONLY", "SATVRMID"]].head()
```

	WOMENONLY	SATVRMID
INSTNM		
Alabama A & M University	0.0	424.0
University of Alabama at Birmingham	0.0	570.0
Amridge University	0.0	NaN
University of Alabama in Huntsville	0.0	595.0
Alabama State University	0.0	425.0

3. Select disjointed rows and columns:

```
>>> college.iloc[[100, 200], [7, 15]]
```

	SATMTMID	UGDS_NHPI
INSTNM		
GateWay Community College	NaN	0.0029
American Baptist Seminary of the West	NaN	NaN

```
>>> rows = [
...     "GateWay Community College",
...     "American Baptist Seminary of the West",
... ]
>>> columns = ["SATMTMID", "UGDS_NHPI"]
>>> college.loc[rows, columns]
```

	SATMTMID	UGDS_NHPI
INSTNM		
GateWay Community College	NaN	0.0029
American Baptist Seminary of the West	NaN	NaN

4. Select a single scalar value:

```
>>> college.iloc[5, -4]
0.401
>>> college.loc["The University of Alabama", "PCTFLOAN"]
0.401
```

5. Slice the rows and select a single column:

```
>>> college.iloc[90:80:-2, 5]
INSTNM
Empire Beauty School-Flagstaff        0
Charles of Italy Beauty College       0
Central Arizona College               0
University of Arizona                  0
Arizona State University-Tempe        0
Name: RELAFFIL, dtype: int64
```

```
>>> start = "Empire Beauty School-Flagstaff"
>>> stop = "Arizona State University-Tempe"
>>> college.loc[start:stop:-2, "RELAFFIL"]
INSTNM
Empire Beauty School-Flagstaff        0
Charles of Italy Beauty College       0
Central Arizona College               0
University of Arizona                  0
Arizona State University-Tempe        0
Name: RELAFFIL, dtype: int64
```

How it works...

One of the keys to selecting rows and columns at the same time is to understand the use of the comma in the brackets. The selection to the left of the comma always selects rows based on the row index. The selection to the right of the comma always selects columns based on the column index.

It is not necessary to make a selection for both rows and columns simultaneously. *Step 2* shows how to select all the rows and a subset of columns. The colon (:) represents a slice object that returns all the values for that dimension.

There's more...

To select only rows (along with all the columns), it is not necessary to use a colon following a comma. The default behavior is to select all the columns if there is no comma present. The previous recipe selected rows in exactly this manner. You can, however, use a colon to represent a slice of all the columns. The following lines of code are equivalent:

```
college.iloc[:10]
college.iloc[:10, :]
```

Selecting data with both integers and labels

Sometimes, you want the functionality of both .iloc and .loc, to select data by both position and label. In earlier versions of pandas, .ix was available to select data by both position and label. While this conveniently worked for those specific situations, it was ambiguous by nature and was a source of confusion for many pandas users. The .ix indexer has subsequently been deprecated and thus should be avoided.

Before the .ix deprecation, it was possible to select the first five rows and the columns of the college dataset from UGDS_WHITE through UGDS_UNKN using college.ix[:5, 'UGDS_WHITE':'UGDS_UNKN']. This is now impossible to do directly using .loc or .iloc. The following recipe shows how to find the integer location of the columns and then use .iloc to complete the selection.

How to do it...

1. Read in the college dataset and assign the institution name (INSTNM) as the index:
```
>>> college = pd.read_csv(
...        "data/college.csv", index_col="INSTNM"
... )
```

2. Use the Index method .get_loc to find the integer position of the desired columns:
```
>>> col_start = college.columns.get_loc("UGDS_WHITE")
>>> col_end = college.columns.get_loc("UGDS_UNKN") + 1
>>> col_start, col_end
(10, 19)
```

3. Use col_start and col_end to select columns by position using .iloc:
```
>>> college.iloc[:5, col_start:col_end]
              UGDS_WHITE   UGDS_BLACK   ...   UGDS_NRA   UGDS_UNKN
```

```
INSTNM                                  . . .
Alabama A...      0.0333      0.9353    . . .    0.0059      0.0138
Universit...      0.5922      0.2600    . . .    0.0179      0.0100
Amridge U...      0.2990      0.4192    . . .    0.0000      0.2715
Universit...      0.6988      0.1255    . . .    0.0332      0.0350
Alabama S...      0.0158      0.9208    . . .    0.0243      0.0137
<BLANKLINE>
[5 rows x 9 columns]
```

How it works...

Step 2 first retrieves the column index through the `.columns` attribute. Indexes have a `.get_loc` method, which accepts an index label and returns its integer location. We find both the start and end integer locations for the columns that we wish to slice. We add one because slicing with `.iloc` uses the half-open interval and is exclusive of the last item. *Step 3* uses slice notation with the row and column positions.

There's more...

We can do a very similar operation to use positions to get the labels for `.loc` to work. The following shows how to select the 10th through 15th (inclusive) rows, along with columns `UGDS_WHITE` through `UGDS_UNKN`:

```
>>> row_start = college.index[10]
>>> row_end = college.index[15]
>>> college.loc[row_start:row_end, "UGDS_WHITE":"UGDS_UNKN"]
            UGDS_WHITE    UGDS_BLACK    . . .    UGDS_NRA    UGDS_UNKN
INSTNM                                  . . .
Birmingha...      0.7983      0.1102    . . .    0.0000      0.0051
Chattahoo...      0.4661      0.4372    . . .    0.0000      0.0139
Concordia...      0.0280      0.8758    . . .    0.0466      0.0000
South Uni...      0.3046      0.6054    . . .    0.0019      0.0326
Enterpris...      0.6408      0.2435    . . .    0.0012      0.0069
James H F...      0.6979      0.2259    . . .    0.0007      0.0009
<BLANKLINE>
[6 rows x 9 columns]
```

Doing this same operation with `.ix` (which is removed from pandas 1.0, so don't do this) would look like this (in versions prior to 1.0):

```
>>> college.ix[10:16, "UGDS_WHITE":"UGDS_UNKN"]
```

	UGDS_WHITE	UGDS_BLACK	...	UGDS_NRA	UGDS_UNKN
INSTNM			...		
Birmingha...	0.7983	0.1102	...	0.0000	0.0051
Chattahoo...	0.4661	0.4372	...	0.0000	0.0139
Concordia...	0.0280	0.8758	...	0.0466	0.0000
South Uni...	0.3046	0.6054	...	0.0019	0.0326
Enterpris...	0.6408	0.2435	...	0.0012	0.0069
James H F...	0.6979	0.2259	...	0.0007	0.0009

```
<BLANKLINE>
```

`[6 rows x 9 columns]`

It is possible to achieve the same results by chaining .loc and `.iloc` together, but chaining indexers is typically a bad idea. It can be slower, and it is also undetermined whether it returns a view or a copy (which is not problematic when viewing the data, but can be when updating data. You might see the infamous `SettingWithCopyWarning` warning):

```
>>> college.iloc[10:16].loc[:, "UGDS_WHITE":"UGDS_UNKN"]
```

	UGDS_WHITE	UGDS_BLACK	...	UGDS_NRA	UGDS_UNKN
INSTNM			...		
Birmingha...	0.7983	0.1102	...	0.0000	0.0051
Chattahoo...	0.4661	0.4372	...	0.0000	0.0139
Concordia...	0.0280	0.8758	...	0.0466	0.0000
South Uni...	0.3046	0.6054	...	0.0019	0.0326
Enterpris...	0.6408	0.2435	...	0.0012	0.0069
James H F...	0.6979	0.2259	...	0.0007	0.0009

```
<BLANKLINE>
```

`[6 rows x 9 columns]`

Slicing lexicographically

The `.loc` attribute typically selects data based on the exact string label of the index. However, it also allows you to select data based on the lexicographic order of the values in the index. Specifically, `.loc` allows you to select all rows with an index lexicographically using slice notation. This only works if the index is sorted.

In this recipe, you will first sort the index and then use slice notation inside the .loc indexer to select all rows between two strings.

How to do it...

1. Read in the college dataset, and set the institution name as the index:

```
>>> college = pd.read_csv(
...         "data/college.csv", index_col="INSTNM"
... )
```

2. Attempt to select all colleges with names lexicographically between Sp and Su:

```
>>> college.loc["Sp":"Su"]
Traceback (most recent call last):
  ...
ValueError: index must be monotonic increasing or decreasing


During handling of the above exception, another exception
occurred:


Traceback (most recent call last):
  ...
KeyError: 'Sp'
```

3. As the index is not sorted, the preceding command fails. Let's go ahead and sort the index:

```
>>> college = college.sort_index()
```

4. Now, let's rerun the same command from *step 2*:

```
>>> college.loc["Sp":"Su"]
                       CITY STABBR  ...  MD_EARN_WNE_P10  GRAD_DEBT_
MDN_SUPP
INSTNM                              ...
Spa Tech ...    Ipswich     MA  ...             21500         6333
Spa Tech ...    Plymouth    MA  ...             21500         6333
Spa Tech ...    Westboro    MA  ...             21500         6333
Spa Tech ...    Westbrook   ME  ...             21500         6333
Spalding ...    Louisville  KY  ...             41700        25000

  ...              ...      ...  ...              ...           ...
```

Studio Ac...	Chandler	AZ	...	NaN	6333
Studio Je...	New York	NY	...	PrivacyS...	PrivacyS...
Stylemast...	Longview	WA	...	17000	13320
Styles an...	Selmer	TN	...	PrivacyS...	PrivacyS...
Styletren...	Rock Hill	SC	...	PrivacyS...	9495.5

```
<BLANKLINE>
[201 rows x 26 columns]
```

How it works...

The normal behavior of `.loc` is to make selections of data based on the exact labels passed to it. It raises a `KeyError` when these labels are not found in the index. However, one special exception to this behavior exists whenever the index is lexicographically sorted, and a slice is passed to it. Selection is now possible between the start and stop labels of the slice, even if those values are not found in the index.

There's more...

With this recipe, it is easy to select colleges between two letters of the alphabet. For instance, to select all colleges that begin with the letters *D* through *S*, you would use `college.loc['D':'T']`. Slicing like this is still closed and includes the last index, so this would technically return a college with the exact name `T`.

This type of slicing also works when the index is sorted in the opposite direction. You can determine in which direction the index is sorted with the index attribute `.is_monotonic_increasing` or `.is_monotonic_decreasing`. Either of these must be `True` in order for lexicographic slicing to work. For instance, the following code lexicographically sorts the index from *Z* to *A*:

```
>>> college = college.sort_index(ascending=False)
>>> college.index.is_monotonic_decreasing
True
>>> college.loc["E":"B"]
                                             CITY  ...
INSTNM                                             ...
Dyersburg State Community College      Dyersburg  ...
Dutchess Community College           Poughkeepsie  ...
Dutchess BOCES-Practical Nursing Program Poughkeepsie  ...
Durham Technical Community College        Durham  ...
```

```
Durham Beauty Academy                        Durham    ...

...                                             ...     ...

Bacone College                             Muskogee    ...

Babson College                            Wellesley    ...

BJ's Beauty & Barber College                 Auburn    ...

BIR Training Center                         Chicago    ...

B M Spurr School of Practical Nursing      Glen Dale    ...
```

7
Filtering Rows

Introduction

Filtering data from a dataset is one of the most common and basic operations. There are numerous ways to filter (or subset) data in pandas with Boolean indexing. Boolean indexing (also known as Boolean selection) can be a confusing term, but in pandas-land, it refers to selecting rows by providing a *Boolean array*, a pandas Series with the same index, but a True or False for each row. The name comes from NumPy, where similar filtering logic works, so while it is really a Series with Boolean values in it, it is also referred to as a Boolean array.

We will begin by creating Boolean Series and calculating statistics on them and then move on to creating more complex conditionals before using Boolean indexing in a wide variety of ways to filter data.

Calculating Boolean statistics

It can be informative to calculate basic summary statistics on Boolean arrays. Each value of a Boolean array, the True or False, evaluates to 1 or 0 respectively, so all the Series methods that work with numerical values also work with Booleans.

In this recipe, we create a Boolean array by applying a condition to a column of data and then calculate summary statistics from it.

How to do it...

1. Read in the movie dataset, set the index to the movie title, and inspect the first few rows of the `duration` column:

```
>>> import pandas as pd
>>> import numpy as np
>>> movie = pd.read_csv(
...      "data/movie.csv", index_col="movie_title"
... )
>>> movie[["duration"]].head()
```

	Duration
movie_title	
Avatar	178.0
Pirates of the Caribbean: At World's End	169.0
Spectre	148.0
The Dark Knight Rises	164.0
Star Wars: Episode VII - The Force Awakens	NaN

2. Determine whether the duration of each movie is longer than two hours by using the *greater than* comparison operator with the `duration` column:

```
>>> movie_2_hours = movie["duration"] > 120
>>> movie_2_hours.head(10)
```

movie_title	
Avatar	True
Pirates of the Caribbean: At World's End	True
Spectre	True
The Dark Knight Rises	True
Star Wars: Episode VII - The Force Awakens	False
John Carter	True
Spider-Man 3	True
Tangled	False
Avengers: Age of Ultron	True
Harry Potter and the Half-Blood Prince	True

```
Name: duration, dtype: bool
```

3. We can now use this Series to determine the number of movies that are longer than two hours:

```
>>> movie_2_hours.sum()
```

```
1039
```

4. To find the percentage of movies in the dataset longer than two hours, use the `.mean` method:

```
>>> movie_2_hours.mean() * 100

21.13506916192026
```

5. Unfortunately, the output from *step 4* is misleading. The duration column has a few missing values. If you look back at the DataFrame output from *step 1*, you will see that the last row is missing a value for `duration`. The Boolean condition in *step 2* returns `False` for this. We need to drop the missing values first, then evaluate the condition and take the mean:

```
>>> movie["duration"].dropna().gt(120).mean() * 100

21.199755152009794
```

6. Use the `.describe` method to output summary statistics on the Boolean array:

```
>>> movie_2_hours.describe()
count          4916
unique            2
top           False
freq           3877
Name: duration, dtype: object
```

How it works...

Most DataFrames will not have columns of Booleans like our movie dataset. The most straightforward method to produce a Boolean array is to apply a conditional operator to one of the columns. In *step 2*, we use the *greater than* comparison operator to test whether the duration of each movie was more than 120 minutes. *Steps 3* and *4* calculate two important quantities from a Boolean Series, its sum and mean. These methods are possible as Python evaluates `False` and `True` as 0 and 1, respectively.

You can prove to yourself that the mean of a Boolean array represents the percentage of `True` values. To do this, use the `.value_counts` method to count with the `normalize` parameter set to `True` to get its distribution:

```
>>> movie_2_hours.value_counts(normalize=True)
False     0.788649
True      0.211351
Name: duration, dtype: float64
```

Step 5 alerts us to the incorrect result from *step 4*. Even though the `duration` column had missing values, the Boolean condition evaluated all these comparisons against missing values as `False`. Dropping these missing values allows us to calculate the correct statistic. This is done in one step through method chaining.

Important takeaway: You want to make sure you have dealt with missing values before making calculations!

Step 6 shows that pandas applies the `.describe` method to Boolean arrays the same way it applies it to a column of objects or strings, by displaying frequency information. This is a natural way to think about Boolean arrays, rather than displaying quantiles.

If you wanted quantile information, you could cast the Series into integers:

```
>>> movie_2_hours.astype(int).describe()
count    4916.000000
mean        0.211351
std         0.408308
min         0.000000
25%         0.000000
50%         0.000000
75%         0.000000
max         1.000000
Name: duration, dtype: float64
```

There's more...

It is possible to compare two columns from the same DataFrame to produce a Boolean Series. For instance, we could determine the percentage of movies that have actor 1 with more Facebook likes than actor 2. To do this, we would select both of these columns and then drop any of the rows that had missing values for either movie. Then we would make the comparison and calculate the mean:

```
>>> actors = movie[
...     ["actor_1_facebook_likes", "actor_2_facebook_likes"]
... ].dropna()
>>> (
...     actors["actor_1_facebook_likes"]
...     > actors["actor_2_facebook_likes"]
... ).mean()
0.9777687130328371
```

Constructing multiple Boolean conditions

In Python, Boolean expressions use the built-in logical operators **and, or,** and **not**. These keywords do not work with Boolean indexing in pandas and are respectively replaced with &, |, and ~. Additionally, when combining expressions, each expression must be wrapped in parentheses, or an error will be raised (due to operator precedence).

Constructing a filter for your dataset might require combining multiple Boolean expressions together to pull out the rows you need. In this recipe, we construct multiple Boolean expressions before combining them to find all the movies that have an `imdb_score` greater than 8, a `content_rating` of PG-13, and a `title_year` either before 2000 or after 2009.

How to do it...

1. Load in the movie dataset and set the title as the index:

```
>>> movie = pd.read_csv(
...     "data/movie.csv", index_col="movie_title"
... )
```

2. Create a variable to hold each filter as a Boolean array:

```
>>> criteria1 = movie.imdb_score > 8
>>> criteria2 = movie.content_rating == "PG-13"
>>> criteria3 = (movie.title_year < 2000) | (
...     movie.title_year > 2009
... )
```

3. Combine all the filters into a single Boolean array:

```
>>> criteria_final = criteria1 & criteria2 & criteria3
>>> criteria_final.head()
movie_title
Avatar                                      False
Pirates of the Caribbean: At World's End    False
Spectre                                     False
The Dark Knight Rises                        True
Star Wars: Episode VII - The Force Awakens   False
dtype: bool
```

How it works...

All values in a Series can be compared against a scalar value using the standard comparison operators (`<`, `>`, `==`, `!=`, `<=`, and `>=`). The expression `movie.imdb_score > 8` yields a Boolean array where all `imdb_score` values exceeding 8 are `True` and those less than or equal to 8 are `False`. The index of this Boolean array has the same index as the `movie` DataFrame.

The `criteria3` variable is created by combining two Boolean arrays. Each expression must be enclosed in parentheses to function properly. The pipe character, `|`, is used to create a logical or condition between each of the values in both Series.

All three criteria need to be True to match the requirements of the recipe. They are each combined using the ampersand character, `&`, which creates a logical **and** condition between each Series value.

There's more...

A consequence of pandas using different syntax for the logical operators is that operator precedence is no longer the same. The comparison operators have a higher precedence than **and**, **or**, and **not**. However, the operators that pandas uses (the bitwise operators `&`, `|`, and `~`) have a higher precedence than the comparison operators, hence the need for parentheses. An example can help clear this up. Take the following expression:

```
>>> 5 < 10 and 3 > 4
False
```

In the preceding expression, `5 < 10` evaluates first, followed by `3 > 4`, and finally, the `and` evaluates. Python progresses through the expression as follows:

```
>>> 5 < 10 and 3 > 4
False
>>> True and 3 > 4
False
>>> True and False
False
>>> False
False
```

Let's take a look at what would happen if the expression in `criteria3` was written as follows:

```
>>> movie.title_year < 2000 | movie.title_year > 2009
```

```
Traceback (most recent call last):

    ...

TypeError: ufunc 'bitwise_or' not supported for the input types, and the
inputs could not be safely coerced to any supported types according to
the casting rule ''safe''


During handling of the above exception, another exception occurred:


Traceback (most recent call last):

    ...

TypeError: cannot compare a dtyped [float64] array with a scalar of type
[bool]
```

As the bitwise operators have higher precedence than the comparison operators, `2000 | movie.title_year` is evaluated first, which is nonsensical and raises an error. Therefore, we need parentheses to enforce operator precedence.

Why can't pandas use **and**, **or**, and **not**? When these keywords are evaluated, Python attempts to find the truthiness of the objects as a whole. As it does not make sense for a Series as a whole to be either `True` or `False` – only each element – pandas raises an error.

All objects in Python have a Boolean representation, which is often referred to as *truthiness*. For instance, all integers except 0 are considered `True`. All strings except the empty string are `True`. All non-empty sets, tuples, dictionaries, and lists are `True`. In general, to evaluate the truthiness of a Python object, pass it to the `bool` function. An empty DataFrame or Series does not evaluate as `True` or `False`, and instead, an error is raised.

Filtering with Boolean arrays

Both Series and DataFrame can be filtered with Boolean arrays. You can index this directly off of the object or off of the `.loc` attribute.

This recipe constructs two complex filters for different rows of movies. The first filters movies with an `imdb_score` greater than 8, a `content_rating` of PG-13, and a `title_year` either before 2000 or after 2009. The second filter consists of those with an `imdb_score` less than 5, a `content_rating` of R, and a `title_year` between 2000 and 2010. Finally, we will combine these filters.

How to do it...

1. Read in the movie dataset, set the index to `movie_title`, and create the first set of criteria:

```
>>> movie = pd.read_csv(
...     "data/movie.csv", index_col="movie_title"
... )
>>> crit_a1 = movie.imdb_score > 8
>>> crit_a2 = movie.content_rating == "PG-13"
>>> crit_a3 = (movie.title_year < 2000) | (
...     movie.title_year > 2009
... )
>>> final_crit_a = crit_a1 & crit_a2 & crit_a3
```

2. Create criteria for the second set of movies:

```
>>> crit_b1 = movie.imdb_score < 5
>>> crit_b2 = movie.content_rating == "R"
>>> crit_b3 = (movie.title_year >= 2000) & (
...     movie.title_year <= 2010
... )
>>> final_crit_b = crit_b1 & crit_b2 & crit_b3
```

3. Combine the two sets of criteria using the pandas or operator. This yields a Boolean array of all movies that are members of either set:

```
>>> final_crit_all = final_crit_a | final_crit_b
>>> final_crit_all.head()
movie_title
Avatar                                       False
Pirates of the Caribbean: At World's End     False
Spectre                                      False
The Dark Knight Rises                         True
Star Wars: Episode VII - The Force Awakens   False
dtype: bool
```

4. Once you have your Boolean array, you pass it to the index operator to filter the data:

```
>>> movie[final_crit_all].head()
                         color  ... movie/likes
```

```
movie_title                                   ...
The Dark Knight Rises            Color   ...      164000
The Avengers                     Color   ...      123000
Captain America: Civil War  Color   ...       72000
Guardians of the Galaxy          Color   ...       96000
Interstellar                     Color   ...      349000
```

5. We can also filter off of the `.loc` attribute:

```
>>> movie.loc[final_crit_all].head()
                                 color   ... movie/likes
movie_title                              ...
The Dark Knight Rises            Color   ...      164000
The Avengers                     Color   ...      123000
Captain America: Civil War  Color   ...       72000
Guardians of the Galaxy          Color   ...       96000
Interstellar                     Color   ...      349000
```

6. In addition, we can specify columns to select with the `.loc` attribute:

```
>>> cols = ["imdb_score", "content_rating", "title_year"]
>>> movie_filtered = movie.loc[final_crit_all, cols]
>>> movie_filtered.head(10)
                imdb_score content_rating  title_year
movie_title
The Dark ...           8.5          PG-13      2012.0
The Avengers           8.1          PG-13      2012.0
Captain A...           8.2          PG-13      2016.0
Guardians...           8.1          PG-13      2014.0
Interstellar           8.6          PG-13      2014.0
Inception              8.8          PG-13      2010.0
The Martian            8.1          PG-13      2015.0
Town & Co...           4.4              R      2001.0
Sex and t...           4.3              R      2010.0
Rollerball             3.0              R      2002.0
```

How it works...

In *step 1* and *step 2*, each set of criteria is built from simpler Boolean arrays. It is not necessary to create a different variable for each Boolean expression as done here, but it does make it far easier to read and debug any logic mistakes. As we desire both sets of movies, *step 3* uses the pandas logical or operator to combine them.

In *step 4*, we pass the Series of Booleans created from *step 3* directly to the index operator. Only the movies with True values from `final_crit_all` are selected.

Filtering also works with the `.loc` attribute, as seen in *step 6*, by simultaneously selecting rows (using the Boolean array) and columns. This slimmed DataFrame is far easier to check manually as to whether the logic was implemented correctly.

The `.iloc` attribute does not support Boolean arrays! If you pass in a Boolean Series to it, an exception will get raised. However, it does work with NumPy arrays, so if you call the `.to_numpy()` method, you can filter with it:

```
>>> movie.iloc[final_crit_all]
Traceback (most recent call last):
  ...
ValueError: iLocation based boolean indexing cannot use an indexable
as a mask
```

```
>>> movie.iloc[final_crit_all.to_numpy()]
```

	color	...	movie/likes
movie_title		...	
The Dark Knight Rises	Color	...	164000
The Avengers	Color	...	123000
Captain America: Civil War	Color	...	72000
Guardians of the Galaxy	Color	...	96000
Interstellar	Color	...	349000
...	...	...	...
The Young Unknowns	Color	...	4
Bled	Color	...	128
Hoop Dreams	Color	...	0
Death Calls	Color	...	16
The Legend of God's Gun	Color	...	13

There's more...

As was stated earlier, it is possible to use one long Boolean expression in place of several other shorter ones. To replicate the `final_crit_a` variable from *step 1* with one long line of code, we can do the following:

```
>>> final_crit_a2 = (
...        (movie.imdb_score > 8)
...        & (movie.content_rating == "PG-13")
...        & (
...            (movie.title_year < 2000)
...            | (movie.title_year > 2009)
...        )
... )
>>> final_crit_a2.equals(final_crit_a)
True
```

Comparing row filtering and index filtering

It is possible to replicate specific cases of Boolean selection by taking advantage of the index.

In this recipe, we use the college dataset to select all institutions from a particular state with both Boolean indexing and index selection and then compare each of their performances against one another.

Personally, I prefer to filter by columns (using Boolean arrays) rather than on the index. Column filtering is more powerful as you can use other logical operators and filter on multiple columns.

How to do it...

1. Read in the college dataset and use Boolean indexing to select all institutions from the state of Texas (TX):

```
>>> college = pd.read_csv("data/college.csv")
>>> college[college["STABBR"] == "TX"].head()
                           INSTNM  ...    GRAD_/_SUPP
3610   Abilene Christian University  ...          25985
3611         Alvin Community College  ...           6750
3612             Amarillo College  ...          10950
```

```
3613              Angelina College   ...   PrivacySuppressed
3614        Angelo State University  ...             21319.5
```

2. To repeat this using index selection, move the `STABBR` column into the index. We can then use label-based selection with the `.loc` indexer:

```
>>> college2 = college.set_index("STABBR")
>>> college2.loc["TX"].head()
```

```
                          INSTNM  ...       GRAD_/_SUPP
3610  Abilene Christian University  ...             25985
3611        Alvin Community College  ...              6750
3612             Amarillo College  ...             10950
3613             Angelina College  ...   PrivacySuppressed
3614       Angelo State University  ...           21319.5
```

3. Let's compare the speed of both methods:

```
>>> %timeit college[college['STABBR'] == 'TX']
1.75 ms ± 187 µs per loop (mean ± std. dev. of 7 runs, 1000 loops
each)
```

```
>>> %timeit college2.loc['TX']
882 µs ± 69.3 µs per loop (mean ± std. dev. of 7 runs, 1000 loops
each)
```

4. Boolean indexing takes two times as long as index selection. As setting the index does not come for free, let's time that operation as well:

```
>>> %timeit college2 = college.set_index('STABBR')
2.01 ms ± 107 µs per loop (mean ± std. dev. of 7 runs, 100 loops
each)
```

How it works...

Step 1 creates a Boolean Series by determining which rows of data have `STABBR` equal to `TX`. This Series is passed to the indexing operator, which selects the data. This process may be replicated by moving that same column to the index and using basic label-based index selection with `.loc`. Selection via the index is much faster than Boolean selection.

However, if you need to filter on multiple columns, you will have the overhead (and confusing code) from repeatedly switching the index. Again, my recommendation is not to switch the index, just to filter by it.

There's more...

This recipe only selects a single state. It is possible to select multiple states with both Boolean and index selection. Let's select Texas (TX), California (CA), and New York (NY). With Boolean selection, you can use the .isin method, but with indexing, just pass a list to .loc:

```
>>> states = ["TX", "CA", "NY"]
>>> college[college["STABBR"].isin(states)]
```

	INSTNM	CITY	...	MD_EARN_WNE_P10	GRAD_DEBT_MDN_SUPP
192	Academy ...	San Fran...	...	36000	35093
193	ITT Tech...	Rancho C...	...	38800	25827.5
194	Academy ...	Oakland	...	NaN	PrivacyS...
195	The Acad...	Huntingt...	...	28400	9500
196	Avalon S...	Alameda	...	21600	9860
...	...	...	...	...	...
7528	WestMed ...	Merced	...	NaN	15623.5
7529	Vantage ...	El Paso	...	NaN	9500
7530	SAE Inst...	Emeryville	...	NaN	9500
7533	Bay Area...	San Jose	...	NaN	PrivacyS...
7534	Excel Le...	San Antonio	...	NaN	12125

```
>>> college2.loc[states]
```

	INSTNM	CITY	...	MD_EARN_WNE_P10	GRAD_DEBT_MDN_SUPP
STABBR			...		
TX	Abilene ...	Abilene	...	40200	25985
TX	Alvin Co...	Alvin	...	34500	6750
TX	Amarillo...	Amarillo	...	31700	10950
TX	Angelina...	Lufkin	...	26900	PrivacyS...
TX	Angelo S...	San Angelo	...	37700	21319.5
...	...	...	...	...	...
NY	Briarcli...	Patchogue	...	38200	28720.5
NY	Jamestow...	Salamanca	...	NaN	12050
NY	Pratt Ma...	New York	...	40900	26691
NY	Saint Jo...	Patchogue	...	52000	22143.5
NY	Franklin...	Brooklyn	...	20000	PrivacyS...

There is quite a bit more to the story than what this recipe explains. pandas implements the index differently based on whether the index is unique or sorted. See the following recipe for more details.

Selecting with unique and sorted indexes

Index selection performance drastically improves when the index is unique or sorted. The prior recipe used an unsorted index that contained duplicates, which makes for relatively slow selections.

In this recipe, we use the college dataset to form unique or sorted indexes to increase the performance of index selection. We will continue to compare the performance to Boolean indexing as well.

If you are only selecting from a single column and that is a bottleneck for you, this recipe can save you ten times the effort

How to do it...

1. Read in the college dataset, create a separate DataFrame with STABBR as the index, and check whether the index is sorted:

   ```
   >>> college = pd.read_csv("data/college.csv")
   >>> college2 = college.set_index("STABBR")
   >>> college2.index.is_monotonic
   False
   ```

2. Sort the index from college2 and store it as another object:

   ```
   >>> college3 = college2.sort_index()
   >>> college3.index.is_monotonic
   True
   ```

3. Time the selection of the state of Texas (TX) from all three DataFrames:

   ```
   >>> %timeit college[college['STABBR'] == 'TX']
   1.75 ms ± 187 µs per loop (mean ± std. dev. of 7 runs, 1000 loops
   each)
   ```

   ```
   >>> %timeit college2.loc['TX']
   1.09 ms ± 232 µs per loop (mean ± std. dev. of 7 runs, 1000 loops
   each)
   ```

```
>>> %timeit college3.loc['TX']
304 µs ± 17.8 µs per loop (mean ± std. dev. of 7 runs, 1000 loops
each)
```

4. The sorted index performs nearly an order of magnitude faster than Boolean selection. Let's now turn toward unique indexes. For this, we use the institution name as the index:

```
>>> college_unique = college.set_index("INSTNM")
>>> college_unique.index.is_unique
True
```

5. Let's select Stanford University with Boolean indexing. Note that this returns a DataFrame:

```
>>> college[college["INSTNM"] == "Stanford University"]
           INSTNM       CITY  ...  MD_EARN_WNE_P10   GRAD_DEBT_MDN_
SUPP
4217  Stanford...   Stanford  ...           86000            12782
```

6. Let's select Stanford University with index selection. Note that this returns a Series:

```
>>> college_unique.loc["Stanford University"]
CITY                  Stanford
STABBR                      CA
HBCU                         0
MENONLY                      0
WOMENONLY                    0
                         ...
PCTPELL                 0.1556
PCTFLOAN                0.1256
UG25ABV                 0.0401
MD_EARN_WNE_P10          86000
GRAD_DEBT_MDN_SUPP       12782
Name: Stanford University, Length: 26, dtype: object
```

7. If we want a DataFrame rather than a Series, we need to pass in a list of index values into .loc:

```
>>> college_unique.loc[["Stanford University"]]
           INSTNM       CITY  ...  MD_EARN_WNE_P10   GRAD_DEBT_MDN_
SUPP
4217  Stanford...   Stanford  ...           86000            12782
```

8. They both produce the same data, just with different objects. Let's time each approach:

```
>>> %timeit college[college['INSTNM'] == 'Stanford University']
1.92 ms ± 396 µs per loop (mean ± std. dev. of 7 runs, 1000 loops
each)
```

```
>>> %timeit college_unique.loc[['Stanford University']]
988 µs ± 122 µs per loop (mean ± std. dev. of 7 runs, 1000 loops
each)
```

How it works...

When the index is not sorted and contains duplicates, as with `college2`, pandas will need to check every single value in the index to make the correct selection. When the index is sorted, as with `college3`, pandas takes advantage of an algorithm called binary search to improve search performance.

In the second half of the recipe, we use a unique column as the index. pandas implements unique indexes with a hash table, which makes for even faster selection. Each index location can be looked up in nearly the same time regardless of its length.

There's more...

Boolean selection gives much more flexibility than index selection as it is possible to condition on any number of columns. In this recipe, we used a single column as the index. It is possible to concatenate multiple columns together to form an index. For instance, in the following code, we set the index equal to the concatenation of the city and state columns:

```
>>> college.index = (
...       college["CITY"] + ", " + college["STABBR"]
... )
>>> college = college.sort_index()
>>> college.head()
```

	INSTNM	CITY	...	MD_EARN_WNE_P10	GRAD_DEBT_MDN_SUPP
ARTESIA, CA	Angeles ...	ARTESIA	...	NaN	16850
Aberdeen, SD	Presenta...	Aberdeen	...	35900	25000
Aberdeen, SD	Northern...	Aberdeen	...	33600	24847
Aberdeen, WA	Grays Ha...	Aberdeen	...	27000	11490
Abilene, TX	Hardin-S...	Abilene	...	38700	25864

From here, we can select all colleges from a particular city and state combination without Boolean indexing. Let's select all colleges from Miami, FL:

```
>>> college.loc["Miami, FL"].head()
              INSTNM    CITY  ... MD_EARN_WNE_P10  GRAD_DEBT_MDN_SUPP
Miami, FL  New Prof...  Miami  ...          18700              8682
Miami, FL  Manageme...  Miami  ...      PrivacyS...            12182
Miami, FL  Strayer ...  Miami  ...          49200            36173.5
Miami, FL  Keiser U...  Miami  ...          29700              26063
Miami, FL  George T...  Miami  ...          38600          PrivacyS...
```

We can compare the speed of this compound index selection with Boolean indexing. There is almost an order of magnitude difference:

```
>>> %%timeit
>>> crit1 = college["CITY"] == "Miami"
>>> crit2 = college["STABBR"] == "FL"
>>> college[crit1 & crit2]
3.05 ms ± 66.4 µs per loop (mean ± std. dev. of 7 runs, 100 loops each)

>>> %timeit college.loc['Miami, FL']
369 µs ± 130 µs per loop (mean ± std. dev. of 7 runs, 1000 loops each)
```

Translating SQL WHERE clauses

Many pandas users will have experience of interacting with a database using **Structured Query Language** (**SQL**). SQL is a standard to define, manipulate, and control data stored in a database

SQL is an important language for data scientists to know. Much of the world's data is stored in databases that require SQL to retrieve and manipulate it SQL syntax is fairly simple and easy to learn. There are many different SQL implementations from companies such as Oracle, Microsoft, IBM, and more.

Within a SQL SELECT statement, the WHERE clause is very common and filters data. This recipe will write pandas code that is equivalent to a SQL query that selects a certain subset of the employee dataset.

Suppose we are given a task to find all the female employees who work in the police or fire departments who have a base salary of between 80 and 120 thousand dollars.

The following SQL statement would answer this query for us:

```
SELECT
    UNIQUE_ID,
    DEPARTMENT,
    GENDER,
    BASE_SALARY
FROM
    EMPLOYEE
WHERE
    DEPARTMENT IN ('Houston Police Department-HPD',
                    'Houston Fire Department (HFD)') AND
    GENDER = 'Female' AND
    BASE_SALARY BETWEEN 80000 AND 120000;
```

This recipe assumes that you have a dump of the EMPLOYEE database in a CSV file and that you want to replicate the above query using pandas.

How to do it...

1. Read in the employee dataset as a DataFrame:

   ```
   >>> employee = pd.read_csv("data/employee.csv")
   ```

2. Before filtering out the data, it is helpful to do some manual inspection of each of the filtered columns to know the exact values that will be used in the filter:

   ```
   >>> employee.dtypes
   UNIQUE_ID            int64
   POSITION_TITLE       object
   DEPARTMENT           object
   BASE_SALARY          float64
   RACE                 object
   EMPLOYMENT_TYPE      object
   GENDER               object
   EMPLOYMENT_STATUS    object
   HIRE_DATE            object
   JOB_DATE             object
   dtype: object
   ```

```
>>> employee.DEPARTMENT.value_counts().head()
Houston Police Department-HPD       638
Houston Fire Department (HFD)       384
Public Works & Engineering-PWE      343
Health & Human Services             110
Houston Airport System (HAS)        106
Name: DEPARTMENT, dtype: int64


>>> employee.GENDER.value_counts()
Male      1397
Female     603
Name: GENDER, dtype: int64


>>> employee.BASE_SALARY.describe()
count      1886.000000
mean      55767.931601
std       21693.706679
min       24960.000000
25%       40170.000000
50%       54461.000000
75%       66614.000000
max      275000.000000
Name: BASE_SALARY, dtype: float64
```

3. Write a single statement for each of the criteria. Use the `isin` method to test equality to one of many values:

```
>>> depts = [
...        "Houston Police Department-HPD",
...        "Houston Fire Department (HFD)",
... ]
>>> criteria_dept = employee.DEPARTMENT.isin(depts)
>>> criteria_gender = employee.GENDER == "Female"
>>> criteria_sal = (employee.BASE_SALARY >= 80000) & (
...        employee.BASE_SALARY <= 120000
... )
```

4. Combine all the Boolean arrays:

```
>>> criteria_final = (
...        criteria_dept & criteria_gender & criteria_sal
... )
```

5. Use Boolean indexing to select only the rows that meet the final criteria:

```
>>> select_columns = [
...        "UNIQUE_ID",
...        "DEPARTMENT",
...        "GENDER",
...        "BASE_SALARY",
... ]
>>> employee.loc[criteria_final, select_columns].head()
      UNIQUE_ID   DEPARTMENT   GENDER   BASE_SALARY
61           61   Houston ...  Female       96668.0
136         136   Houston ...  Female       81239.0
367         367   Houston ...  Female       86534.0
474         474   Houston ...  Female       91181.0
513         513   Houston ...  Female       81239.0
```

How it works...

Before any filtering is done, you will need to know the exact string names that you want to filter by. The `.value_counts` method is one way to get both the exact string name and number of occurrences of string values.

The `.isin` method is equivalent to the SQL `IN` operator and accepts a list of all possible values that you would like to keep. It is possible to use a series of `OR` conditions to replicate this expression, but it would not be as efficient or idiomatic.

The criteria for salary, `criteria_sal`, is formed by combining two simple inequality expressions. All the criteria are combined with the pandas **and** operator, `&`, to yield a single Boolean array as the filter.

There's more...

For many operations, pandas has multiple ways to do the same thing. In the preceding recipe, the criteria for salary uses two separate Boolean expressions. Similar to SQL, Series have a `.between` method, with the salary criteria equivalently written as follows. We will stick in an underscore in the hardcoded numbers to help with legibility:

```
''' {.sourceCode .pycon}
>>> criteria_sal = employee.BASE_SALARY.between(
...     80_000, 120_000
... )
'''
```

Another useful application of `.isin` is to provide a sequence of values automatically generated by some other pandas statements. This would avoid any manual investigating to find the exact string names to store in a list. Conversely, let's try to exclude the rows from the top five most frequently occurring departments:

```
>>> top_5_depts = employee.DEPARTMENT.value_counts().index[
...     :5
... ]
>>> criteria = ~employee.DEPARTMENT.isin(top_5_depts)
>>> employee[criteria]
      UNIQUE_ID POSITION_TITLE  ...    HIRE_DATE    JOB_DATE
0             0 ASSISTAN...     ...   2006-06-12  2012-10-13
1             1 LIBRARY ...     ...   2000-07-19  2010-09-18
4             4 ELECTRICIAN     ...   1989-06-19  1994-10-22
18           18 MAINTENA...     ...   2008-12-29  2008-12-29
32           32 SENIOR A...     ...   1991-02-11  2016-02-13
...         ...         ...     ...          ...         ...
1976       1976 SENIOR S...     ...   2015-07-20  2016-01-30
1983       1983 ADMINIST...     ...   2006-10-16  2006-10-16
1985       1985 TRUCK DR...     ...   2013-06-10  2015-08-01
1988       1988 SENIOR A...     ...   2013-01-23  2013-03-02
1990       1990 BUILDING...     ...   1995-10-14  2010-03-20
```

The SQL equivalent of this would be as follows:

```
SELECT *
   FROM
       EMPLOYEE
   WHERE
       DEPARTMENT not in
       (
          SELECT
              DEPARTMENT
```

```
FROM ( SELECT
DEPARTMENT,

          COUNT(1) as CT
     FROM
          EMPLOYEE
     GROUP BY
          DEPARTMENT
     ORDER BY
          CT DESC
     LIMIT 5

) );
```

Notice the use of the pandas `not` operator, ~, which negates all Boolean values of a Series.

Improving the readability of Boolean indexing with the query method

Boolean indexing is not necessarily the most pleasant syntax to read or write, especially when using a single line to write a complex filter. pandas has an alternative string-based syntax through the DataFrame query method that can provide more clarity.

This recipe replicates the earlier recipe in this chapter, *Translating SQL WHERE clauses*, but instead takes advantage of the `.query` method of the DataFrame. The goal here is to filter the employee data for female employees from the police or fire departments who earn a salary of between 80 and 120 thousand dollars.

How to do it...

1. Read in the employee data, assign the chosen departments, and import columns to variables:

    ```
    >>> employee = pd.read_csv("data/employee.csv")
    >>> depts = [
    ...      "Houston Police Department-HPD",
    ```

```
...         "Houston Fire Department (HFD)",
... ]
>>> select_columns = [
...         "UNIQUE_ID",
...         "DEPARTMENT",
...         "GENDER",
...         "BASE_SALARY",
... ]
```

2. Build the query string and execute the method. Note that the `.query` method does not like triple quoted strings spanning multiple lines, hence the ugly concatenation:

```
>>> qs = (
...         "DEPARTMENT in @depts "
...         " and GENDER == 'Female' "
...         " and 80000 <= BASE_SALARY <= 120000"
... )
>>> emp_filtered = employee.query(qs)
>>> emp_filtered[select_columns].head()
```

	UNIQUE_ID	DEPARTMENT	GENDER	BASE_SALARY
61	61	Houston ...	Female	96668.0
136	136	Houston ...	Female	81239.0
367	367	Houston ...	Female	86534.0
474	474	Houston ...	Female	91181.0
513	513	Houston ...	Female	81239.0

How it works...

Strings passed to the `.query` method are going to look more like plain English than normal pandas code. It is possible to reference Python variables using the at symbol (@), as with `depts`. All DataFrame column names are available in the query namespace by referencing their names without extra quotes. If a string is needed, such as `Female`, inner quotes will need to wrap it.

Another nice feature of the query syntax is the ability to combine Boolean operators using `and`, `or`, and `not`.

There's more...

Instead of manually typing in a list of department names, we could have programmatically created it. For instance, if we wanted to find all the female employees who were not a member of the top 10 departments by frequency, we can run the following code:

```
>>> top10_depts = (
...        employee.DEPARTMENT.value_counts()
...        .index[:10]
...        .tolist()
... )
>>> qs = "DEPARTMENT not in @top10_depts and GENDER == 'Female'"
>>> employee_filtered2 = employee.query(qs)
>>> employee_filtered2.head()
     UNIQUE_ID POSITION_TITLE  ...    HIRE_DATE    JOB_DATE
0            0  ASSISTAN...     ...   2006-06-12  2012-10-13
73          73  ADMINIST...     ...   2011-12-19  2013-11-23
96          96  ASSISTAN...     ...   2013-06-10  2013-06-10
117        117  SENIOR A...     ...   1998-03-20  2012-07-21
146        146  SENIOR S...     ...   2014-03-17  2014-03-17
```

Preserving Series size with the .where method

When you filter with Boolean arrays, the resulting Series or DataFrame is typically smaller. The `.where` method preserves the size of your Series or DataFrame and either sets the values that don't meet the criteria to missing or replaces them with something else. Instead of dropping all these values, it is possible to keep them.

When you combine this functionality with the `other` parameter, you can create functionality similar to *coalesce* found in databases.

In this recipe, we pass the `.where` method Boolean conditions to put a floor and ceiling on the minimum and maximum number of Facebook likes for actor 1 in the movie dataset.

How to do it...

1. Read the movie dataset, set the movie title as the index, and select all the values in the `actor_1_facebook_likes` column that are not missing:

```
>>> movie = pd.read_csv(
...     "data/movie.csv", index_col="movie_title"
... )
>>> fb_likes = movie["actor_1_facebook_likes"].dropna()
>>> fb_likes.head()
movie_title
Avatar                                          1000.0
Pirates of the Caribbean: At World's End       40000.0
Spectre                                         11000.0
The Dark Knight Rises                           27000.0
Star Wars: Episode VII - The Force Awakens        131.0
Name: actor_1_facebook_likes, dtype: float64
```

2. Let's use the `describe` method to get a sense of the distribution:

```
>>> fb_likes.describe()
count      4909.000000
mean       6494.488491
std       15106.986884
min           0.000000
25%         607.000000
50%         982.000000
75%       11000.000000
max      640000.000000
Name: actor_1_facebook_likes, dtype: float64
```

3. Additionally, we may plot a histogram of this Series to visually inspect the distribution. The code below calls `plt.subplots` to specify the figure size, but is not needed in general:

```
>>> import matplotlib.pyplot as plt
>>> fig, ax = plt.subplots(figsize=(10, 8))
>>> fb_likes.hist(ax=ax)
```

```
>>> fig.savefig(
...     "c7-hist.png", dpi=300
... )
```

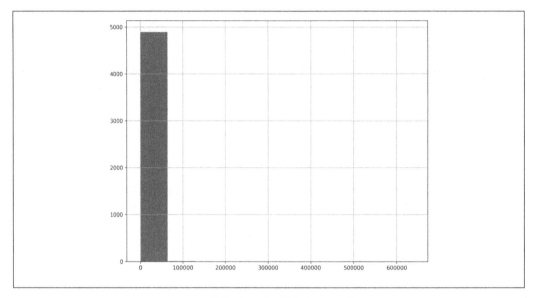

Default pandas histogram

4. This visualization makes it difficult to get a sense of the distribution. On the other hand, the summary statistics from *step 2* appear to be telling us that the data is highly skewed to the right with a few very large observations (more than an order of magnitude greater than the median). Let's create criteria to test whether the number of likes is fewer than 20,000:

```
>>> criteria_high = fb_likes < 20_000
>>> criteria_high.mean().round(2)
0.91
```

5. About 91% of the movies have an actor 1 with fewer than 20,000 likes. We will now use the `.where` method, which accepts a Boolean array. The default behavior is to return a Series the same size as the original, but which has all the `False` locations replaced with a missing value:

```
>>> fb_likes.where(criteria_high).head()
movie_title
Avatar                                    1000.0
Pirates of the Caribbean: At World's End     NaN
Spectre                                  11000.0
```

```
The Dark Knight Rises                            NaN
Star Wars: Episode VII - The Force Awakens      131.0
Name: actor_1_facebook_likes, dtype: float64
```

6. The second parameter to the `.where` method, `other`, allows you to control the replacement value. Let's change all the missing values to 20,000:

```
>>> fb_likes.where(criteria_high, other=20000).head()
movie_title
Avatar                                         1000.0
Pirates of the Caribbean: At World's End      20000.0
Spectre                                       11000.0
The Dark Knight Rises                         20000.0
Star Wars: Episode VII - The Force Awakens      131.0
Name: actor_1_facebook_likes, dtype: float64
```

7. Similarly, we can create criteria to put a floor on the minimum number of likes. Here, we chain another `.where` method and replace the values not satisfying the condition to 300:

```
>>> criteria_low = fb_likes > 300
>>> fb_likes_cap = fb_likes.where(
...        criteria_high, other=20_000
... ).where(criteria_low, 300)
>>> fb_likes_cap.head()
movie_title
Avatar                                         1000.0
Pirates of the Caribbean: At World's End      20000.0
Spectre                                       11000.0
The Dark Knight Rises                         20000.0
Star Wars: Episode VII - The Force Awakens      300.0
Name: actor_1_facebook_likes, dtype: float64
```

8. The lengths of the original Series and the modified Series are the same:

```
>>> len(fb_likes), len(fb_likes_cap)
(4909, 4909)
```

9. Let's make a histogram with the modified Series. With the data in a much tighter range, it should produce a better plot:

```
>>> fig, ax = plt.subplots(figsize=(10, 8))
>>> fb_likes_cap.hist(ax=ax)
```

```
>>> fig.savefig(
...        "c7-hist2.png", dpi=300
... )
```

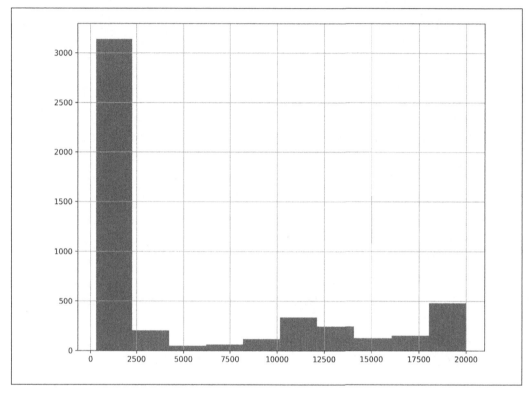

A pandas histogram with a tighter range

How it works...

The .where method again preserves the size and shape of the calling object and does not modify the values where the passed Boolean is True. It was important to drop the missing values in *step 1* as the .where method would have eventually replaced them with a valid number in future steps.

The summary statistics in *step 2* give us some idea of where it would make sense to cap our data. The histogram from *step 3*, on the other hand, appears to clump all the data into one bin. The data has too many outliers for a plain histogram to make a good plot. The .where method allows us to place a ceiling and floor on our data, which results in a histogram with less variance.

There's more...

pandas actually has built-in methods, `.clip`, `.clip_lower`, and `.clip_upper`, that replicate this operation. The `.clip` method can set a floor and ceiling at the same time:

```
>>> fb_likes_cap2 = fb_likes.clip(lower=300, upper=20000)
>>> fb_likes_cap2.equals(fb_likes_cap)
True
```

Masking DataFrame rows

The `.mask` method performs the complement of the `.where` method. By default, it creates missing values wherever the Boolean condition is `True`. In essence, it is literally masking, or covering up, values in your dataset.

In this recipe, we will mask all rows of the movie dataset that were made after 2010 and then filter all the rows with missing values.

How to do it...

1. Read the movie dataset, set the movie title as the index, and create the criteria:

```
>>> movie = pd.read_csv(
...     "data/movie.csv", index_col="movie_title"
... )
>>> c1 = movie["title_year"] >= 2010
>>> c2 = movie["title_year"].isna()
>>> criteria = c1 | c2
```

2. Use the `.mask` method on a DataFrame to remove the values for all the values in rows with movies that were made from 2010. Any movie that originally had a missing value for `title_year` is also masked:

```
>>> movie.mask(criteria).head()
```

	color	...
movie_title		...
Avatar	Color	...
Pirates of the Caribbean: At World's End	Color	...
Spectre	NaN	...
The Dark Knight Rises	NaN	...
Star Wars: Episode VII - The Force Awakens	NaN	...

3. Notice how all the values in the third, fourth, and fifth rows from the preceding DataFrame are missing. Chain the `.dropna` method to remove rows that have all values missing:

```
>>> movie_mask = movie.mask(criteria).dropna(how="all")
>>> movie_mask.head()
```

	color	...
movie_title		...
Avatar	Color	...
Pirates of the Caribbean: At World's End	Color	...
Spider-Man 3	Color	...
Harry Potter and the Half-Blood Prince	Color	...
Superman Returns	Color	...

4. The operation in *step 3* is just a complex way of doing basic Boolean indexing. We can check whether the two methods produce the same DataFrame:

```
>>> movie_boolean = movie[movie["title_year"] < 2010]
>>> movie_mask.equals(movie_boolean)
False
```

5. The `.equals` method informs us that they are not equal. Something is wrong. Let's do some sanity checking and see whether they are the same shape:

```
>>> movie_mask.shape == movie_boolean.shape
True
```

6. When we used the preceding `.mask` method, it created many missing values. Missing values are `float` data types, so any column that was an `integer` type that got missing values was converted to a `float` type. The `.equals` method returns `False` if the data types of the columns are different, even if the values are the same. Let's check the equality of the data types to see whether this scenario happened:

```
>>> movie_mask.dtypes == movie_boolean.dtypes
```

color	True
director_name	True
num_critic_for_reviews	True
duration	True
director_facebook_likes	True
...	
title_year	True
actor_2_facebook_likes	True
imdb_score	True

```
    aspect_ratio                 True
    movie_facebook_likes         False
    Length: 27, dtype: bool
```

7. It turns out that a couple of columns don't have the same data type. pandas has an alternative for these situations. In its `testing` module, which is primarily used by developers, there is a function, `assert_frame_equal`, that allows you to check the equality of Series and DataFrames without also checking the equality of the data types:

```
>>> from pandas.testing import assert_frame_equal
>>> assert_frame_equal(
...     movie_boolean, movie_mask, check_dtype=False
... )
```

How it works...

By default, the `.mask` method fills in rows where the Boolean array is `True` with NaN. The first parameter to the `.mask` method is a Boolean array. Because the `.mask` method is called from a DataFrame, all of the values in each row where the condition is `True` change to `missing`. *Step 3* uses this masked DataFrame to drop the rows that contain all missing values. Step 4 shows how to do this same procedure with index operations.

During data analysis, it is important to continually validate results. Checking the equality of a Series and a DataFrame is one approach to validation. Our first attempt, in *step 4*, yielded an unexpected result. Some basic sanity checking, such as ensuring that the number of rows and columns are the same, or that the row and column names are the same, are good checks before going deeper.

Step 6 compares the data types of the two Series. It is here where we uncover the reason why the DataFrames were not equivalent. The `.equals` method checks that both the values and data types are the same. The `assert_frame_equal` function from step 7 has many available parameters to test equality in a variety of ways. Notice that there is no output after calling `assert_frame_equal`. This method returns `None` when two DataFrames are equal and raises an error when they are not.

There's more...

Let's compare the speed difference between masking and dropping missing rows and filtering with Boolean arrays. Filtering is about an order of magnitude faster in this case:

```
>>> %timeit movie.mask(criteria).dropna(how='all')
11.2 ms ± 144 µs per loop (mean ± std. dev. of 7 runs, 100 loops each)
```

```
>>> %timeit movie[movie['title_year'] < 2010]
1.07 ms ± 34.9 µs per loop (mean ± std. dev. of 7 runs, 1000 loops each)
```

Selecting with Booleans, integer location, and labels

Previously, we covered a wide range of recipes on selecting different subsets of data through the .iloc and .loc attributes. Both of these select rows and columns simultaneously by either integer location or label.

In this recipe, we will filter both rows and columns with the .iloc and .loc attributes.

How to do it...

1. Read in the movie dataset, set the index as the title, and then create a Boolean array matching all movies with a content rating of G and an IMDB score less than 4:

    ```
    >>> movie = pd.read_csv(
    ...       "data/movie.csv", index_col="movie_title"
    ... )
    >>> c1 = movie["content_rating"] == "G"
    >>> c2 = movie["imdb_score"] < 4
    >>> criteria = c1 & c2
    ```

2. Let's first pass these criteria to .loc to filter the rows:

    ```
    >>> movie_loc = movie.loc[criteria]
    >>> movie_loc.head()
                                        color  ... movie/likes
    movie_title                                ...
    The True Story of Puss'N Boots      Color  ...          90
    Doogal                              Color  ...         346
    Thomas and the Magic Railroad       Color  ...         663
    Barney's Great Adventure            Color  ...         436
    Justin Bieber: Never Say Never      Color  ...       62000
    ```

3. Let's check whether this DataFrame is exactly equal to the one generated directly from the indexing operator:

    ```
    >>> movie_loc.equals(movie[criteria])
    True
    ```

4. Now, let's attempt the same Boolean indexing with the `.iloc` indexer:

```
>>> movie_iloc = movie.iloc[criteria]
Traceback (most recent call last):

   ...

ValueError: iLocation based boolean indexing cannot use an
indexable as a mask
```

5. It turns out that we cannot directly use a Series of Booleans because of the index. We can, however, use an ndarray of Booleans. To get the array, use the `.to_numpy()` method:

```
>>> movie_iloc = movie.iloc[criteria.to_numpy()]
>>> movie_iloc.equals(movie_loc)
True
```

6. Although not very common, it is possible to do Boolean indexing to select particular columns. Here, we select all the columns that have a data type of 64-bit integers:

```
>>> criteria_col = movie.dtypes == np.int64
>>> criteria_col.head()
color                        False
director_name                False
num_critic_for_reviews       False
duration                     False
director_facebook_likes      False
dtype: bool

>>> movie.loc[:, criteria_col].head()
             num_voted_users  cast_total_facebook_likes  movie_
facebook_likes
movie_title
Avatar               886204                       4834
33000
Pirates o...         471220                      48350
0
Spectre              275868                      11700
85000
The Dark ...        1144337                     106759
164000
Star Wars...              8                        143
0
```

7. As `criteria_col` is a Series, which always has an index, you must use the underlying ndarray to make it work with `.iloc`. The following produces the same result as *step 6*:

```
>>> movie.iloc[:, criteria_col.to_numpy()].head()
```

	num_voted_users	cast_total_facebook_likes	movie_facebook_likes
movie_title			
Avatar	886204	4834	33000
Pirates o...	471220	48350	0
Spectre	275868	11700	85000
The Dark ...	1144337	106759	164000
Star Wars...	8	143	0

8. When using `.loc`, you can use a Boolean array to select rows, and specify the columns you want with a list of labels. Remember, you need to put a comma between the row and column selections. Let's keep the same row criteria and select the `content_rating`, `imdb_score`, `title_year`, and `gross` columns:

```
>>> cols = [
...     "content_rating",
...     "imdb_score",
...     "title_year",
...     "gross",
... ]
>>> movie.loc[criteria, cols].sort_values("imdb_score")
```

	content_rating	imdb_score	title_year	gross
movie_title				
Justin Bi...	G	1.6	2011.0	73000942.0
Sunday Sc...	G	2.5	2008.0	NaN
Doogal	G	2.8	2006.0	7382993.0
Barney's ...	G	2.8	1998.0	11144518.0
The True ...	G	2.9	2009.0	NaN
Thomas an...	G	3.6	2000.0	15911333.0

9. You can create this same operation with `.iloc`, but you need to specify the position of the columns:

```
>>> col_index = [movie.columns.get_loc(col) for col in cols]
>>> col_index
[20, 24, 22, 8]
>>> movie.iloc[criteria.to_numpy(), col_index].sort_values(
...     "imdb_score"
... )
```

	content_rating	imdb_score	title_year	gross
movie_title				
Justin Bi...	G	1.6	2011.0	73000942.0
Sunday Sc...	G	2.5	2008.0	NaN
Doogal	G	2.8	2006.0	7382993.0
Barney's ...	G	2.8	1998.0	11144518.0
The True ...	G	2.9	2009.0	NaN
Thomas an...	G	3.6	2000.0	15911333.0

How it works...

Both the `.iloc` and `.loc` attributes have some support filtering with Boolean arrays (with the caveat that `.iloc` cannot be passed a Series but the underlying ndarray.) Let's take a look at the one-dimensional ndarray underlying `criteria`:

```
>>> a = criteria.to_numpy()
>>> a[:5]
array([False, False, False, False, False])
>>> len(a), len(criteria)
(4916, 4916)
```

The array is the same length as the Series, which is the same length as the movie DataFrame. The integer location for the Boolean array aligns with the integer location of the DataFrame, and the filter happens as expected. These arrays also work with the `.loc` attribute as well, but they are a necessity with `.iloc`.

Steps 6 and *7* show how to filter by columns instead of by rows. The colon, `:`, is needed to indicate the selection of all the rows. The comma following the colon separates the row and column selections. However, there is actually a much easier way to select columns with integer data types and that is through the `.select_dtypes` method:

```
>>> movie.select_dtypes(int)
```

movie_title	num_voted_users	cast_total_facebook_likes
Avatar	886204	4834
Pirates o...	471220	48350
Spectre	275868	11700
The Dark ...	1144337	106759
Star Wars...	8	143
...	...	...
Signed Se...	629	2283
The Follo...	73839	1753
A Plague ...	38	0
Shanghai ...	1255	2386
My Date w...	4285	163

Steps 8 and *9* show how to do row and column selections simultaneously. The rows were specified by a Boolean array and the columns were specified with a list of columns. You place a comma between the row and column selections. *Step 9* uses a list comprehension to loop through all the desired column names to find their integer location with the index method `.get_loc`.

8
Index Alignment

Introduction

When Series or DataFrames are combined, each dimension of the data automatically aligns on each axis first before any computation happens. This silent and automatic alignment of axes can confuse the uninitiated, but it gives flexibility to the power user. This chapter explores the Index object in-depth before showcasing a variety of recipes that take advantage of its automatic alignment.

Examining the Index object

As was discussed previously, each axis of a Series and a DataFrame has an Index object that labels the values. There are many different types of Index objects, but they all share common behavior. All Index objects, except for the MultiIndex, are single-dimensional data structures that combine the functionality of Python sets and NumPy ndarrays.

In this recipe, we will examine the column index of the college dataset and explore much of its functionality.

How to do it...

1. Read in the college dataset, and create a variable `columns` that holds the column index:

    ```
    >>> import pandas as pd
    >>> import numpy as np
    ```

```
>>> college = pd.read_csv("data/college.csv")
>>> columns = college.columns
>>> columns
Index(['INSTNM', 'CITY', 'STABBR', 'HBCU', 'MENONLY', 'WOMENONLY',
'RELAFFIL',
       'SATVRMID', 'SATMTMID', 'DISTANCEONLY', 'UGDS', 'UGDS_
WHITE',
       'UGDS_BLACK', 'UGDS_HISP', 'UGDS_ASIAN', 'UGDS_AIAN',
'UGDS_NHPI',
       'UGDS_2MOR', 'UGDS_NRA', 'UGDS_UNKN', 'PPTUG_EF',
'CURROPER', 'PCTPELL',
       'PCTFLOAN', 'UG25ABV', 'MD_EARN_WNE_P10', 'GRAD_DEBT_MDN_
SUPP'],
       dtype='object')
```

2. Use the `.values` attribute to access the underlying NumPy array:

```
>>> columns.values
array(['INSTNM', 'CITY', 'STABBR', 'HBCU', 'MENONLY', 'WOMENONLY',
       'RELAFFIL', 'SATVRMID', 'SATMTMID', 'DISTANCEONLY', 'UGDS',
       'UGDS_WHITE', 'UGDS_BLACK', 'UGDS_HISP', 'UGDS_ASIAN',
'UGDS_AIAN',
       'UGDS_NHPI', 'UGDS_2MOR', 'UGDS_NRA', 'UGDS_UNKN', 'PPTUG_
EF',
       'CURROPER', 'PCTPELL', 'PCTFLOAN', 'UG25ABV', 'MD_EARN_WNE_
P10',
       'GRAD_DEBT_MDN_SUPP'], dtype=object)
```

3. Select items from the index by position with a scalar, list, or slice:

```
>>> columns[5]
'WOMENONLY'
>>> columns[[1, 8, 10]]
Index(['CITY', 'SATMTMID', 'UGDS'], dtype='object')
>>> columns[-7:-4]
Index(['PPTUG_EF', 'CURROPER', 'PCTPELL'], dtype='object')
```

4. Indexes share many of the same methods as Series and DataFrames:

```
>>> columns.min(), columns.max(), columns.isnull().sum()
('CITY', 'WOMENONLY', 0)
```

5. You can use basic arithmetic and comparison operators on Index objects:

```
>>> columns + "_A"
```

```
Index(['INSTNM_A', 'CITY_A', 'STABBR_A', 'HBCU_A', 'MENONLY_A',
'WOMENONLY_A',
        'RELAFFIL_A', 'SATVRMID_A', 'SATMTMID_A', 'DISTANCEONLY_A',
'UGDS_A',
        'UGDS_WHITE_A', 'UGDS_BLACK_A', 'UGDS_HISP_A', 'UGDS_
ASIAN_A',
        'UGDS_AIAN_A', 'UGDS_NHPI_A', 'UGDS_2MOR_A', 'UGDS_NRA_A',
        'UGDS_UNKN_A', 'PPTUG_EF_A', 'CURROPER_A', 'PCTPELL_A',
'PCTFLOAN_A',
        'UG25ABV_A', 'MD_EARN_WNE_P10_A', 'GRAD_DEBT_MDN_SUPP_A'],
       dtype='object')


>>> columns > "G"
array([ True, False,  True,  True,  True,  True,  True,  True,
True,
       False,  True,  True,  True,  True,  True,  True,  True,
True,
        True,  True,  True, False,  True,  True,  True,  True,
True])
```

6. Trying to change an Index value after its creation fails. Indexes are immutable objects:

```
>>> columns[1] = "city"
Traceback (most recent call last):
  ...
TypeError: Index does not support mutable operations
```

How it works...

As you can see from many of the Index object operations, it appears to have quite a bit in common with both Series and ndarrays. One of the most significant differences comes in *step 6*. Indexes are immutable and their values cannot be changed once created.

There's more...

Indexes support the set operations—union, intersection, difference, and symmetric difference:

```
>>> c1 = columns[:4]
>>> c1
```

```
Index(['INSTNM', 'CITY', 'STABBR', 'HBCU'], dtype='object')

>>> c2 = columns[2:6]
>>> c2
Index(['STABBR', 'HBCU', 'MENONLY', 'WOMENONLY'], dtype='object')

>>> c1.union(c2)   # or 'c1 | c2'
Index(['CITY', 'HBCU', 'INSTNM', 'MENONLY', 'STABBR', 'WOMENONLY'],
dtype='object')

>>> c1.symmetric_difference(c2)   # or 'c1 ^ c2'
Index(['CITY', 'INSTNM', 'MENONLY', 'WOMENONLY'], dtype='object')
```

Indexes have many of the same operations as Python sets, and are similar to Python sets in another vital way. They are (usually) implemented using hash tables, which make for extremely fast access when selecting rows or columns from a DataFrame. Because the values need to be hashable, the values for the Index object need to be immutable types, such as a string, integer, or tuple, just like the keys in a Python dictionary.

Indexes support duplicate values, and if there happens to be a duplicate in any Index, then a hash table can no longer be used for its implementation, and object access becomes much slower.

Producing Cartesian products

Whenever a Series or DataFrame operates with another Series or DataFrame, the indexes (both the row index and column index) of each object align first before any operation begins. This index alignment happens behind the scenes and can be very surprising for those new to pandas. This alignment always creates a Cartesian product between the indexes unless the indexes are identical.

A Cartesian product is a mathematical term that usually appears in set theory. A Cartesian product between two sets is all the combinations of pairs of both sets. For example, the 52 cards in a standard playing card deck represent a Cartesian product between the 13 ranks (A, 2, 3,..., Q, K) and the four suits.

Producing a Cartesian product isn't always the intended outcome, but it's essential to be aware of how and when it occurs so as to avoid unintended consequences. In this recipe, two Series with overlapping but non-identical indexes are added together, yielding a surprising result. We will also show what happens if they have the same index.

How to do it...

Follow these steps to create a Cartesian product:

1. Construct two Series that have indexes that are different but contain some of the same values:

    ```
    >>> s1 = pd.Series(index=list("aaab"), data=np.arange(4))
    >>> s1
    a    0
    a    1
    a    2
    b    3
    dtype: int64

    >>> s2 = pd.Series(index=list("cababb"), data=np.arange(6))
    >>> s2
    c    0
    a    1
    b    2
    a    3
    b    4
    b    5
    dtype: int64
    ```

2. Add the two Series together to produce a Cartesian product. For each a index value in s1, we add every a in s2:

    ```
    >>> s1 + s2
    a    1.0
    a    3.0
    a    2.0
    a    4.0
    a    3.0
    a    5.0
    b    5.0
    b    7.0
    b    8.0
    c    NaN
    dtype: float64
    ```

How it works...

Each a label in s1 pairs up with each a label in s2. This pairing produces six a labels, three b labels, and one c label in the resulting Series. A Cartesian product happens between all identical index labels.

As the element with label c is unique to the Series s2, pandas defaults its value to missing, as there is no label for it to align to in s1. pandas defaults to a missing value whenever an index label is unique to one object. This has the unfortunate consequence of changing the data type of the Series to a float, whereas each Series had only integers as values. The type change occurred because NumPy's missing value object, np.nan, only exists for floats but not for integers. Series and DataFrame columns must have homogeneous numeric data types. Therefore, each value in the column was converted to a float. Changing types makes little difference for this small dataset, but for larger datasets, this can have a significant memory impact.

There's more...

The Cartesian product is not created when the indexes are unique or contain both the same exact elements and elements in the same order. When the index values are unique or they are the same and have the same order, a Cartesian product is not created, and the indexes instead align by their position. Notice here that each element aligned exactly by position and that the data type remained an integer:

```
>>> s1 = pd.Series(index=list("aaabb"), data=np.arange(5))
>>> s2 = pd.Series(index=list("aaabb"), data=np.arange(5))
>>> s1 + s2
a    0
a    2
a    4
b    6
b    8
dtype: int64
```

If the elements of the index are identical, but the order is different between the Series, the Cartesian product occurs. Let's change the order of the index in s2 and rerun the same operation:

```
>>> s1 = pd.Series(index=list("aaabb"), data=np.arange(5))
>>> s2 = pd.Series(index=list("bbaaa"), data=np.arange(5))
>>> s1 + s2
a    2
a    3
```

```
a     4
a     3
a     4

      ..
a     6
b     3
b     4
b     4
b     5
Length: 13, dtype: int64
```

Be aware of this as pandas has two drastically different outcomes for this same operation. Another instance where this can happen is during a `groupby` operation. If you do a `groupby` with multiple columns and one is of the type `categorical`, you will get a Cartesian product where each outer index will have every inner index value.

Finally, we will add two Series that have index values in a different order but do not have duplicate values. When we add these, we do not get a Cartesian product:

```
>>> s3 = pd.Series(index=list("ab"), data=np.arange(2))
>>> s4 = pd.Series(index=list("ba"), data=np.arange(2))
>>> s3 + s4
a     1
b     1
dtype: int64
```

In this recipe, each Series had a different number of elements. Typically, array-like data structures in Python and other languages do not allow operations to take place when the operating dimensions do not contain the same number of elements. pandas allows this to happen by aligning the indexes first before completing the operation.

In the previous chapter, I showed that you can set a column to the index and then filter on them. My preference is to leave the index alone and filter on the columns. This section gives another example of when you need to be very careful with the index.

Exploding indexes

The previous recipe walked through a trivial example of two small Series being added together with unequal indexes. This recipe is more of an "anti-recipe" of what not to do. The Cartesian product of index alignment can produce comically incorrect results when dealing with larger amounts of data.

In this recipe, we add two larger Series that have indexes with only a few unique values but in different orders. The result will explode the number of values in the indexes.

How to do it...

1. Read in the employee data and set the index to the RACE column:

    ```
    >>> employee = pd.read_csv(
    ...       "data/employee.csv", index_col="RACE"
    ... )
    >>> employee.head()
                    UNIQUE_ID POSITION_TITLE  ...    HIRE_DATE      JOB_
    DATE
    RACE                                      ...
    Hispanic/...            0  ASSISTAN...    ...  2006-06-12  2012-10-
    13
    Hispanic/...            1  LIBRARY ...    ...  2000-07-19  2010-09-
    18
    White                   2  POLICE O...    ...  2015-02-03  2015-02-
    03
    White                   3  ENGINEER...    ...  1982-02-08  1991-05-
    25
    White                   4  ELECTRICIAN    ...  1989-06-19  1994-10-
    22
    ```

2. Select the BASE_SALARY column as two different Series. Check to see whether this operation created two new objects:

    ```
    >>> salary1 = employee["BASE_SALARY"]
    >>> salary2 = employee["BASE_SALARY"]
    >>> salary1 is salary2
    True
    ```

3. The salary1 and salary2 variables are referring to the same object. This means that any change to one will change the other. To ensure that you receive a brand new copy of the data, use the .copy method:

    ```
    >>> salary2 = employee["BASE_SALARY"].copy()
    >>> salary1 is salary2
    False
    ```

4. Let's change the order of the index for one of the Series by sorting it:

    ```
    >>> salary1 = salary1.sort_index()
    >>> salary1.head()
    ```

```
RACE
American Indian or Alaskan Native     78355.0
American Indian or Alaskan Native     26125.0
American Indian or Alaskan Native     98536.0
American Indian or Alaskan Native         NaN
American Indian or Alaskan Native     55461.0
Name: BASE_SALARY, dtype: float64


>>> salary2.head()
RACE
Hispanic/Latino     121862.0
Hispanic/Latino      26125.0
White                45279.0
White                63166.0
White                56347.0
Name: BASE_SALARY, dtype: float64
```

5. Let's add these salary Series together:

```
>>> salary_add = salary1 + salary2


>>> salary_add.head()
RACE
American Indian or Alaskan Native     138702.0
American Indian or Alaskan Native     156710.0
American Indian or Alaskan Native     176891.0
American Indian or Alaskan Native     159594.0
American Indian or Alaskan Native     127734.0
Name: BASE_SALARY, dtype: float64
```

6. The operation completed successfully. Let's create one more Series of `salary1` added to itself and then output the lengths of each Series. We just exploded the index from 2,000 values to more than one million:

```
>>> salary_add1 = salary1 + salary1
>>> len(salary1), len(salary2), len(salary_add), len(
...      salary_add1
... )
(2000, 2000, 1175424, 2000)
```

How it works...

Step 2 appears at first to create two unique objects, but in fact, it creates a single object that is referred to by two different variable names. The expression `employee['BASE_SALARY']`, technically creates a view, and not a brand new copy. This is verified with the `is` operator.

In pandas, a view is not a new object but just a reference to another object, usually some subset of a DataFrame. This shared object can be a cause for many issues.

To ensure that the variables reference completely different objects, we use the `.copy` method and then verify that they are different objects with the `is` operator. *Step 4* uses the `.sort_index` method to sort the Series by race. Note that this Series has the same index entries, but they are now in a different order than `salary1`. *Step 5* adds these different Series together to produce the sum. By inspecting the head, it is still not clear what has been produced.

Step 6 adds `salary1` to itself to show a comparison between the two different Series additions. The lengths of all the Series in this recipe are printed and we clearly see that `salary_add` has now exploded to over one million values. A Cartesian product took place because the indexes were not unique and in the same order. This recipe shows a more dramatic example of what happens when the indexes differ.

There's more...

We can verify the number of values of `salary_add` by doing a little mathematics. As a Cartesian product takes place between all of the same index values, we can sum the square of their counts. Even missing values in the index produce Cartesian products with themselves:

```
>>> index_vc = salary1.index.value_counts(dropna=False)
>>> index_vc
Black or African American          700
White                              665
Hispanic/Latino                    480
Asian/Pacific Islander             107
NaN                                 35
American Indian or Alaskan Native   11
Others                               2
Name: RACE, dtype: int64

>>> index_vc.pow(2).sum()
1175424
```

Filling values with unequal indexes

When two Series are added together using the plus operator and one of the index labels does not appear in the other, the resulting value is always missing. pandas has the .add method, which provides an option to fill the missing value. Note that these Series do not include duplicate entries, hence there is no need to worry about a Cartesian product exploding the number of entries.

In this recipe, we add together multiple Series from the baseball dataset with unequal (but unique) indexes using the .add method with the fill_value parameter to ensure that there are no missing values in the result.

How to do it...

1. Read in the three baseball datasets and set `playerID` as the index:

```
>>> baseball_14 = pd.read_csv(
...       "data/baseball14.csv", index_col="playerID"
... )
>>> baseball_15 = pd.read_csv(
...       "data/baseball15.csv", index_col="playerID"
... )
>>> baseball_16 = pd.read_csv(
...       "data/baseball16.csv", index_col="playerID"
... )
>>> baseball_14.head()
           yearID  stint  teamID  lgID  ...  HBP  SH   SF   GIDP
playerID                                ...
altuvjo01    2014      1     HOU    AL  ...  5.0  1.0  5.0  20.0
cartech02    2014      1     HOU    AL  ...  5.0  0.0  4.0  12.0
castrja01    2014      1     HOU    AL  ...  9.0  1.0  3.0  11.0
corpoca01    2014      1     HOU    AL  ...  3.0  1.0  2.0   3.0
dominma01    2014      1     HOU    AL  ...  5.0  2.0  7.0  23.0
```

2. Use the .difference method on the index to discover which index labels are in baseball_14 and not in baseball_15, and vice versa:

```
>>> baseball_14.index.difference(baseball_15.index)
Index(['corpoca01', 'dominma01', 'fowlede01', 'grossro01',
'guzmaje01',
         'hoeslj01', 'krausma01', 'preslal01', 'singljo02'],
```

```
              dtype='object', name='playerID')


>>> baseball_15.index.difference(baseball_14.index)
Index(['congeha01', 'correca01', 'gattiev01', 'gomezca01',
'lowrije01',
        'rasmuco01', 'tuckepr01', 'valbulu01'],
       dtype='object', name='playerID')
```

3. There are quite a few players unique to each index. Let's find out how many hits each player has in total over the three-year period. The H column contains the number of hits:

    ```
    >>> hits_14 = baseball_14["H"]
    >>> hits_15 = baseball_15["H"]
    >>> hits_16 = baseball_16["H"]
    >>> hits_14.head()
    playerID
    altuvjo01    225
    cartech02    115
    castrja01    103
    corpoca01     40
    dominma01    121
    Name: H, dtype: int64
    ```

4. Let's first add together two Series using the plus operator:

    ```
    >>> (hits_14 + hits_15).head()
    playerID
    altuvjo01    425.0
    cartech02    193.0
    castrja01    174.0
    congeha01      NaN
    corpoca01      NaN
    Name: H, dtype: float64
    ```

5. Even though players congeha01 and corpoca01 have values for 2015, their result is missing. Let's use the .add method with the fill_value parameter to avoid missing values:

    ```
    >>> hits_14.add(hits_15, fill_value=0).head()
    playerID
    altuvjo01    425.0
    ```

```
cartech02      193.0
castrja01      174.0
congeha01       46.0
corpoca01       40.0
Name: H, dtype: float64
```

6. We add hits from 2016 by chaining the add method once more:

```
>>> hits_total = hits_14.add(hits_15, fill_value=0).add(
...        hits_16, fill_value=0
... )
>>> hits_total.head()
playerID
altuvjo01      641.0
bregmal01       53.0
cartech02      193.0
castrja01      243.0
congeha01       46.0
Name: H, dtype: float64
```

7. Check for missing values in the result:

```
>>> hits_total.hasnans
False
```

How it works...

The .add method works in a similar way to the plus operator, but allows for more flexibility by providing the fill_value parameter to take the place of a non-matching index. In this problem, it makes sense to default the non-matching index value to 0, but you could have used any other number.

There will be occasions when each Series contains index labels that correspond to missing values. In this specific instance, when the two Series are added, the index label will still correspond to a missing value regardless of whether the fill_value parameter is used. To clarify this, take a look at the following example where the index label a corresponds to a missing value in each Series:

```
>>> s = pd.Series(
...        index=["a", "b", "c", "d"],
...        data=[np.nan, 3, np.nan, 1],
... )
```

```
>>> s
a    NaN
b    3.0
c    NaN
d    1.0
dtype: float64

>>> s1 = pd.Series(
...     index=["a", "b", "c"], data=[np.nan, 6, 10]
... )
>>> s1
a     NaN
b     6.0
c    10.0
dtype: float64

>>> s.add(s1, fill_value=5)
a     NaN
b     9.0
c    15.0
d     6.0
dtype: float64
```

There's more...

This recipe shows how to add Series with only a single index together. It is also possible to add DataFrames together. Adding two DataFrames together will align both the index and columns before computation and insert missing values for non-matching indexes. Let's start by selecting a few of the columns from the 2014 baseball dataset:

```
>>> df_14 = baseball_14[["G", "AB", "R", "H"]]
>>> df_14.head()
            G   AB   R    H
playerID
altuvjo01  158  660  85  225
cartech02  145  507  68  115
castrja01  126  465  43  103
```

```
corpoca01    55   170   22    40
dominma01   157   564   51   121
```

Let's also select a few of the same and a few different columns from the 2015 baseball dataset:

```
>>> df_15 = baseball_15[["AB", "R", "H", "HR"]]
>>> df_15.head()
            AB    R     H   HR
playerID
altuvjo01   638   86   200   15
cartech02   391   50    78   24
castrja01   337   38    71   11
congeha01   201   25    46   11
correca01   387   52   108   22
```

Adding the two DataFrames together creates missing values wherever rows or column labels cannot align. You can use the `.style` attribute and call the `.highlight_null` method to see where the missing values are:

```
(df_14 + df_15).head(10).style.highlight_null('yellow')
```

playerID	AB	G	H	HR	R
altuvjo01	1298	nan	425	nan	171
cartech02	898	nan	193	nan	118
castrja01	802	nan	174	nan	81
congeha01	nan	nan	nan	nan	nan
corpoca01	nan	nan	nan	nan	nan
correca01	nan	nan	nan	nan	nan
dominma01	nan	nan	nan	nan	nan
fowlede01	nan	nan	nan	nan	nan
gattiev01	nan	nan	nan	nan	nan
gomezca01	nan	nan	nan	nan	nan

Highlight null values when using the plus operator

Only the rows where **playerID** appears in both DataFrames will be available. Similarly, the columns **AB**, **H**, and **R** are the only ones that appear in both DataFrames. Even if we use the .add method with the `fill_value` parameter specified, we still might have missing values. This is because some combinations of rows and columns never existed in our input data; for example, the intersection of **playerID congeha01** and column **G**. That player only appeared in the 2015 dataset that did not have the **G** column. Therefore, that value was missing:

```
(df_14
    .add(df_15, fill_value=0)
    .head(10)
    .style.highlight_null('yellow')
)
```

playerID	AB	G	H	HR	R
altuvjo01	1298	158	425	15	171
cartech02	898	145	193	24	118
castrja01	802	126	174	11	81
congeha01	201	nan	46	11	25
corpoca01	170	55	40	nan	22
correca01	387	nan	108	22	52
dominma01	564	157	121	nan	51
fowlede01	434	116	120	nan	61
gattiev01	566	nan	139	27	66
gomezca01	149	nan	36	4	19

Highlight null values when using the .add method

Adding columns from different DataFrames

All DataFrames can add new columns to themselves. However, as usual, whenever a DataFrame is adding a new column from another DataFrame or Series, the indexes align first, and then the new column is created.

This recipe uses the employee dataset to append a new column containing the maximum salary of that employee's department.

How to do it...

1. Import the employee data and select the DEPARTMENT and BASE_SALARY columns in a new DataFrame:

```
>>> employee = pd.read_csv("data/employee.csv")
>>> dept_sal = employee[["DEPARTMENT", "BASE_SALARY"]]
```

2. Sort this smaller DataFrame by salary within each department:

```
>>> dept_sal = dept_sal.sort_values(
...     ["DEPARTMENT", "BASE_SALARY"],
...     ascending=[True, False],
... )
```

3. Use the .drop_duplicates method to keep the first row of each DEPARTMENT:

```
>>> max_dept_sal = dept_sal.drop_duplicates(
...     subset="DEPARTMENT"
... )
>>> max_dept_sal.head()
        DEPARTMENT  BASE_SALARY
                   DEPARTMENT   BASE_SALARY
1494    Admn. & Regulatory Affairs    140416.0
149          City Controller's Office     64251.0
236                    City Council    100000.0
647    Convention and Entertainment     38397.0
1500    Dept of Neighborhoods (DON)     89221.0
```

4. Put the DEPARTMENT column into the index for each DataFrame:

```
>>> max_dept_sal = max_dept_sal.set_index("DEPARTMENT")
>>> employee = employee.set_index("DEPARTMENT")
```

5. Now that the indexes contain matching values, we can add a new column to the employee DataFrame:

```
>>> employee = employee.assign(
...     MAX_DEPT_SALARY=max_dept_sal["BASE_SALARY"]
... )
>>> employee
                             UNIQUE_ID  ...  MAX_D/ALARY
DEPARTMENT                              ...
Municipal Courts Department          0  ...     121862.0
```

```
Library                               1  ...      107763.0
Houston Police Department-HPD         2  ...      199596.0
Houston Fire Department (HFD)         3  ...      210588.0
General Services Department           4  ...       89194.0
...                                  ...  ...          ...
Houston Police Department-HPD      1995  ...      199596.0
Houston Fire Department (HFD)      1996  ...      210588.0
Houston Police Department-HPD      1997  ...      199596.0
Houston Police Department-HPD      1998  ...      199596.0
Houston Fire Department (HFD)      1999  ...      210588.0
```

6. We can validate our results with the query method to check whether there exist any rows where BASE_SALARY is greater than MAX_DEPT_SALARY:

```
>>> employee.query("BASE_SALARY > MAX_DEPT_SALARY")
Empty DataFrame
Columns: [UNIQUE_ID, POSITION_TITLE, BASE_SALARY, RACE,
EMPLOYMENT_TYPE, GENDER, EMPLOYMENT_STATUS, HIRE_DATE, JOB_DATE,
MAX_DEPT_SALARY]
Index: []
```

7. Refactor our code into a chain:

```
>>> employee = pd.read_csv("data/employee.csv")
>>> max_dept_sal = (
...     employee
...     [["DEPARTMENT", "BASE_SALARY"]]
...     .sort_values(
...         ["DEPARTMENT", "BASE_SALARY"],
...         ascending=[True, False],
...     )
...     .drop_duplicates(subset="DEPARTMENT")
...     .set_index("DEPARTMENT")
... )

>>> (
...     employee
...     .set_index("DEPARTMENT")
...     .assign(
...         MAX_DEPT_SALARY=max_dept_sal["BASE_SALARY"]
```

```
...        )
...  )
                    UNIQUE_ID POSITION_TITLE  ...    JOB_DATE MAX_DEPT_
SALARY
DEPARTMENT                                ...
Municipal...         0  ASSISTAN...  ...  2012-10-13
121862.0
Library              1  LIBRARY ...  ...  2010-09-18
107763.0
Houston P...         2  POLICE O...  ...  2015-02-03
199596.0
Houston F...         3  ENGINEER...  ...  1991-05-25
210588.0
General S...         4  ELECTRICIAN  ...  1994-10-22
89194.0
...                ...          ...  ...         ...
...
Houston P...      1995  POLICE O...  ...  2015-06-09
199596.0
Houston F...      1996  COMMUNIC...  ...  2013-10-06
210588.0
Houston P...      1997  POLICE O...  ...  2015-10-13
199596.0
Houston P...      1998  POLICE O...  ...  2011-07-02
199596.0
Houston F...      1999  FIRE FIG...  ...  2010-07-12
210588.0
```

How it works...

Steps 2 and *3* find the maximum salary for each department. For automatic index alignment to work properly, we set each DataFrame index as the department. *Step 5* works because each row index from the left DataFrame, `employee`, aligns with one, and only one, index from the right DataFrame, `max_dept_sal`. If `max_dept_sal` has duplicates of any departments in its index, then we will get a Cartesian product.

For instance, let's see what happens when we use a DataFrame on the right-hand side of the equality that has repeated index values. We use the `.sample` DataFrame method to randomly choose 10 rows without replacement:

```
>>> random_salary = dept_sal.sample(
...      n=10, random_state=42
```

```
... ).set_index("DEPARTMENT")
>>> random_salary
```

	BASE_SALARY
DEPARTMENT	
Public Works & Engineering-PWE	34861.0
Houston Airport System (HAS)	29286.0
Houston Police Department-HPD	31907.0
Houston Police Department-HPD	66614.0
Houston Police Department-HPD	42000.0
Houston Police Department-HPD	43443.0
Houston Police Department-HPD	66614.0
Public Works & Engineering-PWE	52582.0
Finance	93168.0
Houston Police Department-HPD	35318.0

Notice how there are several repeated departments in the index. When we attempt to create a new column, an error is raised alerting us that there are duplicates. At least one index label in the employee DataFrame is joining with two or more index labels from `random_salary`:

```
>>> employee["RANDOM_SALARY"] = random_salary["BASE_SALARY"]
Traceback (most recent call last):
...
ValueError: cannot reindex from a duplicate axis
```

There's more...

During alignment, if there is nothing for the DataFrame index to align to, the resulting value will be missing. Let's create an example where this happens. We will use only the first three rows of the `max_dept_sal` Series to create a new column:

```
>>> (
...     employee
...     .set_index("DEPARTMENT")
...     .assign(
...         MAX_SALARY2=max_dept_sal["BASE_SALARY"].head(3)
...     )
...     .MAX_SALARY2
...     .value_counts(dropna=False)
... )
```

```
NaN          1955
140416.0       29
100000.0       11
64251.0         5
Name: MAX_SALARY2, dtype: int64
```

The operation completed successfully but filled in salaries for only three of the departments. All the other departments that did not appear in the first three rows of the `max_dept_sal` Series resulted in a missing value.

My preference is to use the following code rather than the code in *step 7*. This code uses the `.groupby` method combined with the `.transform` method, which is discussed in a later chapter. This code reads much cleaner to me. It is shorter and does not mess with reassigning the index:

```
>>> max_sal = (
...       employee
...       .groupby("DEPARTMENT")
...       .BASE_SALARY
...       .transform("max")
... )
```

```
>>> (employee.assign(MAX_DEPT_SALARY=max_sal))
UNIQUE_ID POSITION_TITLE  ...    JOB_DATE  MAX_DEPT_SALARY
0               0  ASSISTAN...  ...  2012-10-13       121862.0
1               1  LIBRARY ...  ...  2010-09-18       107763.0
2               2  POLICE O...  ...  2015-02-03       199596.0
3               3  ENGINEER...  ...  1991-05-25       210588.0
4               4  ELECTRICIAN  ...  1994-10-22        89194.0
...           ...         ...   ...         ...            ...
1995         1995  POLICE O...  ...  2015-06-09       199596.0
1996         1996  COMMUNIC...  ...  2013-10-06       210588.0
1997         1997  POLICE O...  ...  2015-10-13       199596.0
1998         1998  POLICE O...  ...  2011-07-02       199596.0
1999         1999  FIRE FIG...  ...  2010-07-12       210588.0
```

This works because `.transform` preserves the original index. If you did a `.groupby` that creates a new index, you can use the `.merge` method to combine the data. We just need to tell it to merge on DEPARTMENT for the left side and the index for the right side:

```
>>> max_sal = (
...       employee
```

```
...        .groupby("DEPARTMENT")
...        .BASE_SALARY
...        .max()
... )

>>> (
...        employee.merge(
...            max_sal.rename("MAX_DEPT_SALARY"),
...            how="left",
...            left_on="DEPARTMENT",
...            right_index=True,
...        )
... )
UNIQUE_ID POSITION_TITLE  ...      JOB_DATE  MAX_DEPT_SALARY
0                 0 ASSISTAN...    ... 2012-10-13      121862.0
1                 1 LIBRARY ...    ... 2010-09-18      107763.0
2                 2 POLICE O...    ... 2015-02-03      199596.0
3                 3 ENGINEER...    ... 1991-05-25      210588.0
4                 4 ELECTRICIAN    ... 1994-10-22       89194.0
...             ...        ...     ...        ...           ...
1995           1995 POLICE O...    ... 2015-06-09      199596.0
1996           1996 COMMUNIC...    ... 2013-10-06      210588.0
1997           1997 POLICE O...    ... 2015-10-13      199596.0
1998           1998 POLICE O...    ... 2011-07-02      199596.0
1999           1999 FIRE FIG...    ... 2010-07-12      210588.0
```

Highlighting the maximum value from each column

The college dataset has many numeric columns describing different metrics about each school. Many people are interested in schools that perform the best for specific metrics.

This recipe discovers the school that has the maximum value for each numeric column and styles the DataFrame to highlight the information.

How to do it...

1. Read the college dataset with the institution name as the index:

```
>>> college = pd.read_csv(
...        "data/college.csv", index_col="INSTNM"
... )
>>> college.dtypes
CITY                    object
STABBR                  object
HBCU                    float64
MENONLY                 float64
WOMENONLY               float64
                          ...
PCTPELL                 float64
PCTFLOAN                float64
UG25ABV                 float64
MD_EARN_WNE_P10         object
GRAD_DEBT_MDN_SUPP      object
Length: 26, dtype: object
```

2. All the other columns besides CITY and STABBR appear to be numeric. Examining the data types from the preceding step reveals unexpectedly that the MD_EARN_WNE_P10 and GRAD_DEBT_MDN_SUPP columns are of the object type and not numeric. To help get a better idea of what kinds of values are in these columns, let's examine a sample from them:

```
>>> college.MD_EARN_WNE_P10.sample(10, random_state=42)
INSTNM
Career Point College                              20700
Ner Israel Rabbinical College                  PrivacyS...
Reflections Academy of Beauty                       NaN
Capital Area Technical College                    26400
West Virginia University Institute of Technology  43400
Mid-State Technical College                       32000
Strayer University-Huntsville Campus              49200
National Aviation Academy of Tampa Bay            45000
University of California-Santa Cruz               43000
Lexington Theological Seminary                      NaN
Name: MD_EARN_WNE_P10, dtype: object
```

```
>>> college.GRAD_DEBT_MDN_SUPP.sample(10, random_state=42)
INSTNM
Career Point College                                      14977
Ner Israel Rabbinical College                          PrivacyS...
Reflections Academy of Beauty                          PrivacyS...
Capital Area Technical College                         PrivacyS...
West Virginia University Institute of Technology          23969
Mid-State Technical College                                8025
Strayer University-Huntsville Campus                     36173.5
National Aviation Academy of Tampa Bay                    22778
University of California-Santa Cruz                       19884
Lexington Theological Seminary                         PrivacyS...
Name: GRAD_DEBT_MDN_SUPP, dtype: object
```

3. These values are strings, but we would like them to be numeric. I like to use the
   `.value_counts` method in this case to see whether it reveals any characters that
   forced the column to be non-numeric:

```
>>> college.MD_EARN_WNE_P10.value_counts()
PrivacySuppressed    822
38800                151
21500                 97
49200                 78
27400                 46
                     ...
66700                  1
163900                 1
64400                  1
58700                  1
64100                  1
Name: MD_EARN_WNE_P10, Length: 598, dtype: int64


>>> set(college.MD_EARN_WNE_P10.apply(type))
{<class 'float'>, <class 'str'>}


>>> college.GRAD_DEBT_MDN_SUPP.value_counts()
PrivacySuppressed    1510
9500                  514
```

```
27000                      306
25827.5                    136
25000                      124

                           ...

16078.5                      1
27763.5                      1
6382                         1
27625                        1
11300                        1
Name: GRAD_DEBT_MDN_SUPP, Length: 2038, dtype: int64
```

4. The culprit appears to be that some schools have privacy concerns about these two columns of data. To force these columns to be numeric, use the pandas function to_numeric. If we use the errors='coerce' parameter, it will convert those values to NaN:

```
>>> cols = ["MD_EARN_WNE_P10", "GRAD_DEBT_MDN_SUPP"]
>>> for col in cols:
...     college[col] = pd.to_numeric(
...         college[col], errors="coerce"
...     )

>>> college.dtypes.loc[cols]
MD_EARN_WNE_P10        float64
GRAD_DEBT_MDN_SUPP     float64
dtype: object
```

5. Use the .select_dtypes method to filter for only numeric columns. This will exclude STABBR and CITY columns, where a maximum value doesn't make sense with this problem:

```
>>> college_n = college.select_dtypes("number")
>>> college_n.head()
              HBCU    MENONLY  ...  MD_EARN_WNE_P10  GRAD_DEBT_MDN_
SUPP
INSTNM                         ...
Alabama A...   1.0       0.0   ...          30300.0          33888.0
Universit...   0.0       0.0   ...          39700.0          21941.5
Amridge U...   0.0       0.0   ...          40100.0          23370.0
Universit...   0.0       0.0   ...          45500.0          24097.0
Alabama S...   1.0       0.0   ...          26600.0          33118.5
```

6. Several columns have binary only (0 or 1) values that will not provide useful information for maximum values. To find these columns, we can create a Boolean Series and find all the columns that have two unique values with the `.nunique` method:

```
>>> binary_only = college_n.nunique() == 2
>>> binary_only.head()
HBCU          True
MENONLY       True
WOMENONLY     True
RELAFFIL      True
SATVRMID      False
dtype: bool
```

7. Use the Boolean array to create a list of binary columns:

```
>>> binary_cols = binary_only[binary_only].index
>>> binary_cols
Index(['HBCU', 'MENONLY', 'WOMENONLY', 'RELAFFIL', 'DISTANCEONLY',
'CURROPER'], dtype='object')
```

8. Since we are looking for the maximum values, we can drop the binary columns using the `.drop` method:

```
>>> college_n2 = college_n.drop(columns=binary_cols)
>>> college_n2.head()
```

	SATVRMID	SATMTMID	...	MD_EARN_WNE_P10	GRAD_DEBT_ MDN_SUPP
INSTNM			...		
Alabama A...	424.0	420.0	...	30300.0	33888.0
Universit...	570.0	565.0	...	39700.0	21941.5
Amridge U...	NaN	NaN	...	40100.0	23370.0
Universit...	595.0	590.0	...	45500.0	24097.0
Alabama S...	425.0	430.0	...	26600.0	33118.5

9. Now we can use the `.idxmax` method to find the index label of the maximum value for each column:

```
>>> max_cols = college_n2.idxmax()
>>> max_cols
```

SATVRMID	California Institute of Technology
SATMTMID	California Institute of Technology
UGDS	University of Phoenix-Arizona
UGDS_WHITE	Mr Leon's School of Hair Design-Moscow
UGDS_BLACK	Velvatex College of Beauty Culture

. . .

PCTPELL	MTI Business College Inc
PCTFLOAN	ABC Beauty College Inc
UG25ABV	Dongguk University-Los Angeles
MD_EARN_WNE_P10	Medical College of Wisconsin
GRAD_DEBT_MDN_SUPP	Southwest University of Visual Arts-Tucson

```
Length: 18, dtype: object
```

10. Call the `.unique` method on the `max_cols` Series. This returns an ndarray of the index values in `college_n2` that has the maximum values:

```
>>> unique_max_cols = max_cols.unique()
>>> unique_max_cols[:5]
array(['California Institute of Technology',
       'University of Phoenix-Arizona',
       "Mr Leon's School of Hair Design-Moscow",
       'Velvatex College of Beauty Culture',
       'Thunderbird School of Global Management'], dtype=object)
```

11. Use the values of `max_cols` to select only those rows that have schools with a maximum value and then use the `.style` attribute to highlight these values:

```
college_n2.loc[unique_max_cols].style.highlight_max()
```

college_n2.loc[unique_max_cols].style.highlight_max()												
INSTNM	SATVRMID	SATMTMID	UGDS	UGDS_WHITE	UGDS_BLACK	UGDS_HISP	UGDS_ASIAN	UGDS_AIAN	UGDS_NHPI	UGDS_2MOR	UGDS_NRA	UGD
California Institute of Technology	765	785	983	0.2787	0.0153	0.1221	0.4385	0.001	0	0.057	0.0875	
University of Phoenix-Arizona	nan	nan	151558	0.3098	0.1555	0.076	0.0082	0.0042	0.005	0.1131	0.0131	
Mr Leon's School of Hair Design-Moscow	nan	nan	16	1	0	0	0	0	0	0	0	
Velvatex College of Beauty Culture	nan	nan	25	0	1	0	0	0	0	0	0	
Thunderbird School of Global Management	nan	nan	1	0	0	1	0	0	0	0	0	
Cosmopolitan Beauty and Tech School	nan	nan	110	0.0091	0	0.0182	0.9727	0	0	0	0	
Haskell Indian Nations University	430	440	805	0	0	0	0	1	0	0	0	

Display maximum column values

12. Refactor the code to make it easier to read:

```
>>> def remove_binary_cols(df):
...     binary_only = df.nunique() == 2
...     cols = binary_only[binary_only].index.tolist()
...     return df.drop(columns=cols)


>>> def select_rows_with_max_cols(df):
...     max_cols = df.idxmax()
...     unique = max_cols.unique()
...     return df.loc[unique]


>>> (
...     college
...     .assign(
...         MD_EARN_WNE_P10=pd.to_numeric(
...             college.MD_EARN_WNE_P10, errors="coerce"
```

```
...              ),
...              GRAD_DEBT_MDN_SUPP=pd.to_numeric(
...                  college.GRAD_DEBT_MDN_SUPP, errors="coerce"
...              ),
...          )
...      .select_dtypes("number")
...      .pipe(remove_binary_cols)
...      .pipe(select_rows_with_max_cols)
... )
```

	SATVRMID	SATMTMID	...	MD_EARN_WNE_P10	GRAD_DEBT_ MDN_SUPP
INSTNM			...		
Californi...	765.0	785.0	...	77800.0	11812.5
Universit...	NaN	NaN	...	NaN	33000.0
Mr Leon's...	NaN	NaN	...	NaN	15710.0
Velvatex ...	NaN	NaN	...	NaN	NaN
Thunderbi...	NaN	NaN	...	118900.0	NaN
...	...	...	...	...	...
MTI Busin...	NaN	NaN	...	23000.0	9500.0
ABC Beaut...	NaN	NaN	...	NaN	16500.0
Dongguk U...	NaN	NaN	...	NaN	NaN
Medical C...	NaN	NaN	...	233100.0	NaN
Southwest...	NaN	NaN	...	27200.0	49750.0

How it works...

The .idxmax method is a useful method, especially when the index is meaningfully labeled. It was unexpected that both MD_EARN_WNE_P10 and GRAD_DEBT_MDN_SUPP were of the object data type. When loading CSV files, pandas lists the column as an object type (even though it might contain both number and string types) if the column contains at least one string.

By examining a specific column value in *step 2*, we were able to discover that we had strings in these columns. In *step 3*, we use the `.value_counts` method to reveal offending characters. We uncover the `PrivacySuppressed` values that are causing havoc.

pandas can force all strings that contain only numeric characters to numeric data types with the `to_numeric` function. We do this in *step 4*. To override the default behavior of raising an error when `to_numeric` encounters a string that cannot be converted, you must pass `coerce` to the `errors` parameter. This forces all non-numeric character strings to become missing values (`np.nan`).

Several columns do not have useful or meaningful maximum values. They were removed in *step 5* through *step 8*. The `.select_dtypes` method can be beneficial for wide DataFrames with many columns.

In *step 9*, `.idxmax` iterates through all the columns to find the index of the maximum value for each column. It outputs the results as a Series. The school with both the highest SAT math and verbal scores is California Institute of Technology, while Dongguk University Los Angeles has the highest number of students older than 25.

Although the information provided by `.idxmax` is convenient, it does not yield the corresponding maximum value. To do this, we gather all the unique school names from the values of the `max_cols` Series in *step 10*.

Next, in *step 11*, we index off a `.loc` to select rows based on the index label, which was set to school names when loading the CSV in the first step. This filters for only schools that have a maximum value. DataFrames have a `.style` attribute that itself has some methods to alter the appearance of the displayed DataFrame. Highlighting the maximum value makes the result much clearer.

Finally, we refactor the code to make it a clean pipeline.

There's more...

By default, the `.highlight_max` method highlights the maximum value of each column. We can use the `axis` parameter to highlight the maximum value of each row instead. Here, we select just the race percentage columns of the college dataset and highlight the race with the highest percentage for each school:

```
>>> college = pd.read_csv(
...     "data/college.csv", index_col="INSTNM"
... )
>>> college_ugds = college.filter(like="UGDS_").head()
```

```
college_ugds.style.highlight_max(axis='columns')
```

INSTNM	UGDS_WHITE	UGDS_BLACK	UGDS_HISP	UGDS_ASIAN	UGDS_AIAN	UGDS_NHPI	UGDS_2MOR	UGDS_NRA	UGDS_UNKN
Alabama A & M University	0.0333	0.9353	0.0055	0.0019	0.0024	0.0019	0	0.0059	0.0138
University of Alabama at Birmingham	0.5922	0.26	0.0283	0.0518	0.0022	0.0007	0.0368	0.0179	0.01
Amridge University	0.299	0.4192	0.0069	0.0034	0	0	0	0	0.2715
University of Alabama in Huntsville	0.6988	0.1255	0.0382	0.0376	0.0143	0.0002	0.0172	0.0332	0.035
Alabama State University	0.0158	0.9208	0.0121	0.0019	0.001	0.0006	0.0098	0.0243	0.0137

Display maximum column values

Replicating idxmax with method chaining

A good exercise is to attempt an implementation of a built-in DataFrame method on your own. This type of replication can give you a deeper understanding of other pandas methods that you normally wouldn't have come across. `.idxmax` is a challenging method to replicate using only the methods covered thus far in the book.

This recipe slowly chains together basic methods to eventually find all the row index values that contain a maximum column value.

How to do it...

1. Load in the college dataset and execute the same operations as the previous recipe to get only the numeric columns that are of interest:

```
>>> def remove_binary_cols(df):
...     binary_only = df.nunique() == 2
...     cols = binary_only[binary_only].index.tolist()
...     return df.drop(columns=cols)

>>> college_n = (
...     college
...     .assign(
...         MD_EARN_WNE_P10=pd.to_numeric(
...             college.MD_EARN_WNE_P10, errors="coerce"
...         ),
...         GRAD_DEBT_MDN_SUPP=pd.to_numeric(
...             college.GRAD_DEBT_MDN_SUPP, errors="coerce"
...         ),
```

```
...        )
...        .select_dtypes("number")
...        .pipe(remove_binary_cols)
...    )
```

2. Find the maximum of each column with the .max method:

```
>>> college_n.max().head()
SATVRMID          765.0
SATMTMID          785.0
UGDS           151558.0
UGDS_WHITE          1.0
UGDS_BLACK          1.0
dtype: float64
```

3. Use the .eq DataFrame method to test each value against the column .max method. By default, the .eq method aligns the columns of the column DataFrame with the labels of the passed Series index:

```
>>> college_n.eq(college_n.max()).head()
                  SATVRMID  SATMTMID  ...  MD_EARN_WNE_P10  GRAD_DEBT_
MDN_SUPP
INSTNM                                ...
Alabama A...      False     False     ...      False
False
Universit...      False     False     ...      False
False
Amridge U...      False     False     ...      False
False
Universit...      False     False     ...      False
False
Alabama S...      False     False     ...      False
False
```

4. All the rows in this DataFrame that have at least one True value must contain a column maximum. Let's use the .any method to find all such rows that have at least one True value:

```
>>> has_row_max = (
...        college_n
...        .eq(college_n.max())
...        .any(axis="columns")
...    )
```

```
>>> has_row_max.head()

INSTNM

Alabama A & M University                    False

University of Alabama at Birmingham         False

Amridge University                          False

University of Alabama in Huntsville         False

Alabama State University                    False

dtype: bool
```

5. There are only 18 columns, which means that there should only be at most 18 `True` values in `has_row_max`. Let's find out how many there are:

```
>>> college_n.shape

(7535, 18)

>>> has_row_max.sum()

401
```

6. This was a bit unexpected, but it turns out that there are columns with many rows that equal the maximum value. This is common with many of the percentage columns that have a maximum of 1. `.idxmax` returns the first occurrence of the maximum value. Let's back up a bit, remove the `.any` method, and look at the output from *step 3*. Let's run the `.cumsum` method instead to accumulate all the `True` values:

```
>>> college_n.eq(college_n.max()).cumsum()
```

	SATVRMID	SATMTMID	...	MD_EARN_WNE_P10	GRAD_DEBT_ MDN_SUPP
INSTNM			...		
Alabama A...	0	0	...	0	0
Universit...	0	0	...	0	0
Amridge U...	0	0	...	0	0
Universit...	0	0	...	0	0
Alabama S...	0	0	...	0	0
...	...	...	...	...	...
SAE Insti...	1	1	...	1	2
Rasmussen...	1	1	...	1	2

National ... 2	1	1 ...		1
Bay Area ... 2	1	1 ...		1
Excel Lea... 2	1	1 ...		1

7. Some columns have one unique maximum, like SATVRMID and SATMTMID, while others like UGDS_WHITE have many. 109 schools have 100% of their undergraduates as White. If we chain the .cumsum method one more time, the value 1 would only appear once in each column and it would be the first occurrence of the maximum:

```
>>> (college_n.eq(college_n.max()).cumsum().cumsum())
```

INSTNM	SATVRMID	SATMTMID	...	MD_EARN_WNE_P10	GRAD_DEBT_MDN_SUPP
			...		
Alabama A...	0	0	...	0	0
Universit...	0	0	...	0	0
Amridge U...	0	0	...	0	0
Universit...	0	0	...	0	0
Alabama S...	0	0	...	0	0
...	...	... ...		...	...
SAE Insti...	7305	7305	...	3445	10266
Rasmussen...	7306	7306	...	3446	10268
National ...	7307	7307	...	3447	10270
Bay Area ...	7308	7308	...	3448	10272
Excel Lea...	7309	7309	...	3449	10274

8. We can now test the equality of each value against 1 with the .eq method and then use the .any method to find rows that have at least one True value:

```
>>> has_row_max2 = (
...     college_n.eq(college_n.max())
```

```
...        .cumsum()
...        .cumsum()
...        .eq(1)
...        .any(axis="columns")
... )
```

```
>>> has_row_max2.head()
INSTNM
Alabama A & M University                    False
University of Alabama at Birmingham         False
Amridge University                          False
University of Alabama in Huntsville         False
Alabama State University                    False
dtype: bool
```

9. Check that `has_row_max2` has no more `True` values than the number of columns:

```
>>> has_row_max2.sum()
16
```

10. We need all the institutions where `has_row_max2` is `True`. We can use Boolean indexing on the Series itself:

```
>>> idxmax_cols = has_row_max2[has_row_max2].index
>>> idxmax_cols
Index(['Thunderbird School of Global Management',
       'Southwest University of Visual Arts-Tucson', 'ABC Beauty
College Inc',
       'Velvatex College of Beauty Culture',
       'California Institute of Technology',
       'Le Cordon Bleu College of Culinary Arts-San Francisco',
       'MTI Business College Inc', 'Dongguk University-Los
Angeles',
       'Mr Leon's School of Hair Design-Moscow',
       'Haskell Indian Nations University', 'LIU Brentwood',
       'Medical College of Wisconsin', 'Palau Community College',
       'California University of Management and Sciences',
       'Cosmopolitan Beauty and Tech School', 'University of
Phoenix-Arizona'],
       dtype='object', name='INSTNM')
```

11. All 16 of these institutions are the index of the first maximum occurrence for at least one of the columns. We can check whether they are the same as the ones found with the `.idxmax` method:

```
>>> set(college_n.idxmax().unique()) == set(idxmax_cols)
True
```

12. Refactor to an `idx_max` function:

```
>>> def idx_max(df):
...         has_row_max = (
...             df
...             .eq(df.max())
...             .cumsum()
...             .cumsum()
...             .eq(1)
...             .any(axis="columns")
...         )
...         return has_row_max[has_row_max].index

>>> idx_max(college_n)
Index(['Thunderbird School of Global Management',
       'Southwest University of Visual Arts-Tucson', 'ABC Beauty
College Inc',
       'Velvatex College of Beauty Culture',
       'California Institute of Technology',
       'Le Cordon Bleu College of Culinary Arts-San Francisco',
       'MTI Business College Inc', 'Dongguk University-Los
Angeles',
       'Mr Leon's School of Hair Design-Moscow',
       'Haskell Indian Nations University', 'LIU Brentwood',
       'Medical College of Wisconsin', 'Palau Community College',
       'California University of Management and Sciences',
       'Cosmopolitan Beauty and Tech School', 'University of
Phoenix-Arizona'],
       dtype='object', name='INSTNM')
```

How it works...

The first step replicates work from the previous recipe by converting two columns to numeric and eliminating the binary columns. We find the maximum value of each column in *step 2*. Care needs to be taken here as pandas silently drops columns that cannot produce a maximum. If this happens, then *step 3* will still complete but provide `False` values for each column without an available maximum.

Step 4 uses the `.any` method to scan across each row in search of at least one `True` value. Any row with at least one `True` value contains a maximum value for a column. We sum up the resulting Boolean Series in *step 5* to determine how many rows contain a maximum. Somewhat unexpectedly, there are far more rows than columns. *Step 6* gives an insight into why this happens. We take a cumulative sum of the output from *step 3* and detect the total number of rows that equal the maximum for each column.

Many colleges have 100% of their student population as only a single race. This is by far the largest contributor to the multiple rows with maximums. As you can see, there is only one row with a maximum value for both SAT score columns and undergraduate population, but several of the race columns have a tie for the maximum.

Our goal is to find the first row with the maximum value. We need to take the cumulative sum once more so that each column has only a single row equal to 1. *Step 8* formats the code to have one method per line and runs the `.any` method as was done in *step 4*. If this step is successful, then we should have no more `True` values than the number of columns. *Step 9* asserts that this is true.

To validate that we have found the same columns as `.idxmax` in the previous columns, we use Boolean selection on `has_row_max2` with itself. The columns will be in a different order, so we convert the sequence of column names to sets, which are inherently unordered to compare equality.

There's more...

It is possible to complete this recipe in one long line of code chaining the indexing operator with an anonymous function. This little trick removes the need for *step 10*. We can time the difference between the `.idxmax` method and our manual effort in this recipe:

```
>>> def idx_max(df):
...     has_row_max = (
...         df
...         .eq(df.max())
...         .cumsum()
...         .cumsum()
...         .eq(1)
```

```
...           .any(axis="columns")
...           [lambda df_: df_]
...           .index
...      )
...      return has_row_max
```

```
>>> %timeit college_n.idxmax().values
1.12 ms ± 28.4 µs per loop (mean ± std. dev. of 7 runs, 1000 loops each)
>>> %timeit idx_max(college_n)
5.35 ms ± 55.2 µs per loop (mean ± std. dev. of 7 runs, 100 loops each)
```

Our effort is, unfortunately, five times as slow as the built-in `.idxmax` pandas method, but regardless of its performance regression, many creative and practical solutions use the accumulation methods like `.cumsum` with Boolean Series to find streaks or specific patterns along an axis.

Finding the most common maximum of columns

The college dataset contains the undergraduate population percentage of eight different races for over 7,500 colleges. It would be interesting to find the race with the highest undergrad population for each school and then find the distribution of this result for the entire dataset. We would be able to answer a question like, "What percentage of institutions have more White students than any other race?"

In this recipe, we find the race with the highest percentage of the undergraduate population for each school with the `.idxmax` method and then find the distribution of these maximums.

How to do it...

1. Read in the college dataset and select just those columns with undergraduate race percentage information:

   ```
   >>> college = pd.read_csv(
   ...      "data/college.csv", index_col="INSTNM"
   ... )
   >>> college_ugds = college.filter(like="UGDS_")
   >>> college_ugds.head()
                    UGDS_WHITE  UGDS_BLACK  ...  UGDS_NRA  UGDS_UNKN
   ```

INSTNM			...		
Alabama A...	0.0333	0.9353	...	0.0059	0.0138
Universit...	0.5922	0.2600	...	0.0179	0.0100
Amridge U...	0.2990	0.4192	...	0.0000	0.2715
Universit...	0.6988	0.1255	...	0.0332	0.0350
Alabama S...	0.0158	0.9208	...	0.0243	0.0137

2. Use the `.idxmax` method applied against the column axis to get the college name with the highest race percentage for each row:

```
>>> highest_percentage_race = college_ugds.idxmax(
...      axis="columns"
... )
>>> highest_percentage_race.head()
INSTNM
Alabama A & M University
University of Alabama at Birmingham
Amridge University
University of Alabama in Huntsville
Alabama State University
dtype: object
```

3. Use the `.value_counts` method to return the distribution of maximum occurrences. Add the `normalize=True` parameter so that it sums to 1:

```
>>> highest_percentage_race.value_counts(normalize=True)
UGDS_WHITE    0.670352
UGDS_BLACK    0.151586
UGDS_HISP     0.129473
UGDS_UNKN     0.023422
UGDS_ASIAN    0.012074
UGDS_AIAN     0.006110
UGDS_NRA      0.004073
UGDS_NHPI     0.001746
UGDS_2MOR     0.001164
dtype: float64
```

How it works...

The key to this recipe is recognizing that the columns all represent the same unit of information. We can compare these columns with each other, which is usually not the case. For instance, it wouldn't make sense to compare SAT verbal scores with the undergraduate population. As the data is structured in this manner, we can apply the `.idxmax` method to each row of data to find the column with the largest value. We need to alter its default behavior with the `axis` parameter.

Step 3 completes this operation and returns a Series, to which we can now apply the `.value_counts` method to return the distribution. We pass `True` to the normalize parameter as we are interested in the distribution (relative frequency) and not the raw counts.

There's more...

We might want to explore more and answer the question: For those schools with more Black students than any other race, what is the distribution of its second highest race percentage?

```
>>> (
...      college_ugds
...      [highest_percentage_race == "UGDS_BLACK"]
...      .drop(columns="UGDS_BLACK")
...      .idxmax(axis="columns")
...      .value_counts(normalize=True)
... )
UGDS_WHITE     0.661228
UGDS_HISP      0.230326
UGDS_UNKN      0.071977
UGDS_NRA       0.018234
UGDS_ASIAN     0.009597
UGDS_2MOR      0.006718
UGDS_AIAN      0.000960
UGDS_NHPI      0.000960
dtype: float64
```

We needed to drop the `UGDS_BLACK` column before applying the same method from this recipe. It seems that these schools with higher Black populations tend to have higher Hispanic populations.

9

Grouping for Aggregation, Filtration, and Transformation

Introduction

One of the most fundamental tasks during data analysis involves splitting data into independent groups before performing a calculation on each group. This methodology has been around for quite some time but has more recently been referred to as *split-apply-combine*. This chapter covers the powerful `.groupby` method, which allows you to group your data in any way imaginable and apply any type of function independently to each group before returning a single dataset.

Before we get started with the recipes, we will need to know just a little terminology. All basic groupby operations have grouping columns, and each unique combination of values in these columns represents an independent grouping of the data. The syntax looks as follows:

```
df.groupby(['list', 'of', 'grouping', 'columns'])
df.groupby('single_column')  # when grouping by a single column
```

The result of calling the `.groupby` method is a `groupby` object. It is this `groupby` object that will be the engine that drives all the calculations for this entire chapter. pandas does very little when creating this `groupby` object, merely validating that grouping is possible. You will have to chain methods on this `groupby` object to unleash its powers.

The most common use of the `.groupby` method is to perform an aggregation. What is an aggregation? An aggregation takes place when a sequence of many inputs get summarized or combined into a single value output. For example, summing up all the values of a column or finding its maximum are aggregations applied to a sequence of data. An aggregation takes a sequence and reduces it to a single value.

In addition to the grouping columns defined during the introduction, most aggregations have two other components, the aggregating columns and aggregating functions. The aggregating columns are the columns whose values will be aggregated. The aggregating functions define what aggregations take place. Aggregation functions include `sum`, `min`, `max`, `mean`, `count`, `variance`, `std`, and so on.

Defining an aggregation

In this recipe, we examine the flights dataset and perform the simplest aggregation involving only a single grouping column, a single aggregating column, and a single aggregating function. We will find the average arrival delay for each airline. pandas has different syntaxes to create an aggregation, and this recipe will show them.

How to do it...

1. Read in the flights dataset:

    ```
    >>> import pandas as pd
    >>> import numpy as np
    >>> flights = pd.read_csv('data/flights.csv')
    >>> flights.head()
    ```

0	1	1	4	...	65.0	0	0
1	1	1	4	...	-13.0	0	0
2	1	1	4	...	35.0	0	0
3	1	1	4	...	-7.0	0	0
4	1	1	4	...	39.0	0	0

2. Define the grouping columns (`AIRLINE`), aggregating columns (`ARR_DELAY`), and aggregating functions (`mean`). Place the grouping column in the `.groupby` method and then call the `.agg` method with a dictionary pairing the aggregating column with its aggregating function. If you pass in a dictionary, it returns back a DataFrame instance:

    ```
    >>> (flights
    ...     .groupby('AIRLINE')
    ...     .agg({'ARR_DELAY':'mean'})
    ```

```
... )
        ARR_DELAY
AIRLINE
AA         5.542661
AS        -0.833333
B6         8.692593
DL         0.339691
EV         7.034580
...            ...
OO         7.593463
UA         7.765755
US         1.681105
VX         5.348884
WN         6.397353
```

Alternatively, you may place the aggregating column in the index operator and then pass the aggregating function as a string to .agg. This will return a Series:

```
>>> (flights
...     .groupby('AIRLINE')
...     ['ARR_DELAY']
...     .agg('mean')
... )
AIRLINE
AA    5.542661
AS   -0.833333
B6    8.692593
DL    0.339691
EV    7.034580
         ...
OO    7.593463
UA    7.765755
US    1.681105
VX    5.348884
WN    6.397353
Name: ARR_DELAY, Length: 14, dtype: float64
```

3. The string names used in the previous step are a convenience that pandas offers you to refer to a particular aggregation function. You can pass any aggregating function directly to the `.agg` method, such as the NumPy `mean` function. The output is the same as the previous step:

```
>>> (flights
...      .groupby('AIRLINE')
...      ['ARR_DELAY']
...      .agg(np.mean)
... )
AIRLINE
AA     5.542661
AS    -0.833333
B6     8.692593
DL     0.339691
EV     7.034580
       ...
OO     7.593463
UA     7.765755
US     1.681105
VX     5.348884
WN     6.397353
Name: ARR_DELAY, Length: 14, dtype: float64
```

4. It's possible to skip the `agg` method altogether in this case and use the code in text method directly. This output is also the same as *step 3*:

```
>>> (flights
...      .groupby('AIRLINE')
...      ['ARR_DELAY']
...      .mean()
... )
AIRLINE
AA     5.542661
AS    -0.833333
B6     8.692593
DL     0.339691
EV     7.034580
       ...
OO     7.593463
```

```
UA    7.765755
US    1.681105
VX    5.348884
WN    6.397353
Name: ARR_DELAY, Length: 14, dtype: float64
```

How it works...

The syntax for the `.groupby` method is not as straightforward as other methods. Let's intercept the chain of methods in *step 2* by storing the result of the `.groupby` method as its own variable:

```
>>> grouped = flights.groupby('AIRLINE')
>>> type(grouped)
<class 'pandas.core.groupby.generic.DataFrameGroupBy'>
```

A completely new intermediate object is first produced with its own distinct attributes and methods. No calculations take place at this stage. pandas merely validates the grouping columns. This `groupby` object has an `.agg` method to perform aggregations. One of the ways to use this method is to pass it a dictionary mapping the aggregating column to the aggregating function, as done in *step 2*. If you pass in a dictionary, the result will be a DataFrame.

The pandas library often has more than one way to perform the same operation. *Step 3* shows another way to perform a groupby. Instead of identifying the aggregating column in the dictionary, place it inside the index operator as if you were selecting it as a column from a DataFrame. The function string name is then passed as a scalar to the `.agg` method. The result, in this case, is a Series.

You may pass any aggregating function to the `.agg` method. pandas allows you to use the string names for simplicity, but you may also explicitly call an aggregating function as done in *step 4*. NumPy provides many functions that aggregate values.

Step 5 shows one last syntax flavor. When you are only applying a single aggregating function as in this example, you can often call it directly as a method on the `groupby` object itself without `.agg`. Not all aggregation functions have a method equivalent, but most do.

There's more...

If you do not use an aggregating function with `.agg`, pandas raises an exception. For instance, let's see what happens when we apply the square root function to each group:

```
>>> (flights
```

```
...     .groupby('AIRLINE')
...     ['ARR_DELAY']
...     .agg(np.sqrt)
... )
Traceback (most recent call last):
  ...
ValueError: function does not reduce
```

Grouping and aggregating with multiple columns and functions

It is possible to group and aggregate with multiple columns. The syntax is slightly different than it is for grouping and aggregating with a single column. As usual with any kind of grouping operation, it helps to identify the three components: the grouping columns, aggregating columns, and aggregating functions.

In this recipe, we showcase the flexibility of the `.groupby` method by answering the following queries:

▶ Finding the number of canceled flights for every airline per weekday

▶ Finding the number and percentage of canceled and diverted flights for every airline per weekday

▶ For each origin and destination, finding the total number of flights, the number and percentage of canceled flights, and the average and variance of the airtime

How to do it...

1. Read in the flights dataset, and answer the first query by defining the grouping columns (AIRLINE, WEEKDAY), the aggregating column (CANCELLED), and the aggregating function (sum):

```
>>> (flights
...     .groupby(['AIRLINE', 'WEEKDAY'])
...     ['CANCELLED']
...     .agg('sum')
... )
AIRLINE  WEEKDAY
AA       1          41
         2           9
```

	3	16
	4	20
	5	18
		..
WN	3	18
	4	10
	5	7
	6	10
	7	7

```
Name: CANCELLED, Length: 98, dtype: int64
```

2. Answer the second query by using a list for each pair of grouping and aggregating columns, and use a list for the aggregating functions:

```
>>> (flights
...      .groupby(['AIRLINE', 'WEEKDAY'])
...      [['CANCELLED', 'DIVERTED']]
...      .agg(['sum', 'mean'])
... )
```

AIRLINE	WEEKDAY	CANCELLED sum	CANCELLED mean	DIVERTED sum	DIVERTED mean
AA	1	41	0.032106	6	0.004699
	2	9	0.007341	2	0.001631
	3	16	0.011949	2	0.001494
	4	20	0.015004	5	0.003751
	5	18	0.014151	1	0.000786
...		...	...	...	...
WN	3	18	0.014118	2	0.001569
	4	10	0.007911	4	0.003165
	5	7	0.005828	0	0.000000
	6	10	0.010132	3	0.003040
	7	7	0.006066	3	0.002600

3. Answer the third query using a dictionary in the .agg method to map specific aggregating columns to specific aggregating functions:

```
>>> (flights
...      .groupby(['ORG_AIR', 'DEST_AIR'])
```

```
...         .agg({'CANCELLED':['sum', 'mean', 'size'],
...              'AIR_TIME':['mean', 'var']})
... )
```

		CANCELLED		...	AIR_TIME	
		sum	mean	...	mean	var
ORG_AIR	DEST_AIR			...		
ATL	ABE	0	0.000000	...	96.387097	45.778495
	ABQ	0	0.000000	...	170.500000	87.866667
	ABY	0	0.000000	...	28.578947	6.590643
	ACY	0	0.000000	...	91.333333	11.466667
	AEX	0	0.000000	...	78.725000	47.332692
...		...	...	...	...	...
SFO	SNA	4	0.032787	...	64.059322	11.338331
	STL	0	0.000000	...	198.900000	101.042105
	SUN	0	0.000000	...	78.000000	25.777778
	TUS	0	0.000000	...	100.200000	35.221053
	XNA	0	0.000000	...	173.500000	0.500000

4. In pandas 0.25, there is a *named aggregation* object that can create non-hierarchical columns. We will repeat the above query using them:

```
>>> (flights
...       .groupby(['ORG_AIR', 'DEST_AIR'])
...       .agg(sum_cancelled=pd.NamedAgg(column='CANCELLED',
aggfunc='sum'),
...            mean_cancelled=pd.NamedAgg(column='CANCELLED',
aggfunc='mean'),
...            size_cancelled=pd.NamedAgg(column='CANCELLED',
aggfunc='size'),
...            mean_air_time=pd.NamedAgg(column='AIR_TIME',
aggfunc='mean'),
...            var_air_time=pd.NamedAgg(column='AIR_TIME',
aggfunc='var'))
... )
```

		sum_cancelled	mean_cancelled	...	mean_air_time
ORG_AIR	DEST_AIR			...	
ATL	ABE	0	0.000000	...	96.387097
	ABQ	0	0.000000	...	170.500000

	ABY	0	0.000000	...	28.578947
	ACY	0	0.000000	...	91.333333
	AEX	0	0.000000	...	78.725000
...		...	...	...	...
SFO	SNA	4	0.032787	...	64.059322
	STL	0	0.000000	...	198.900000
	SUN	0	0.000000	...	78.000000
	TUS	0	0.000000	...	100.200000
	XNA	0	0.000000	...	173.500000

How it works...

To group by multiple columns as in *step 1*, we pass a list of the string names to the `.groupby` method. Each unique combination of AIRLINE and WEEKDAY forms its own group. Within each of these groups, the sum of the canceled flights is calculated and then returned as a Series.

Step 2 groups by both AIRLINE and WEEKDAY, but this time aggregates two columns. It applies each of the two aggregation functions, using the strings sum and mean, to each column, resulting in four returned columns per group.

Step 3 goes even further, and uses a dictionary to map specific aggregating columns to different aggregating functions. Notice that the size aggregating function returns the total number of rows per group. This is different than the count aggregating function, which returns the number of non-missing values per group.

Step 4 shows the new syntax to create flat columns, named aggregations.

There's more...

To flatten the columns in *step 3*, you can use the `.to_flat_index` method (available since pandas 0.24):

```
>>> res = (flights
...        .groupby(['ORG_AIR', 'DEST_AIR'])
...        .agg({'CANCELLED':['sum', 'mean', 'size']
...              'AIR_TIME':['mean', 'var']})
... )
>>> res.columns = ['_'.join(x) for x in
...       res.columns.to_flat_index()]
```

```
>>> res
```

		CANCELLED_sum	CANCELLED_mean	...	AIR_TIME_mean
ORG_AIR	DEST_AIR			...	
ATL	ABE	0	0.000000	...	96.387097
	ABQ	0	0.000000	...	170.500000
	ABY	0	0.000000	...	28.578947
	ACY	0	0.000000	...	91.333333
	AEX	0	0.000000	...	78.725000
...		...	...	...	...
SFO	SNA	4	0.032787	...	64.059322
	STL	0	0.000000	...	198.900000
	SUN	0	0.000000	...	78.000000
	TUS	0	0.000000	...	100.200000
	XNA	0	0.000000	...	173.500000

That is kind of ugly and I would prefer a chain operation to flatten the columns. Unfortunately, the .reindex method does not support flattening. Instead, we will have to leverage the .pipe method:

```
>>> def flatten_cols(df):
...     df.columns = ['_'.join(x) for x in
...         df.columns.to_flat_index()]
...     return df


>>> res = (flights
...     .groupby(['ORG_AIR', 'DEST_AIR'])
...     .agg({'CANCELLED':['sum', 'mean', 'size'],
...         'AIR_TIME':['mean', 'var']})
...     .pipe(flatten_cols)
... )


>>> res
```

		CANCELLED_sum	CANCELLED_mean	...	AIR_TIME_mean
ORG_AIR	DEST_AIR			...	
ATL	ABE	0	0.000000	...	96.387097
	ABQ	0	0.000000	...	170.500000
	ABY	0	0.000000	...	28.578947

	ACY	0	0.000000	...	91.333333
	AEX	0	0.000000	...	78.725000
...		...	...	...	...
SFO	SNA	4	0.032787	...	64.059322
	STL	0	0.000000	...	198.900000
	SUN	0	0.000000	...	78.000000
	TUS	0	0.000000	...	100.200000
	XNA	0	0.000000	...	173.500000

Be aware that when grouping with multiple columns, pandas creates a hierarchical index, or multi-index. In the preceding example, it returned 1,130 rows. However, if one of the columns that we group by is categorical (and has a `category` type, not an `object` type), then pandas will create a Cartesian product of all combinations for each level. In this case, it returns 2,710 rows. However, if you have categorical columns with higher cardinality, you can get many more values:

```
>>> res = (flights
...        .assign(ORG_AIR=flights.ORG_AIR.astype('category'))
...        .groupby(['ORG_AIR', 'DEST_AIR'])
...        .agg({'CANCELLED':['sum', 'mean', 'size'],
...              'AIR_TIME':['mean', 'var']})
... )
>>> res
```

ORG_AIR	DEST_AIR	CANCELLED sum	mean	...	AIR_TIME mean	var
ATL	ABE	0.0	0.0	...	96.387097	45.778495
	ABI	NaN	NaN	...	NaN	NaN
	ABQ	0.0	0.0	...	170.500000	87.866667
	ABR	NaN	NaN	...	NaN	NaN
	ABY	0.0	0.0	...	28.578947	6.590643
...		...	...	...	...	...
SFO	TYS	NaN	NaN	...	NaN	NaN
	VLD	NaN	NaN	...	NaN	NaN
	VPS	NaN	NaN	...	NaN	NaN
	XNA	0.0	0.0	...	173.500000	0.500000
	YUM	NaN	NaN	...	NaN	NaN

To remedy the combinatoric explosion, use the `observed=True` parameter. This makes the categorical group `by`s work like grouping with string types, and only shows the observed values and not the Cartesian product:

```
>>> res = (flights
...        .assign(ORG_AIR=flights.ORG_AIR.astype('category'))
...        .groupby(['ORG_AIR', 'DEST_AIR'], observed=True)
...        .agg({'CANCELLED':['sum', 'mean', 'size'],
...              'AIR_TIME':['mean', 'var']})
... )
>>> res
```

		CANCELLED		...	AIR_TIME	
		sum	mean	...	mean	var
ORG_AIR	DEST_AIR			...		
LAX	ABQ	1	0.018182	...	89.259259	29.403215
	ANC	0	0.000000	...	307.428571	78.952381
	ASE	1	0.038462	...	102.920000	102.243333
	ATL	0	0.000000	...	224.201149	127.155837
	AUS	0	0.000000	...	150.537500	57.897310
...		...	...	...	...	...
MSP	TTN	1	0.125000	...	124.428571	57.952381
	TUL	0	0.000000	...	91.611111	63.075163
	TUS	0	0.000000	...	176.000000	32.000000
	TVC	0	0.000000	...	56.600000	10.300000
	XNA	0	0.000000	...	90.642857	115.939560

Removing the MultiIndex after grouping

Inevitably, when using groupby, you will create a MultiIndex. MultiIndexes can happen in both the index and the columns. DataFrames with MultiIndexes are more difficult to navigate and occasionally have confusing column names as well.

In this recipe, we perform an aggregation with the `.groupby` method to create a DataFrame with a MultiIndex for the rows and columns. Then, we manipulate the index so that it has a single level and the column names are descriptive.

How to do it...

1. Read in the flights dataset, write a statement to find the total and average miles flown, and the maximum and minimum arrival delay for each airline for each weekday:

```
>>> flights = pd.read_csv('data/flights.csv')
>>> airline_info = (flights
...        .groupby(['AIRLINE', 'WEEKDAY'])
...        .agg({'DIST':['sum', 'mean'],
...              'ARR_DELAY':['min', 'max']})
...        .astype(int)
... )
>>> airline_info
```

		DIST		ARR_DELAY	
		sum	mean	min	max
AIRLINE	WEEKDAY				
AA	1	1455386	1139	-60	551
	2	1358256	1107	-52	725
	3	1496665	1117	-45	473
	4	1452394	1089	-46	349
	5	1427749	1122	-41	732
...		...	...	...	...
WN	3	997213	782	-38	262
	4	1024854	810	-52	284
	5	981036	816	-44	244
	6	823946	834	-41	290
	7	945679	819	-45	261

2. Both the rows and columns are labeled by a MultiIndex with two levels. Let's squash both down to just a single level. To address the columns, we use the MultiIndex method, `.to_flat_index`. Let's display the output of each level and then concatenate both levels before setting it as the new column values:

```
>>> airline_info.columns.get_level_values(0)
Index(['DIST', 'DIST', 'ARR_DELAY', 'ARR_DELAY'], dtype='object')
>>> airline_info.columns.get_level_values(1)
Index(['sum', 'mean', 'min', 'max'], dtype='object')

>>> airline_info.columns.to_flat_index()
```

```
Index([('DIST', 'sum'), ('DIST', 'mean'), ('ARR_DELAY', 'min'),
       ('ARR_DELAY', 'max')],
      dtype='object')


>>> airline_info.columns = ['_'.join(x) for x in
...     airline_info.columns.to_flat_index()]

>>> airline_info
```

		DIST_sum	DIST_mean	ARR_DELAY_min	ARR_DELAY_max
AIRLINE	WEEKDAY				
AA	1	1455386	1139	-60	551
	2	1358256	1107	-52	725
	3	1496665	1117	-45	473
	4	1452394	1089	-46	349
	5	1427749	1122	-41	732
...		...	...	...	...
WN	3	997213	782	-38	262
	4	1024854	810	-52	284
	5	981036	816	-44	244
	6	823946	834	-41	290
	7	945679	819	-45	261

3. A quick way to get rid of the row MultiIndex is to use the `.reset_index` method:

```
>>> airline_info.reset_index()
```

	AIRLINE	WEEKDAY	...	ARR_DELAY_min	ARR_DELAY_max
0	AA	1	...	-60	551
1	AA	2	...	-52	725
2	AA	3	...	-45	473
3	AA	4	...	-46	349
4	AA	5	...	-41	732
..	...	...	...	...	...
93	WN	3	...	-38	262
94	WN	4	...	-52	284
95	WN	5	...	-44	244
96	WN	6	...	-41	290
97	WN	7	...	-45	261

4. Refactor the code to make it readable. Use the pandas 0.25 functionality to flatten columns automatically:

```
>>> (flights
...      .groupby(['AIRLINE', 'WEEKDAY'])
...      .agg(dist_sum=pd.NamedAgg(column='DIST', aggfunc='sum'),
...           dist_mean=pd.NamedAgg(column='DIST', aggfunc='mean'),
...           arr_delay_min=pd.NamedAgg(column='ARR_DELAY',
aggfunc='min'),
...           arr_delay_max=pd.NamedAgg(column='ARR_DELAY',
aggfunc='max'))
...      .astype(int)
...      .reset_index()
... )
```

	AIRLINE	WEEKDAY	...	ARR_DELAY_min	ARR_DELAY_max
0	AA	1	...	-60	551
1	AA	2	...	-52	725
2	AA	3	...	-45	473
3	AA	4	...	-46	349
4	AA	5	...	-41	732
..	...	...	...	...	...
93	WN	3	...	-38	262
94	WN	4	...	-52	284
95	WN	5	...	-44	244
96	WN	6	...	-41	290
97	WN	7	...	-45	261

How it works...

When using the `.agg` method to perform an aggregation on multiple columns, pandas creates an index object with two levels. The aggregating columns become the top level, and the aggregating functions become the bottom level. pandas displays MultiIndex levels differently to single-level columns. Except for the innermost levels, repeated index values do not get displayed in Jupyter or a Python shell. You can inspect the DataFrame from *step 1* to verify this. For instance, the `DIST` column shows up only once, but it refers to both of the first two columns.

Step 2 defines new columns by first retrieving the underlying values of each of the levels with the MultiIndex method, `.get_level_values`. This method accepts an integer identifying the index level. They are numbered beginning with zero from the outside (top/left). We use the recently added index method, `.to_flat_index`, in combination with a list comprehension to create strings for each column. We assign these new values to the columns attribute.

In *step 3*, we make use of the `.reset_index` method to push both index levels into columns. This is easy, and I wish there was a similar method for column name compaction.

In *step 4,* we use the `NamedAgg` class (new in pandas 0.25) to create flat aggregate columns.

There's more...

By default, at the end of a `groupby` operation, pandas puts all of the grouping columns in the index. The `as_index` parameter in the `.groupby` method can be set to `False` to avoid this behavior. You can chain the `.reset_index` method after grouping to get the same effect as seen in *step 3*. Let's see an example of this by finding the average distance traveled per flight from each airline:

```
>>> (flights
...        .groupby(['AIRLINE'], as_index=False)
...        ['DIST']
...        .agg('mean')
...        .round(0)
... )
   AIRLINE    DIST
0       AA  1114.0
1       AS  1066.0
2       B6  1772.0
3       DL   866.0
4       EV   460.0
..      ...    ...
9       OO   511.0
10      UA  1231.0
11      US  1181.0
12      VX  1240.0
13      WN   810.0
```

Take a look at the order of the airlines in the previous result. By default, pandas sorts the grouping columns. The `sort` parameter exists within the `.groupby` method and defaults to `True`. You may set it to `False` to keep the order of the grouping columns the same as how they are encountered in the dataset. There is a small performance improvement by not sorting your data.

Grouping with a custom aggregation function

pandas provides a number of aggregation functions to use with the `groupby` object. At some point, you may need to write your own custom user-defined function that does not exist in pandas or NumPy.

In this recipe, we use the college dataset to calculate the mean and standard deviation of the undergraduate student population per state. We then use this information to find the maximum number of standard deviations from the mean that any single population value is per state.

How to do it...

1. Read in the college dataset, and find the mean and standard deviation of the undergraduate population by state:

```
>>> college = pd.read_csv('data/college.csv')
>>> (college
...      .groupby('STABBR')
...      ['UGDS']
...      .agg(['mean', 'std'])
...      .round(0)
... )
            mean        std
STABBR
AK        2493.0     4052.0
AL        2790.0     4658.0
AR        1644.0     3143.0
AS        1276.0        NaN
AZ        4130.0    14894.0
...          ...        ...
VT        1513.0     2194.0
```

```
WA      2271.0    4124.0

WI      2655.0    4615.0

WV      1758.0    5957.0

WY      2244.0    2745.0
```

2. This output isn't quite what we desire. We are not looking for the mean and standard deviations of the entire group but the maximum number of standard deviations away from the mean for any one institution. To calculate this, we need to subtract the mean undergraduate population by state from each institution's undergraduate population and then divide by the standard deviation. This standardizes the undergraduate population for each group. We can then take the maximum of the absolute value of these scores to find the one that is farthest away from the mean. pandas does not provide a function capable of doing this. Instead, we will need to create a custom function:

```
>>> def max_deviation(s):
...         std_score = (s - s.mean()) / s.std()
...         return std_score.abs().max()
```

3. After defining the function, pass it directly to the .agg method to complete the aggregation:

```
>>> (college
...      .groupby('STABBR')
...      ['UGDS']
...      .agg(max_deviation)
...      .round(1)
... )
STABBR
AK      2.6
AL      5.8
AR      6.3
AS      NaN
AZ      9.9
        ...
VT      3.8
WA      6.6
WI      5.8
WV      7.2
WY      2.8
Name: UGDS, Length: 59, dtype: float64
```

How it works...

There is no predefined pandas function to calculate the maximum number of standard deviations away from the mean. We need to write our own function. Notice that this custom function, `max_deviation`, accepts a single parameter, s.

In *step 3*, you will notice that the function name is placed inside the `.agg` method without directly being called. Nowhere is the parameter s explicitly passed to `max_deviation`. Instead, pandas implicitly passes the `UGDS` column as a Series to `max_deviation`.

The `max_deviation` function is called once for each group. As s is a Series, all normal Series methods are available. It subtracts the mean of that particular grouping from each of the values in the group before dividing by the standard deviation in a process called standardization.

As we are interested in absolute deviation from the mean, we take the absolute value from all the standardized scores and return the maximum. The `.agg` method requires that we return a scalar from the function, or else an exception will be raised.

pandas defaults to using the sample standard deviation, which is undefined for any groups with just a single value. For instance, the state abbreviation `AS` (American Samoa) has a missing value returned as it has only a single institution in the dataset.

There's more...

It is possible to apply our custom function to multiple aggregating columns. We simply add more column names to the indexing operator. The `max_deviation` function only works with numeric columns:

```
>>> (college
...     .groupby('STABBR')
...     [['UGDS', 'SATVRMID', 'SATMTMID']]
...     .agg(max_deviation)
...     .round(1)
... )
```

	UGDS	SATVRMID	SATMTMID
STABBR			
AK	2.6	NaN	NaN
AL	5.8	1.6	1.8
AR	6.3	2.2	2.3
AS	NaN	NaN	NaN
AZ	9.9	1.9	1.4

...	...	...	...
VT	3.8	1.9	1.9
WA	6.6	2.2	2.0
WI	5.8	2.4	2.2
WV	7.2	1.7	2.1
WY	2.8	NaN	NaN

You can also use your custom aggregation function along with the prebuilt functions. The following does this and groups by state and religious affiliation:

```
>>> (college
...      .groupby(['STABBR', 'RELAFFIL'])
...      [['UGDS', 'SATVRMID', 'SATMTMID']]
...      .agg([max_deviation, 'mean', 'std'])
...      .round(1)
... )
```

		UGDS			SATMTMID	
		max_deviation	mean	...	mean	std
STABBR	RELAFFIL			...		
AK	0	2.1	3508.9	...	NaN	NaN
	1	1.1	123.3	...	503.0	NaN
AL	0	5.2	3248.8	...	515.8	56.7
	1	2.4	979.7	...	485.6	61.4
AR	0	5.8	1793.7	...	503.6	39.0
...		...	...	...	...	...
WI	0	5.3	2879.1	...	591.2	85.7
	1	3.4	1716.2	...	526.6	42.5
WV	0	6.9	1873.9	...	480.0	27.7
	1	1.3	716.4	...	484.8	17.7
WY	0	2.8	2244.4	...	540.0	NaN

Notice that pandas uses the name of the function as the name for the returned column. You can change the column name directly with the .rename method or you can modify the function attribute .__name__:

```
>>> max_deviation.__name__
'max_deviation'
>>> max_deviation.__name__ = 'Max Deviation'
>>> (college
```

```
...        .groupby(['STABBR', 'RELAFFIL'])
...        [['UGDS', 'SATVRMID', 'SATMTMID']]
...        .agg([max_deviation, 'mean', 'std'])
...        .round(1)
... )
```

		UGDS		...	SATMTMID	
		Max Deviation	mean	...	mean	std
STABBR	RELAFFIL			...		
AK	0	2.1	3508.9	...	NaN	NaN
	1	1.1	123.3	...	503.0	NaN
AL	0	5.2	3248.8	...	515.8	56.7
	1	2.4	979.7	...	485.6	61.4
AR	0	5.8	1793.7	...	503.6	39.0
...		...	...	...	...	...
WI	0	5.3	2879.1	...	591.2	85.7
	1	3.4	1716.2	...	526.6	42.5
WV	0	6.9	1873.9	...	480.0	27.7
	1	1.3	716.4	...	484.8	17.7
WY	0	2.8	2244.4	...	540.0	NaN

Customizing aggregating functions with *args and **kwargs

When writing your own user-defined customized aggregation function, pandas implicitly passes it each of the aggregating columns one at a time as a Series. Occasionally, you will need to pass more arguments to your function than just the Series itself. To do so, you need to be aware of Python's ability to pass an arbitrary number of arguments to functions.

The signature to .agg is agg(func, *args, **kwargs). The func parameter is a reducing function, the string name of a reducing method, a list of reducing functions, or a dictionary mapping columns to functions or a list of functions. Additionally, as we have seen, you can use keyword arguments to create named aggregations.

If you have a reducing function that takes additional arguments that you would like to use, you can leverage the *args and **kwargs parameters to pass arguments to the reduction function. You can use *args to pass an arbitrary number of positional arguments to your customized aggregation function. Similarly, **kwargs allows you to pass an arbitrary number of keyword arguments.

In this recipe, we will build a customized function for the college dataset that finds the percentage of schools by state and religious affiliation that have an undergraduate population between two values.

How to do it...

1. Define a function that returns the percentage of schools with an undergraduate population of between 1,000 and 3,000:

```
>>> def pct_between_1_3k(s):
...     return (s
...         .between(1_000, 3_000)
...         .mean()
...         * 100
...     )
```

2. Calculate this percentage grouping by state and religious affiliation:

```
>>> (college
...     .groupby(['STABBR', 'RELAFFIL'])
...     ['UGDS']
...     .agg(pct_between_1_3k)
...     .round(1)
... )
STABBR  RELAFFIL
AK      0              14.3
        1               0.0
AL      0              23.6
AR      0              27.9
                       ...
WI      0              13.8
        1              36.0
WV      0              24.6
        1              37.5
WY      0              54.5
Name: UGDS, Length: 112, dtype: float64
```

3. This function works, but it does not give the user any flexibility to choose the lower and upper bound. Let's create a new function that allows the user to parameterize these bounds:

```
>>> def pct_between(s, low, high):
...     return s.between(low, high).mean() * 100
```

4. Pass this new function to the `.agg` method along with the lower and upper bounds:

```
>>> (college
...        .groupby(['STABBR', 'RELAFFIL'])
...        ['UGDS']
...        .agg(pct_between, 1_000, 10_000)
...        .round(1)
... )
STABBR   RELAFFIL
AK       0                  42.9
         1                   0.0
AL       0                  45.8
         1                  37.5
AR       0                  39.7
                           ...
WI       0                  31.0
         1                  44.0
WV       0                  29.2
         1                  37.5
WY       0                  72.7
Name: UGDS, Length: 112, dtype: float64
```

How it works...

Step 1 creates a function that doesn't accept any extra arguments. The upper and lower bounds are hardcoded into the function, which isn't very flexible. *Step 2* shows the results of this aggregation.

We create a more flexible function in *step 3* where we parameterize both the lower and upper bounds dynamically. *Step 4* is where the magic of `*args` and `**kwargs` comes into play. In this particular example, we pass two non-keyword arguments, `1_000` and `10_000`, to the `.agg` method. pandas passes these two arguments respectively to the `low` and `high` parameters of `pct_between`.

There are a few ways we could achieve the same result in *step 4*. We could have explicitly used keyword parameters to produce the same result:

```
(college
    .groupby(['STABBR', 'RELAFFIL'])
    ['UGDS']
```

```
        .agg(pct_between, high=10_000, low=1_000)
        .round(1)
)
```

There's more...

If we want to call multiple aggregation functions and some of them need parameters, we can utilize Python's closure functionality to create a new function that has the parameters closed over in its calling environment:

```
>>> def between_n_m(n, m):
...     def wrapper(ser):
...         return pct_between(ser, n, m)
...     wrapper.__name__ = f'between_{n}_{m}'
...     return wrapper

>>> (college
...     .groupby(['STABBR', 'RELAFFIL'])
...     ['UGDS']
...     .agg([between_n_m(1_000, 10_000), 'max', 'mean'])
...     .round(1)
... )
                 between_1000_10000       max     mean
STABBR RELAFFIL
AK     0                       42.9   12865.0   3508.9
       1                        0.0     275.0    123.3
AL     0                       45.8   29851.0   3248.8
       1                       37.5    3033.0    979.7
AR     0                       39.7   21405.0   1793.7
...                             ...       ...      ...
WI     0                       31.0   29302.0   2879.1
       1                       44.0    8212.0   1716.2
WV     0                       29.2   44924.0   1873.9
       1                       37.5    1375.0    716.4
WY     0                       72.7    9910.0   2244.4
```

Examining the groupby object

The immediate result from using the `.groupby` method on a DataFrame is a `groupby` object. Usually, we chain operations on this object to do aggregations or transformations without ever storing the intermediate values in variables.

In this recipe, we examine the `groupby` object to examine individual groups.

How to do it...

1. Let's get started by grouping the state and religious affiliation columns from the college dataset, saving the result to a variable and confirming its type:

```
>>> college = pd.read_csv('data/college.csv')
>>> grouped = college.groupby(['STABBR', 'RELAFFIL'])
>>> type(grouped)
<class 'pandas.core.groupby.generic.DataFrameGroupBy'>
```

2. Use the `dir` function to discover the attributes of a `groupby` object:

```
>>> print([attr for attr in dir(grouped) if not
...       attr.startswith('_')])
['CITY', 'CURROPER', 'DISTANCEONLY', 'GRAD_DEBT_MDN_SUPP', 'HBCU',
'INSTNM',

'MD_EARN_ WNE_P10', 'MENONLY', 'PCTFLOAN', 'PCTPELL', 'PPTUG_EF',
'RELAFFIL',

'SATMTMID', 'SATVRMID' , 'STABBR', 'UG25ABV', 'UGDS', 'UGDS_2MOR',
'UGDS_AIAN',

'UGDS_ASIAN', 'UGDS_BLACK', 'UGDS _HISP', 'UGDS_NHPI', 'UGDS_NRA',
'UGDS_UNKN',

'UGDS_WHITE', 'WOMENONLY', 'agg', 'aggregate ', 'all', 'any',
'apply',

'backfill', 'bfill', 'boxplot', 'corr', 'corrwith', 'count', 'co
v', 'cumcount',

'cummax', 'cummin', 'cumprod', 'cumsum', 'describe', 'diff',
'dtypes', 'ex

panding', 'ffill', 'fillna', 'filter', 'first', 'get_group',
'groups', 'head',

'hist', 'id xmax', 'idxmin', 'indices', 'last', 'mad', 'max',
'mean', 'median',

'min', 'ndim', 'ngroup ', 'ngroups', 'nth', 'nunique', 'ohlc',
'pad',
```

```
'pct_change', 'pipe', 'plot', 'prod', 'quan tile', 'rank',
'resample',
'rolling', 'sem', 'shift', 'size', 'skew', 'std', 'sum', 'tail' ,
'take',
'transform', 'tshift', 'var']
```

3. Find the number of groups with the `.ngroups` attribute:

```
>>> grouped.ngroups
112
```

4. To find the uniquely identifying labels for each group, look in the `.groups` attribute, which contains a dictionary of each unique group mapped to all the corresponding index labels of that group. Because we grouped by two columns, each of the keys has a tuple, one value for the STABBR column and another for the RELAFFIL column:

```
>>> groups = list(grouped.groups)
>>> groups[:6]
[('AK', 0), ('AK', 1), ('AL', 0), ('AL', 1), ('AR', 0), ('AR', 1)]
```

5. Retrieve a single group with the `.get_group` method by passing it a tuple of an exact group label. For example, to get all the religiously affiliated schools in the state of Florida, do the following:

```
>>> grouped.get_group(('FL', 1))
```

	INSTNM	CITY	...	MD_EARN_WNE_P10	GRAD_DEBT_MDN_SUPP
712	The Bapt...	Graceville	...	30800	20052
713	Barry Un...	Miami	...	44100	28250
714	Gooding ...	Panama City	...	NaN	PrivacyS...
715	Bethune-...	Daytona ...	...	29400	36250
724	Johnson ...	Kissimmee	...	26300	20199
...	...	...	...	...	...
7486	Strayer ...	Coral Sp...	...	49200	36173.5
7487	Strayer ...	Fort Lau...	...	49200	36173.5
7488	Strayer ...	Miramar	...	49200	36173.5
7489	Strayer ...	Miami	...	49200	36173.5
7490	Strayer ...	Miami	...	49200	36173.5

6. You may want to take a peek at each individual group. This is possible because `groupby` objects are iterable. If you are in Jupyter, you can leverage the `display` function to show each group in a single cell (otherwise, Jupyter will only show the result of the last statement of the cell):

```
from IPython.display import display
```

```
for name, group in grouped:
    print(name)
    display(group.head(3))
```

Displaying multiple dataframes

However, I typically want to see some example data from a single group to figure out what function I want to apply to the groups. If I know the names of the values from the columns I grouped by, I can use the previous step. Often, I don't know those names, but I also don't need to see all of the groups. The following is some debugging of the code that is usually sufficient to understand what a group looks like:

```
>>> for name, group in grouped:
...     print(name)
...     print(group)
...     break
('AK', 0)
         INSTNM        CITY  ...  MD_EARN_WNE_P10  GRAD_DEBT_MDN_
SUPP
60   Universi...   Anchorage  ...          42500          19449.5
62   Universi...   Fairbanks  ...          36200          19355
```

63	Universi...	Juneau	...	37400	16875
65	AVTEC-Al...	Seward	...	33500	PrivacyS...
66	Charter ...	Anchorage	...	39200	13875
67	Alaska C...	Anchorage	...	28700	8994
5171	Ilisagvi...	Barrow	...	24900	PrivacyS...

7. You can also call the `.head` method on your `groupby` object to get the first rows of each group together in a single DataFrame:

```
>>> grouped.head(2)
```

	INSTNM	CITY	...	MD_EARN_WNE_P10	GRAD_DEBT_MDN_SUPP
0	Alabama ...	Normal	...	30300	33888
1	Universi...	Birmingham	...	39700	21941.5
2	Amridge ...	Montgomery	...	40100	23370
10	Birmingh...	Birmingham	...	44200	27000
43	Prince I...	Elmhurst	...	PrivacyS...	20992
...	...	...	...	...	...
5289	Pacific ...	Mangilao	...	PrivacyS...	PrivacyS...
6439	Touro Un...	Henderson	...	NaN	PrivacyS...
7352	Marinell...	Henderson	...	21200	9796.5
7404	Universi...	St. Croix	...	31800	15150
7419	Computer...	Las Cruces	...	21300	14250

How it works...

Step 1 creates our `groupby` object. We can display all the public attributes and methods to reveal the functionality of an object as was done in *step 2*. Each group is uniquely identified by a tuple containing a unique combination of the values in the grouping columns. pandas allows you to select a specific group as a DataFrame with the `.get_group` method shown in *step 5*.

It is rare that you will need to iterate through your groups. In fact, you should avoid doing so, as it can be quite slow. Occasionally, however, you will have no other choice. When iterating through a `groupby` object, you are given a tuple containing the group name and the DataFrame with the grouping columns moved into the index. This tuple is unpacked into the `name` and `group` variables in the `for` loop in *step 6*.

One thing you can do while iterating through your groups is to display a few of the rows from each group directly in the notebook. To do this, you can either use the `print` function or the `display` function from the `IPython.display` module if you are using Jupyter.

There's more...

There are several useful methods that were not explored from the list in *step 2*. Take, for instance, the .nth method, which, when provided with a list of integers, selects those specific rows from each group. For example, the following operation selects the first and last rows from each group:

```
>>> grouped.nth([1, -1])
```

		INSTNM	CITY	...	MD_EARN_WNE_P10
STABBR	RELAFFIL			...	
AK	0	Universi...	Fairbanks	...	36200
	0	Ilisagvi...	Barrow	...	24900
	1	Alaska P...	Anchorage	...	47000
	1	Alaska C...	Soldotna	...	NaN
AL	0	Universi...	Birmingham	...	39700
...		...	...	...	...
WV	0	BridgeVa...	South C...	...	NaN
	1	Appalach...	Mount Hope	...	28700
	1	West Vir...	Nutter Fort	...	16700
WY	0	Central ...	Riverton	...	25200
	0	CollegeA...	Cheyenne	...	25600

Filtering for states with a minority majority

Previously, we examined using Boolean arrays to filter rows. In a similar fashion, when using the .groupby method, we can filter out groups. The .filter method of the groupby object accepts a function that must return either True or False to indicate whether a group is kept.

This .filter method applied after a call to the .groupby method is completely different to the DataFrame .filter method covered in the *Selecting columns with methods* recipe from *Chapter 2, Essential DataFrame Operations*.

One thing to be aware of is that when the .filter method is applied, the result does not use the grouping columns as the index, but keeps the original index! The DataFrame .filter method filters columns, not values.

In this recipe, we use the college dataset to find all the states that have more non-white undergraduate students than white. This is a dataset from the US, where whites form the majority and therefore, we are looking for states with a minority majority.

How to do it...

1. Read in the college dataset, group by state, and display the total number of groups. This should equal the number of unique states retrieved from the `.nunique` Series method:

    ```
    >>> college = pd.read_csv('data/college.csv', index_col='INSTNM')
    >>> grouped = college.groupby('STABBR')
    >>> grouped.ngroups
    59
    >>> college['STABBR'].nunique() # verifying the same number
    59
    ```

2. The grouped variable has a `.filter` method, which accepts a custom function that determines whether a group is kept. The custom function accepts a DataFrame of the current group and is required to return a Boolean. Let's define a function that calculates the total percentage of minority students and returns `True` if this percentage is greater than a user-defined threshold:

    ```
    >>> def check_minority(df, threshold):
    ...     minority_pct = 1 - df['UGDS_WHITE']
    ...     total_minority = (df['UGDS'] * minority_pct).sum()
    ...     total_ugds = df['UGDS'].sum()
    ...     total_minority_pct = total_minority / total_ugds
    ...     return total_minority_pct > threshold
    ```

3. Use the `.filter` method passed with the `check_minority` function and a threshold of 50% to find all states that have a minority majority:

    ```
    >>> college_filtered = grouped.filter(check_minority,
    threshold=.5)
    >>> college_filtered
    ```

	CITY	STABBR	...	MD_EARN_WNE_P10	GRAD_DEBT_ MDN_SUPP
INSTNM			...		
Everest C...	Phoenix	AZ	...	28600	9500
Collins C...	Phoenix	AZ	...	25700	47000
Empire Be...	Phoenix	AZ	...	17800	9588
Empire Be...	Tucson	AZ	...	18200	9833
Thunderbi...	Glendale	AZ	...	118900	

```
PrivacyS...

...                     ...     ...   ...              ...
...
WestMed C...        Merced      CA    ...      NaN
15623.5Vantage C...     El Paso      TX   ...              NaN
9500

SAE Insti...    Emeryville      CA    ...      NaN
9500

Bay Area ...    San Jose        CA    ...      NaN
PrivacyS...

Excel Lea...  San Antonio       TX    ...      NaN
12125
```

4. Just looking at the output may not be indicative of what happened. The DataFrame starts with the state of Arizona (AZ) and not Alaska (AK), so we can visually confirm that something changed. Let's compare the shape of this filtered DataFrame with the original. Looking at the results, about 60% of the rows have been filtered, and only 20 states remain that have a minority majority:

```
>>> college.shape
(7535, 26)
>>> college_filtered.shape
(3028, 26)
>>> college_filtered['STABBR'].nunique()
20
```

How it works...

This recipe takes a look at the total population of all the institutions on a state-by-state basis. The goal is to keep all the rows from the states, as a whole, that have a minority majority. This requires us to group our data by state, which we do in *step 1*. We find that there are 59 independent groups.

The `.filter` groupby method either keeps all the rows in a group or filters them out. It does not change the number of columns. The `.filter` groupby method performs this gatekeeping through a user-defined function, `check_minority`, in this recipe. This function accepts a DataFrame of each group and needs to return a Boolean.

Inside the `check_minority` function, the percentage and the total number of non-white students for each institution are first calculated followed by the total number of all students. Finally, the percentage of non-white students for the entire state is checked against the given threshold, which produces a Boolean.

The final result is a DataFrame with the same columns as the original (and the same index, not the grouped index), but with the rows from the states that don't meet the threshold filtered out. As it is possible that the head of the filtered DataFrame is the same as the original, you need to do some inspection to ensure that the operation completed successfully. We verify this by checking the number of rows and unique states.

There's more...

Our function, `check_minority`, is flexible and accepts a parameter to lower or raise the percentage of minority threshold. Let's check the shape and number of unique states for a couple of other thresholds:

```
>>> college_filtered_20 = grouped.filter(check_minority, threshold=.2)
>>> college_filtered_20.shape
(7461, 26)
>>> college_filtered_20['STABBR'].nunique()
57
>>> college_filtered_70 = grouped.filter(check_minority, threshold=.7)
>>> college_filtered_70.shape
(957, 26)
>>> college_filtered_70['STABBR'].nunique()
10
```

Transforming through a weight loss bet

One method to increase motivation to lose weight is to make a bet with someone else. The scenario in this recipe will track weight loss from two individuals throughout a four-month period and determine a winner.

In this recipe, we use simulated data from two individuals to track the percentage of weight loss over four months. At the end of each month, a winner will be declared based on the individual who lost the highest percentage of body weight for that month. To track weight loss, we group our data by month and person, and then call the `.transform` method to find the percentage weight loss change for each week against the start of the month.

We will use the `.transform` method in this recipe. This method returns a new object that preserves the index of the original DataFrame but allows you to do calculations on groups of the data.

How to do it...

1. Read in the raw `weight_loss` dataset, and examine the first month of data from the two people, Amy and Bob. There are a total of four weigh-ins per month:

```
>>> weight_loss = pd.read_csv('data/weight_loss.csv')
>>> weight_loss.query('Month == "Jan"')
```

	Name	Month	Week	Weight
0	Bob	Jan	Week 1	291
1	Amy	Jan	Week 1	197
2	Bob	Jan	Week 2	288
3	Amy	Jan	Week 2	189
4	Bob	Jan	Week 3	283
5	Amy	Jan	Week 3	189
6	Bob	Jan	Week 4	283
7	Amy	Jan	Week 4	190

2. To determine the winner for each month, we only need to compare weight loss from the first week to the last week of each month. But, if we wanted to have weekly updates, we can also calculate weight loss from the current week to the first week of each month. Let's create a function that is capable of providing weekly updates. It will take a Series and return a Series of the same size:

```
>>> def percent_loss(s):
...         return ((s - s.iloc[0]) / s.iloc[0]) * 100
```

3. Let's test out this function for Bob during the month of January:

```
>>> (weight_loss
...         .query('Name=="Bob" and Month=="Jan"')
...         ['Weight']
...         .pipe(percent_loss)
... )
0    0.000000
2   -1.030928
4   -2.749141
6   -2.749141
Name: Weight, dtype: float64
```

4. After the first week, Bob lost 1% of his body weight. He continued losing weight during the second week but made no progress during the last week. We can apply this function to every single combination of person and month to get the weight loss per week in relation to the first week of the month. To do this, we need to group our data by `Name` and `Month`, and then use the `.transform` method to apply this custom function. The function we pass to `.transform` needs to maintain the index of the group that is passed into it, so we can use `percent_loss` here:

```
>>> (weight_loss
...         .groupby(['Name', 'Month'])
...         ['Weight']
...         .transform(percent_loss)
... )
0       0.000000
1       0.000000
2      -1.030928
3      -4.060914
4      -2.749141
         ...
27     -3.529412
28     -3.065134
29     -3.529412
30     -4.214559
31     -5.294118
Name: Weight, Length: 32, dtype: float64
```

5. The `.transform` method takes a function that returns an object with the same index (and the same number of rows) as was passed into it. Because it has the same index, we can insert it as a column. The `.transform` method is useful for summarizing information from the groups and then adding it back to the original DataFrame. We will also filter down to two months of data for Bob:

```
>>> (weight_loss
...         .assign(percent_loss=(weight_loss
...             .groupby(['Name', 'Month'])
...             ['Weight']
...             .transform(percent_loss)
...             .round(1)))
...         .query('Name=="Bob" and Month in ["Jan", "Feb"]')
... )
```

```
     Name Month    Week  Weight  percent_loss
0    Bob   Jan   Week 1    291           0.0
2    Bob   Jan   Week 2    288          -1.0
4    Bob   Jan   Week 3    283          -2.7
6    Bob   Jan   Week 4    283          -2.7
8    Bob   Feb   Week 1    283           0.0
10   Bob   Feb   Week 2    275          -2.8
12   Bob   Feb   Week 3    268          -5.3
14   Bob   Feb   Week 4    268          -5.3
```

6. Notice that the percentage of weight loss resets after the new month. With this new `percent_loss` column, we can manually determine a winner but let's see whether we can find a way to do this automatically. As the only week that matters is the last week, let's select week 4:

```
>>> (weight_loss
...       .assign(percent_loss=(weight_loss
...           .groupby(['Name', 'Month'])
...           ['Weight']
...           .transform(percent_loss)
...           .round(1)))
...       .query('Week == "Week 4"')
... )
     Name Month    Week  Weight  percent_loss
6    Bob   Jan   Week 4    283          -2.7
7    Amy   Jan   Week 4    190          -3.6
14   Bob   Feb   Week 4    268          -5.3
15   Amy   Feb   Week 4    173          -8.9
22   Bob   Mar   Week 4    261          -2.6
23   Amy   Mar   Week 4    170          -1.7
30   Bob   Apr   Week 4    250          -4.2
31   Amy   Apr   Week 4    161          -5.3
```

7. This narrows down the weeks but still doesn't automatically find out the winner of each month. Let's reshape this data with the `.pivot` method so that Bob's and Amy's percent weight loss is side by side for each month:

```
>>> (weight_loss
...       .assign(percent_loss=(weight_loss
...           .groupby(['Name', 'Month'])
```

```
...              ['Weight']
...                .transform(percent_loss)
...                .round(1)))
...          .query('Week == "Week 4"')
...          .pivot(index='Month', columns='Name',
...                values='percent_loss')
... )
Name    Amy   Bob
Month
Apr    -5.3  -4.2
Feb    -8.9  -5.3
Jan    -3.6  -2.7
Mar    -1.7  -2.6
```

8. This output makes it clearer who has won each month, but we can still go a couple of steps further. NumPy has a vectorized `if then else` function called `where`, which can map a Series or array of Booleans to other values. Let's create a column, `winner`, with the name of the winner:

```
>>> (weight_loss
...        .assign(percent_loss=(weight_loss
...            .groupby(['Name', 'Month'])
...            ['Weight']
...            .transform(percent_loss)
...            .round(1)))
...          .query('Week == "Week 4"')
...          .pivot(index='Month', columns='Name',
...                values='percent_loss')
...          .assign(winner=lambda df_:
...                np.where(df_.Amy < df_.Bob, 'Amy', 'Bob'))
... )
Name    Amy   Bob  winner
Month
Apr    -5.3  -4.2      Amy
Feb    -8.9  -5.3      Amy
Jan    -3.6  -2.7      Amy
Mar    -1.7  -2.6      Bob
```

In Jupyter, you can highlight the winning percentage for each month using the `.style` attribute:

```
(weight_loss
    .assign(percent_loss=(weight_loss
        .groupby(['Name', 'Month'])
        ['Weight']
        .transform(percent_loss)
        .round(1)))
    .query('Week == "Week 4"')
    .pivot(index='Month', columns='Name',
           values='percent_loss')
    .assign(winner=lambda df_:
            np.where(df_.Amy < df_.Bob, 'Amy', 'Bob'))
    .style.highlight_min(axis=1)
)
```

```
In [112]: (weight_loss
              .assign(percent_loss=(weight_loss
                  .groupby(['Name', 'Month'])
                  ['Weight']
                  .transform(percent_loss)
                  .round(1)))
              .query('Week == "Week 4"')
              .pivot(index='Month', columns='Name',
                     values='percent_loss')
              .assign(winner=lambda df_:
                      np.where(df_.Amy < df_.Bob, 'Amy', 'Bob'))
              .style.highlight_min(axis=1)
          )
```

Out[112]:

Name	Amy	Bob	winner
Month			
Apr	-5.3	-4.2	Amy
Feb	-8.9	-5.3	Amy
Jan	-3.6	-2.7	Amy
Mar	-1.7	-2.6	Bob

The highlight minimum

9. Use the `.value_counts` method to return the final score as the number of months won:

```
>>> (weight_loss
...     .assign(percent_loss=(weight_loss
```

```
   ...              .groupby(['Name', 'Month'])
   ...              ['Weight']
   ...              .transform(percent_loss)
   ...              .round(1)))
   ...          .query('Week == "Week 4"')
   ...          .pivot(index='Month', columns='Name',
   ...                 values='percent_loss')
   ...          .assign(winner=lambda df_:
   ...                  np.where(df_.Amy < df_.Bob, 'Amy', 'Bob'))
   ...          .winner
   ...          .value_counts()
   ... )
Amy     3
Bob     1
Name: winner, dtype: int64
```

How it works...

Throughout this recipe, the `.query` method is used to filter data instead of using Boolean arrays. Refer to the *Improving readability of Boolean indexing with the query method* recipe in *Chapter 7, Filtering Rows* for more information.

Our goal is to find the percentage weight loss for each month for each person. One way to accomplish this task is to calculate each week's weight loss relative to the start of each month. This specific task is perfectly suited to the `.transform` groupby method. The `.transform` method requires a function as a parameter. This function gets passed each group (which can be a Series or DataFrame). It must return a sequence of values the same length as the group that was passed in or else an exception will be raised. No aggregation or filtering takes place.

Step 2 creates a function that calculates the percent age loss (or gain) relative to the first value. It subtracts the first value of the passed Series from all of its values and then divides this result by the first value. In *step 3*, we test this function on one person during one month.

In *step 4*, we use `.groupby` with `.transform` to run this function over every combination of person and month. We are transforming the `Weight` column into the percentage of weight lost in the current week.

The first month of data is outputted for each person in *step 6*. pandas returns the new data as a Series. This Series isn't all that useful by itself and makes more sense appended to the original DataFrame as a new column. We complete this operation in *step 5*.

To determine the winner, only week 4 of each month is necessary. We could stop here and manually determine the winner, but pandas supplies us with the functionality to automate this. The .pivot function in *step 7* reshapes our dataset by pivoting the unique values of one column into new column names. The index parameter is used for the column that you do not want to pivot. The column passed to the values parameter gets tiled over each unique combination of the columns in the index and columns parameters.

The .pivot method only works if there is just a single occurrence of each unique combination of the columns in the index and columns parameters. If there is more than one unique combination, an exception is raised. You can use the .pivot_table or .groupby method in that situation.

Here is an example of using .groupby with .unstack to emulate the pivot functionality:

```
>>> (weight_loss
...      .assign(percent_loss=(weight_loss
...          .groupby(['Name', 'Month'])
...          ['Weight']
...          .transform(percent_loss)
...          .round(1)))
...      .query('Week == "Week 4"')
...      .groupby(['Month', 'Name'])
...      ['percent_loss']
...      .first()
...      .unstack()
... )
Name    Amy   Bob
Month
Apr     -5.3  -4.2
Feb     -8.9  -5.3
Jan     -3.6  -2.7
Mar     -1.7  -2.6
```

After pivoting, we utilize the NumPy where function, whose first argument is a condition that produces a Series of Booleans. True values get mapped to Amy, and False values get mapped to Bob. We highlight the winner of each month and tally the final score with the .value_counts method.

There's more...

Take a look at the DataFrame output from *step 7*. Did you notice that the months are in alphabetical and not chronological order? pandas unfortunately, in this case at least, orders the months for us alphabetically. We can solve this issue by changing the data type of `Month` to a categorical variable. Categorical variables map all the values of each column to an integer. We can choose this mapping to be the normal chronological order for the months. pandas uses this underlying integer mapping during the `.pivot` method to order the months chronologically:

```
>>> (weight_loss
...        .assign(percent_loss=(weight_loss
...            .groupby(['Name', 'Month'])
...            ['Weight']
...            .transform(percent_loss)
...            .round(1)),
...                Month=pd.Categorical(weight_loss.Month,
...                    categories=['Jan', 'Feb', 'Mar', 'Apr'],
...                    ordered=True))
...        .query('Week == "Week 4"')
...        .pivot(index='Month', columns='Name',
...            values='percent_loss')
... )
Name    Amy   Bob
Month
Jan    -3.6  -2.7
Feb    -8.9  -5.3
Mar    -1.7  -2.6
Apr    -5.3  -4.2
```

To convert `Month` to an ordered category column, use the `Categorical` constructor. Pass it the original column as a Series and a unique sequence of all the categories in the desired order to the `categories` parameter. In general, to sort columns of the `object` data type by something other than alphabetical, convert them to categorical.

Calculating weighted mean SAT scores per state with apply

The `groupby` object has four methods that accept a function (or functions) to perform a calculation on each group. These four methods are `.agg`, `.filter`, `.transform`, and `.apply`. Each of the first three of these methods has a very specific output that the function must return. `.agg` must return a scalar value, `.filter` must return a Boolean, and `.transform` must return a Series or DataFrame with the same length as the passed group. The `.apply` method, however, may return a scalar value, a Series, or even a DataFrame of any shape, therefore making it very flexible. It is also called only once per group (on a DataFrame), while the `.transform` and `.agg` methods get called once for each aggregating column (on a Series). The `.apply` method's ability to return a single object when operating on multiple columns at the same time makes the calculation in this recipe possible.

In this recipe, we calculate the weighted average of both the math and verbal SAT scores per state from the college dataset. We weight the scores by the population of undergraduate students per school.

How to do it...

1. Read in the college dataset, and drop any rows that have missing values in the UGDS, SATMTMID, or SATVRMID columns. We do not want any missing values for those columns:

```
>>> college = pd.read_csv('data/college.csv')
>>> subset = ['UGDS', 'SATMTMID', 'SATVRMID']
>>> college2 = college.dropna(subset=subset)
>>> college.shape
(7535, 27)
>>> college2.shape
(1184, 27)
```

2. The vast majority of institutions do not have data for our three required columns, but this is still more than enough data to continue. Next, create a user-defined function to calculate the weighted average of the SAT math scores:

```
>>> def weighted_math_average(df):
...     weighted_math = df['UGDS'] * df['SATMTMID']
...     return int(weighted_math.sum() / df['UGDS'].sum())
```

3. Group by state and pass this function to the `.apply` method. Because each group has multiple columns and we want to reduce those to a single value, we need to use `.apply`. The `weighted_math_average` function will be called once for each group (not on the individual columns in the group):

```
>>> college2.groupby('STABBR').apply(weighted_math_average)
STABBR
AK     503
AL     536
AR     529
AZ     569
CA     564

      . . .

VT     566
WA     555
WI     593
WV     500
WY     540
Length: 53, dtype: int64
```

4. We successfully returned a scalar value for each group. Let's take a small detour and see what the outcome would have been by passing the same function to the `.agg` method (which calls the function for every column):

```
>>> (college2
...        .groupby('STABBR')
...        .agg(weighted_math_average)
... )
Traceback (most recent call last):
    . . .
KeyError: 'UGDS'
```

5. The `weighted_math_average` function gets applied to each non-aggregating column in the DataFrame. If you try and limit the columns to just SATMTMID, you will get an error as you won't have access to UGDS. So, the best way to complete operations that act on multiple columns is with `.apply`:

```
>>> (college2
...        .groupby('STABBR')
...        ['SATMTMID']
...        .agg(weighted_math_average)
... )
```

```
Traceback (most recent call last):

    ...

KeyError: 'UGDS'
```

6. A nice feature of `.apply` is that you can create multiple new columns by returning a Series. The index of this returned Series will be the new column names. Let's modify our function to calculate the weighted and arithmetic average for both SAT scores along with the count of the number of institutions from each group. We return these five values in a Series:

```
>>> def weighted_average(df):
...     weight_m = df['UGDS'] * df['SATMTMID']
...     weight_v = df['UGDS'] * df['SATVRMID']
...     wm_avg = weight_m.sum() / df['UGDS'].sum()
...     wv_avg = weight_v.sum() / df['UGDS'].sum()
...     data = {'w_math_avg': wm_avg,
...             'w_verbal_avg': wv_avg,
...             'math_avg': df['SATMTMID'].mean(),
...             'verbal_avg': df['SATVRMID'].mean(),
...             'count': len(df)
...     }
...     return pd.Series(data)
>>> (college2
...     .groupby('STABBR')
...     .apply(weighted_average)
...     .astype(int)
... )
```

STABBR	w_math_avg	w_verbal_avg	math_avg	verbal_avg	count
AK	503	555	503	555	1
AL	536	533	504	508	21
AR	529	504	515	491	16
AZ	569	557	536	538	6
CA	564	539	562	549	72
...	...	...	...	...	...
VT	566	564	526	527	8
WA	555	541	551	548	18
WI	593	556	545	516	14
WV	500	487	481	473	17
WY	540	535	540	535	1

How it works...

In order for this recipe to complete correctly, we need to filter for institutions that do not have missing values for UGDS, SATMTMID, and SATVRMID. By default, the .dropna method drops rows that have one or more missing values. We must use the subset parameter to limit the columns it looks at. It only considers the UGDS, SATMTMID, or SATVRMID columns for missing values.

If we do not remove the missing values, it will throw off the computations for the weighted averages. Next, you can see that the weighted scores for AK are 5 and 6, which does not make sense:

```
>>> (college
...       .groupby('STABBR')
...       .apply(weighted_average)
... )
```

STABBR	w_math_avg	w_verbal_avg	math_avg	verbal_avg	count
AK	5.548091	6.121651	503.000000	555.000000	10.0
AL	261.895658	260.550109	504.285714	508.476190	96.0
AR	301.054792	287.264872	515.937500	491.875000	86.0
AS	0.000000	0.000000	NaN	NaN	1.0
AZ	61.815821	60.511712	536.666667	538.333333	133.0
...	...	...	...	...	...
VT	389.967094	388.696848	526.875000	527.500000	27.0
WA	274.885878	267.880280	551.222222	548.333333	123.0
WI	153.803086	144.160115	545.071429	516.857143	112.0
WV	224.697582	218.843452	481.705882	473.411765	73.0
WY	216.761180	214.754132	540.000000	535.000000	11.0

In *step 2*, we define a function that calculates the weighted average for just the SATMTMID column. The weighted average differs from the arithmetic mean because each value is multiplied by a weight. This quantity is then summed and divided by the sum of the weights. In this case, our weight is the undergraduate student population.

In *step 3*, we pass this function to the .apply method. Our function, weighted_math_average, gets passed a DataFrame of all the original columns for each group. It returns a single scalar value, the weighted average of SATMTMID. At this point, you might think that this calculation is possible using the .agg method. Directly replacing .apply with .agg does not work as .agg returns a value for each of its aggregating columns.

Step 6 shows the versatility of `.apply`. We build a new function that calculates the weighted and arithmetic average of both SAT columns as well as the number of rows for each group. To use `.apply` to create multiple columns, you must return a Series. The index values are used as column names in the resulting DataFrame. You can return as many values as you want with this method.

Note that because I'm using a Python version greater than 3.5, I can use a normal dictionary in `weighted_average` to create a Series. This is because since Python 3.6, the dictionary is sorted by default.

There's more...

In this recipe, we returned a single row as a Series for each group. It's possible to return any number of rows and columns for each group by returning a DataFrame.

In addition to finding just the arithmetic and weighted means, let's also find the geometric and harmonic means of both SAT columns and return the results as a DataFrame with rows as the name of the type of mean and columns as the SAT type. To ease the burden on us, we use the NumPy function average to compute the weighted average and the SciPy functions `gmean` and `hmean` for geometric and harmonic means:

```
>>> from scipy.stats import gmean, hmean
>>> def calculate_means(df):
...     df_means = pd.DataFrame(index=['Arithmetic', 'Weighted',
...                                     'Geometric', 'Harmonic'])
...     cols = ['SATMTMID', 'SATVRMID']
...     for col in cols:
...         arithmetic = df[col].mean()
...         weighted = np.average(df[col], weights=df['UGDS'])
...         geometric = gmean(df[col])
...         harmonic = hmean(df[col])
...         df_means[col] = [arithmetic, weighted,
...                          geometric, harmonic]
...     df_means['count'] = len(df)
...     return df_means.astype(int)
>>> (college2
...     .groupby('STABBR')
...     .apply(calculate_means)
... )
```

	SATMTMID	SATVRMID	count

STABBR				
AK	Arithmetic	503	555	1
	Weighted	503	555	1
	Geometric	503	555	1
	Harmonic	503	555	1
AL	Arithmetic	504	508	21
...		...	...	...
WV	Harmonic	480	472	17
WY	Arithmetic	540	535	1
	Weighted	540	535	1
	Geometric	540	534	1
	Harmonic	540	535	1

Grouping by continuous variables

When grouping in pandas, you typically use columns with discrete repeating values. If there are no repeated values, then grouping would be pointless as there would only be one row per group. Continuous numeric columns typically have few repeated values and are generally not used to form groups. However, if we can transform columns with continuous values into a discrete column by placing each value in a bin, rounding them, or using some other mapping, then grouping with them makes sense.

In this recipe, we explore the flights dataset to discover the distribution of airlines for different travel distances. This allows us, for example, to find the airline that makes the most flights between 500 and 1,000 miles. To accomplish this, we use the pandas cut function to discretize the distance of each flight flown.

How to do it...

1. Read in the flights dataset:

```
>>> flights = pd.read_csv('data/flights.csv')
>>> flights
```

	MONTH	DAY	WEEKDAY	...	ARR_DELAY	DIVERTED	CANCELLED
0	1	1	4	...	65.0	0	0
1	1	1	4	...	-13.0	0	0
2	1	1	4	...	35.0	0	0
3	1	1	4	...	-7.0	0	0
4	1	1	4	...	39.0	0	0

...	...	...	...	...	...	...	...
58487	12	31	4	...	-19.0	0	0
58488	12	31	4	...	4.0	0	0
58489	12	31	4	...	-5.0	0	0
58490	12	31	4	...	34.0	0	0
58491	12	31	4	...	-1.0	0	0

2. If we want to find the distribution of airlines over a range of distances, we need to place the values of the DIST column into discrete bins. Let's use the pandas cut function to split the data into five bins:

```
>>> bins = [-np.inf, 200, 500, 1000, 2000, np.inf]
>>> cuts = pd.cut(flights['DIST'], bins=bins)
>>> cuts
0           (500.0, 1000.0]
1          (1000.0, 2000.0]
2           (500.0, 1000.0]
3          (1000.0, 2000.0]
4          (1000.0, 2000.0]
                 ...
58487      (1000.0, 2000.0]
58488        (200.0, 500.0]
58489        (200.0, 500.0]
58490       (500.0, 1000.0]
58491       (500.0, 1000.0]
Name: DIST, Length: 58492, dtype: category
Categories (5, interval[float64]): [(-inf, 200.0] < (200.0, 500.0]
< (500.0, 1000.0] <
                           (1000.0, 2000.0] < (2000.0, inf]]
```

3. An ordered categorical Series is created. To help get an idea of what happened, let's count the values of each category:

```
>>> cuts.value_counts()
(500.0, 1000.0]     20659
(200.0, 500.0]      15874
(1000.0, 2000.0]    14186
(2000.0, inf]        4054
(-inf, 200.0]        3719
Name: DIST, dtype: int64
```

4. The `cuts` Series can now be used to form groups. pandas allows you to pass many types into the `.groupby` method. Pass the `cuts` Series to the `.groupby` method and then call the `.value_counts` method on the `AIRLINE` column to find the distribution for each distance group. Notice that SkyWest (OO) makes up 33% of flights of less than 200 miles but only 16% of those between 200 and 500 miles:

```
>>> (flights
...       .groupby(cuts)
...       ['AIRLINE']
...       .value_counts(normalize=True)
...       .round(3)
... )
DIST            AIRLINE
(-inf, 200.0]   OO          0.326
                EV          0.289
                MQ          0.211
                DL          0.086
                AA          0.052
                            ...
(2000.0, inf]   WN          0.046
                HA          0.028
                NK          0.019
                AS          0.012
                F9          0.004
Name: AIRLINE, Length: 57, dtype: float64
```

How it works...

In *step 2*, the `.cut` function places each value of the `DIST` column into one of five bins. The bins are created by a sequence of six numbers defining the edges. You always need one more edge than the number of bins. You can pass the `bins` parameter an integer, which automatically creates that number of equal-width bins. Negative infinity and positive infinity values are available in NumPy and ensure that all values get placed in a bin. If you have values that are outside the bin edges, they will be made missing and not be placed in a bin.

The `cuts` variable is now a Series of five ordered categories. It has all the normal Series methods and, in *step 3*, the `.value_counts` method is used to get a sense of its distribution.

The `.groupby` method allows you to pass any object to group on. This means that you are able to form groups from something completely unrelated to the current DataFrame. Here, we group by the values in the `cuts` variable. For each grouping, we find the percentage of flights per airline with `.value_counts` by setting `normalize` to `True`.

Some interesting insights can be drawn from this result. Looking at the full result, SkyWest is the leading airline for under 200 miles but has no flights over 2,000 miles. In contrast, American Airlines has the fifth highest total for flights under 200 miles but has by far the most flights between 1,000 and 2,000 miles.

There's more...

We can find more results when grouping by the `cuts` variable. For instance, we can find the 25th, 50th, and 75th percentile airtime for each distance grouping. As airtime is in minutes, we can divide by 60 to get hours. This will return a Series with a MultiIndex:

```
>>> (flights
...     .groupby(cuts)
...     ['AIR_TIME']
...     .quantile(q=[.25, .5, .75])
...     .div(60)
...     .round(2)
... )
DIST
(-inf, 200.0]      0.25     0.43
                   0.50     0.50
                   0.75     0.57
(200.0, 500.0]     0.25     0.77
                   0.50     0.92
                             ...
(1000.0, 2000.0]   0.50     2.93
                   0.75     3.40
(2000.0, inf]      0.25     4.30
                   0.50     4.70
                   0.75     5.03
Name: AIR_TIME, Length: 15, dtype: float64
```

We can use this information to create informative string labels when using the `cut` function. These labels replace the interval notation found in the index. We can also chain the `.unstack` method, which transposes the inner index level to column names:

```
>>> labels=['Under an Hour', '1 Hour', '1-2 Hours',
...         '2-4 Hours', '4+ Hours']
>>> cuts2 = pd.cut(flights['DIST'], bins=bins, labels=labels)
>>> (flights
...      .groupby(cuts2)
...      ['AIRLINE']
...      .value_counts(normalize=True)
...      .round(3)
...      .unstack()
... )
```

AIRLINE	AA	AS	B6	...	US	VX	WN
DIST				...			
Under an Hour	0.052	NaN	NaN	...	NaN	NaN	0.009
1 Hour	0.071	0.001	0.007	...	0.016	0.028	0.194
1-2 Hours	0.144	0.023	0.003	...	0.025	0.004	0.138
2-4 Hours	0.264	0.016	0.003	...	0.040	0.012	0.160
4+ Hours	0.212	0.012	0.080	...	0.065	0.074	0.046

Counting the total number of flights between cities

In the flights dataset, we have data on the origin and destination airport. It is trivial to count the number of flights originating in Houston and landing in Atlanta, for instance. What is more difficult is counting the total number of flights between the two cities.

In this recipe, we count the total number of flights between two cities, regardless of which one is the origin or destination. To accomplish this, we sort the origin and destination airports alphabetically so that each combination of airports always occurs in the same order. We can then use this new column arrangement to form groups and then to count.

How to do it...

1. Read in the flights dataset, and find the total number of flights between each origin and destination airport:

```
>>> flights = pd.read_csv('data/flights.csv')
>>> flights_ct = flights.groupby(['ORG_AIR', 'DEST_AIR']).size()
>>> flights_ct
ORG_AIR   DEST_AIR
ATL       ABE          31
          ABQ          16
          ABY          19
          ACY           6
          AEX          40
                       ...
SFO       SNA         122
          STL          20
          SUN          10
          TUS          20
          XNA           2
Length: 1130, dtype: int64
```

2. Select the total number of flights between Houston (IAH) and Atlanta (ATL) in both directions:

```
>>> flights_ct.loc[[('ATL', 'IAH'), ('IAH', 'ATL')]]
ORG_AIR   DEST_AIR
ATL       IAH         121
IAH       ATL         148
dtype: int64
```

3. We could simply sum these two numbers together to find the total flights between the cities, but there is a more efficient and automated solution that can work for all flights. Let's sort the origin and destination columns for each row alphabetically. We will use `axis='columns'` to do that:

```
>>> f_part3 = (flights
...     [['ORG_AIR', 'DEST_AIR']]
...     .apply(lambda ser:
...             ser.sort_values().reset_index(drop=True),
...             axis='columns')
... )
>>> f_part3
     DEST_AIR ORG_AIR
0         SLC     LAX
```

1	IAD	DEN
2	VPS	DFW
3	DCA	DFW
4	MCI	LAX
...	...	...
58487	DFW	SFO
58488	SFO	LAS
58489	SBA	SFO
58490	ATL	MSP
58491	BOI	SFO

4. Now that the origin and destination values in each row are sorted, the column names are not correct. Let's rename them to something more generic and then again find the total number of flights between all cities:

```
>>> rename_dict = {0:'AIR1', 1:'AIR2'}
>>> (flights
...    [['ORG_AIR', 'DEST_AIR']]
...    .apply(lambda ser:
...            ser.sort_values().reset_index(drop=True),
...            axis='columns')
...    .rename(columns=rename_dict)
...    .groupby(['AIR1', 'AIR2'])
...    .size()
... )
AIR1  AIR2
ATL   ABE    31
      ABQ    16
      ABY    19
      ACY     6
      AEX    40
             ...
SFO   SNA   122
      STL    20
      SUN    10
      TUS    20
      XNA     2
Length: 1130, dtype: int64
```

5. Let's select all the flights between Atlanta and Houston and verify that they match the sum of the values in *step 2*:

```
>>> (flights
...     [['ORG_AIR', 'DEST_AIR']]
...     .apply(lambda ser:
...             ser.sort_values().reset_index(drop=True),
...             axis='columns')
...     .rename(columns=rename_dict)
...     .groupby(['AIR1', 'AIR2'])
...     .size()
...     .loc[('ATL', 'IAH')]
... )
269
```

6. If we try and select flights with Houston followed by Atlanta, we get an error:

```
>>> (flights
...     [['ORG_AIR', 'DEST_AIR']]
...     .apply(lambda ser:
...             ser.sort_values().reset_index(drop=True),
...             axis='columns')
...     .rename(columns=rename_dict)
...     .groupby(['AIR1', 'AIR2'])
...     .size()
...     .loc[('IAH', 'ATL')]
... )
Traceback (most recent call last)
    ...
KeyError: 'ATL'
```

How it works...

In *step 1*, we form groups by the origin and destination airport columns and then apply the `.size` method to the `groupby` object, which returns the total number of rows for each group. Notice that we could have passed the string `size` to the `.agg` method to achieve the same result. In *step 2*, the total number of flights for each direction between Atlanta and Houston are selected. The result is a Series that has a MultiIndex with two levels. One way to select rows from a MultiIndex is to pass the `.loc` index operator a tuple of the exact level values. Here, we select two different rows, (`'ATL'`, `'HOU'`) and (`'HOU'`, `'ATL'`). We use a list of tuples to do this correctly.

Step 3 is the most important step in the recipe. We would like to have just one label for all flights between Atlanta and Houston and so far we have two. If we sort each combination of origin and destination airports alphabetically, we would then have a single label for flights between airports. To do this, we use the `.apply` method on a DataFrame. This is different from the groupby `.apply` method. No groups are formed in *step 3*.

The DataFrame `.apply` method must be passed a function. In this case, it's a lambda function that sorts each row. By default, this function is passed each column. We can change the direction of computation by using `axis='columns'` (or `axis=1`). The lambda function has each row of data passed to it implicitly as a Series. It returns a Series with sorted airport codes. We have to call `.reset_index` so that the columns do not realign after the application of the function.

The `.apply` method iterates over all rows using the lambda function. After completion of this operation, the values in the two columns are sorted for each row. The column names are now meaningless. We rename the column names in the next step and then perform the same grouping and aggregation as was done in *step 2*. This time, all flights between Atlanta and Houston fall under the same label.

There's more...

Steps 3 through *6* are expensive operations and take several seconds to complete. There are only about 60,000 rows, so this solution would not scale well to larger data. Calling the `.apply` method with `axis='columns'` (or `axis=1`) is one of the least performant operations in all of pandas. Internally, pandas loops over each row and does not provide any speed boosts from NumPy. If possible, avoid using `.apply` with `axis=1`.

We can get a massive speed increase with the NumPy sort function. Let's go ahead and use this function and analyze its output. By default, it sorts each row:

```
>>> data_sorted = np.sort(flights[['ORG_AIR', 'DEST_AIR']])
>>> data_sorted[:10]
array([['LAX', 'SLC'],
       ['DEN', 'IAD'],
       ['DFW', 'VPS'],
       ['DCA', 'DFW'],
       ['LAX', 'MCI'],
       ['IAH', 'SAN'],
       ['DFW', 'MSY'],
       ['PHX', 'SFO'],
       ['ORD', 'STL'],
       ['IAH', 'SJC']], dtype=object)
```

A two-dimensional NumPy array is returned. NumPy does not do grouping operations so let's use the DataFrame constructor to create a new DataFrame and check whether it equals the DataFrame from *step 3*:

```
>>> flights_sort2 = pd.DataFrame(data_sorted, columns=['AIR1', 'AIR2'])
>>> flights_sort2.equals(f_part3.rename(columns={0:'AIR1', 1:'AIR2'}))
True
```

Because the DataFrames are the same, you can replace *step 3* with the previous faster sorting routine. Let's time the difference between each of the different sorting methods:

```
>>> %%timeit
>>> flights_sort = (flights
...       [['ORG_AIR', 'DEST_AIR']]
...     .apply(lambda ser:
...             ser.sort_values().reset_index(drop=True),
...             axis='columns')
... )
1min 5s ± 2.67 s per loop (mean ± std. dev. of 7 runs, 1 loop each)
```

```
>>> %%timeit
>>> data_sorted = np.sort(flights[['ORG_AIR', 'DEST_AIR']])
>>> flights_sort2 = pd.DataFrame(data_sorted,
...       columns=['AIR1', 'AIR2'])
14.6 ms ± 173 µs per loop (mean ± std. dev. of 7 runs, 100 loops each)
```

The NumPy solution is 4,452 times faster than using `.apply` with pandas in this example.

Finding the longest streak of on-time flights

One of the most important metrics for airlines is their on-time flight performance. The Federal Aviation Administration considers a flight delayed when it arrives at least 15 minutes later than its scheduled arrival time. pandas includes methods to calculate the total and percentage of on-time flights per airline. While these basic summary statistics are an important metric, there are other non-trivial calculations that are interesting, such as finding the length of consecutive on-time flights for each airline at each of its origin airports.

In this recipe, we find the longest consecutive streak of on-time flights for each airline at each origin airport. This requires each value in a column to be aware of the value immediately following it. We make clever use of the `.diff` and `.cumsum` methods to find streaks before applying this methodology to each of the groups.

> The `max_streak` function we develop in this section exposes a regression in pandas 1.0 and 1.0.1. This bug (`https://github.com/pandas-dev/pandas/issues/31802`) should be fixed in pandas 1.0.2.

How to do it...

1. Before we get started with the flights dataset, let's practice counting streaks of ones with a small sample Series:

```
>>> s = pd.Series([0, 1, 1, 0, 1, 1, 1, 0])
>>> s
0    0
1    1
2    1
3    0
4    1
5    1
6    1
7    0
dtype: int64
```

2. Our final representation of the streaks of ones will be a Series of the same length as the original with an independent count beginning from one for each streak. To get started, let's use the `.cumsum` method:

```
>>> s1 = s.cumsum()
>>> s1
0    0
1    1
2    2
3    2
4    3
5    4
6    5
7    5
dtype: int64
```

3. We have now accumulated all the ones going down the Series. Let's multiply this Series by the original:

```
>>> s.mul(s1)
0    0
1    1
2    2
3    0
4    3
5    4
6    5
7    0
dtype: int64
```

4. We have only non-zero values where we originally had ones. This result is fairly close to what we desire. We just need to restart each streak at one instead of where the cumulative sum left off. Let's chain the `.diff` method, which subtracts the previous value from the current:

```
>>> s.mul(s1).diff()
0    NaN
1    1.0
2    1.0
3   -2.0
4    3.0
5    1.0
6    1.0
7   -5.0
dtype: float64
```

5. A negative value represents the end of a streak. We need to propagate the negative values down the Series and use them to subtract away the excess accumulation from *step 2*. To do this, we will make all non-negative values missing with the `.where` method:

```
>>> (s
...       .mul(s.cumsum())
...       .diff()
...       .where(lambda x: x < 0)
... )
0    NaN
```

```
1    NaN
2    NaN
3    -2.0
4    NaN
5    NaN
6    NaN
7    -5.0
dtype: float64
```

6. We can now propagate these values down with the `.ffill` method:

```
>>> (s
...       .mul(s.cumsum())
...       .diff()
...       .where(lambda x: x < 0)
...       .ffill()
... )
0    NaN
1    NaN
2    NaN
3    -2.0
4    -2.0
5    -2.0
6    -2.0
7    -5.0
dtype: float64
```

7. Finally, we can add this Series back to the cumulative sum to clear out the excess accumulation:

```
>>> (s
...       .mul(s.cumsum())
...       .diff()
...       .where(lambda x: x < 0)
...       .ffill()
...       .add(s.cumsum(), fill_value=0)
... )
0    0.0
1    1.0
```

```
2    2.0
3    0.0
4    1.0
5    2.0
6    3.0
7    0.0
dtype: float64
```

8. Now that we have a working consecutive streak finder, we can find the longest streak per airline and origin airport. Let's read in the flights dataset and create a column to represent on-time arrival:

```
>>> flights = pd.read_csv('data/flights.csv')
>>> (flights
...       .assign(ON_TIME=flights['ARR_DELAY'].lt(15).astype(int))
...       [['AIRLINE', 'ORG_AIR', 'ON_TIME']]
... )
       AIRLINE ORG_AIR  ON_TIME
0           WN     LAX        0
1           UA     DEN        1
2           MQ     DFW        0
3           AA     DFW        1
4           WN     LAX        0
...        ...     ...      ...
58487       AA     SFO        1
58488       F9     LAS        1
58489       OO     SFO        1
58490       WN     MSP        0
58491       OO     SFO        1
```

9. Use our logic from the first seven steps to define a function that returns the maximum streak of ones for a given Series:

```
>>> def max_streak(s):
...     s1 = s.cumsum()
...     return (s
...         .mul(s1)
...         .diff()
...         .where(lambda x: x < 0)
...         .ffill()
```

```
...          .add(s1, fill_value=0)
...          .max()
...      )
```

10. Find the maximum streak of on-time arrivals per airline and origin airport along with the total number of flights and the percentage of on-time arrivals. First, sort the day of the year and the scheduled departure time:

```
>>> (flights
...      .assign(ON_TIME=flights['ARR_DELAY'].lt(15).astype(int))
...      .sort_values(['MONTH', 'DAY', 'SCHED_DEP'])
...      .groupby(['AIRLINE', 'ORG_AIR'])
...      ['ON_TIME']
...      .agg(['mean', 'size', max_streak])
...      .round(2)
... )
```

AIRLINE	ORG_AIR	mean	size	max_streak
AA	ATL	0.82	233	15
	DEN	0.74	219	17
	DFW	0.78	4006	64
	IAH	0.80	196	24
	LAS	0.79	374	29
...		...	...	...
WN	LAS	0.77	2031	39
	LAX	0.70	1135	23
	MSP	0.84	237	32
	PHX	0.77	1724	33
	SFO	0.76	445	17

How it works...

Finding streaks in the data is not a straightforward operation in pandas and requires methods that look ahead or behind, such as .diff or .shift, or those that remember their current state, such as .cumsum. The final result from the first seven steps is a Series the same length as the original that keeps track of all consecutive ones. Throughout these steps, we use the .mul and .add methods instead of their operator equivalents, (*) and (+). In my opinion, this allows for a slightly cleaner progression of calculations from left to right. You, of course, can replace these with the actual operators.

Ideally, we would like to tell pandas to apply the `.cumsum` method to the start of each streak and reset itself after the end of each one. It takes many steps to convey this message to pandas. *Step 2* accumulates all the ones in the Series as a whole. The rest of the steps slowly remove any excess accumulation. To identify this excess accumulation, we need to find the end of each streak and subtract this value from the beginning of the next streak.

To find the end of each streak, we cleverly make all values not part of the streak zero by multiplying the cumulative sum by the original Series of zeros and ones in *step 3*. The first zero following a non-zero, marks the end of a streak. That's good, but again, we need to eliminate the excess accumulation. Knowing where the streak ends doesn't exactly get us there.

In *step 4*, we use the `.diff` method to find this excess. The `.diff` method takes the difference between the current value and any value located a set number of rows away from it. By default, the difference between the current and the immediately preceding value is returned.

Only negative values are meaningful in *step 4*. Those are the ones immediately following the end of a streak. These values need to be propagated down until the end of the following streak. To eliminate (make missing) all the values we don't care about, we use the `.where` method (this is different from the NumPy `where` function), which takes a Boolean array of the same size as the calling Series. By default, all the `True` values remain the same, while the `False` values become missing. The `.where` method allows you to use the calling Series as part of the conditional by taking a function as its first parameter. An anonymous function is used, which gets passed the calling Series implicitly and checks whether each value is less than zero. The result of *step 5* is a Series where only the negative values are preserved, with the rest changed to missing.

The `.ffill` method in *step 6* replaces missing values with the last non-missing value going down a Series. As the first three values don't follow a non-missing value, they remain missing. We finally have our Series that removes the excess accumulation. We add our accumulation Series to the result of *step 6* to get the streaks all beginning from zero. The `.add` method allows us to replace the missing values with the `fill_value` parameter. This completes the process of finding streaks of ones in the dataset. When doing complex logic like this, it is a good idea to use a small dataset where you know what the final output will be. It would be quite a difficult task to start at *step 8* and build this streak-finding logic while grouping.

In *step 8*, we create the ON_TIME column. One item of note is that the canceled flights have missing values for ARR_DELAY, which do not pass the Boolean condition and therefore result in a zero for the ON_TIME column. Canceled flights are treated the same as delayed.

Step 9 turns our logic from the first seven steps into a function and chains the `.max` method to return the longest streak. As our function returns a single value, it is formally an aggregating function and can be passed to the `.agg` method in *step 10*. To ensure that we are looking at consecutive flights, we use the `.sort_values` method to sort by date and scheduled departure time.

There's more...

Now that we have found the longest streaks of on-time arrivals, we can easily find the opposite – the longest streak of delayed arrivals. The following function returns two rows for each group passed to it. The first row is the start of the streak, and the last row is the end of the streak. Each row contains the month and day that the streak started and ended, along with the total streak length:

```
>>> def max_delay_streak(df):
...     df = df.reset_index(drop=True)
...     late = 1 - df['ON_TIME']
...     late_sum = late.cumsum()
...     streak = (late
...         .mul(late_sum)
...         .diff()
...         .where(lambda x: x < 0)
...         .ffill()
...         .add(late_sum, fill_value=0)
...     )
...     last_idx = streak.idxmax()
...     first_idx = last_idx - streak.max() + 1
...     res = (df
...         .loc[[first_idx, last_idx], ['MONTH', 'DAY']]
...         .assign(streak=streak.max())
...     )
...     res.index = ['first', 'last']
...     return res

>>> (flights
...     .assign(ON_TIME=flights['ARR_DELAY'].lt(15).astype(int))
...     .sort_values(['MONTH', 'DAY', 'SCHED_DEP'])
...     .groupby(['AIRLINE', 'ORG_AIR'])
...     .apply(max_delay_streak)
...     .sort_values('streak', ascending=False)
... )
                       MONTH   DAY   streak
AIRLINE ORG_AIR
AA      DFW    first   2.0   26.0    38.0
```

		last	3.0	1.0	38.0
MQ	ORD	last	1.0	12.0	28.0
		first	1.0	6.0	28.0
	DFW	last	2.0	26.0	25.0
...			...	...	...
US	LAS	last	1.0	7.0	1.0
AS	ATL	first	5.0	4.0	1.0
OO	LAS	first	2.0	8.0	1.0
EV	PHX	last	8.0	1.0	0.0
		first	NaN	NaN	0.0

As we are using the `.apply` groupby method, a DataFrame of each group is passed to the `max_delay_streak` function. Inside this function, the index of the DataFrame is dropped and replaced by a `RangeIndex` in order for us to easily find the first and last row of the streak. The `ON_TIME` column is inverted and then the same logic is used to find streaks of delayed flights. The index of the first and last rows of the streak are stored as variables. These indexes are then used to select the month and day when the streaks ended. We use a DataFrame to return our results. We label and name the index to make the final result clearer.

Our final results show the longest delayed streaks accompanied by the first and last date. Let's investigate to see whether we can find out why these delays happened. Inclement weather is a common reason for delayed or canceled flights. Looking at the first row, American Airlines (AA) started a streak of 38 delayed flights in a row from the Dallas Fort-Worth (DFW) airport beginning February 26 until March 1,2015. Looking at historical weather data from February 27, 2015, two inches of snow fell, which was a record for that day. This was a major weather event for DFW and caused problems for the entire city. Notice that DFW makes another appearance as the third longest streak, but this time a few days earlier and for a different airline.

10

Restructuring Data into a Tidy Form

Introduction

All the datasets used in the preceding chapters have not had much or any work done to change their structure. We immediately began processing the datasets in their original shape. Many datasets in the wild will need a significant amount of restructuring before commencing a more detailed analysis. In some cases, an entire project might only concern itself with formatting the data in such a way that it can be easily processed by someone else.

There are many terms that are used to describe the process of data restructuring, with tidy data being the most common to data scientists. Tidy data is a term coined by Hadley Wickham to describe a form of data that makes analysis easy to do. This chapter will cover many ideas formulated by Hadley and how to accomplish them with pandas. To learn a great deal more about tidy data, read Hadley's paper (http://vita.had.co.nz/papers/tidy-data.pdf).

The following is an example of untidy data:

Name	Category	Value
Jill	Bank	2,300
Jill	Color	Red
John	Bank	1,100
Jill	Age	40
John	Color	Purple

The following is an example of tidy data:

Name	Age	Bank	Color
Jill	40	2,300	Red
John	38		Purple

What is tidy data? Hadley puts forth three guiding principles that determine whether a dataset is tidy:

- ▶ Each variable forms a column
- ▶ Each observation forms a row
- ▶ Each type of observational unit forms a table

Any dataset that does not meet these guidelines is considered messy. This definition will make more sense once we start restructuring our data into tidy form, but for now, we'll need to know what variables, observations, and observational units are.

Using this jargon, a variable is not referring to a Python variable, it is a piece of data. It is good to think about the distinction between a variable name and the variable value. The variable names are labels, such as gender, race, salary, and position. The variable values are those things liable to change for every observation, such as male, female, or other for gender.

A single observation is the collection of all variable values for a single observational unit. To help understand what an observational unit might be, consider a retail store, which has data for each transaction, employee, customer, item, and the store itself. Each of these can be viewed as an observational unit and would require its own table. Combining employee information (like the number of hours worked) with customer information (like the amount spent) in the same table would break this tidy principle.

The first step to resolving messy data is to recognize it when it exists, and there are boundless possibilities. Hadley explicitly mentions five of the most common types of messy data:

- ▶ Column names are values, not variable names
- ▶ Multiple variables are stored in column names
- ▶ Variables are stored in both rows and columns
- ▶ Multiple types of observational units are stored in the same table
- ▶ A single observational unit is stored in multiple tables

It is important to understand that tidying data does not typically involve changing the values of your dataset, filling in missing values, or doing any sort of analysis. Tidying data consists in changing the shape or structure of the data to meet the tidy principles. Tidy data is akin to having all your tools in the toolbox instead of scattered randomly throughout your house. Having the tools properly in the toolbox allows all other tasks to be completed easily. Once the data is in the correct form, it becomes much easier to perform further analysis.

Once you have spotted messy data, you will use the pandas library to restructure the data, so that it is tidy. The main tidy tools that pandas has available for you are the DataFrame methods `.stack`, `.melt`, `.unstack`, and `.pivot`. More complex tidying involves ripping apart text, which necessitates the `.str` accessor. Other helper methods, such as `.rename`, `.rename_axis`, `.reset_index`, and `.set_index`, will help with applying the final touches to tidy data.

Tidying variable values as column names with stack

To help understand the differences between tidy and messy data, let's take a look at a table that may or may not be in tidy form:

```
>>> import pandas as pd
>>> import numpy as np
>>> state_fruit = pd.read_csv('data/state_fruit.csv', index_col=0)
>>> state_fruit
```

	Apple	Orange	Banana
Texas	12	10	40
Arizona	9	7	12
Florida	0	14	190

There does not appear to be anything messy about this table, and the information is easily consumable. However, according to the tidy principles, it isn't tidy. Each column name is the value of a variable. In fact, none of the variable names are even present in the DataFrame. One of the first steps to transform a messy dataset into tidy data is to identify all of the variables. In this particular dataset, we have variables for state and fruit. There's also the numeric data that wasn't identified anywhere in the context of the problem. We can label this variable as weight or any other sensible name.

This particular messy dataset contains variable values as column names. We will need to transpose these column names into column values. In this recipe, we use the stack method to restructure our DataFrame into tidy form.

How to do it...

1. First, take note that the state names are in the index of the DataFrame. These states are correctly placed vertically and do not need to be restructured. It is the column names that are the problem. The `.stack` method takes all of the column names and pivots them into the index. Typically, when you call the `.stack` method, the data becomes taller.

2. Note that in this case, the result collapses from a DataFrame to a Series:

```
>>> state_fruit.stack()
Texas     Apple      12
          Orange     10
          Banana     40
Arizona   Apple       9
          Orange      7
          Banana     12
Florida   Apple       0
          Orange     14
          Banana    190
dtype: int64
```

3. Notice that we now have a Series with a MultiIndex. There are now two levels in the index. The original index has been pushed to the left to make room for the fruit column names. With this one command, we now essentially have tidy data. Each variable, state, fruit, and weight is vertical. Let's use the `.reset_index` method to turn the result into a DataFrame:

```
>>> (state_fruit
...     .stack()
...     .reset_index()
... )
    level_0 level_1    0
0     Texas   Apple   12
1     Texas  Orange   10
2     Texas  Banana   40
3   Arizona   Apple    9
4   Arizona  Orange    7
5   Arizona  Banana   12
6   Florida   Apple    0
7   Florida  Orange   14
8   Florida  Banana  190
```

4. Our structure is now correct, but the column names are meaningless. Let's replace them with proper identifiers:

```
>>> (state_fruit
...     .stack()
...     .reset_index()
```

```
...         .rename(columns={'level_0':'state',
...             'level_1': 'fruit', 0: 'weight'})
... )
       state     fruit  weight
0       Texas     Apple      12
1       Texas    Orange      10
2       Texas    Banana      40
3     Arizona     Apple       9
4     Arizona    Orange       7
5     Arizona    Banana      12
6     Florida     Apple       0
7     Florida    Orange      14
8     Florida    Banana     190
```

5. Instead of using the .rename method, it is possible to use the lesser-known Series method .rename_axis to set the names of the index levels before using .reset_index:

```
>>> (state_fruit
...         .stack()
...         .rename_axis(['state', 'fruit'])
... )
state     fruit
Texas     Apple      12
          Orange     10
          Banana     40
Arizona   Apple       9
          Orange      7
          Banana     12
Florida   Apple       0
          Orange     14
          Banana     190
dtype: int64
```

6. From here, we can chain the .reset_index method with the name parameter to reproduce the output from *step 3*:

```
>>> (state_fruit
...         .stack()
```

```
...          .rename_axis(['state', 'fruit'])
...          .reset_index(name='weight')
... )
```

	state	fruit	weight
0	Texas	Apple	12
1	Texas	Orange	10
2	Texas	Banana	40
3	Arizona	Apple	9
4	Arizona	Orange	7
5	Arizona	Banana	12
6	Florida	Apple	0
7	Florida	Orange	14
8	Florida	Banana	190

How it works...

The `.stack` method is powerful, and it takes time to understand and appreciate fully. By default, it takes the (innermost level in hierarchical columns of) column names and transposes them, so they become the new innermost index level. Notice how each old column name still labels its original value by being paired with each state. There were nine original values in a 3 x 3 DataFrame, which got transformed into a single Series with the same number of values. The original first row of data became the first three values in the resulting Series.

After resetting the index in *step 2*, pandas defaults our DataFrame columns to `level_0`, `level_1`, and `0` (two strings and one integer). This is because the Series calling this method has two index levels that were formally unnamed. pandas also refers to indexes by integer, beginning from zero from the outside.

Step 3 shows an intuitive way to rename the columns with the `.rename` method.

Alternatively, it is possible to set the column names by chaining the `.rename_axis` method that uses a list of values as the index level names. pandas uses these index level names as the new column names when the index is reset. Additionally, the `.reset_index` method has a `name` parameter corresponding to the new column name of the Series values.

All Series have a name attribute that can be assigned or changed with the `.rename` method. It is this attribute that becomes the column name when using `.reset_index`.

There's more...

One of the keys to using `.stack` is to place all of the columns that you do not wish to transform in the index. The dataset in this recipe was initially read with the states in the index. Let's take a look at what would have happened if we did not read the states into the index:

```
>>> state_fruit2 = pd.read_csv('data/state_fruit2.csv')
>>> state_fruit2
     State  Apple  Orange  Banana
0    Texas     12      10      40
1  Arizona      9       7      12
2  Florida      0      14     190
```

As the state names are not in the index, using `.stack` on this DataFrame reshapes all values into one long Series of values:

```
>>> state_fruit2.stack()
0  State      Texas
   Apple         12
   Orange        10
   Banana        40
1  State    Arizona
              ...
   Banana        12
2  State    Florida
   Apple          0
   Orange        14
   Banana       190
Length: 12, dtype: object
```

This command reshapes all the columns, this time including the states, and is not at all what we need. To reshape this data correctly, you will need to put all the non-reshaped columns into the index first with the `.set_index` method, and then use `.stack`. The following code gives a similar result to *step 1*:

```
>>> state_fruit2.set_index('State').stack()
State
Texas    Apple     12
         Orange    10
         Banana    40
Arizona  Apple      9
```

```
            Orange      7

            Banana     12

Florida    Apple        0

            Orange     14

            Banana    190

dtype:  int64
```

Tidying variable values as column names with melt

Like most large Python libraries, pandas has many different ways to accomplish the same task, the differences usually being readability and performance. A DataFrame has a method named `.melt` that is similar to the `.stack` method described in the previous recipe but gives a bit more flexibility.

In this recipe, we use the `.melt` method to tidy a DataFrame with variable values as column names.

How to do it...

1. Read in the `state_fruit2.csv` dataset:

```
>>> state_fruit2 = pd.read_csv('data/state_fruit2.csv')
>>> state_fruit2
        State  Apple  Orange  Banana
0        Texas     12      10      40
1      Arizona      9       7      12
2      Florida      0      14     190
```

2. Use the `.melt` method by passing the appropriate columns to the `id_vars` and `value_vars` parameters:

```
>>> state_fruit2.melt(id_vars=['State'],
...        value_vars=['Apple', 'Orange', 'Banana'])
        State  variable  value
0        Texas     Apple     12
1      Arizona     Apple      9
2      Florida     Apple      0
3        Texas    Orange     10
```

4	Arizona	Orange	7
5	Florida	Orange	14
6	Texas	Banana	40
7	Arizona	Banana	12
8	Florida	Banana	190

3. This one step creates tidy data for us. By default, `.melt` refers to the transformed column names as variables and the corresponding values as values. Conveniently, `.melt` has two additional parameters, `var_name` and `value_name`, that give you the ability to rename these two columns:

```
>>> state_fruit2.melt(id_vars=['State'],
...                   value_vars=['Apple', 'Orange', 'Banana'],
...                   var_name='Fruit',
...                   value_name='Weight')
```

	State	Fruit	Weight
0	Texas	Apple	12
1	Arizona	Apple	9
2	Florida	Apple	0
3	Texas	Orange	10
4	Arizona	Orange	7
5	Florida	Orange	14
6	Texas	Banana	40
7	Arizona	Banana	12
8	Florida	Banana	190

How it works...

The `.melt` method reshapes your DataFrame. It takes up to five parameters, with two of them being crucial to understanding how to reshape your data correctly:

▶ `id_vars` is a list of column names that you want to preserve as columns and not reshape

▶ `value_vars` is a list of column names that you want to reshape into a single column

The `id_vars`, or the identification variables, remain in the same column but repeat for each of the columns passed to `value_vars`. One crucial aspect of `.melt` is that it ignores values in the index, and it silently drops your index and replaces it with a default `RangeIndex`. This means that if you do have values in your index that you would like to keep, you will need to reset the index first before using melt.

There's more...

All the parameters for the `.melt` method are optional, and if you desire all your values to be in a single column and their old column labels to be in the other, you may call `.melt` with the default parameters:

```
>>> state_fruit2.melt()
```

	variable	value
0	State	Texas
1	State	Arizona
2	State	Florida
3	Apple	12
4	Apple	9
..	...	...
7	Orange	7
8	Orange	14
9	Banana	40
10	Banana	12
11	Banana	190

More realistically, you might have lots of variables that need melting and would like to specify only the identification variables. In that case, calling `.melt` in the following manner will yield the same result as in *step 2*. You don't even need a list when melting a single column and can pass its string value:

```
>>> state_fruit2.melt(id_vars='State')
```

	State	variable	value
0	Texas	Apple	12
1	Arizona	Apple	9
2	Florida	Apple	0
3	Texas	Orange	10
4	Arizona	Orange	7
5	Florida	Orange	14
6	Texas	Banana	40
7	Arizona	Banana	12
8	Florida	Banana	190

Stacking multiple groups of variables simultaneously

Some datasets contain multiple groups of variables as column names that need to be stacked simultaneously into their own columns. An example involving the movie dataset can help clarify this. Let's begin by selecting all columns containing the actor names and their corresponding Facebook likes:

```
>>> movie = pd.read_csv('data/movie.csv')
>>> actor = movie[['movie_title', 'actor_1_name',
...                 'actor_2_name', 'actor_3_name',
...                 'actor_1_facebook_likes',
...                 'actor_2_facebook_likes',
...                 'actor_3_facebook_likes']]
>>> actor.head()
                                       movie_title  ...
0                                           Avatar  ...
1        Pirates of the Caribbean: At World's End  ...
2                                          Spectre  ...
3                          The Dark Knight Rises  ...
4    Star Wars: Episode VII - The Force Awakens  ...
```

If we define our variables as the title of the movie, the actor name, and the number of Facebook likes, then we will need to stack two sets of columns, which is not possible using a single call to `.stack` or `.melt`.

In this recipe, we will tidy our actor DataFrame by simultaneously stacking the actor names and their corresponding Facebook likes with the `wide_to_long` function.

How to do it...

1. We will be using the `wide_to_long` function to reshape our data into tidy form. To use this function, we will need to change the column names that we are stacking, so that they end with a digit. We first create a user-defined function to change the column names:

```
>>> def change_col_name(col_name):
...     col_name = col_name.replace('_name', '')
...     if 'facebook' in col_name:
...         fb_idx = col_name.find('facebook')
```

```
...            col_name = (col_name[:5] + col_name[fb_idx - 1:]
...                         + col_name[5:fb_idx-1])
...            return col_name
```

2. Pass this function to the `rename` method to transform all the column names:

```
>>> actor2 = actor.rename(columns=change_col_name)
>>> actor2
```

	movie_title	actor_1	...	actor_facebook_likes_2
0	Avatar	CCH Pounder	...	936.0
1	Pirates ...	Johnny Depp	...	5000.0
2	Spectre	Christop...	...	393.0
3	The Dark...	Tom Hardy	...	23000.0
4	Star War...	Doug Walker	...	12.0
...	...	...	...	...
4911	Signed S...	Eric Mabius	...	470.0
4912	The Foll...	Natalie Zea	...	593.0
4913	A Plague...	Eva Boehnke	...	0.0
4914	Shanghai...	Alan Ruck	...	719.0
4915	My Date ...	John August	...	23.0

3. Use the `wide_to_long` function to stack the actor and Facebook sets of columns simultaneously:

```
>>> stubs = ['actor', 'actor_facebook_likes']
>>> actor2_tidy = pd.wide_to_long(actor2,
...         stubnames=stubs,
...         i=['movie_title'],
...         j='actor_num',
...         sep='_')
>>> actor2_tidy.head()
```

movie_title	actor_num	actor	actor_facebook_likes
Avatar	1	CCH Pounder	1000.0
Pirates o...	1	Johnny Depp	40000.0
Spectre	1	Christop...	11000.0
The Dark ...	1	Tom Hardy	27000.0
Star Wars...	1	Doug Walker	131.0

How it works...

The `wide_to_long` function works in a fairly specific manner. Its main parameter is `stubnames`, which is a list of strings. Each string represents a single column grouping. All columns that begin with this string will be stacked into a single column. In this recipe, there are two groups of columns: `actor`, and `actor_facebook_likes`. By default, each of these groups of columns will need to end in a digit. This digit will subsequently be used to label the reshaped data. Each of these column groups has an underscore character separating the `stubname` from the ending digit. To account for this, you must use the `sep` parameter.

The original column names do not match the pattern needed for `wide_to_long` to work. The column names could have been changed manually by specifying their values with a list. This could quickly become a lot of typing so instead, we define a function that automatically converts our columns to a format that works. The `change_col_name` function removes *_name* from the actor columns and rearranges the Facebook columns so that now they both end in digits.

To accomplish the column renaming, we use the `.rename` method in *step 2*. It accepts many different types of arguments, one of which is a function. When passing it to a function, every column name gets implicitly passed to it one at a time.

We have now correctly created two groups of columns, those beginning with `actor` and `actor_facebook_likes` that will be stacked. In addition to this, `wide_to_long` requires a unique column, parameter `i`, to act as an identification variable that will not be stacked. Also required is the parameter `j`, which renames the identifying digit stripped from the end of the original column names. By default, the `suffix` parameter contains the regular expression, `r'\d+'`, that searches for one or more digits. The `\d` is a special token that matches the digits 0-9. The plus sign, +, makes the expression match for one or more of these digits.

There's more...

The function `wide_to_long` works when all groupings of variables have the same numeric ending like they did in this recipe. When your variables do not have the same ending or don't end in a digit, you can still use `wide_to_long` to do simultaneous column stacking. For instance, let's take a look at the following dataset:

```
>>> df = pd.read_csv('data/stackme.csv')
>>> df
```

	State	Country	a1	b2	Test	d	e
0	TX	US	0.45	0.3	Test1	2	6
1	MA	US	0.03	1.2	Test2	9	7
2	ON	CAN	0.70	4.2	Test3	4	2

Let's say we wanted columns a1 and b1 stacked together, as well as columns d and e. Additionally, we wanted to use a1 and b1 as labels for the rows. To accomplish this task, we would need to rename the columns so that they ended in the label we desired:

```
>>> df.rename(columns = {'a1':'group1_a1', 'b2':'group1_b2',
...                       'd':'group2_a1', 'e':'group2_b2'})
   State Country  ...  group2_a1  group2_b2
0    TX      US   ...          2          6
1    MA      US   ...          9          7
2    ON     CAN   ...          4          2
```

We would then need to modify the suffix parameter, which normally defaults to a regular expression that selects digits. Here, we tell it to find any number of characters:

```
>>> pd.wide_to_long(
...         df.rename(columns = {'a1':'group1_a1',
...                    'b2':'group1_b2',
...                    'd':'group2_a1', 'e':'group2_b2'}),
...      stubnames=['group1', 'group2'],
...      i=['State', 'Country', 'Test'],
...      j='Label',
...      suffix='.+',
...      sep='_')
                            group1  group2
State Country Test  Label
TX    US      Test1 a1        0.45       2
                    b2        0.30       6
MA    US      Test2 a1        0.03       9
                    b2        1.20       7
ON    CAN     Test3 a1        0.70       4
                    b2        4.20       2
```

Inverting stacked data

DataFrames have two similar methods, .stack and .melt, to convert horizontal column names into vertical column values. DataFrames can invert these two operations with the .unstack and .pivot methods, respectively. .stack and .unstack are methods that allow control over only the column and row indexes, while .melt and .pivot give more flexibility to choose which columns are reshaped.

In this recipe, we will call `.stack` and `.melt` on a dataset and promptly invert the operation with the `.unstack` and `.pivot` methods.

How to do it...

1. Read in the college dataset with the institution name as the index, and with only the undergraduate race columns:

    ```
    >>> def usecol_func(name):
    ...     return 'UGDS_' in name or name == 'INSTNM'
    >>> college = pd.read_csv('data/college.csv',
    ...     index_col='INSTNM',
    ...     usecols=usecol_func)
    >>> college
    ```

	UGDS_WHITE	UGDS_BLACK	...	UGDS_NRA	UGDS_UNKN
INSTNM			...		
Alabama A...	0.0333	0.9353	...	0.0059	0.0138
Universit...	0.5922	0.2600	...	0.0179	0.0100
Amridge U...	0.2990	0.4192	...	0.0000	0.2715
Universit...	0.6988	0.1255	...	0.0332	0.0350
Alabama S...	0.0158	0.9208	...	0.0243	0.0137
...	...	...	...	...	...
SAE Insti...	NaN	NaN	...	NaN	NaN
Rasmussen...	NaN	NaN	...	NaN	NaN
National ...	NaN	NaN	...	NaN	NaN
Bay Area ...	NaN	NaN	...	NaN	NaN
Excel Lea...	NaN	NaN	...	NaN	NaN

2. Use the `.stack` method to convert each horizontal column name to a vertical index level:

    ```
    >>> college_stacked = college.stack()
    >>> college_stacked
    INSTNM
    Alabama A & M University        UGDS_WHITE    0.0333
                                    UGDS_BLACK    0.9353
                                    UGDS_HISP     0.0055
                                    UGDS_ASIAN    0.0019
                                    UGDS_AIAN     0.002
    ```

```
                                        . . .
Coastal Pines Technical College  UGDS_AIAN    0.0034
                                 UGDS_NHPI    0.0017
                                 UGDS_2MOR    0.0191
                                 UGDS_NRA     0.0028
                                 UGDS_UNKN    0.0056
Length: 61866, dtype: float64
```

3. Invert this stacked data back to its original form with the `.unstack` method:

```
>>> college_stacked.unstack()
```

INSTNM	UGDS_WHITE	UGDS_BLACK	...	UGDS_NRA	UGDS_UNKN
			...		
Alabama A...	0.0333	0.9353	...	0.0059	0.0138
Universit...	0.5922	0.2600	...	0.0179	0.0100
Amridge U...	0.2990	0.4192	...	0.0000	0.2715
Universit...	0.6988	0.1255	...	0.0332	0.0350
Alabama S...	0.0158	0.9208	...	0.0243	0.0137
...	...	...	...	...	...
Hollywood...	0.2182	0.4182	...	0.0182	0.0909
Hollywood...	0.1200	0.3333	...	0.0000	0.0667
Coachella...	0.3284	0.1045	...	0.0000	0.0000
Dewey Uni...	0.0000	0.0000	...	0.0000	0.0000
Coastal P...	0.6762	0.2508	...	0.0028	0.0056

4. A similar sequence of operations can be done with `.melt` followed by `.pivot`. First, read in the data without putting the institution name in the index:

```
>>> college2 = pd.read_csv('data/college.csv',
...     usecols=usecol_func)
>>> college2
```

	INSTNM	UGDS_WHITE	...	UGDS_NRA	UGDS_UNKN
0	Alabama ...	0.0333	...	0.0059	0.0138
1	Universi...	0.5922	...	0.0179	0.0100
2	Amridge ...	0.2990	...	0.0000	0.2715
3	Universi...	0.6988	...	0.0332	0.0350
4	Alabama ...	0.0158	...	0.0243	0.0137
...	...	...	...	...	...
7530	SAE Inst...	NaN	...	NaN	NaN

7531	Rasmusse...	NaN	...	NaN	NaN
7532	National...	NaN	...	NaN	NaN
7533	Bay Area...	NaN	...	NaN	NaN
7534	Excel Le...	NaN	...	NaN	NaN

5. Use the `.melt` method to transpose all the race columns into a single column:

```
>>> college_melted = college2.melt(id_vars='INSTNM',
...         var_name='Race',
...         value_name='Percentage')
>>> college_melted
```

	INSTNM	Race	Percentage
0	Alabama ...	UGDS_WHITE	0.0333
1	Universi...	UGDS_WHITE	0.5922
2	Amridge ...	UGDS_WHITE	0.2990
3	Universi...	UGDS_WHITE	0.6988
4	Alabama ...	UGDS_WHITE	0.0158
...	...	...	...
67810	SAE Inst...	UGDS_UNKN	NaN
67811	Rasmusse...	UGDS_UNKN	NaN
67812	National...	UGDS_UNKN	NaN
67813	Bay Area...	UGDS_UNKN	NaN
67814	Excel Le...	UGDS_UNKN	NaN

6. Use the `.pivot` method to invert this previous result:

```
>>> melted_inv = college_melted.pivot(index='INSTNM',
...         columns='Race',
...         values='Percentage')
>>> melted_inv
```

Race	UGDS_2MOR	UGDS_AIAN	...	UGDS_UNKN	UGDS_WHITE
INSTNM			...		
A & W Hea...	0.0000	0.0000	...	0.0000	0.0000
A T Still...	NaN	NaN	...	NaN	NaN
ABC Beaut...	0.0000	0.0000	...	0.0000	0.0000
ABC Beaut...	0.0000	0.0000	...	0.0000	0.2895
AI Miami ...	0.0018	0.0000	...	0.4644	0.0324
...	...	...	...	...	...
Yukon Bea...	0.0000	0.1200	...	0.0000	0.8000

Z Hair Ac...	0.0211	0.0000	...	0.0105	0.9368
Zane Stat...	0.0218	0.0029	...	0.2399	0.6995
duCret Sc...	0.0976	0.0000	...	0.0244	0.4634
eClips Sc...	0.0000	0.0000	...	0.0000	0.1446

7. Notice that the institution names are now shuttled over into the index and are not in their original order. The column names are not in their original order. To get an exact replication of our starting DataFrame from *step 4*, use the `.loc` index operator to select rows and columns simultaneously and then reset the index:

```
>>> college2_replication = (melted_inv
...         .loc[college2['INSTNM'], college2.columns[1:]]
...         .reset_index()
... )
>>> college2.equals(college2_replication)
True
```

How it works...

There are multiple ways to accomplish the same thing in *step 1*. Here, we show the versatility of the `read_csv` function. The `usecols` parameter accepts either a list of the columns that we would like to import or a function that dynamically determines them. We use a function that checks whether the column name contains `UGDS_` or is equal to `INSTNM`. The function is passed each column name as a string and must return a Boolean. A considerable amount of memory can be saved in this manner.

The stack method in *step 2* puts all column names into the innermost index level and returns a Series. In *step 3*, the `.unstack` method inverts this operation by taking all the values in the innermost index level and converting them to column names. Note that the sizes of the results of *steps 1* and *3* are different because `.stack` drops missing values by default. If you pass in the `dropna=False` parameter, it will round-trip correctly.

Step 4 reads in the same dataset as in *step 1* but does not put the institution name in the index because the `.melt` method isn't able to access it. *Step 5* uses the `.melt` method to transpose all the Race columns. It does this by leaving the `value_vars` parameter as its default value, `None`. When not specified, all the columns not present in the `id_vars` parameter get transposed.

Step 6 inverts the operation from *step 5* with the `.pivot` method, which accepts three parameters. Most parameters take a single column as a string (the `values` parameter may also accept a list of column names). The column referenced by the index parameter remains vertical and becomes the new index. The values of the column referenced by the `columns` parameter become the column names. The values referenced by the `values` parameter become tiled to correspond with the intersection of their former index and columns label.

To make a replication with `pivot`, we need to sort the rows and columns in the same order as the original. As the institution name is in the index, we use the `.loc` index operator to sort the DataFrame by its original index.

There's more...

To help further understand `.stack` and `.unstack`, let's use them to transpose the college DataFrame. In this context, we are using the precise mathematical definition of the transposing of a matrix, where the new rows are the old columns of the original data matrix.

If you take a look at the output from *step 2*, you'll notice that there are two index levels. By default, the `.unstack` method uses the innermost index level as the new column values. Index levels are numbered beginning from zero from the outside. pandas defaults the level parameter of the `.unstack` method to -1, which refers to the innermost index. We can instead `.unstack` the outermost column using `level=0`:

```
>>> college.stack().unstack(0)
INSTNM        Alaba/rsity   ...   Coast/llege
UGDS_WHITE        0.0333    ...      0.6762
UGDS_BLACK        0.9353    ...      0.2508
UGDS_HISP         0.0055    ...      0.0359
UGDS_ASIAN        0.0019    ...      0.0045
UGDS_AIAN         0.0024    ...      0.0034
UGDS_NHPI         0.0019    ...      0.0017
UGDS_2MOR         0.0000    ...      0.0191
UGDS_NRA          0.0059    ...      0.0028
UGDS_UNKN         0.0138    ...      0.0056
```

There is a way to transpose a DataFrame that does not require `.stack` or `.unstack`. Use the `.transpose` method or the `.T` attribute like this:

```
>>> college.T
>>> college.transpose()
INSTNM        Alaba/rsity   ...   Coast/llege
UGDS_WHITE        0.0333    ...      0.6762
UGDS_BLACK        0.9353    ...      0.2508
UGDS_HISP         0.0055    ...      0.0359
UGDS_ASIAN        0.0019    ...      0.0045
UGDS_AIAN         0.0024    ...      0.0034
UGDS_NHPI         0.0019    ...      0.0017
```

UGDS_2MOR	0.0000	...	0.0191
UGDS_NRA	0.0059	...	0.0028
UGDS_UNKN	0.0138	...	0.0056

Unstacking after a groupby aggregation

Grouping data by a single column and performing an aggregation on a single column returns a result that is easy to consume. When grouping by more than one column, a resulting aggregation might not be structured in a manner that makes consumption easy. Since .groupby operations, by default, put the unique grouping columns in the index, the .unstack method can be beneficial to rearrange the data so that it is presented in a manner that is more useful for interpretation.

In this recipe, we use the employee dataset to perform an aggregation, grouping by multiple columns. We then use the .unstack method to reshape the result into a format that makes for easier comparisons of different groups.

How to do it...

1. Read in the employee dataset and find the mean salary by *race*:

```
>>> employee = pd.read_csv('data/employee.csv')
>>> (employee
...      .groupby('RACE')
...      ['BASE_SALARY']
...      .mean()
...      .astype(int)
... )
RACE
American Indian or Alaskan Native    60272
Asian/Pacific Islander               61660
Black or African American            50137
Hispanic/Latino                      52345
Others                               51278
White                                64419
Name: BASE_SALARY, dtype: int64
```

2. This is a `groupby` operation that results in a Series that is easy to read and has no need to reshape. Let's now find the average salary for all races by gender. Note that the result is a Series:

```
>>> (employee
...      .groupby(['RACE', 'GENDER'])
...      ['BASE_SALARY']
...      .mean()
...      .astype(int)
... )
```

RACE	GENDER	
American Indian or Alaskan Native	Female	60238
	Male	60305
Asian/Pacific Islander	Female	63226
	Male	61033
Black or African American	Female	48915
	...	
Hispanic/Latino	Male	54782
Others	Female	63785
	Male	38771
White	Female	66793
	Male	63940

```
Name: BASE_SALARY, Length: 12, dtype: int64
```

3. This aggregation is more complex and can be reshaped to make different comparisons easier. For instance, it would be easier to compare male versus female salaries for each race if they were side by side and not vertical as they are now. Let's call on `.unstack` on the *gender* index level:

```
>>> (employee
...      .groupby(['RACE', 'GENDER'])
...      ['BASE_SALARY']
...      .mean()
...      .astype(int)
...      .unstack('GENDER')
... )
```

GENDER	Female	Male
RACE		
American Indian or Alaskan Native	60238	60305

Asian/Pacific Islander	63226	61033
Black or African American	48915	51082
Hispanic/Latino	46503	54782
Others	63785	38771
White	66793	63940

4. Similarly, we can unstack the race index level:

```
>>> (employee
...      .groupby(['RACE', 'GENDER'])
...      ['BASE_SALARY']
...      .mean()
...      .astype(int)
...      .unstack('RACE')
... )
```

RACE	American Indian or Alaskan Native	...	White
GENDER		...	
Female	60238	...	66793
Male	60305	...	63940

How it works...

Step 1 has the simplest possible aggregation with a single grouping column (RACE), a single aggregating column (BASE_SALARY), and a single aggregating function (.mean). This result is easy to consume and doesn't require any more processing to evaluate. *Step 2* groups by both race and gender together. The resulting Series (which has a MultiIndex) contains all the values in a single dimension, which makes comparisons more difficult. To make the information easier to consume, we use the .unstack method to convert the values in one (or more) of the levels to columns.

By default, .unstack uses the innermost index level as the new columns. You can specify the level you would like to unstack with the level parameter, which accepts either the level name as a string or the level integer location. It is preferable to use the level name over the integer location to avoid ambiguity. *Steps 3* and *4* unstack each level, which results in a DataFrame with a single-level index. It is now much easier to compare salaries from each race by gender.

There's more...

If there are multiple aggregating functions when performing a groupby with a single column from a DataFrame, then the immediate result will be a DataFrame and not a Series. For instance, let's calculate more aggregations than just the mean, as was done in *step 2*:

```
>>> (employee
...      .groupby(['RACE', 'GENDER'])
...      ['BASE_SALARY']
...      .agg(['mean', 'max', 'min'])
...      .astype(int)
... )
```

		mean	max	min
RACE	GENDER			
American Indian or Alaskan Native	Female	60238	98536	26125
	Male	60305	81239	26125
Asian/Pacific Islander	Female	63226	130416	26125
	Male	61033	163228	27914
Black or African American	Female	48915	150416	24960
...		...	...	...
Hispanic/Latino	Male	54782	165216	26104
Others	Female	63785	63785	63785
	Male	38771	38771	38771
White	Female	66793	178331	27955
	Male	63940	210588	26125

Unstacking the `Gender` column will result in columns with a `MultiIndex`. From here, you can keep swapping row and column levels with both the `.unstack` and `.stack` methods until you achieve the structure of data you desire:

```
>>> (employee
...      .groupby(['RACE', 'GENDER'])
...      ['BASE_SALARY']
...      .agg(['mean', 'max', 'min'])
...      .astype(int)
...      .unstack('GENDER')
... )
```

	mean		...	min	
GENDER	Female	Male	...	Female	Male

```
RACE                      ...
American ...   60238   60305   ...   26125   26125
Asian/Pac...   63226   61033   ...   26125   27914
Black or ...   48915   51082   ...   24960   26125
Hispanic/...   46503   54782   ...   26125   26104
Others         63785   38771   ...   63785   38771
White          66793   63940   ...   27955   26125
```

Replicating pivot_table with a groupby aggregation

At first glance, it may seem that the `.pivot_table` method provides a unique way to analyze data. However, after a little massaging, it is possible to replicate its functionality with the `.groupby` method. Knowing this equivalence can help shrink the universe of pandas functionality.

In this recipe, we use the flights dataset to create a pivot table and then recreate it using the `.groupby` method.

How to do it...

1. Read in the flights dataset, and use the `.pivot_table` method to find the total number of canceled flights per origin airport for each *airline*:

```
>>> flights = pd.read_csv('data/flights.csv')
>>> fpt = flights.pivot_table(index='AIRLINE',
...         columns='ORG_AIR',
...         values='CANCELLED',
...         aggfunc='sum',
...         fill_value=0)
>>> fpt
```

ORG_AIR	ATL	DEN	DFW	IAH	LAS	LAX	MSP	ORD	PHX	SFO
AIRLINE										
AA	3	4	86	3	3	11	3	35	4	2
AS	0	0	0	0	0	0	0	0	0	0
B6	0	0	0	0	0	0	0	0	0	1
DL	28	1	0	0	1	1	4	0	1	2
EV	18	6	27	36	0	0	6	53	0	0
...	...	...	...	...	...	...	...	...	...	...

OO	3	25	2	10	0	15	4	41	9	33
UA	2	9	1	23	3	6	2	25	3	19
US	0	0	2	2	1	0	0	6	7	3
VX	0	0	0	0	0	3	0	0	0	3
WN	9	13	0	0	7	32	1	0	6	25

2. To replicate this with the `.groupby` method, we will need to groupby two columns and then unstack them. A groupby aggregation cannot replicate this table. The trick is to group by all the columns in both the index and columns parameters first:

```
>>> (flights
...        .groupby(['AIRLINE', 'ORG_AIR'])
...        ['CANCELLED']
...        .sum()
... )
AIRLINE   ORG_AIR
AA        ATL          3
          DEN          4
          DFW          86
          IAH          3
          LAS          3
                       ..
WN        LAS          7
          LAX          32
          MSP          1
          PHX          6
          SFO          25
Name: CANCELLED, Length: 114, dtype: int64
```

3. Use the `.unstack` method to pivot the `ORG_AIR` index level to column names:

```
>>> fpg = (flights
...        .groupby(['AIRLINE', 'ORG_AIR'])
...        ['CANCELLED']
...        .sum()
...        .unstack('ORG_AIR', fill_value=0)
... )

>>> fpt.equals(fpg)
True
```

How it works...

The `.pivot_table` method is very versatile and flexible but performs a rather similar operation to a groupby aggregation with *step 1* showing an example. The `index` parameter takes a column (or list of columns) that will not be pivoted and whose unique values will be placed in the index. The `columns` parameter takes a column (or list of columns) that will be pivoted and whose unique values will be made into column names. The `values` parameter takes a column (or list of columns) that will be aggregated.

There also exists an `aggfunc` parameter that takes an aggregating function (or list of functions) that determines how the columns in the `values` parameter get aggregated. It defaults to the string `mean`, and, in this example, we change it to calculate the sum. Additionally, some unique combinations of `AIRLINE` and `ORG_AIR` do not exist. These missing combinations will default to missing values in the resulting DataFrame. Here, we use the `fill_value` parameter to change them to zero.

Step 2 begins the replication process using all the columns in the `index` and `columns` parameter as the grouping columns. This is the key to making this recipe work. A pivot table is an intersection of all the unique combinations of the grouping columns. *Step 3* finishes the replication by pivoting the innermost index level into column names with the `.unstack` method. Just like with `.pivot_table`, not all combinations of `AIRLINE` and `ORG_AIR` exist; we again use the `fill_value` parameter to force these missing intersections to zero.

There's more...

It is possible to replicate much more complex pivot tables with the `.groupby` method. For instance, take the following result from `.pivot_table`:

```
>>> flights.pivot_table(index=['AIRLINE', 'MONTH'],
...        columns=['ORG_AIR', 'CANCELLED'],
...        values=['DEP_DELAY', 'DIST'],
...        aggfunc=['sum', 'mean'],
...        fill_value=0)
```

		sum		...	mean	
		DEP_DELAY		...	DIST	
ORG_AIR		ATL		...	SFO	
CANCELLED		0	1	...	0	1
AIRLINE	MONTH			...		
AA	1	-13	0	...	1860.166667	0.0
	2	-39	0	...	1337.916667	2586.0
	3	-2	0	...	1502.758621	0.0

```
    4            1  0  ...  1646.903226    0.0
    5           52  0  ...  1436.892857    0.0
...         ...  .. ...          ...       ...
WN  7         2604  0  ...   636.210526    0.0
    8         1718  0  ...   644.857143  392.0
    9         1033  0  ...   731.578947  354.5
    11         700  0  ...   580.875000  392.0
    12        1679  0  ...   782.256410    0.0
```

To replicate this with the `.groupby` method, follow the same pattern from the recipe, place all the columns from the `index` and `columns` parameters into the `.groupby` method, and then call `.unstack` to pull the index levels out to the columns:

```
>>> (flights
...      .groupby(['AIRLINE', 'MONTH', 'ORG_AIR', 'CANCELLED'])
...      [['DEP_DELAY', 'DIST']]
...      .agg(['mean', 'sum'])
...      .unstack(['ORG_AIR', 'CANCELLED'], fill_value=0)
...      .swaplevel(0, 1, axis='columns')
... )
                      mean        ...       sum
                 DEP_DELAY        ...      DIST
ORG_AIR                ATL        ...       SFO
CANCELLED            0    1  ...      0      1
AIRLINE MONTH                     ...
AA      1      -3.250000  NaN ...  33483.0    NaN
        2      -3.000000  NaN ...  32110.0  2586.0
        3      -0.166667  NaN ...  43580.0    NaN
        4       0.071429  NaN ...  51054.0    NaN
        5       5.777778  NaN ...  40233.0    NaN
...                 ...   .. ...      ...     ...
WN      7      21.700000  NaN ...  24176.0    NaN
        8      16.207547  NaN ...  18056.0   784.0
        9       8.680672  NaN ...  27800.0   709.0
        11      5.932203  NaN ...  23235.0   784.0
        12     15.691589  NaN ...  30508.0    NaN
```

The order of the column levels differs, with `.pivot_table` putting the aggregation functions at a level preceding the columns in the `values` parameter. You can use the `.swaplevel` method to remedy this. It will swap the outermost column (level 0) with the level below that (level 1). Also note that the column order is different.

Renaming axis levels for easy reshaping

Reshaping with the `.stack` and `.unstack` methods is far easier when each axis (both index and column) level has a name. pandas allows users to reference each axis level by integer location or by name. Since integer location is implicit and not explicit, you should consider using level names whenever possible. This advice follows from *The Zen of Python* (type `import this` if you are not familiar with it), a short list of guiding principles for Python, of which the second one is "Explicit is better than implicit."

When grouping or aggregating with multiple columns, the resulting pandas object will have multiple levels in one or both of the axes. In this recipe, we will name each level of each axis and then use the `.stack` and `.unstack` methods to reshape the data to the desired form.

How to do it...

1. Read in the college dataset, and find a few basic summary statistics on the undergraduate population and SAT math scores by institution and religious affiliation:

```
>>> college = pd.read_csv('data/college.csv')
>>> (college
...      .groupby(['STABBR', 'RELAFFIL'])
...      [['UGDS', 'SATMTMID']]
...      .agg(['size', 'min', 'max'])
... )
```

	UGDS			SATMTMID		
	size	min	max	size	min	max
STABBR RELAFFIL						
AK 0	7	109.0	12865.0	7	NaN	NaN
1	3	27.0	275.0	3	503.0	503.0
AL 0	72	12.0	29851.0	72	420.0	590.0
1	24	13.0	3033.0	24	400.0	560.0
AR 0	68	18.0	21405.0	68	427.0	565.0
...	...	...	...	...	...	...
WI 0	87	20.0	29302.0	87	480.0	680.0

	1	25	4.0	8212.0	25	452.0	605.0
WV	0	65	20.0	44924.0	65	430.0	530.0
	1	8	63.0	1375.0	8	455.0	510.0
WY	0	11	52.0	9910.0	11	540.0	540.0

2. Notice that both index levels have names and are the old column names. The column levels, on the other hand, do not have names. Use the `.rename_axis` method to give them level names:

```
>>> (college
...     .groupby(['STABBR', 'RELAFFIL'])
...     [['UGDS', 'SATMTMID']]
...     .agg(['size', 'min', 'max'])
...     .rename_axis(['AGG_COLS', 'AGG_FUNCS'], axis='columns')
... )
```

AGG_COLS		UGDS			SATMTMID		
AGG_FUNCS		size	min	max	size	min	max
STABBR	RELAFFIL						
AK	0	7	109.0	12865.0	7	NaN	NaN
	1	3	27.0	275.0	3	503.0	503.0
AL	0	72	12.0	29851.0	72	420.0	590.0
	1	24	13.0	3033.0	24	400.0	560.0
AR	0	68	18.0	21405.0	68	427.0	565.0
...		...	...	...	...	...	...
WI	0	87	20.0	29302.0	87	480.0	680.0
	1	25	4.0	8212.0	25	452.0	605.0
WV	0	65	20.0	44924.0	65	430.0	530.0
	1	8	63.0	1375.0	8	455.0	510.0
WY	0	11	52.0	9910.0	11	540.0	540.0

3. Now that each axis level has a name, reshaping is a breeze. Use the `.stack` method to move the AGG_FUNCS column to an index level:

```
>>> (college
...     .groupby(['STABBR', 'RELAFFIL'])
...     [['UGDS', 'SATMTMID']]
...     .agg(['size', 'min', 'max'])
...     .rename_axis(['AGG_COLS', 'AGG_FUNCS'], axis='columns')
...     .stack('AGG_FUNCS')
... )
```

AGG_COLS			UGDS	SATMTMID
STABBR	RELAFFIL	AGG_FUNCS		
AK	0	size	7.0	7.0
		min	109.0	NaN
		max	12865.0	NaN
	1	size	3.0	3.0
		min	27.0	503.0
...			...	...
WV	1	min	63.0	455.0
		max	1375.0	510.0
WY	0	size	11.0	11.0
		min	52.0	540.0
		max	9910.0	540.0

4. By default, stacking places the new column level in the innermost index position. Use the `.swaplevel` method to move AGG_FUNCS from the innermost level to the outer level:

```
>>> (college
...       .groupby(['STABBR', 'RELAFFIL'])
...       [['UGDS', 'SATMTMID']]
...       .agg(['size', 'min', 'max'])
...       .rename_axis(['AGG_COLS', 'AGG_FUNCS'], axis='columns')
...       .stack('AGG_FUNCS')
...       .swaplevel('AGG_FUNCS', 'STABBR',
...          axis='index')
... )
```

AGG_COLS			UGDS	SATMTMID
AGG_FUNCS	RELAFFIL	STABBR		
size	0	AK	7.0	7.0
min	0	AK	109.0	NaN
max	0	AK	12865.0	NaN
size	1	AK	3.0	3.0
min	1	AK	27.0	503.0
...			...	...
		WV	63.0	455.0
max	1	WV	1375.0	510.0
size	0	WY	11.0	11.0

min	0	WY	52.0	540.0
max	0	WY	9910.0	540.0

5. We can continue to make use of the axis level names by sorting levels with the
   `.sort_index` method:

```
>>> (college
...       .groupby(['STABBR', 'RELAFFIL'])
...       [['UGDS', 'SATMTMID']]
...       .agg(['size', 'min', 'max'])
...       .rename_axis(['AGG_COLS', 'AGG_FUNCS'], axis='columns')
...       .stack('AGG_FUNCS')
...       .swaplevel('AGG_FUNCS', 'STABBR', axis='index')
...       .sort_index(level='RELAFFIL', axis='index')
...       .sort_index(level='AGG_COLS', axis='columns')
... )
```

AGG_COLS			SATMTMID	UGDS
AGG_FUNCS	RELAFFIL	STABBR		
max	0	AK	NaN	12865.0
		AL	590.0	29851.0
		AR	565.0	21405.0
		AS	NaN	1276.0
		AZ	580.0	151558.0
...			...	...
size	1	VI	1.0	1.0
		VT	5.0	5.0
		WA	17.0	17.0
		WI	25.0	25.0
		WV	8.0	8.0

6. To completely reshape your data, you might need to stack some columns while
   unstacking others. Chain the two methods together:

```
>>> (college
...       .groupby(['STABBR', 'RELAFFIL'])
...       [['UGDS', 'SATMTMID']]
...       .agg(['size', 'min', 'max'])
...       .rename_axis(['AGG_COLS', 'AGG_FUNCS'], axis='columns')
...       .stack('AGG_FUNCS')
```

```
...         .unstack(['RELAFFIL', 'STABBR'])
... )
```

AGG_COLS	UGDS		...	SATMTMID	
RELAFFIL	0	1	...	1	0
STABBR	AK	AK	...	WV	WY
AGG_FUNCS			...		
size	7.0	3.0	...	8.0	11.0
min	109.0	27.0	...	455.0	540.0
max	12865.0	275.0	...	510.0	540.0

7. Stack all the columns at once to return a Series:

```
>>> (college
...         .groupby(['STABBR', 'RELAFFIL'])
...         [['UGDS', 'SATMTMID']]
...         .agg(['size', 'min', 'max'])
...         .rename_axis(['AGG_COLS', 'AGG_FUNCS'], axis='columns')
...         .stack(['AGG_FUNCS', 'AGG_COLS'])
... )
```

STABBR	RELAFFIL	AGG_FUNCS	AGG_COLS	
AK	0	size	UGDS	7.0
			SATMTMID	7.0
		min	UGDS	109.0
		max	UGDS	12865.0
	1	size	UGDS	3.0
				...
WY	0	size	SATMTMID	11.0
		min	UGDS	52.0
			SATMTMID	540.0
		max	UGDS	9910.0
			SATMTMID	540.0

```
Length: 640, dtype: float64
```

8. We can also unstack everything in the index. In this case, it collapses to a very wide result, which pandas displays as a Series:

```
>>> (college
...         .groupby(['STABBR', 'RELAFFIL'])
...         [['UGDS', 'SATMTMID']]
```

```
...         .agg(['size', 'min', 'max'])
...         .rename_axis(['AGG_COLS', 'AGG_FUNCS'], axis='columns')
...         .unstack(['STABBR', 'RELAFFIL'])
... )
AGG_COLS   AGG_FUNCS   STABBR   RELAFFIL
UGDS       size        AK       0                   7.0
                                1                   3.0
                       AL       0                  72.0
                                1                  24.0
                       AR       0                  68.0
                                                    ...
SATMTMID   max         WI       1                 605.0
                       WV       0                 530.0
                                1                 510.0
                       WY       0                 540.0
                                1                   NaN

Length: 708, dtype: float64
```

How it works...

It is common for the result of a call to the `.groupby` method to produce a DataFrame or Series with multiple axis levels. The resulting DataFrame from the groupby operation in *step 1* has multiple levels for each axis. The column levels are not named, which would require us to reference them only by their integer location. To ease our ability to reference the column levels, we rename them with the `.rename_axis` method.

The `.rename_axis` method is a bit strange in that it can modify both the level names and the level values based on the type of the first argument passed to it. Passing it a list (or a scalar if there is only one level) changes the names of the levels. In *step 2*, we pass the `.rename_axis` method a list and are returned a DataFrame with all axis levels named.

Once all the axis levels have names, we can control the structure of data. *Step 3* stacks the AGG_FUNCS column into the innermost index level. The `.swaplevel` method in *step 4* accepts the name or position of the levels that you want to swap as the first two arguments. In *step 5*, the `.sort_index` method is called twice and sorts the values of each level. Notice that the values of the column level are the column names SATMTMID and UGDS.

We can get vastly different output by both stacking and unstacking, as done in *step 6*. It is also possible to stack or unstack every single column or index level, and both will collapse into a Series.

There's more...

If you wish to dispose of the level values altogether, you may set them to None. You can do this when you want to reduce visual clutter or when it is obvious what the column levels represent and no further processing will take place:

```
>>> (college
...        .groupby(['STABBR', 'RELAFFIL'])
...        [['UGDS', 'SATMTMID']]
...        .agg(['size', 'min', 'max'])
...        .rename_axis([None, None], axis='index')
...        .rename_axis([None, None], axis='columns')
... )
```

		UGDS			SATMTMID		
		size	min	max	size	min	max
AK	0	7	109.0	12865.0	7	NaN	NaN
	1	3	27.0	275.0	3	503.0	503.0
AL	0	72	12.0	29851.0	72	420.0	590.0
	1	24	13.0	3033.0	24	400.0	560.0
AR	0	68	18.0	21405.0	68	427.0	565.0
...		...	...	...	...	...	...
WI	0	87	20.0	29302.0	87	480.0	680.0
	1	25	4.0	8212.0	25	452.0	605.0
WV	0	65	20.0	44924.0	65	430.0	530.0
	1	8	63.0	1375.0	8	455.0	510.0
WY	0	11	52.0	9910.0	11	540.0	540.0

Tidying when multiple variables are stored as column names

One particular flavor of messy data appears whenever the column names contain multiple different variables themselves. A common example of this scenario occurs when age and sex are concatenated together. To tidy datasets like this, we must manipulate the columns with the pandas .str attribute. This attribute contains additional methods for string processing.

In this recipe, we will first identify all the variables, of which some will be concatenated together as column names. We then reshape the data and parse the text to extract the correct variable values.

How to do it...

1. Read in the men's weightlifting dataset, and identify the variables:

```
>>> weightlifting = pd.read_csv('data/weightlifting_men.csv')
>>> weightlifting
```

	Weight Category	M35 35-39	...	M75 75-79	M80 80+
0	56	137	...	62	55
1	62	152	...	67	57
2	69	167	...	75	60
3	77	182	...	82	65
4	85	192	...	87	70
5	94	202	...	90	75
6	105	210	...	95	80
7	105+	217	...	100	85

2. The variables are the `Weight Category`, a combination of sex and age, and the qualifying total. The age and sex variables have been concatenated together into a single cell. Before we can separate them, let's use the `.melt` method to transpose the age and sex column names into a single vertical column:

```
>>> (weightlifting
...     .melt(id_vars='Weight Category',
...           var_name='sex_age',
...           value_name='Qual Total')
... )
```

	Weight Category	sex_age	Qual Total
0	56	M35 35-39	137
1	62	M35 35-39	152
2	69	M35 35-39	167
3	77	M35 35-39	182
4	85	M35 35-39	192
..	...	...	...
75	77	M80 80+	65
76	85	M80 80+	70
77	94	M80 80+	75
78	105	M80 80+	80
79	105+	M80 80+	85

3. Select the `sex_age` column, and use the `.split` method available from the `.str` attribute to split the column into two different columns:

```
>>> (weightlifting
...     .melt(id_vars='Weight Category',
...           var_name='sex_age',
...           value_name='Qual Total')
...     ['sex_age']
...     .str.split(expand=True)
... )
          0       1
0       M35    35-39
1       M35    35-39
2       M35    35-39
3       M35    35-39
4       M35    35-39
..      ...     ...
75      M80     80+
76      M80     80+
77      M80     80+
78      M80     80+
79      M80     80+
```

4. This operation returned a DataFrame with meaningless column names. Let's rename the columns:

```
>>> (weightlifting
...     .melt(id_vars='Weight Category',
...           var_name='sex_age',
...           value_name='Qual Total')
...     ['sex_age']
...     .str.split(expand=True)
...     .rename(columns={0:'Sex', 1:'Age Group'})
... )
        Sex   Age Group
0       M35      35-39
1       M35      35-39
2       M35      35-39
3       M35      35-39
```

4	M35	35-39
..	...	...
75	M80	80+
76	M80	80+
77	M80	80+
78	M80	80+
79	M80	80+

5. Create a `Sex` column using an index operation after the `.str` attribute to select the first character from the renamed `Sex` column:

```
>>> (weightlifting
...      .melt(id_vars='Weight Category',
...           var_name='sex_age',
...           value_name='Qual Total')
...      ['sex_age']
...      .str.split(expand=True)
...      .rename(columns={0:'Sex', 1:'Age Group'})
...      .assign(Sex=lambda df_: df_.Sex.str[0])
... )
```

	Sex	Age Group
0	M	35-39
1	M	35-39
2	M	35-39
3	M	35-39
4	M	35-39
..	..	...
75	M	80+
76	M	80+
77	M	80+
78	M	80+
79	M	80+

6. Use the `pd.concat` function to concatenate this DataFrame with the `Weight Category` and `Qual Total` columns:

```
>>> melted = (weightlifting
...      .melt(id_vars='Weight Category',
...           var_name='sex_age',
```

```
...             value_name='Qual Total')
... )
>>> tidy = pd.concat([melted
...             ['sex_age']
...             .str.split(expand=True)
...             .rename(columns={0:'Sex', 1:'Age Group'})
...             .assign(Sex=lambda df_: df_.Sex.str[0]),
...         melted[['Weight Category', 'Qual Total']]],
...         axis='columns'
... )
>>> tidy
```

	Sex	Age Group	Weight Category	Qual Total
0	M	35-39	56	137
1	M	35-39	62	152
2	M	35-39	69	167
3	M	35-39	77	182
4	M	35-39	85	192
..	..	...	...	...
75	M	80+	77	65
76	M	80+	85	70
77	M	80+	94	75
78	M	80+	105	80
79	M	80+	105+	85

7. This same result could have been created with the following:

```
>>> melted = (weightlifting
...         .melt(id_vars='Weight Category',
...             var_name='sex_age',
...             value_name='Qual Total')
... )
>>> (melted
...         ['sex_age']
...         .str.split(expand=True)
...         .rename(columns={0:'Sex', 1:'Age Group'})
...         .assign(Sex=lambda df_: df_.Sex.str[0],
...             Category=melted['Weight Category'],
```

```
...            Total=melted['Qual Total'])
... )
```

	Sex	Age Group	Category	Total
0	M	35-39	56	137
1	M	35-39	62	152
2	M	35-39	69	167
3	M	35-39	77	182
4	M	35-39	85	192
..	..	...	...	...
75	M	80+	77	65
76	M	80+	85	70
77	M	80+	94	75
78	M	80+	105	80
79	M	80+	105+	85

How it works...

The weightlifting dataset, like many datasets, has easily digestible information in its raw form. Still, technically it is messy, as all but one of the column names contain information for sex and age. Once the variables are identified, we can begin to tidy the dataset. Whenever column names contain variables, you will need to use the .melt (or .stack) method. The Weight Category variable is already in the correct position, so we keep it as an identifying variable by passing it to the id_vars parameter. Note that we don't explicitly need to name all the columns that we are melting with value_vars. By default, all the columns not present in id_vars get melted.

The sex_age column needs to be parsed, and split into two variables. For this, we turn to the extra functionality provided by the .str attribute, only available to Series (a single DataFrame column) or an index (this is not hierarchical). The .split method is one of the more common methods in this situation, as it can separate different parts of the string into their own columns.By default, it splits on an empty space, but you may also specify a string or regular expression with the pat parameter. When the expand parameter is set to True, a new column forms for each independent split character segment. When False, a single column is returned, containing a list of all the segments.

After renaming the columns in *step 4*, we need to use the .str attribute again. This attribute allows us to index or slice off of it, just like a string. Here, we select the first character, which is the variable for sex. We could go further and split the ages into two separate columns for minimum and maximum age, but it is common to refer to the entire age group in this manner, so we leave it as is.

Step 6 shows one of two different methods to join all the data together. The `concat` function accepts a collection of DataFrames and either concatenates them vertically (`axis='index'`) or horizontally (`axis='columns'`). Because the two DataFrames are indexed identically, it is possible to assign the values of one DataFrame to new columns in the other, as done in *step 7*.

There's more...

Another way to complete this recipe, beginning after *step 2*, is by assigning new columns from the `sex_age` column without using the `.split` method. The `.assign` method may be used to add these new columns dynamically:

```
>>> tidy2 = (weightlifting
...         .melt(id_vars='Weight Category',
...               var_name='sex_age',
...               value_name='Qual Total')
...         .assign(Sex=lambda df_:df_.sex_age.str[0],
...             **{'Age Group':(lambda df_: (df_
...                 .sex_age
...                 .str.extract(r'(\d{2}[-+](?:\d{2})?)',
...                              expand=False)))})
...         .drop(columns='sex_age')
... )
```

```
>>> tidy2
    Weight Category  Qual Total Sex Age Group
0               56          137   M    35-39
1               62          152   M    35-39
2               69          167   M    35-39
3               77          182   M    35-39
4               85          192   M    35-39
..             ...          ...  ..      ...
75              77           65   M      80+
76              85           70   M      80+
77              94           75   M      80+
78             105           80   M      80+
79            105+           85   M      80+
```

```
>>> tidy.sort_index(axis=1).equals(tidy2.sort_index(axis=1))
True
```

The Sex column is found in the same manner as done in *step 5*. Because we are not using .split, the Age Group column must be extracted in a different manner. The .extract method uses a complex regular expression to extract very specific portions of the string. To use .extract correctly, your pattern must contain capture groups. A capture group is formed by enclosing parentheses around a portion of the pattern. In this example, the entire expression is one large capture group. It begins with \d{2}, which searches for exactly two digits, followed by either a literal plus or minus, optionally followed by two more digits. Although the last part of the expression, (?:\d{2})?, is surrounded by parentheses, the ?: denotes that it is not a capture group. It is technically a non-capturing group used to express two digits together as optional. The sex_age column is no longer needed and is dropped.

Finally, the two tidy DataFrames are compared against one another and are found to be equivalent.

Tidying when multiple variables are stored as a single column

Tidy datasets must have a single column for each variable. Occasionally, multiple variable names are placed in a single column with their corresponding value placed in another.

In this recipe, we identify the column containing the improperly structured variables and pivot it to create tidy data.

How to do it...

1. Read in the restaurant inspections dataset, and convert the Date column data type to datetime64:

    ```
    >>> inspections = pd.read_csv('data/restaurant_inspections.csv',
    ...     parse_dates=['Date'])
    >>> inspections
                              Name    ...
    0            E & E Grill House    ...
    1            E & E Grill House    ...
    2            E & E Grill House    ...
    3            E & E Grill House    ...
    4            E & E Grill House    ...
    ..                         ...    ...
    ```

```
495   PIER SIXTY ONE-THE LIGHTHOUSE   ...
496   PIER SIXTY ONE-THE LIGHTHOUSE   ...
497   PIER SIXTY ONE-THE LIGHTHOUSE   ...
498   PIER SIXTY ONE-THE LIGHTHOUSE   ...
499   PIER SIXTY ONE-THE LIGHTHOUSE   ...
```

2. This dataset has two columns, `Name` and `Date`, that are each correctly contained in a single column. The `Info` column has five different variables: Borough, Cuisine, Description, Grade, and Score. Let's attempt to use the `.pivot` method to keep the `Name` and `Date` columns vertical, create new columns out of all the values in the `Info` column, and use the `Value` column as their intersection:

```
>>> inspections.pivot(index=['Name', 'Date'],
...       columns='Info', values='Value')
Traceback (most recent call last):
   ...
NotImplementedError: > 1 ndim Categorical are not supported at
this time
```

3. Unfortunately, pandas developers have not implemented this functionality for us. Thankfully, for the most part, pandas has multiple ways of accomplishing the same task. Let's put `Name`, `Date`, and `Info` into the index:

```
>>> inspections.set_index(['Name','Date', 'Info'])
                                        Value
Name          Date         Info
E & E Gri... 2017-08-08 Borough        MANHATTAN
                        Cuisine        American
                        Description    Non-food...
                        Grade          A
                        Score          9.0
...                                    ...
PIER SIXT... 2017-09-01 Borough        MANHATTAN
                        Cuisine        American
                        Description    Filth fl...
                        Grade          Z
                        Score          33.0
```

4. Use the `.unstack` method to pivot all the values in the `Info` column:

```
>>> (inspections
...       .set_index(['Name','Date', 'Info'])
```

```
...       .unstack('Info')
... )
```

Info		Value		...		
		Borough	Cuisine	...	Grade	Score
Name	Date			...		
3 STAR JU...	2017-05-10	BROOKLYN	Juice, S...	...	A	12.0
A & L PIZ...	2017-08-22	BROOKLYN	Pizza	...	A	9.0
AKSARAY T...	2017-07-25	BROOKLYN	Turkish	...	A	13.0
ANTOJITOS...	2017-06-01	BROOKLYN	Latin (C...	...	A	10.0
BANGIA	2017-06-16	MANHATTAN	Korean	...	A	9.0
...		...	...	...	...	...
VALL'S PI...	2017-03-15	STATEN I...	Pizza/It...	...	A	9.0
VIP GRILL	2017-06-12	BROOKLYN	Jewish/K...	...	A	10.0
WAHIZZA	2017-04-13	MANHATTAN	Pizza	...	A	10.0
WANG MAND...	2017-08-29	QUEENS	Korean	...	A	12.0
XIAOYAN Y...	2017-08-29	QUEENS	Korean	...	Z	49.0

5. Make the index levels into columns with the `.reset_index` method:

```
>>> (inspections
...       .set_index(['Name','Date', 'Info'])
...       .unstack('Info')
...       .reset_index(col_level=-1)
... )
```

Info	Name	Date	...	Value	
			...	Grade	Score
0	3 STAR J...	2017-05-10	...	A	12.0
1	A & L PI...	2017-08-22	...	A	9.0
2	AKSARAY ...	2017-07-25	...	A	13.0
3	ANTOJITO...	2017-06-01	...	A	10.0
4	BANGIA	2017-06-16	...	A	9.0
..	...	...	...	...	...
95	VALL'S P...	2017-03-15	...	A	9.0
96	VIP GRILL	2017-06-12	...	A	10.0
97	WAHIZZA	2017-04-13	...	A	10.0
98	WANG MAN...	2017-08-29	...	A	12.0
99	XIAOYAN ...	2017-08-29	...	Z	49.0

6. The dataset is tidy, but there is some annoying leftover pandas debris that needs to be removed. Let's use the `.droplevel` method to remove the top column level and then rename the index level to `None`:

```
>>> (inspections
...      .set_index(['Name','Date', 'Info'])
...      .unstack('Info')
...      .reset_index(col_level=-1)
...      .droplevel(0, axis=1)
...      .rename_axis(None, axis=1)
... )
            Name        Date  ... Grade Score
0    3 STAR J... 2017-05-10  ...     A  12.0
1    A & L PI... 2017-08-22  ...     A   9.0
2    AKSARAY ... 2017-07-25  ...     A  13.0
3    ANTOJITO... 2017-06-01  ...     A  10.0
4        BANGIA 2017-06-16  ...     A   9.0
..          ...        ...  ...   ...   ...
95   VALL'S P... 2017-03-15  ...     A   9.0
96    VIP GRILL 2017-06-12  ...     A  10.0
97      WAHIZZA 2017-04-13  ...     A  10.0
98   WANG MAN... 2017-08-29  ...     A  12.0
99   XIAOYAN ... 2017-08-29  ...     Z  49.0
```

7. The creation of the column MultiIndex in *step 4* could have been avoided by converting that one column DataFrame in *step 3* into a Series with the `.squeeze` method. The following code produces the same result as the previous step:

```
>>> (inspections
...      .set_index(['Name','Date', 'Info'])
...      .squeeze()
...      .unstack('Info')
...      .reset_index()
...      .rename_axis(None, axis='columns')
... )
            Name        Date  ... Grade Score
0    3 STAR J... 2017-05-10  ...     A  12.0
1    A & L PI... 2017-08-22  ...     A   9.0
2    AKSARAY ... 2017-07-25  ...     A  13.0
3    ANTOJITO... 2017-06-01  ...     A  10.0
```

4	BANGIA	2017-06-16	...	A	9.0
..	...	...	...	...	...
95	VALL'S P...	2017-03-15	...	A	9.0
96	VIP GRILL	2017-06-12	...	A	10.0
97	WAHIZZA	2017-04-13	...	A	10.0
98	WANG MAN...	2017-08-29	...	A	12.0
99	XIAOYAN ...	2017-08-29	...	Z	49.0

How it works...

In *step 1*, we notice that there are five variables placed vertically in the `Info` column with their corresponding value in the `Value` column. Because we need to pivot each of these five variables as horizontal column names, it would seem that the `.pivot` method would work. Unfortunately, pandas developers have yet to implement this special case when there is more than one non-pivoted column. We are forced to use a different method.

The `.unstack` method also pivots vertical data, but only for data in the index. *Step 3* begins this process by moving both the columns that will and will not be pivoted into the index with the `.set_index` method. Once these columns are in the index, the `.unstack` method can be put to work, as done in *step 4*.

Notice that as we are unstacking a DataFrame, pandas keeps the original column names (here, it is just a single column, `Value`) and creates a `MultiIndex` with the old column names as the upper level. The dataset is now essentially tidy, but we go ahead and make our non-pivoted columns normal columns with the `.reset_index` method. Because we have `MultiIndex` columns, we can choose which level the new column names will belong to with the `col_level` parameter. By default, the names are inserted into the uppermost level (level 0). We use -1 to indicate the bottommost level.

After all this, we have some excess DataFrame names and indexes that need to be discarded. We use `.droplevel` and `.rename_axis` to remedy that. These columns still have a useless `.name` attribute, `Info`, which is renamed `None`.

Cleaning up the `MultiIndex` columns could have been avoided by forcing the resulting DataFrame from *step 3* to a Series. The `.squeeze` method works on single-column DataFrames and turns them into Series.

There's more...

It is possible to use the `.pivot_table` method, which has no restrictions on how many non-pivoted columns are allowed. The `.pivot_table` method differs from `.pivot` by performing an aggregation for all the values that correspond to the intersection between the columns in the `index` and `columns` parameters.

Because there may be multiple values in this intersection, `.pivot_table` requires the user to pass it an aggregating function to output a single value. We use the `first` aggregating function, which takes the first of the values of the group. In this particular example, there is exactly one value for each intersection, so there is nothing to be aggregated. The default aggregation function is the `mean`, which will produce an error here, since some of the values are strings:

```
>>> (inspections
...        .pivot_table(index=['Name', 'Date'],
...                     columns='Info',
...                     values='Value',
...                     aggfunc='first')
...        .reset_index()
...        .rename_axis(None, axis='columns')
... )
```

	Name	Date	...	Grade	Score
0	3 STAR J...	2017-05-10	...	A	12.0
1	A & L PI...	2017-08-22	...	A	9.0
2	AKSARAY ...	2017-07-25	...	A	13.0
3	ANTOJITO...	2017-06-01	...	A	10.0
4	BANGIA	2017-06-16	...	A	9.0
..	...	...	...	...	...
95	VALL'S P...	2017-03-15	...	A	9.0
96	VIP GRILL	2017-06-12	...	A	10.0
97	WAHIZZA	2017-04-13	...	A	10.0
98	WANG MAN...	2017-08-29	...	A	12.0
99	XIAOYAN ...	2017-08-29	...	Z	49.0

Tidying when two or more values are stored in the same cell

Tabular data, by nature, is two-dimensional, and thus, there is a limited amount of information that can be presented in a single cell. As a workaround, you will occasionally see datasets with more than a single value stored in the same cell. Tidy data allows for just a single value for each cell. To rectify these situations, you will typically need to parse the string data into multiple columns with the methods from the `.str` attribute.

In this recipe, we examine a dataset that has a column containing multiple different variables in each cell. We use the `.str` attribute to parse these strings into separate columns to tidy the data.

How to do it...

1. Read in the Texas cities dataset:

```
>>> cities = pd.read_csv('data/texas_cities.csv')
>>> cities
        City              Geolocation
0   Houston    29.7604° N,  95.3698° W
1    Dallas    32.7767° N,  96.7970° W
2    Austin    30.2672° N,  97.7431° W
```

2. The `City` column looks good and contains exactly one value. The `Geolocation` column, on the other hand, contains four variables: latitude, latitude direction, longitude, and longitude direction. Let's split the `Geolocation` column into four separate columns. We will use the regular expression that matches any character followed by a space:

```
>>> geolocations = cities.Geolocation.str.split(pat='. ',
...     expand=True)
>>> geolocations.columns = ['latitude', 'latitude direction',
...     'longitude', 'longitude direction']
```

3. Because the original data type for the `Geolocation` was an `object`, all the new columns are also objects. Let's change `latitude` and `longitude` into `float` types:

```
>>> geolocations = geolocations.astype({'latitude':'float',
...     'longitude':'float'})
>>> geolocations.dtypes
latitude               float64
latitude direction      object
longitude              float64
longitude direction     object
dtype: object
```

4. Combine these new columns with the `City` column from the original:

```
>>> (geolocations
...     .assign(city=cities['City'])
... )
```

	latitude	latitude direction	...	longitude direction	city
0	29.7604	N	...	W	Houston
1	32.7767	N	...	W	Dallas
2	30.2672	N	...	W	Austin

How it works...

After reading the data, we decide how many variables there are in the dataset. Here, we chose to split the `Geolocation` column into four variables, but we could have just chosen two for `latitude` and `longitude` and used a negative sign to differentiate between west and east and south and north.

There are a few ways to parse the `Geolocation` column with the methods from the `.str` attribute. The easiest way is to use the `.split` method. We pass it a regular expression defined by any character (the period) and a space. When a space follows any character, a split is made, and a new column is formed. The first occurrence of this pattern takes place at the end of the latitude. A space follows the degree character, and a split is formed. The splitting characters are discarded and not kept in the resulting columns. The next split matches the comma and space following directly after the latitude direction.

A total of three splits are made, resulting in four columns. The second line in *step 2* provides them with meaningful names. Even though the resulting `latitude` and `longitude` columns appear to be `float` types, they are not. They were originally parsed from an `object` column and therefore remain `object` data types. *Step 3* uses a dictionary to map the column names to their new types.

Instead of using a dictionary, which would require a lot of typing if you had many column names, you can use the function `to_numeric` to attempt to convert each column to either `integer` or `float`. To apply this function iteratively over each column, use the `.apply` method with the following:

```
>>> geolocations.apply(pd.to_numeric, errors='ignore')
```

	latitude	latitude direction	longitude	longitude direction
0	29.7604	N	95.3698	W
1	32.7767	N	96.7970	W
2	30.2672	N	97.7431	W

Step 4 concatenates the city to the DataFrame to complete the process of making tidy data.

There's more...

The `.split` method worked well in this example with a regular expression. For other examples, some columns might require you to create splits on several different patterns. To search for multiple regular expressions, use the pipe character (|). For instance, if we wanted to split only the degree symbol and comma, each followed by a space, we would do the following:

```
>>> cities.Geolocation.str.split(pat=r'° |, ', expand=True)
        0   1      2   3
0   29.7604   N   95.3698   W
1   32.7767   N   96.7970   W
2   30.2672   N   97.7431   W
```

This returns the same DataFrame from *step 2*. Any number of additional split patterns may be appended to the preceding string pattern with the pipe character.

The `.extract` method is another method that allows you to extract specific groups within each cell. These capture groups must be enclosed in parentheses. Anything that matches outside the parentheses is not present in the result. The following line produces the same output as *step 2*:

```{.sourceCode .pycon}
>>> cities.Geolocation.str.extract(r'([0-9.]+). (N|S), ([0-9.]+). (E|W)',
...     expand=True)
        0   1      2   3
0   29.7604   N   95.3698   W
1   32.7767   N   96.7970   W
2   30.2672   N   97.7431   W


```

This regular expression has four capture groups. The first and third groups search for at least one or more consecutive digits with decimals. The second and fourth groups search for a single character (the direction). The first and third capture groups are separated by any character followed by a space. The second capture group is separated by a comma and then a space.

Tidying when variables are stored in column names and values

One particularly difficult form of messy data to diagnose appears whenever variables are stored both horizontally across the column names and vertically down column values. This type of dataset usually is not found in a database, but from a summarized report that someone else has already generated.

How to do it...

In this recipe, data is reshaped into tidy data with the `.melt` and `.pivot_table` methods.

1. Read in the sensors dataset:

```
>>> sensors = pd.read_csv('data/sensors.csv')
>>> sensors
```

	Group	Property	2012	2013	2014	2015	2016
0	A	Pressure	928	873	814	973	870
1	A	Temperature	1026	1038	1009	1036	1042
2	A	Flow	819	806	861	882	856
3	B	Pressure	817	877	914	806	942
4	B	Temperature	1008	1041	1009	1002	1013
5	B	Flow	887	899	837	824	873

2. The only variable placed correctly in a vertical column is `Group`. The `Property` column appears to have three unique variables, `Pressure`, `Temperature`, and `Flow`. The rest of the columns 2012 to 2016 are themselves a single variable, which we can sensibly name `Year`. It isn't possible to restructure this kind of messy data with a single DataFrame method. Let's begin with the `.melt` method to pivot the years into their own column:

```
>>> sensors.melt(id_vars=['Group', 'Property'], var_name='Year')
```

	Group	Property	Year	value
0	A	Pressure	2012	928
1	A	Temperature	2012	1026
2	A	Flow	2012	819
3	B	Pressure	2012	817
4	B	Temperature	2012	1008
..	...	...	...	...
25	A	Temperature	2016	1042

```
26    A            Flow  2016   856
27    B        Pressure  2016   942
28    B     Temperature  2016  1013
29    B            Flow  2016   873
```

3. This takes care of one of our issues. Let's use the `.pivot_table` method to pivot the `Property` column into new column names:

```
>>> (sensors
...      .melt(id_vars=['Group', 'Property'], var_name='Year')
...      .pivot_table(index=['Group', 'Year'],
...                   columns='Property', values='value')
...      .reset_index()
...      .rename_axis(None, axis='columns')
... )
   Group  Year  Flow  Pressure  Temperature
0      A  2012   819       928         1026
1      A  2013   806       873         1038
2      A  2014   861       814         1009
3      A  2015   882       973         1036
4      A  2016   856       870         1042
5      B  2012   887       817         1008
6      B  2013   899       877         1041
7      B  2014   837       914         1009
8      B  2015   824       806         1002
9      B  2016   873       942         1013
```

How it works...

Once we have identified the variables in *step 1*, we can begin our restructuring. pandas does not have a method to pivot columns simultaneously, so we must take on this task one step at a time. We correct the years by keeping the `Property` column vertical by passing it to the `id_vars` parameter in the `.melt` method.

The result is now the pattern of messy data found in the recipe before last. As explained in the *There's more...* section of that recipe, we must use `.pivot_table` to pivot a DataFrame when using more than one column in the `index` parameter. After pivoting, the `Group` and `Year` variables are stuck in the index. We push them back out as columns with `.reset_index`. The `.pivot_table` method preserves the column name used in the `columns` parameter as the name of the column index. After resetting the index, this name is meaningless, and we remove it with `.rename_axis`.

There's more...

Whenever a solution involves `.melt`, `.pivot_table`, or `.pivot`, you can be sure that there is an alternative method using `.stack` and `.unstack`. The trick is first to move the columns that are not currently being pivoted into the index:

```
>>> (sensors
...       .set_index(['Group', 'Property'])
...       .rename_axis('Year', axis='columns')
...       .stack()
...       .unstack('Property')
...       .rename_axis(None, axis='columns')
...       .reset_index()
... )
```

	Group	Year	Flow	Pressure	Temperature
0	A	2012	819	928	1026
1	A	2013	806	873	1038
2	A	2014	861	814	1009
3	A	2015	882	973	1036
4	A	2016	856	870	1042
5	B	2012	887	817	1008
6	B	2013	899	877	1041
7	B	2014	837	914	1009
8	B	2015	824	806	1002
9	B	2016	873	942	1013

11
Combining Pandas Objects

A wide variety of options are available to combine two or more DataFrames or Series together. The `append` method is the least flexible and only allows for new rows to be appended to a DataFrame. The `concat` method is very versatile and can combine any number of DataFrames or Series on either axis. The `join` method provides fast lookups by aligning a column of one DataFrame to the index of others. The `merge` method provides SQL-like capabilities to join two DataFrames together.

Appending new rows to DataFrames

When performing data analysis, it is far more common to create new columns than new rows. This is because a new row of data usually represents a new observation, and as an analyst, it is typically not your job to continually capture new data. Data capture is usually left to other platforms like relational database management systems. Nevertheless, it is a necessary feature to know as it will crop up from time to time.

In this recipe, we will begin by appending rows to a small dataset with the `.loc` attribute and then transition to using the `.append` method.

How to do it...

1. Read in the `names` dataset, and output it:

```
>>> import pandas as pd
>>> import numpy as np
>>> names = pd.read_csv('data/names.csv')
>>> names
       Name  Age
0  Cornelia   70
1     Abbas   69
2  Penelope    4
3      Niko    2
```

2. Let's create a list that contains some new data and use the `.loc` attribute to set a single row label equal to this new data:

```
>>> new_data_list = ['Aria', 1]
>>> names.loc[4] = new_data_list
>>> names
       Name  Age
0  Cornelia   70
1     Abbas   69
2  Penelope    4
3      Niko    2
4      Aria    1
```

3. The `.loc` attribute uses labels to refer to the rows. In this case, the row labels exactly match the integer location. It is possible to append more rows with non-integer labels:

```
>>> names.loc['five'] = ['Zach', 3]
>>> names
          Name  Age
0     Cornelia   70
1        Abbas   69
2     Penelope    4
3         Niko    2
4         Aria    1
five      Zach    3
```

4. To be more explicit in associating variables to values, you may use a dictionary. Also, in this step, we can dynamically choose the new index label to be the length of the DataFrame:

```
>>> names.loc[len(names)] = {'Name':'Zayd', 'Age':2}
>>> names
```

	Name	Age
0	Cornelia	70
1	Abbas	69
2	Penelope	4
3	Niko	2
4	Aria	1
five	Zach	3
6	Zayd	2

5. A Series can hold the new data as well and works exactly the same as a dictionary:

```
>>> names.loc[len(names)] = pd.Series({'Age':32, 'Name':'Dean'})
>>> names
```

	Name	Age
0	Cornelia	70
1	Abbas	69
2	Penelope	4
3	Niko	2
4	Aria	1
five	Zach	3
6	Zayd	2
7	Dean	32

6. The preceding operations all use the `.loc` attribute to make changes to the `names` DataFrame in-place. There is no separate copy of the DataFrame that is returned. In the next few steps, we will look at the `.append` method, which does not modify the calling DataFrame. Instead, it returns a new copy of the DataFrame with the appended row(s). Let's begin with the original `names` DataFrame and attempt to append a row. The first argument to `.append` must be either another DataFrame, Series, dictionary, or a list of these, but not a list like the one in *step 2*. Let's see what happens when we attempt to use a dictionary with `.append`:

```
>>> names = pd.read_csv('data/names.csv')
>>> names.append({'Name':'Aria', 'Age':1})
Traceback (most recent call last):
    ...
TypeError: Can only append a Series if ignore_index=True or if the
Series has a name
```

7. This error message appears to be slightly incorrect. We are passing a dictionary and not a Series but nevertheless, it gives us instructions on how to correct it, we need to pass the `ignore_index=True` parameter:

```
>>> names.append({'Name':'Aria', 'Age':1}, ignore_index=True)
        Name   Age
0    Cornelia    70
1       Abbas    69
2    Penelope     4
3        Niko     2
4        Aria     1
```

8. This works but `ignore_index` is a sneaky parameter. When set to `True`, the old index will be removed completely and replaced with a `RangeIndex` from 0 to *n-1*. For instance, let's specify an index for the `names` DataFrame:

```
>>> names.index = ['Canada', 'Canada', 'USA', 'USA']
>>> names
            Name   Age
Canada  Cornelia    70
Canada     Abbas    69
USA     Penelope     4
USA         Niko     2
```

9. Rerun the code from *step 7*, and you will get the same result. The original index is completely ignored.

10. Let's continue with this names DataFrame with the country strings in the index. Let's append a Series that has a `name` attribute with the `.append` method:

```
>>> s = pd.Series({'Name': 'Zach', 'Age': 3}, name=len(names))
>>> s
Name    Zach
Age        3
Name: 4, dtype: object

>>> names.append(s)
            Name   Age
Canada  Cornelia    70
Canada     Abbas    69
USA     Penelope     4
USA         Niko     2
4           Zach     3
```

11. The `.append` method is more flexible than the `.loc` attribute. It supports appending multiple rows at the same time. One way to accomplish this is by passing in a list of Series:

```
>>> s1 = pd.Series({'Name': 'Zach', 'Age': 3}, name=len(names))
>>> s2 = pd.Series({'Name': 'Zayd', 'Age': 2}, name='USA')
>>> names.append([s1, s2])
```

	Name	Age
Canada	Cornelia	70
Canada	Abbas	69
USA	Penelope	4
USA	Niko	2
4	Zach	3
USA	Zayd	2

12. Small DataFrames with only two columns are simple enough to manually write out all the column names and values. When they get larger, this process will be quite painful. For instance, let's take a look at the 2016 baseball dataset:

```
>>> bball_16 = pd.read_csv('data/baseball16.csv')
>>> bball_16
```

	playerID	yearID	stint	teamID	...	HBP	SH	SF	GIDP
0	altuv...	2016	1	HOU	...	7.0	3.0	7.0	15.0
1	bregm...	2016	1	HOU	...	0.0	0.0	1.0	1.0
2	castr...	2016	1	HOU	...	1.0	1.0	0.0	9.0
3	corre...	2016	1	HOU	...	5.0	0.0	3.0	12.0
4	gatti...	2016	1	HOU	...	4.0	0.0	5.0	12.0
..	...	...	...	...	...	...	...	...	...
11	reedaj01	2016	1	HOU	...	0.0	0.0	1.0	1.0
12	sprin...	2016	1	HOU	...	11.0	0.0	1.0	12.0
13	tucke...	2016	1	HOU	...	2.0	0.0	0.0	2.0
14	valbu...	2016	1	HOU	...	1.0	3.0	2.0	5.0
15	white...	2016	1	HOU	...	2.0	0.0	2.0	6.0

13. This dataset contains 22 columns and it would be easy to mistype a column name or forget one altogether if you were manually entering new rows of data. To help protect against these mistakes, let's select a single row as a Series and chain the `.to_dict` method to it to get an example row as a dictionary:

```
>>> data_dict = bball_16.iloc[0].to_dict()
>>> data_dict
```

```
{'playerID': 'altuvjo01', 'yearID': 2016, 'stint': 1, 'teamID':
'HOU', 'lgID': 'AL', 'G': 161, 'AB': 640, 'R': 108, 'H': 216,
'2B': 42, '3B': 5, 'HR': 24, 'RBI': 96.0, 'SB': 30.0, 'CS': 10.0,
'BB': 60, 'SO': 70.0, 'IBB': 11.0, 'HBP': 7.0, 'SH': 3.0, 'SF':
7.0, 'GIDP': 15.0}
```

14. Clear the old values with a dictionary comprehension assigning any previous string value as an empty string and all others as missing values. This dictionary can now serve as a template for any new data you would like to enter:

```
>>> new_data_dict = {k: '' if isinstance(v, str) else
...        np.nan for k, v in data_dict.items()}
>>> new_data_dict
{'playerID': '', 'yearID': nan, 'stint': nan, 'teamID': '',
'lgID': '', 'G': nan, 'AB': nan, 'R': nan, 'H': nan, '2B': nan,
'3B': nan, 'HR': nan, 'RBI': nan, 'SB': nan, 'CS': nan, 'BB': nan,
'SO': nan, 'IBB': nan, 'HBP': nan, 'SH': nan, 'SF': nan, 'GIDP':
nan}
```

How it works...

The `.loc` attribute is used to select and assign data based on the row and column labels. The first value passed to it represents the row label. In *step 2*, `names.loc[4]` refers to the row with a label equal to the integer 4. This label does not currently exist in the DataFrame. The assignment statement creates a new row with data provided by the list. As was mentioned in the recipe, this operation modifies the names DataFrame itself. If there were a previously existing row with a label equal to the integer 4, this command would have written over it. Using in-place modification makes this indexing operator riskier to use than the `.append` method, which never modifies the original calling DataFrame. Throughout this book we have advocated chaining operations, and you should follow suit.

Any valid label may be used with the `.loc` attribute, as seen in *step 3*. Regardless of what the new label value is, the new row is always appended to the end. Even though assigning with a list works, for clarity, it is best to use a dictionary so that we know exactly which columns are associated with each value, as done in *step 4*.

Steps 4 and *5* show a trick to dynamically set the new label to be the current number of rows in the DataFrame. Data stored in a Series will also get assigned correctly as long as the index labels match the column names.

The rest of the steps use the `.append` method, which is a method that only appends new rows to DataFrames. Most DataFrame methods allow both row and column manipulation through an `axis` parameter. One exception is the `.append` method, which can only append rows to DataFrames.

Using a dictionary of column names mapped to values isn't enough information for `.append` to work, as seen by the error message in *step 6*. To correctly append a dictionary without a row name, you will have to set the `.ignore_index` parameter to `True`.

Step 10 shows you how to keep the old index by converting your dictionary to a Series. Make sure to use the `name` parameter, which is then used as the new index label. Any number of rows may be added with `append` in this manner by passing a list of Series as the first argument.

When wanting to append rows in this manner with a much larger DataFrame, you can avoid lots of typing and mistakes by converting a single row to a dictionary with the `.to_dict` method and then using a dictionary comprehension to clear out all the old values replacing them with some defaults. This can serve as a template for new rows.

There's more...

Appending a single row to a DataFrame is a fairly expensive operation and if you find yourself writing a loop to append single rows of data to a DataFrame, then you are doing it wrong. Let's first create 1,000 rows of new data as a list of Series:

```
>>> random_data = []
>>> for i in range(1000):
...       d = dict()
...       for k, v in data_dict.items():
...           if isinstance(v, str):
...               d[k] = np.random.choice(list('abcde'))
...           else:
...               d[k] = np.random.randint(10)
...       random_data.append(pd.Series(d, name=i + len(bball_16)))
>>> random_data[0]
2B    3
3B    9
AB    3
BB    9
CS    4
Name: 16, dtype: object
```

Let's time how long it takes to loop through each item making one append at a time:

```
>>> %%timeit
>>> bball_16_copy = bball_16.copy()
```

```
>>> for row in random_data:
...      bball_16_copy = bball_16_copy.append(row)
4.88 s ± 190 ms per loop (mean ± std. dev. of 7 runs, 1 loop each)
```

That took nearly five seconds for only 1,000 rows. If we instead pass in the entire list of Series, we get an enormous speed increase:

```
>>> %%timeit
>>> bball_16_copy = bball_16.copy()
>>> bball_16_copy = bball_16_copy.append(random_data)
78.4 ms ± 6.2 ms per loop (mean ± std. dev. of 7 runs, 10 loops each)
```

If you pass in a list of Series objects, the time has been reduced to under one-tenth of a second. Internally, pandas converts the list of Series to a single DataFrame and then appends the data.

Concatenating multiple DataFrames together

The concat function enables concatenating two or more DataFrames (or Series) together, both vertically and horizontally. As per usual, when dealing with multiple pandas objects simultaneously, concatenation doesn't happen haphazardly but aligns each object by their index.

In this recipe, we combine DataFrames both horizontally and vertically with the concat function and then change the parameter values to yield different results.

How to do it...

1. Read in the 2016 and 2017 stock datasets, and make their ticker symbol the index:

```
>>> stocks_2016 = pd.read_csv('data/stocks_2016.csv',
...      index_col='Symbol')
>>> stocks_2017 = pd.read_csv('data/stocks_2017.csv',
...      index_col='Symbol')

>>> stocks_2016
        Shares  Low  High
Symbol
AAPL        80   95   110
```

```
TSLA          50    80    130
WMT           40    55    70


>>> stocks_2017
          Shares   Low   High
Symbol
AAPL          50   120    140
GE           100    30     40
IBM           87    75     95
SLB           20    55     85
TXN          500    15     23
TSLA         100   100    300
```

2. Place all the stock datasets into a single list, and then call the `concat` function to concatenate them together along the default axis (0):

```
>>> s_list = [stocks_2016, stocks_2017]
>>> pd.concat(s_list)
          Shares   Low   High
Symbol
AAPL          80    95    110
TSLA          50    80    130
WMT           40    55     70
AAPL          50   120    140
GE           100    30     40
IBM           87    75     95
SLB           20    55     85
TXN          500    15     23
TSLA         100   100    300
```

3. By default, the `concat` function concatenates DataFrames vertically, one on top of the other. One issue with the preceding DataFrame is that there is no way to identify the year of each row. The `concat` function allows each piece of the resulting DataFrame to be labeled with the `keys` parameter. This label will appear in the outermost index level of the concatenated frame and force the creation of a `MultiIndex`. Also, the `names` parameter has the ability to rename each index level for clarity:

```
>>> pd.concat(s_list, keys=['2016', '2017'],
...     names=['Year', 'Symbol'])
          Shares   Low   High
```

```
      Year  Symbol
      2016  AAPL        80     95    110
            TSLA        50     80    130
            WMT         40     55     70
      2017  AAPL        50    120    140
            GE         100     30     40
            IBM         87     75     95
            SLB         20     55     85
            TXN        500     15     23
            TSLA       100    100    300
```

4. It is also possible to concatenate horizontally by changing the `axis` parameter to `columns` or `1`:

```
>>> pd.concat(s_list, keys=['2016', '2017'],
...       axis='columns', names=['Year', None])
Year    2016                 2017
        Shares   Low   High Shares     Low    High
AAPL    80.0   95.0  110.0   50.0   120.0   140.0
GE       NaN    NaN    NaN  100.0    30.0    40.0
IBM      NaN    NaN    NaN   87.0    75.0    95.0
SLB      NaN    NaN    NaN   20.0    55.0    85.0
TSLA    50.0   80.0  130.0  100.0   100.0   300.0
TXN      NaN    NaN    NaN  500.0    15.0    23.0
WMT     40.0   55.0   70.0    NaN     NaN     NaN
```

5. Notice that missing values appear whenever a stock symbol is present in one year but not the other. The `concat` function, by default, uses an *outer join*, keeping all rows from each DataFrame in the list. However, it gives us an option to keep only rows that have the same index values in both DataFrames. This is referred to as an *inner join*. We set the `join` parameter to `inner` to change the behavior:

```
>>> pd.concat(s_list, join='inner', keys=['2016', '2017'],
...       axis='columns', names=['Year', None])
Year      2016                 2017
          Shares Low High Shares   Low High
Symbol
AAPL        80   95  110     50   120  140
TSLA        50   80  130    100   100  300
```

How it works...

The `concat` function accepts a list as the first parameter. This list must be a sequence of pandas objects, typically a list of DataFrames or Series. By default, all these objects will be stacked vertically, one on top of the other. In this recipe, only two DataFrames are concatenated, but any number of pandas objects work. When we were concatenating vertically, the DataFrames align by their column names.

In this dataset, all the column names were the same so each column in the 2017 data lined up precisely under the same column name in the 2016 data. However, when they were concatenated horizontally, as in *step 4*, only two of the index labels matched from both years – AAPL and TSLA. Therefore, these ticker symbols had no missing values for either year. There are two types of alignment possible using `concat`, `outer` (the default), and `inner` referred to by the `join` parameter.

There's more...

The `.append` method is a heavily watered-down version of `concat` that can only append new rows to a DataFrame. Internally, `.append` just calls the `concat` function. For instance, *step 2* from this recipe may be duplicated with the following:

```
>>> stocks_2016.append(stocks_2017)
```

Shares	Low	High
Symbol		
AAPL	80	95	110
TSLA	50	80	130
WMT	40	55	70
AAPL	50	120	140
GE	100	30	40
IBM	87	75	95
SLB	20	55	85
TXN	500	15	23
TSLA	100	100	300

Understanding the differences between concat, join, and merge

The `.merge` and `.join` DataFrame (and not Series) methods and the `concat` function all provide very similar functionality to combine multiple pandas objects together. As they are so similar and they can replicate each other in certain situations, it can get very confusing regarding when and how to use them correctly.

To help clarify their differences, take a look at the following outline:

`concat`:

- ▶ A pandas function
- ▶ Combines two or more pandas objects vertically or horizontally
- ▶ Aligns only on the index
- ▶ Errors whenever a duplicate appears in the index
- ▶ Defaults to outer join with the option for inner join

`.join`:

- ▶ A DataFrame method
- ▶ Combines two or more pandas objects horizontally
- ▶ Aligns the calling DataFrame's column(s) or index with the other object's index (and not the columns)
- ▶ Handles duplicate values on the joining columns/index by performing a Cartesian product
- ▶ Defaults to left join with options for inner, outer, and right

`.merge`:

- ▶ A DataFrame method
- ▶ Combines exactly two DataFrames horizontally
- ▶ Aligns the calling DataFrame's column(s) or index with the other DataFrame's column(s) or index
- ▶ Handles duplicate values on the joining columns or index by performing a cartesian product
- ▶ Defaults to inner join with options for left, outer, and right

In this recipe, we will combine DataFrames. The first situation is simpler with `concat` while the second is simpler with `.merge`.

How to do it...

1. Let's read in stock data for 2016, 2017, and 2018 into a list of DataFrames using a loop instead of three different calls to the `read_csv` function:

```
>>> years = 2016, 2017, 2018
>>> stock_tables = [pd.read_csv(
...       f'data/stocks_{year}.csv', index_col='Symbol')
```

```
...         for year in years]
>>> stocks_2016, stocks_2017, stocks_2018 = stock_tables
>>> stocks_2016
          Shares   Low   High
Symbol
AAPL          80    95    110
TSLA          50    80    130
WMT           40    55     70


>>> stocks_2017
          Shares   Low   High
Symbol
AAPL          50   120    140
GE           100    30     40
IBM           87    75     95
SLB           20    55     85
TXN          500    15     23
TSLA         100   100    300


>>> stocks_2018
          Shares   Low   High
Symbol
AAPL          40   135    170
AMZN           8   900   1125
TSLA          50   220    400
```

2. The concat function is the only pandas method that is able to combine DataFrames vertically. Let's do this by passing it the list stock_tables:

```
>>> pd.concat(stock_tables, keys=[2016, 2017, 2018])
            Shares   Low   High
     Symbol
2016 AAPL       80    95    110
     TSLA       50    80    130
     WMT        40    55     70
2017 AAPL       50   120    140
     GE        100    30     40
...              ...   ...    ...
```

```
        TXN       500   15    23
        TSLA      100  100   300
2018 AAPL          40  135   170
        AMZN        8  900  1125
        TSLA       50  220   400
```

3. It can also combine DataFrames horizontally by changing the `axis` parameter to `columns`:

```
>>> pd.concat(dict(zip(years, stock_tables)), axis='columns')
```

	2016			...	2018		
	Shares	Low	High	...	Shares	Low	High
AAPL	80.0	95.0	110.0	...	40.0	135.0	170.0
AMZN	NaN	NaN	NaN	...	8.0	900.0	1125.0
GE	NaN	NaN	NaN	...	NaN	NaN	NaN
IBM	NaN	NaN	NaN	...	NaN	NaN	NaN
SLB	NaN	NaN	NaN	...	NaN	NaN	NaN
TSLA	50.0	80.0	130.0	...	50.0	220.0	400.0
TXN	NaN	NaN	NaN	...	NaN	NaN	NaN
WMT	40.0	55.0	70.0	...	NaN	NaN	NaN

4. Now that we have started combining DataFrames horizontally, we can use the `.join` and `.merge` methods to replicate this functionality of concat. Here, we use the `.join` method to combine the `stock_2016` and `stock_2017` DataFrames. By default, the DataFrames align on their index. If any of the columns have the same names, then you must supply a value to the `lsuffix` or `rsuffix` parameters to distinguish them in the result:

```
>>> stocks_2016.join(stocks_2017, lsuffix='_2016',
...      rsuffix='_2017', how='outer')
```

Symbol	Shares_2016	Low_2016	...	Low_2017	High_2017
AAPL	80.0	95.0	...	120.0	140.0
GE	NaN	NaN	...	30.0	40.0
IBM	NaN	NaN	...	75.0	95.0
SLB	NaN	NaN	...	55.0	85.0
TSLA	50.0	80.0	...	100.0	300.0
TXN	NaN	NaN	...	15.0	23.0
WMT	40.0	55.0	...	NaN	NaN

5. To replicate the output of the `concat` function from *step 3*, we can pass a list of DataFrames to the `.join` method:

```
>>> other = [stocks_2017.add_suffix('_2017'),
...         stocks_2018.add_suffix('_2018')]
>>> stocks_2016.add_suffix('_2016').join(other, how='outer')
```

	Shares_2016	Low_2016	...	Low_2018	High_2018
AAPL	80.0	95.0	...	135.0	170.0
TSLA	50.0	80.0	...	220.0	400.0
WMT	40.0	55.0	...	NaN	NaN
GE	NaN	NaN	...	NaN	NaN
IBM	NaN	NaN	...	NaN	NaN
SLB	NaN	NaN	...	NaN	NaN
TXN	NaN	NaN	...	NaN	NaN
AMZN	NaN	NaN	...	900.0	1125.0

6. Let's check whether they are equal:

```
>>> stock_join = stocks_2016.add_suffix('_2016').join(other,
...         how='outer')

>>> stock_concat = (
...     pd.concat(
...             dict(zip(years, stock_tables)), axis="columns")
...     .swaplevel(axis=1)
...     .pipe(lambda df_:
...             df_.set_axis(df_.columns.to_flat_index(), axis=1))
...     .rename(lambda label:
...             "_".join([str(x) for x in label]), axis=1)
... )
>>> stock_join.equals(stock_concat)
True
```

7. Now, let's turn to the `.merge` method that, unlike `concat` and `.join`, can only combine two DataFrames together. By default, `.merge` attempts to align the values in the columns that have the same name for each of the DataFrames. However, you can choose to have it align on the index by setting the Boolean parameters `left_index` and `right_index` to `True`. Let's merge the 2016 and 2017 stock data together:

```
>>> stocks_2016.merge(stocks_2017, left_index=True,
```

```
...        right_index=True)
           Shares_x  Low_x  High_x  Shares_y  Low_y  High_y
Symbol
AAPL            80     95     110        50    120     140
TSLA            50     80     130       100    100     300
```

8. By default, `.merge` uses an inner join and automatically supplies suffixes for identically named columns. Let's change to an outer join and then perform another outer join of the 2018 data to replicate the behavior of `concat`. Note that in pandas 1.0, the `merge` index will be sorted and the `concat` version won't be:

```
>>> stock_merge = (stocks_2016
...        .merge(stocks_2017, left_index=True,
...               right_index=True, how='outer',
...               suffixes=('_2016', '_2017'))
...        .merge(stocks_2018.add_suffix('_2018'),
...               left_index=True, right_index=True,
...               how='outer')
... )
>>> stock_concat.sort_index().equals(stock_merge)
True
```

9. Now let's turn our comparison to datasets where we are interested in aligning together the values of columns and not the index or column labels themselves. The `.merge` method is built for this situation. Let's take a look at two new small datasets, `food_prices` and `food_transactions`:

```
>>> names = ['prices', 'transactions']
>>> food_tables = [pd.read_csv('data/food_{}.csv'.format(name))
...        for name in names]
>>> food_prices, food_transactions = food_tables
>>> food_prices
     item store  price  Date
0    pear     A   0.99  2017
1    pear     B   1.99  2017
2   peach     A   2.99  2017
3   peach     B   3.49  2017
4  banana     A   0.39  2017
5  banana     B   0.49  2017
6   steak     A   5.99  2017
```

```
7    steak    B    6.99    2017
8    steak    B    4.99    2015
```

```
>>> food_transactions
     custid    item  store   quantity
0        1     pear     A           5
1        1   banana     A          10
2        2    steak     B           3
3        2     pear     B           1
4        2    peach     B           2
5        2    steak     B           1
6        2  coconut     B           4
```

10. If we wanted to find the total amount of each transaction, we would need to join these tables on the `item` and `store` columns:

```
>>> food_transactions.merge(food_prices, on=['item', 'store'])
     custid    item  store   quantity   price   Date
0        1     pear     A           5    0.99   2017
1        1   banana     A          10    0.39   2017
2        2    steak     B           3    6.99   2017
3        2    steak     B           3    4.99   2015
4        2    steak     B           1    6.99   2017
5        2    steak     B           1    4.99   2015
6        2     pear     B           1    1.99   2017
7        2    peach     B           2    3.49   2017
```

11. The price is now aligned correctly with its corresponding item and store, but there is a problem. Customer 2 has a total of four `steak` items. As the `steak` item appears twice in each table for store `B`, a Cartesian product takes place between them, resulting in four rows. Also, notice that the item, `coconut`, is missing because there was no corresponding price for it. Let's fix both of these issues:

```
>>> food_transactions.merge(food_prices.query('Date == 2017'),
...       how='left')
     custid    item  store   quantity   price     Date
0        1     pear     A           5    0.99   2017.0
1        1   banana     A          10    0.39   2017.0
2        2    steak     B           3    6.99   2017.0
```

3	2	pear	B	1	1.99	2017.0
4	2	peach	B	2	3.49	2017.0
5	2	steak	B	1	6.99	2017.0
6	2	coconut	B	4	NaN	NaN

12. We can replicate this with the `.join` method, but we must first put the joining columns of the `food_prices` DataFrame into the index:

```
>>> food_prices_join = food_prices.query('Date == 2017') \
...      .set_index(['item', 'store'])
>>> food_prices_join
```

		price	Date
item	store		
pear	A	0.99	2017
	B	1.99	2017
peach	A	2.99	2017
	B	3.49	2017
banana	A	0.39	2017
	B	0.49	2017
steak	A	5.99	2017
	B	6.99	2017

13. The `.join` method only aligns with the index of the passed DataFrame but can use the index or the columns of the calling DataFrame. To use columns for alignment on the calling DataFrame, you will need to pass them to the `on` parameter:

```
>>> food_transactions.join(food_prices_join, on=['item', 'store'])
```

	custid	item	store	quantity	price	Date
0	1	pear	A	5	0.99	2017.0
1	1	banana	A	10	0.39	2017.0
2	2	steak	B	3	6.99	2017.0
3	2	pear	B	1	1.99	2017.0
4	2	peach	B	2	3.49	2017.0
5	2	steak	B	1	6.99	2017.0
6	2	coconut	B	4	NaN	NaN

The output matches the result from *step 11*. To replicate this with the `concat` function, you would need to put the `item` and `store` columns into the index of both DataFrames. However, in this particular case, an error would be produced as a duplicate index value occurs in at least one of the DataFrames (with item `steak` and store B):

```
>>> pd.concat([food_transactions.set_index(['item', 'store']),
...             food_prices.set_index(['item', 'store'])],
...           axis='columns')
Traceback (most recent call last):
  ...
ValueError: cannot handle a non-unique multi-index!
```

How it works...

It can be tedious to repeatedly write the `read_csv` function when importing many DataFrames at the same time. One way to automate this process is to put all the filenames in a list and iterate through them with a `for` loop. This was done in *step 1* with a list comprehension.

At the end of *step 1*, we unpack the list of DataFrames into their own appropriately named variables so that each table may be easily and clearly referenced. The nice thing about having a list of DataFrames is that it is the exact requirement for the `concat` function, as seen in *step 2*. Notice how *step 2* uses the `keys` parameter to name each chunk of data. This can be also be accomplished by passing a dictionary to `concat`, as done in *step 3*.

In *step 4*, we must change the type of `.join` to `outer` to include all of the rows in the passed DataFrame that do not have an index present in the calling DataFrame. In *step 5*, the passed list of DataFrames cannot have any columns in common. Although there is an `rsuffix` parameter, it only works when passing a single DataFrame and not a list of them. To work around this limitation, we change the names of the columns beforehand with the `.add_suffix` method, and then call the `.join` method.

In *step 7*, we use `.merge`, which defaults to aligning on all column names that are the same in both DataFrames. To change this default behavior, and align on the index of either one or both, set the `left_index` or `right_index` parameters to `True`. *Step 8* finishes the replication with two calls to `.merge`. As you can see, when you are aligning multiple DataFrames on their index, `concat` is usually going to be a far better choice than `.merge`.

In *step 9*, we switch gears to focus on a situation where the `.merge` method has the advantage. The `.merge` method is the only one capable of aligning both the calling and passed DataFrame by column values. *Step 10* shows you how easy it is to merge two DataFrames. The `on` parameter is not necessary but provided for clarity.

Unfortunately, it is very easy to duplicate or drop data when combining DataFrames, as shown in *step 10*. It is vital to take some time to do some sanity checks after combining data. In this instance, the `food_prices` dataset had a duplicate price for `steak` in store `B`, so we eliminated this row by querying for only the current year in *step 11*. We also change to a left join to ensure that each transaction is kept regardless if a price is present or not.

It is possible to use `.join` in these instances, but all the columns in the passed DataFrame must be moved into the index first. Finally, `concat` is going to be a poor choice whenever you intend to align data by values in their columns.

In summary, I find myself using `.merge` unless I know that the indexes align.

There's more...

It is possible to read all files from a particular directory into DataFrames without knowing their names. Python provides a few ways to iterate through directories, with the `glob` module being a popular choice. The `gas prices` directory contains five different CSV files, each having weekly prices of a particular grade of gas beginning from 2007. Each file has just two columns – the date for the week and the price. This is a perfect situation to iterate through all the files, read them into DataFrames, and combine them all together with the `concat` function.

The `glob` module has the `glob` function, which takes a single parameter – the location of the directory you would like to iterate through as a string. To get all the files in the directory, use the string *. In this example, `''*.csv'` returns only files that end in `.csv`. The result from the `glob` function is a list of string filenames, which can be passed to the `read_csv` function:

```
>>> import glob
>>> df_list = []
>>> for filename in glob.glob('data/gas prices/*.csv'):
...     df_list.append(pd.read_csv(filename, index_col='Week',
...     parse_dates=['Week']))
>>> gas = pd.concat(df_list, axis='columns')
>>> gas
```

	Midgrade	Premium	Diesel	All Grades	Regular
Week					
2017-09-25	2.859	3.105	2.788	2.701	2.583
2017-09-18	2.906	3.151	2.791	2.750	2.634
2017-09-11	2.953	3.197	2.802	2.800	2.685
2017-09-04	2.946	3.191	2.758	2.794	2.679
2017-08-28	2.668	2.901	2.605	2.513	2.399
...	...	...	...	...	...
2007-01-29	2.277	2.381	2.413	2.213	2.165
2007-01-22	2.285	2.391	2.430	2.216	2.165
2007-01-15	2.347	2.453	2.463	2.280	2.229
2007-01-08	2.418	2.523	2.537	2.354	2.306
2007-01-01	2.442	2.547	2.580	2.382	2.334

Connecting to SQL databases

Learning SQL is a useful skill. Much of the world's data is stored in databases that accept SQL statements. There are many dozens of relational database management systems, with SQLite being one of the most popular and easy to use.

We will be exploring the *chinook* sample database provided by SQLite that contains 11 tables of data for a music store. One of the best things to do when first diving into a proper relational database is to study a database diagram (sometimes called an entity relationship diagram) to understand how tables are related. The following diagram will be immensely helpful when navigating through this recipe:

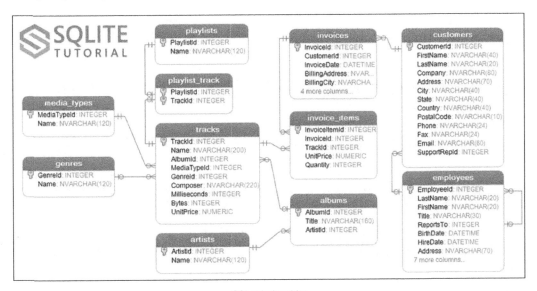

SQL relationships

In order for this recipe to work, you will need to have the `sqlalchemy` Python package installed. If you installed the Anaconda distribution, then it should already be available to you. SQLAlchemy is the preferred pandas tool when making connections to databases. In this recipe, you will learn how to connect to a SQLite database. You will then ask two different queries, and answer them by joining together tables with the `.merge` method.

How to do it...

1. Before we can begin reading tables from the chinook database, we need to set up our SQLAlchemy engine:

```
>>> from sqlalchemy import create_engine
>>> engine = create_engine('sqlite:///data/chinook.db')
```

2. We can now step back into the world of pandas and remain there for the rest of
    the recipe. Let's complete a command and read in the `tracks` table with the
    `read_sql_table` function. The name of the table is the first argument and the
    SQLAlchemy engine is the second:

```
>>> tracks = pd.read_sql_table('tracks', engine)
>>> tracks
        TrackId  ...  UnitPrice
0             1  ...       0.99
1             2  ...       0.99
2             3  ...       0.99
3             4  ...       0.99
4             5  ...       0.99
...         ...  ...        ...
3498       3499  ...       0.99
3499       3500  ...       0.99
3500       3501  ...       0.99
3501       3502  ...       0.99
3502       3503  ...       0.99
```

3. For the rest of the recipe, we will answer a couple of different specific queries with
    help from the database diagram. To begin, let's find the average length of song per
    genre:

```
>>> (pd.read_sql_table('genres', engine)
...         .merge(tracks[['GenreId', 'Milliseconds']],
...               on='GenreId', how='left')
...         .drop('GenreId', axis='columns')
... )
           Name  Milliseconds
0          Rock        343719
1          Rock        342562
2          Rock        230619
3          Rock        252051
4          Rock        375418
...         ...           ...
3498  Classical        286741
3499  Classical        139200
3500  Classical         66639
3501  Classical        221331
3502      Opera        174813
```

4. Now we can easily find the average length of each song per genre. To help ease interpretation, we convert the `Milliseconds` column to the `timedelta` data type:

```
>>> (pd.read_sql_table('genres', engine)
...      .merge(tracks[['GenreId', 'Milliseconds']],
...            on='GenreId', how='left')
...      .drop('GenreId', axis='columns')
...      .groupby('Name')
...      ['Milliseconds']
...      .mean()
...      .pipe(lambda s_: pd.to_timedelta(s_, unit='ms')
...                        .rename('Length'))
...      .dt.floor('s')
...      .sort_values()
... )
Name
Rock And Roll      00:02:14
Opera              00:02:54
Hip Hop/Rap        00:02:58
Easy Listening     00:03:09
Bossa Nova         00:03:39
                      ...
Comedy             00:26:25
TV Shows           00:35:45
Drama              00:42:55
Science Fiction    00:43:45
Sci Fi & Fantasy   00:48:31
Name: Length, Length: 25, dtype: timedelta64[ns]
```

5. Now let's find the total amount spent per customer. We will need the `customers`, `invoices`, and `invoice_items` tables all connected to each other:

```
>>> cust = pd.read_sql_table('customers', engine,
...     columns=['CustomerId','FirstName',
...     'LastName'])
>>> invoice = pd.read_sql_table('invoices', engine,
...     columns=['InvoiceId','CustomerId'])
>>> invoice_items = pd.read_sql_table('invoice_items', engine,
...     columns=['InvoiceId', 'UnitPrice', 'Quantity'])
```

```
>>> (cust
...      .merge(invoice, on='CustomerId')
...      .merge(invoice_items, on='InvoiceId')
... )
```

	CustomerId	FirstName	...	UnitPrice	Quantity
0	1	Luís	...	1.99	1
1	1	Luís	...	1.99	1
2	1	Luís	...	0.99	1
3	1	Luís	...	0.99	1
4	1	Luís	...	0.99	1
...	...	...	...	...	...
2235	59	Puja	...	0.99	1
2236	59	Puja	...	0.99	1
2237	59	Puja	...	0.99	1
2238	59	Puja	...	0.99	1
2239	59	Puja	...	0.99	1

6. We can now multiply the quantity by the unit price and then find the total amount spent per customer:

```
>>> (cust
...      .merge(invoice, on='CustomerId')
...      .merge(invoice_items, on='InvoiceId')
...      .assign(Total=lambda df_:df_.Quantity * df_.UnitPrice)
...      .groupby(['CustomerId', 'FirstName', 'LastName'])
...      ['Total']
...      .sum()
...      .sort_values(ascending=False)
... )
```

CustomerId	FirstName	LastName	
6	Helena	Holý	49.62
26	Richard	Cunningham	47.62
57	Luis	Rojas	46.62
46	Hugh	O'Reilly	45.62
45	Ladislav	Kovács	45.62
			...
32	Aaron	Mitchell	37.62
31	Martha	Silk	37.62

29	Robert	Brown	37.62
27	Patrick	Gray	37.62
59	Puja	Srivastava	36.64

Name: Total, Length: 59, dtype: float64

How it works...

The `create_engine` function requires a connection string to work properly. The connection string for SQLite is the location of the database, which is located in the `data` directory. Other relational database management systems have more complex connection strings. You will need to provide a username, password, hostname, port, and optionally, a database. You will also need to supply the SQL dialect and the driver. The general form for the connection string is as follows: `dialect+driver://username:password@host:port/database`. The driver for your particular relational database might need to be installed separately.

Once we have created the engine, selecting entire tables into DataFrames is very easy with the `read_sql_table` function in *step 2*. Each of the tables in the database has a primary key identifying each row. It is identified graphically with a key symbol in the diagram. In *step 3*, we link `genres` to `tracks` through `GenreId`. As we only care about the track length, we trim the tracks DataFrame down to just the columns we need before performing the merge. Once the tables have merged, we can answer the query with a basic `.groupby` operation.

We go one step further and convert the integer milliseconds into a `Timedelta` object that is far easier to read. The key is passing in the correct unit of measurement as a string. Now that we have a Timedelta Series, we can use the `.dt` attribute to access the `.floor` method, which rounds the time down to the nearest second.

The query required to answer *step 5* involves three tables. We can trim the tables down significantly to only the columns we need by passing them to the `columns` parameter. When using `.merge`, the joining columns are not kept when they have the same name. In *step 6*, we could have assigned a column for the price times quantity with the following:

```
cust_inv['Total'] = cust_inv['Quantity'] * cust_inv['UnitPrice']
```

As has been emphasized through this book, we prefer chaining operations when possible, and hence you see `.assign` used frequently.

There's more...

If you are adept with SQL, you can write a SQL query as a string and pass it to the `read_sql_query` function. For example, the following will reproduce the output from *step 4*:

```
>>> sql_string1 = '''
... SELECT
```

```
...         Name,
...         time(avg(Milliseconds) / 1000, 'unixepoch') as avg_time
... FROM (
...         SELECT
...             g.Name,
...             t.Milliseconds
...         FROM
...             genres as g
...         JOIN
...             tracks as t on
...             g.genreid == t.genreid
...         )
... GROUP BY Name
... ORDER BY avg_time'''
>>> pd.read_sql_query(sql_string1, engine)
                 Name     avg_time
0       Rock And Roll     00:02:14
1               Opera     00:02:54
2         Hip Hop/Rap     00:02:58
3      Easy Listening     00:03:09
4          Bossa Nova     00:03:39
..                ...          ...
20             Comedy     00:26:25
21           TV Shows     00:35:45
22              Drama     00:42:55
23    Science Fiction     00:43:45
24    Sci Fi & Fantasy    00:48:31
```

To reproduce the answer from *step 6*, use the following SQL query:

```
>>> sql_string2 = '''
...     SELECT
...             c.customerid,
...             c.FirstName,
...             c.LastName,
...             sum(ii.quantity * ii.unitprice) as Total
...     FROM
```

```
...          customers as c
...     JOIN
...          invoices as i
...          on c.customerid = i.customerid
...     JOIN
...          invoice_items as ii
...          on i.invoiceid = ii.invoiceid
...     GROUP BY
...          c.customerid, c.FirstName, c.LastName
...     ORDER BY
...          Total desc'''

>>> pd.read_sql_query(sql_string2, engine)
    CustomerId FirstName    LastName   Total
0            6    Helena        Holý   49.62
1           26   Richard  Cunningham   47.62
2           57      Luis       Rojas   46.62
3           45  Ladislav      Kovács   45.62
4           46      Hugh     O'Reilly   45.62
..         ...       ...         ...     ...
54          53      Phil      Hughes   37.62
55          54     Steve      Murray   37.62
56          55      Mark      Taylor   37.62
57          56     Diego   Gutiérrez   37.62
58          59      Puja   Srivastava   36.64
```

12

Time Series Analysis

Introduction

The roots of pandas lay in analyzing financial time series data. Time series are points of data gathered over time. Generally, the time is evenly spaced between each data point. However, there may be gaps in the observations. pandas includes functionality to manipulate dates, aggregate over different time periods, sample different periods of time, and more.

Understanding the difference between Python and pandas date tools

Before we get to pandas, it can help to be aware of and understand core Python's date and time functionality. The `datetime` module provides three data types: `date`, `time`, and `datetime`. Formally, a `date` is a moment in time consisting of just the year, month, and day. For instance, June 7, 2013 would be a `date`. A `time` consists of hours, minutes, seconds, and microseconds (one-millionth of a second) and is unattached to any date. An example of `time` would be 12 hours and 30 minutes. A `datetime` consists of both the elements of a `date` and `time` together.

On the other hand, pandas has a single object to encapsulate date and time called a `Timestamp`. It has nanosecond (one-billionth of a second) precision and is derived from NumPy's `datetime64` data type. Both Python and pandas each have a `timedelta` object that is useful when doing date addition and subtraction.

In this recipe, we will first explore Python's `datetime` module and then turn to the corresponding date tools in pandas.

How to do it...

1. Let's begin by importing the `datetime` module into our namespace and creating a `date`, `time`, and `datetime` object:

```
>>> import pandas as pd
>>> import numpy as np
>>> import datetime
>>> date = datetime.date(year=2013, month=6, day=7)
>>> time = datetime.time(hour=12, minute=30,
...      second=19, microsecond=463198)
>>> dt = datetime.datetime(year=2013, month=6, day=7,
...      hour=12, minute=30, second=19,
...      microsecond=463198)
>>> print(f"date is {date}")
date is 2013-06-07

>>> print(f"time is {time}")
time is 12:30:19.463198

>>> print(f"datetime is {dt}")
datetime is 2013-06-07 12:30:19.463198
```

2. Let's construct and print out a `timedelta` object, the other major data type from the `datetime` module:

```
>>> td = datetime.timedelta(weeks=2, days=5, hours=10,
...      minutes=20, seconds=6.73,
...      milliseconds=99, microseconds=8)
>>> td
datetime.timedelta(days=19, seconds=37206, microseconds=829008)
```

3. Add this `td` to the `date` and `dt` objects from *step 1*:

```
>>> print(f'new date is {date+td}')
new date is 2013-06-26

>>> print(f'new datetime is {dt+td}')
new datetime is 2013-06-26 22:50:26.292206
```

4. Attempting to add a `timedelta` to a `time` object is not possible:

    ```
    >>> time + td
    Traceback (most recent call last):

        ...

    TypeError: unsupported operand type(s) for +: 'datetime.time' and
    'datetime.timedelta'
    ```

5. Let's turn to pandas and its `Timestamp` object, which is a moment in time with nanosecond precision. The `Timestamp` constructor is very flexible, and handles a wide variety of inputs:

    ```
    >>> pd.Timestamp(year=2012, month=12, day=21, hour=5,
    ...      minute=10, second=8, microsecond=99)
    Timestamp('2012-12-21 05:10:08.000099')


    >>> pd.Timestamp('2016/1/10')
    Timestamp('2016-01-10 00:00:00')


    >>> pd.Timestamp('2014-5/10')
    Timestamp('2014-05-10 00:00:00')


    >>> pd.Timestamp('Jan 3, 2019 20:45.56')
    Timestamp('2019-01-03 20:45:33')


    >>> pd.Timestamp('2016-01-05T05:34:43.123456789')
    Timestamp('2016-01-05 05:34:43.123456789')
    ```

6. It's also possible to pass in a single integer or float to the `Timestamp` constructor, which returns a date equivalent to the number of nanoseconds after the Unix epoch (January 1, 1970):

    ```
    >>> pd.Timestamp(500)
    Timestamp('1970-01-01 00:00:00.000000500')


    >>> pd.Timestamp(5000, unit='D')
    Timestamp('1983-09-10 00:00:00')
    ```

7. pandas provides the `to_datetime` function that works similarly to the `Timestamp` constructor, but comes with a few different parameters for special situations. This comes in useful for converting string columns in DataFrames to dates.

But it also works on scalar dates; see the following examples:

```
>>> pd.to_datetime('2015-5-13')
Timestamp('2015-05-13 00:00:00')


>>> pd.to_datetime('2015-13-5', dayfirst=True)
Timestamp('2015-05-13 00:00:00')


>>> pd.to_datetime('Start Date: Sep 30, 2017 Start Time: 1:30 pm',
...     format='Start Date: %b %d, %Y Start Time: %I:%M %p')
Timestamp('2017-09-30 13:30:00')


>>> pd.to_datetime(100, unit='D', origin='2013-1-1')
Timestamp('2013-04-11 00:00:00')
```

8. The to_datetime function comes equipped with even more functionality. It is capable of converting entire lists or Series of strings or integers to Timestamp objects. Since we are far more likely to interact with Series or DataFrames and not single scalar values, you are far more likely to use to_datetime than Timestamp:

```
>>> s = pd.Series([10, 100, 1000, 10000])
>>> pd.to_datetime(s, unit='D')
0    1970-01-11
1    1970-04-11
2    1972-09-27
3    1997-05-19
dtype: datetime64[ns]


>>> s = pd.Series(['12-5-2015', '14-1-2013',
...     '20/12/2017', '40/23/2017'])


>>> pd.to_datetime(s, dayfirst=True, errors='coerce')
0    2015-05-12
1    2013-01-14
2    2017-12-20
3           NaT
dtype: datetime64[ns]


>>> pd.to_datetime(['Aug 3 1999 3:45:56', '10/31/2017'])
DatetimeIndex(['1999-08-03 03:45:56', '2017-10-31 00:00:00'],
dtype='datetime64[ns]', freq=None)
```

9. Like the `Timestamp` constructor and the `to_datetime` function, pandas has `Timedelta` and `to_timedelta` to represent an amount of time. Both the `Timedelta` constructor and the `to_timedelta` function can create a single `Timedelta` object. Like `to_datetime`, `to_timedelta` has a bit more functionality and can convert entire lists or Series into `Timedelta` objects:

```
>>> pd.Timedelta('12 days 5 hours 3 minutes 123456789
nanoseconds')
Timedelta('12 days 05:03:00.123456')


>>> pd.Timedelta(days=5, minutes=7.34)
Timedelta('5 days 00:07:20.400000')


>>> pd.Timedelta(100, unit='W')
Timedelta('700 days 00:00:00')


>>> pd.to_timedelta('67:15:45.454')
Timedelta('2 days 19:15:45.454000')


>>> s = pd.Series([10, 100])
>>> pd.to_timedelta(s, unit='s')
0    00:00:10
1    00:01:40
dtype: timedelta64[ns]


>>> time_strings = ['2 days 24 minutes 89.67 seconds',
...      '00:45:23.6']
>>> pd.to_timedelta(time_strings)
TimedeltaIndex(['2 days 00:25:29.670000', '0 days
00:45:23.600000'], dtype='timedelta64[ns]', freq=None)
```

10. A `Timedelta` may be added or subtracted from another `Timestamp`. They may even be divided from each other to return a float:

```
>>> pd.Timedelta('12 days 5 hours 3 minutes') * 2
Timedelta('24 days 10:06:00')


>>> (pd.Timestamp('1/1/2017') +
...      pd.Timedelta('12 days 5 hours 3 minutes') * 2)
Timestamp('2017-01-25 10:06:00')
```

```
>>> td1 = pd.to_timedelta([10, 100], unit='s')
>>> td2 = pd.to_timedelta(['3 hours', '4 hours'])
>>> td1 + td2
TimedeltaIndex(['03:00:10', '04:01:40'], dtype='timedelta64[ns]',
freq=None)


>>> pd.Timedelta('12 days') / pd.Timedelta('3 days')
4.0
```

11. Both `Timestamp` and `Timedelta` have a large number of features available as attributes and methods. Let's sample a few of them:

```
>>> ts = pd.Timestamp('2016-10-1 4:23:23.9')
>>> ts.ceil('h')
Timestamp('2016-10-01 05:00:00')


>>> ts.year, ts.month, ts.day, ts.hour, ts.minute, ts.second
(2016, 10, 1, 4, 23, 23)


>>> ts.dayofweek, ts.dayofyear, ts.daysinmonth
(5, 275, 31)


>>> ts.to_pydatetime()
datetime.datetime(2016, 10, 1, 4, 23, 23, 900000)


>>> td = pd.Timedelta(125.8723, unit='h')
>>> td
Timedelta('5 days 05:52:20.280000')


>>> td.round('min')
Timedelta('5 days 05:52:00')


>>> td.components
Components(days=5, hours=5, minutes=52, seconds=20,
milliseconds=280, microseconds=0, nanoseconds=0)


>>> td.total_seconds()
453140.28
```

How it works...

The `datetime` module is part of the Python standard library. It is a good idea to have some familiarity with it, as you will likely cross paths with it. The `datetime` module has only six types of objects: `date`, `time`, `datetime`, `timedelta`, `timezone`, and `tzinfo`. The pandas `Timestamp` and `Timedelta` objects have all the functionality of their `datetime` module counterparts and more. It will be possible to remain completely in pandas when working with time series.

Steps 1 and *2* show how to create datetimes, dates, times, and timedeltas with the `datetime` module. Only integers may be used as parameters of the date or time. Compare this to *step 5*, where the pandas `Timestamp` constructor can accept the same parameters, as well as a wide variety of date strings. In addition to integer components and strings, *step 6* shows how a single numeric scalar can be used as a date. The units of this scalar are defaulted to nanoseconds (ns) but are changed to days (D) in the second statement with the other options being hours (h), minutes (m), seconds (s), milliseconds (ms), and microseconds (µs).

Step 2 details the construction of the `datetime` module's `timedelta` object with all of its parameters. Again, compare this to the pandas `Timedelta` constructor shown in *step 9*, which accepts these same parameters along with strings and scalar numerics.

In addition to the `Timestamp` and `Timedelta` constructors, which are only capable of creating a single object, the `to_datetime` and `to_timedelta` functions can convert entire sequences of integers or strings to the desired type. These functions also provide several more parameters not available with the constructors. One of these parameters is `errors`, which is defaulted to the string value `raise` but can also be set to `ignore` or `coerce`.

Whenever a string date is unable to be converted, the `errors` parameter determines what action to take. When set to `raise`, an exception is raised, and program execution stops. When set to `ignore`, the original sequence gets returned as it was prior to entering the function. When set to `coerce`, the `NaT` (not a time) object is used to represent the new value. The second call to `to_datetime` in *step 8* converts all values to a `Timestamp` correctly, except for the last one, which is forced to become `NaT`.

Another one of these parameters available only to `to_datetime` is `format`, which is particularly useful whenever a string contains a particular date pattern that is not automatically recognized by pandas. In the third statement of *step 7*, we have a `datetime` enmeshed inside some other characters. We substitute the date and time pieces of the string with their respective formatting directives.

A date formatting directive appears as a single percent sign (`%`), followed by a single character. Each directive specifies some part of a date or time. See the official Python documentation for a table of all the directives (`http://bit.ly/2kePoRe`).

Slicing time series intelligently

DataFrame selection and slicing was covered previously. When the DataFrame has a `DatetimeIndex`, even more opportunities arise for selection and slicing.

In this recipe, we will use partial date matching to select and slice a DataFrame with a `DatetimeIndex`.

How to do it...

1. Read in the Denver crimes dataset from the hdf5 file `crimes.h5`, and output the column data types and the first few rows. The hdf5 file format allows efficient storage of large amounts of data and is different from a CSV text file:

```
>>> crime = pd.read_hdf('data/crime.h5', 'crime')
>>> crime.dtypes
OFFENSE_TYPE_ID              category
OFFENSE_CATEGORY_ID          category
REPORTED_DATE          datetime64[ns]
GEO_LON                       float64
GEO_LAT                       float64
NEIGHBORHOOD_ID              category
IS_CRIME                        int64
IS_TRAFFIC                      int64
dtype: object
```

2. Notice that there are three categorical columns and a Timestamp (denoted by NumPy's `datetime64` object). These data types were stored whenever the data file was created, unlike a CSV file, which only stores raw text. Set the REPORTED_DATE column as the index to make intelligent Timestamp slicing possible:

```
>>> crime = crime.set_index('REPORTED_DATE')
>>> crime
                            OFFENSE_TYPE_ID    ...
REPORTED_DATE                                  ...
2014-06-29 02:01:00    traffic-accident-dui-duid    ...
2014-06-29 01:54:00    vehicular-eluding-no-chase   ...
2014-06-29 02:00:00        disturbing-the-peace     ...
2014-06-29 02:18:00                      curfew     ...
2014-06-29 04:17:00          aggravated-assault     ...
```

```
...                              ...   ...
2017-09-13 05:48:00    burglary-business-by-force    ...
2017-09-12 20:37:00    weapon-unlawful-discharge-of  ...
2017-09-12 16:32:00    traf-habitual-offender        ...
2017-09-12 13:04:00    criminal-mischief-other       ...
2017-09-12 09:30:00                    theft-other   ...
```

3. As usual, it is possible to select all the rows equal to a single index by passing that value to the `.loc` attribute:

```
>>> crime.loc['2016-05-12 16:45:00']
            OFFENSE_TYPE_ID OFFENSE_CATEGORY_ID   GEO_LON

                              OFFENSE_TYPE_ID  ...  IS_TRAFFIC

REPORTED_DATE                              ...
2016-05-12 16:45:00     traffic-accident  ...           1
2016-05-12 16:45:00     traffic-accident  ...           1
2016-05-12 16:45:00  fraud-identity-theft ...           0
```

4. With a Timestamp in the index, it is possible to select all rows that partially match an index value. For instance, if we wanted all the crimes from May 5, 2016, we would select it as follows:

```
>>> crime.loc['2016-05-12']
                          OFFENSE_TYPE_ID  ...  IS_TRAFFIC

REPORTED_DATE                             ...
2016-05-12 23:51:00  criminal-mischief-other  ...       0
2016-05-12 18:40:00       liquor-possession  ...        0
2016-05-12 22:26:00        traffic-accident  ...        1
2016-05-12 20:35:00           theft-bicycle  ...        0
2016-05-12 09:39:00    theft-of-motor-vehicle  ...      0
...                                 ...  ...      ...
2016-05-12 17:55:00       public-peace-other  ...       0
2016-05-12 19:24:00        threats-to-injure  ...       0
2016-05-12 22:28:00            sex-aslt-rape  ...       0
2016-05-12 15:59:00  menacing-felony-w-weap  ...        0
2016-05-12 16:39:00              assault-dv  ...         0
```

5. Not only can you select a single date inexactly, but you can do so for an entire month, year, or even hour of the day:

```
>>> crime.loc['2016-05'].shape
(8012, 7)
```

```
>>> crime.loc['2016'].shape
(91076, 7)
>>> crime.loc['2016-05-12 03'].shape
(4, 7)
```

6. The selection strings may also contain the name of the month:

```
>>> crime.loc['Dec 2015'].sort_index()
```

	OFFENSE_TYPE_ID	...
REPORTED_DATE		...
2015-12-01 00:48:00	drug-cocaine-possess	...
2015-12-01 00:48:00	theft-of-motor-vehicle	...
2015-12-01 01:00:00	criminal-mischief-other	...
2015-12-01 01:10:00	traf-other	...
2015-12-01 01:10:00	traf-habitual-offender	...
...	...	...
2015-12-31 23:35:00	drug-cocaine-possess	...
2015-12-31 23:40:00	traffic-accident	...
2015-12-31 23:44:00	drug-cocaine-possess	...
2015-12-31 23:45:00	violation-of-restraining-order	...
2015-12-31 23:50:00	weapon-poss-illegal-dangerous	...

7. Many other string patterns with month name included also work:

```
>>> crime.loc['2016 Sep, 15'].shape
(252, 7)
>>> crime.loc['21st October 2014 05'].shape
(4, 7)
```

8. In addition to selection, you may use the slice notation to select a precise range of data. This example will include all values starting from March 4, 2015 through the end of January 1, 2016:

```
>>> crime.loc['2015-3-4':'2016-1-1'].sort_index()
```

	OFFENSE_TYPE_ID	...
REPORTED_DATE		...
2015-03-04 00:11:00	assault-dv	...
2015-03-04 00:19:00	assault-dv	...
2015-03-04 00:27:00	theft-of-services	...
2015-03-04 00:49:00	traffic-accident-hit-and-run	...
2015-03-04 01:07:00	burglary-business-no-force	...

```
...                                            ...   ...
2016-01-01 23:15:00   traffic-accident-hit-and-run   ...
2016-01-01 23:16:00              traffic-accident   ...
2016-01-01 23:40:00              robbery-business   ...
2016-01-01 23:45:00          drug-cocaine-possess   ...
2016-01-01 23:48:00       drug-poss-paraphernalia   ...
```

9. Notice that all crimes committed on the end date regardless of the time are included in the returned result. This is true for any result using the label-based `.loc` attribute. You can provide as much precision (or lack thereof) to any start or end portion of the slice:

```
>>> crime.loc['2015-3-4 22':'2016-1-1 11:22:00'].sort_index()
                                   OFFENSE_TYPE_ID   ...

REPORTED_DATE                                        ...
2015-03-04 22:25:00   traffic-accident-hit-and-run   ...
2015-03-04 22:30:00              traffic-accident   ...
2015-03-04 22:32:00   traffic-accident-hit-and-run   ...
2015-03-04 22:33:00   traffic-accident-hit-and-run   ...
2015-03-04 22:36:00          theft-unauth-use-of-ftd   ...
...                                            ...   ...
2016-01-01 11:10:00          theft-of-motor-vehicle   ...
2016-01-01 11:11:00              traffic-accident   ...
2016-01-01 11:11:00   traffic-accident-hit-and-run   ...
2016-01-01 11:16:00                     traf-other   ...
2016-01-01 11:22:00              traffic-accident   ...
```

How it works...

One of the features of hdf5 files is their ability to preserve the data types of each column, which reduces the memory required. In this case, three of these columns are stored as a pandas category instead of as an object. Storing them as objects will lead to a four times increase in memory usage:

```
>>> mem_cat = crime.memory_usage().sum()
>>> mem_obj = (crime
...     .astype({'OFFENSE_TYPE_ID':'object',
...              'OFFENSE_CATEGORY_ID':'object',
...              'NEIGHBORHOOD_ID':'object'})
```

```
...        .memory_usage(deep=True)
...        .sum()
... )
>>> mb = 2 ** 20
>>> round(mem_cat / mb, 1), round(mem_obj / mb, 1)
(29.4, 122.7)
```

To select and slice rows by date using the indexing operator, the index must contain date values. In *step 2*, we move the REPORTED_DATE column into the index and to create a DatetimeIndex as the new index:

```
>>> crime.index[:2]
DatetimeIndex(['2014-06-29 02:01:00', '2014-06-29 01:54:00'],
dtype='datetime64[ns]', name='REPORTED_DATE', freq=None)
```

With a DatetimeIndex, a huge variety of strings may be used to select rows with the .loc attribute. In fact, all strings that can be sent to the pandas Timestamp constructor will work here. Surprisingly, it is not necessary to use the .loc attribute for any of the selections or slices in this recipe. The index operator by itself will work in the same manner. For instance, the second statement of *step 7* may be written as crime['21st October 2014 05'].

Personally, I prefer using the .loc attribute when selecting rows and would always use it over the index operator on a DataFrame. The .loc indexer is explicit, and it is unambiguous that the first value passed to it is always used to select rows.

Steps 8 and 9 show how slicing works with timestamps. Any date that partially matches either the start or end value of the slice is included in the result.

There's more...

Our original crimes DataFrame was not sorted and slicing still worked as expected. Sorting the index will lead to large gains in performance. Let's see the difference with slicing done from *step 8*:

```
>>> %timeit crime.loc['2015-3-4':'2016-1-1']
12.2 ms ± 1.93 ms per loop (mean ± std. dev. of 7 runs, 100 loops each)


>>> crime_sort = crime.sort_index()
>>> %timeit crime_sort.loc['2015-3-4':'2016-1-1']
1.44 ms ± 41.9 µs per loop (mean ± std. dev. of 7 runs, 1000 loops each)
```

The sorted DataFrame provides an eight times performance improvement over the original.

Filtering columns with time data

The last section showed how to filter data that has a `DatetimeIndex`. Often, you will have columns with dates in them, and it does not make sense to have that column be the index. In this section, we will reproduce the slicing of the preceding section with columns. Sadly, the slicing constructs do not work on columns, so we will have to take a different tack.

How to do it...

1. Read in the Denver crimes dataset from the hdf5 file `crimes.h5` and inspect the column types:

    ```
    >>> crime = pd.read_hdf('data/crime.h5', 'crime')
    >>> crime.dtypes
    OFFENSE_TYPE_ID             category
    OFFENSE_CATEGORY_ID         category
    REPORTED_DATE         datetime64[ns]
    GEO_LON                     float64
    GEO_LAT                     float64
    NEIGHBORHOOD_ID            category
    IS_CRIME                      int64
    IS_TRAFFIC                    int64
    dtype: object
    ```

2. Select all the rows where the `REPORTED_DATE` column has a certain value. We will use a Boolean array to filter. Note, that we can compare the a datetime column to a string:

    ```
    >>> (crime
    ...     [crime.REPORTED_DATE == '2016-05-12 16:45:00']
    ... )
                   OFFEN/PE_ID  ...  IS_TRAFFIC
    300905       traffic-accident  ...           1
    302354       traffic-accident  ...           1
    302373  fraud-identity-theft  ...           0
    ```

3. Select all rows with a partial date match. If we try this with the equality operator, it fails. We do not get an error, but there are no rows returned:

    ```
    >>> (crime
    ...     [crime.REPORTED_DATE == '2016-05-12']
    ```

```
... )
```

```
Empty DataFrame
```

```
Columns: [OFFENSE_TYPE_ID, OFFENSE_CATEGORY_ID, REPORTED_DATE,
GEO_LON, GEO_LAT, NEIGHBORHOOD_ID, IS_CRIME, IS_TRAFFIC]
```

```
Index: []
```

This also fails if we try and compare to the `.dt.date` attribute. That is because this is a series of Python `datetime.date` objects, and they do not support that comparison:

```
>>> (crime

...     [crime.REPORTED_DATE.dt.date == '2016-05-12']

... )
```

```
Empty DataFrame
```

```
Columns: [OFFENSE_TYPE_ID, OFFENSE_CATEGORY_ID, REPORTED_DATE,
GEO_LON, GEO_LAT, NEIGHBORHOOD_ID, IS_CRIME, IS_TRAFFIC]
```

```
Index: []
```

4. If we want a partial date match, we can use the `.between` method, which supports partial date strings. Note that the start and end dates (the parameter names are `left` and `right` respectively) are inclusive by default. If there were a row with a date on midnight May 13, 2016, it would be included here:

```
>>> (crime

...     [crime.REPORTED_DATE.between(

...         '2016-05-12', '2016-05-13')]

... )
```

	OFFEN/PE_ID	...	IS_TRAFFIC
295715	criminal-mischief-other	...	0
296474	liquor-possession	...	0
297204	traffic-accident	...	1
299383	theft-bicycle	...	0
299389	theft-of-motor-vehicle	...	0
...	...	...	...
358208	public-peace-other	...	0
358448	threats-to-injure	...	0
363134	sex-aslt-rape	...	0
365959	menacing-felony-w-weap	...	0
378711	assault-dv	...	0

5. Because `.between` supports partial date strings, we can replicate most of the slicing functionality of the previous section with it. We can match just a month, year, or hour of the day:

```
>>> (crime
...     [crime.REPORTED_DATE.between(
...         '2016-05', '2016-06')]
...     .shape
... )
(8012, 8)
```

```
>>> (crime
...     [crime.REPORTED_DATE.between(
...         '2016', '2017')]
...     .shape
... )
(91076, 8)
```

```
>>> (crime
...     [crime.REPORTED_DATE.between(
...         '2016-05-12 03', '2016-05-12 04')]
...     .shape
... )
(4, 8)
```

6. We can use other string patterns:

```
>>> (crime
...     [crime.REPORTED_DATE.between(
...         '2016 Sep, 15', '2016 Sep, 16')]
...     .shape
... )
(252, 8)
```

```
>>> (crime
...     [crime.REPORTED_DATE.between(
...         '21st October 2014 05', '21st October 2014 06')]
...     .shape
... )
(4, 8)
```

7. Because `.loc` is closed and includes both start and end, the functionality of `.between` mimics that. However, in a partial date string there is a slight difference. Ending a slice on `2016-1-1` will include all values for January 1, 2016. Using that value as the end value will include values up to the start of that day. To replicate the slice `['2015-3-4':'2016-1-1']`, we need to add the last time of the end day:

```
>>> (crime
...      [crime.REPORTED_DATE.between(
...           '2015-3-4','2016-1-1 23:59:59')]
...      .shape
... )
(75403, 8)
```

8. We can tweak this dates as needed. Below replicates the behavior of the last step of the previous recipe:

```
>>> (crime
...      [crime.REPORTED_DATE.between(
...           '2015-3-4 22','2016-1-1 11:22:00')]
...      .shape
... )
(75071, 8)
```

How it works...

The pandas library can slice index values, but not columns. To replicate `DatetimeIndex` slicing on a column, we need to use the `.between` method. The body of this method is just seven lines of code:

```
def between(self, left, right, inclusive=True):
if inclusive:
lmask = self >= left
rmask = self <= right
else:
lmask = self > left
rmask = self < right


return lmask & rmask
```

This gives us insight that we can build up mask and combine them as needed. For example, we can replicate *step 7* using two masks:

```
>>> lmask = crime.REPORTED_DATE >= '2015-3-4 22'
>>> rmask = crime.REPORTED_DATE <= '2016-1-1 11:22:00'
>>> crime[lmask & rmask].shape
(75071, 8)
```

There's more...

Let's compare timing of `.loc` on the index and `.between` on a column:

```
>>> ctseries = crime.set_index('REPORTED_DATE')
>>> %timeit ctseries.loc['2015-3-4':'2016-1-1']
11 ms ± 3.1 ms per loop (mean ± std. dev. of 7 runs, 100 loops each)

>>> %timeit crime[crime.REPORTED_DATE.between('2015-3-4','2016-1-1')]
20.1 ms ± 525 µs per loop (mean ± std. dev. of 7 runs, 10 loops each)
```

Having the date information in the index provides a slight speed improvement. If you need to perform date slicing on a single column, it might make sense to set the index to a date column. Note that there is also overhead for setting the index to a column, and if you are only slicing a single time, the overhead makes the time for these two operations about the same.

Using methods that only work with a DatetimeIndex

There are a number of DataFrame and Series methods that only work with a `DatetimeIndex`. If the index is of any other type, these methods will fail.

In this recipe, we will first use methods to select rows of data by their time component. We will then learn about the powerful `DateOffset` objects and their aliases.

How to do it...

1. Read in the crime hdf5 dataset, set the index as REPORTED_DATE, and ensure that we have a `DatetimeIndex`:

    ```
    >>> crime = (pd.read_hdf('data/crime.h5', 'crime')
    ...          .set_index('REPORTED_DATE')
    ...     )
    ```

```
>>> type(crime.index)

<class 'pandas.core.indexes.datetimes.DatetimeIndex'>
```

2. Use the `.between_time` method to select all crimes that occurred between 2 A.M. and 5 A.M., regardless of the date:

```
>>> crime.between_time('2:00', '5:00', include_end=False)
                                  OFFENSE_TYPE_ID  ...
REPORTED_DATE                                      ...
2014-06-29 02:01:00        traffic-accident-dui-duid  ...
2014-06-29 02:00:00            disturbing-the-peace  ...
2014-06-29 02:18:00                          curfew  ...
2014-06-29 04:17:00              aggravated-assault  ...
2014-06-29 04:22:00  violation-of-restraining-order  ...
...                                             ...  ...
2017-08-25 04:41:00         theft-items-from-vehicle  ...
2017-09-13 04:17:00          theft-of-motor-vehicle  ...
2017-09-13 02:21:00                  assault-simple  ...
2017-09-13 03:21:00        traffic-accident-dui-duid  ...
2017-09-13 02:15:00      traffic-accident-hit-and-run  ...
```

3. Select all dates at a specific time with `.at_time`:

```
>>> crime.at_time('5:47')
                                  OFFENSE_TYPE_ID  ...
REPORTED_DATE                                      ...
2013-11-26 05:47:00          criminal-mischief-other  ...
2017-04-09 05:47:00          criminal-mischief-mtr-veh  ...
2017-02-19 05:47:00          criminal-mischief-other  ...
2017-02-16 05:47:00              aggravated-assault  ...
2017-02-12 05:47:00              police-interference  ...
...                                             ...  ...
2013-09-10 05:47:00                 traffic-accident  ...
2013-03-14 05:47:00                     theft-other  ...
2012-10-08 05:47:00         theft-items-from-vehicle  ...
2013-08-21 05:47:00         theft-items-from-vehicle  ...
2017-08-23 05:47:00      traffic-accident-hit-and-run  ...
```

4. The `.first` methods provide an elegant way of selecting the first *n* segments of time, where *n* is an integer. These segments of time are represented by `DateOffset` objects that can be in the `pd.offsets` module. The DataFrame must be sorted on its index to guarantee that this method will work. Let's select the first six months of crime data:

```
>>> crime_sort = crime.sort_index()
>>> crime_sort.first(pd.offsets.MonthBegin(6))
```

	OFFENSE_TYPE_ID	...
REPORTED_DATE		...
2012-01-02 00:06:00	aggravated-assault	...
2012-01-02 00:06:00	violation-of-restraining-order	...
2012-01-02 00:16:00	traffic-accident-dui-duid	...
2012-01-02 00:47:00	traffic-accident	...
2012-01-02 01:35:00	aggravated-assault	...
...	...	...
2012-06-30 23:40:00	traffic-accident-dui-duid	...
2012-06-30 23:44:00	traffic-accident	...
2012-06-30 23:50:00	criminal-mischief-mtr-veh	...
2012-06-30 23:54:00	traffic-accident-hit-and-run	...
2012-07-01 00:01:00	robbery-street	...

5. This captured the data from January through June but also, surprisingly, selected a single row in July. The reason for this is that pandas uses the time component of the first element in the index, which, in this example, is 6 minutes. Let's use `MonthEnd`, a slightly different offset:

```
>>> crime_sort.first(pd.offsets.MonthEnd(6))
```

	OFFENSE_TYPE_ID	...
REPORTED_DATE		...
2012-01-02 00:06:00	aggravated-assault	...
2012-01-02 00:06:00	violation-of-restraining-order	...
2012-01-02 00:16:00	traffic-accident-dui-duid	...
2012-01-02 00:47:00	traffic-accident	...
2012-01-02 01:35:00	aggravated-assault	...
...	...	...
2012-06-29 23:01:00	aggravated-assault	...
2012-06-29 23:11:00	traffic-accident	...
2012-06-29 23:41:00	robbery-street	...
2012-06-29 23:57:00	assault-simple	...
2012-06-30 00:04:00	traffic-accident	...

6. This captured nearly the same amount of data but if you look closely, only a single row from June 30th was captured. Again, this is because the time component of the first index was preserved. The exact search went to `2012-06-30 00:06:00`. So, how do we get exactly six months of data? There are a couple of ways. All `DateOffset` objects have a `normalize` parameter that, when set to `True`, sets all the time components to zero. The following should get us very close to what we want:

```
>>> crime_sort.first(pd.offsets.MonthBegin(6, normalize=True))
```

	OFFENSE_TYPE_ID	...
REPORTED_DATE		...
2012-01-02 00:06:00	aggravated-assault	...
2012-01-02 00:06:00	violation-of-restraining-order	...
2012-01-02 00:16:00	traffic-accident-dui-duid	...
2012-01-02 00:47:00	traffic-accident	...
2012-01-02 01:35:00	aggravated-assault	...
...	...	...
2012-06-30 23:40:00	traffic-accident-hit-and-run	...
2012-06-30 23:40:00	traffic-accident-dui-duid	...
2012-06-30 23:44:00	traffic-accident	...
2012-06-30 23:50:00	criminal-mischief-mtr-veh	...
2012-06-30 23:54:00	traffic-accident-hit-and-run	...

7. This method has successfully captured all the data for the first six months of the year. With `normalize` set to `True`, the search went to `2012-07-01 00:00:00`, which would include any crimes reported exactly on this date and time. There is no possible way to use the `.first` method to ensure that only data from January to June is captured. The following slice would yield the exact result:

```
>>> crime_sort.loc[:'2012-06']
```

	OFFENSE_TYPE_ID	...
REPORTED_DATE		...
2012-01-02 00:06:00	aggravated-assault	...
2012-01-02 00:06:00	violation-of-restraining-order	...
2012-01-02 00:16:00	traffic-accident-dui-duid	...
2012-01-02 00:47:00	traffic-accident	...
2012-01-02 01:35:00	aggravated-assault	...
...	...	...
2012-06-30 23:40:00	traffic-accident-hit-and-run	...
2012-06-30 23:40:00	traffic-accident-dui-duid	...
2012-06-30 23:44:00	traffic-accident	...
2012-06-30 23:50:00	criminal-mischief-mtr-veh	...
2012-06-30 23:54:00	traffic-accident-hit-and-run	...

8. There are a dozen `DateOffset` objects for moving forward or backward to the next nearest offset. Instead of hunting down the `DateOffset` objects in `pd.offsets`, you can use a string called an *offset alias* instead. For instance, the string for `MonthEnd` is `M` and for `MonthBegin` is `MS`. To denote the number of these offset aliases, place an integer in front of it. Use this table to find all the aliases (https://pandas.pydata.org/pandas-docs/stable/user_guide/timeseries.html#timeseries-offset-aliases). Let's see some examples of offset aliases with the description of what is being selected in the comments:

```
>>> crime_sort.first('5D') # 5 days
                              OFFENSE_TYPE_ID  ...
REPORTED_DATE                                  ...
2012-01-02 00:06:00        aggravated-assault  ...
2012-01-02 00:06:00  violation-of-restraining-order  ...
2012-01-02 00:16:00     traffic-accident-dui-duid  ...
2012-01-02 00:47:00           traffic-accident  ...
2012-01-02 01:35:00        aggravated-assault  ...
...                                       ...  ...
2012-01-06 23:11:00      theft-items-from-vehicle  ...
2012-01-06 23:23:00  violation-of-restraining-order  ...
2012-01-06 23:30:00                 assault-dv  ...
2012-01-06 23:44:00      theft-of-motor-vehicle  ...
2012-01-06 23:55:00          threats-to-injure  ...


>>> crime_sort.first('5B') # 5 business days
                              OFFENSE_TYPE_ID  ...
REPORTED_DATE                                  ...
2012-01-02 00:06:00        aggravated-assault  ...
2012-01-02 00:06:00  violation-of-restraining-order  ...
2012-01-02 00:16:00     traffic-accident-dui-duid  ...
2012-01-02 00:47:00           traffic-accident  ...
2012-01-02 01:35:00        aggravated-assault  ...
...                                       ...  ...
2012-01-08 23:46:00      theft-items-from-vehicle  ...
2012-01-08 23:51:00   burglary-residence-no-force  ...
2012-01-08 23:52:00                theft-other  ...
2012-01-09 00:04:00   traffic-accident-hit-and-run  ...
2012-01-09 00:05:00  fraud-criminal-impersonation  ...
```

```
>>> crime_sort.first('7W') # 7 weeks, with weeks ending on Sunday
                                        OFFENSE_TYPE_ID  ...

REPORTED_DATE                                            ...
2012-01-02 00:06:00              aggravated-assault  ...
2012-01-02 00:06:00   violation-of-restraining-order  ...
2012-01-02 00:16:00           traffic-accident-dui-duid  ...
2012-01-02 00:47:00                 traffic-accident  ...
2012-01-02 01:35:00              aggravated-assault  ...
         ...                                     ...  ...
2012-02-18 21:57:00                 traffic-accident  ...
2012-02-18 22:19:00         criminal-mischief-graffiti  ...
2012-02-18 22:20:00           traffic-accident-dui-duid  ...
2012-02-18 22:44:00           criminal-mischief-mtr-veh  ...
2012-02-18 23:27:00         theft-items-from-vehicle  ...


>>> crime_sort.first('3QS') # 3rd quarter start
                                        OFFENSE_TYPE_ID  ...

REPORTED_DATE                                            ...
2012-01-02 00:06:00              aggravated-assault  ...
2012-01-02 00:06:00   violation-of-restraining-order  ...
2012-01-02 00:16:00           traffic-accident-dui-duid  ...
2012-01-02 00:47:00                 traffic-accident  ...
2012-01-02 01:35:00              aggravated-assault  ...
         ...                                     ...  ...
2012-09-30 23:17:00         drug-hallucinogen-possess  ...
2012-09-30 23:29:00                   robbery-street  ...
2012-09-30 23:29:00           theft-of-motor-vehicle  ...
2012-09-30 23:41:00         traffic-accident-hit-and-run  ...
2012-09-30 23:43:00                 robbery-business  ...


>>> crime_sort.first('A') # one year end
                                        OFFENSE_TYPE_ID  ...

REPORTED_DATE                                            ...
2012-01-02 00:06:00              aggravated-assault  ...
2012-01-02 00:06:00   violation-of-restraining-order  ...
```

```
2012-01-02 00:16:00          traffic-accident-dui-duid   ...
2012-01-02 00:47:00                     traffic-accident   ...
2012-01-02 01:35:00                  aggravated-assault   ...
...                                              ...  ...
2012-12-30 23:13:00                     traffic-accident   ...
2012-12-30 23:14:00     burglary-residence-no-force   ...
2012-12-30 23:39:00          theft-of-motor-vehicle   ...
2012-12-30 23:41:00                     traffic-accident   ...
2012-12-31 00:05:00                     assault-simple   ...
```

How it works...

Once we ensure that our index is a `DatetimeIndex`, we can take advantage of all the methods in this recipe. It is impossible to do selection or slicing based on just the time component of a `Timestamp` with the `.loc` attribute. To select all dates by a range of time, you must use the `.between_time` method, or to select an exact time, use `.at_time`. Make sure that the passed string for start and end times consists of at least the hour and minute. It is also possible to use `time` objects from the `datetime` module. For instance, the following command would yield the same result as in *step 2*:

```
>>> import datetime
>>> crime.between_time(datetime.time(2,0), datetime.time(5,0),
...                    include_end=False)
                               OFFENSE_TYPE_ID   ...
REPORTED_DATE                                     ...
2014-06-29 02:01:00       traffic-accident-dui-duid   ...
2014-06-29 02:00:00          disturbing-the-peace   ...
2014-06-29 02:18:00                          curfew   ...
2014-06-29 04:17:00             aggravated-assault   ...
2014-06-29 04:22:00     violation-of-restraining-order   ...
...                                         ...  ...
2017-08-25 04:41:00        theft-items-from-vehicle   ...
2017-09-13 04:17:00          theft-of-motor-vehicle   ...
2017-09-13 02:21:00                 assault-simple   ...
2017-09-13 03:21:00       traffic-accident-dui-duid   ...
2017-09-13 02:15:00     traffic-accident-hit-and-run   ...
```

In *step 4*, we begin using the `.first` method, but with a complicated parameter `offset`. It must be a `DateOffset` object or an offset alias as a string. To help understand `DateOffset` objects, it's best to see what they do to a single `Timestamp`. For example, let's take the first element of the index and add six months to it in two different ways:

```
>>> first_date = crime_sort.index[0]
>>> first_date
Timestamp('2012-01-02 00:06:00')


>>> first_date + pd.offsets.MonthBegin(6)
Timestamp('2012-07-01 00:06:00')


>>> first_date + pd.offsets.MonthEnd(6)
Timestamp('2012-06-30 00:06:00')
```

Neither the `MonthBegin` not the `MonthEnd` offsets add or subtract an exact amount of time but effectively round up to the next beginning or end of the month regardless of what day it is. Internally, the `.first` method uses the very first index element of the DataFrame and adds the `DateOffset` passed to it. It then slices up until this new date. For instance, *step 4* is equivalent to the following:

```
>>> step4 = crime_sort.first(pd.offsets.MonthEnd(6))
>>> end_dt = crime_sort.index[0] + pd.offsets.MonthEnd(6)
>>> step4_internal = crime_sort[:end_dt]
>>> step4.equals(step4_internal)
True
```

In *step 8*, offset aliases make for a much more compact method of referencing `DateOffsets`.

There's more...

It is possible to build a custom `DateOffset` when those available do not suit your needs:

```
>>> dt = pd.Timestamp('2012-1-16 13:40')
>>> dt + pd.DateOffset(months=1)
Timestamp('2012-02-16 13:40:00')
```

Notice that this custom `DateOffset` increased the `Timestamp` by exactly one month. Let's look at one more example using many more date and time components:

```
>>> do = pd.DateOffset(years=2, months=5, days=3,
```

```
...        hours=8, seconds=10)
>>> pd.Timestamp('2012-1-22 03:22') + do
Timestamp('2014-06-25 11:22:10')
```

Counting the number of weekly crimes

The Denver crime dataset is huge, with over 460,000 rows each marked with a reported date. Counting the number of weekly crimes is one of many queries that can be answered by grouping according to some period of time. The `.resample` method provides an easy interface to grouping by any possible span of time.

In this recipe, we will use both the `.resample` and `.groupby` methods to count the number of weekly crimes.

How to do it...

1. Read in the crime hdf5 dataset, set the index as the REPORTED_DATE, and then sort it to increase performance for the rest of the recipe:

```
>>> crime_sort = (pd.read_hdf('data/crime.h5', 'crime')
...        .set_index('REPORTED_DATE')
...        .sort_index()
... )
```

2. To count the number of crimes per week, we need to form a group for each week. The `.resample` method takes a DateOffset object or alias and returns an object ready to perform an action on all groups. The object returned from the `.resample` method is very similar to the object produced after calling the `.groupby` method:

```
>>> crime_sort.resample('W')
<pandas.core.resample.DatetimeIndexResampler object at
0x10f07acf8>
```

3. The offset alias, W, was used to inform pandas that we want to group by each week. There isn't much that happened in the preceding step. pandas has validated our offset and returned an object that is ready to perform an action on each week as a group. There are several methods that we can chain after calling `.resample` to return some data. Let's chain the `.size` method to count the number of weekly crimes:

```
>>> (crime_sort
...        .resample('W')
...        .size()
```

```
... )
REPORTED_DATE
2012-01-08     877
2012-01-15    1071
2012-01-22     991
2012-01-29     988
2012-02-05     888
                ...
2017-09-03    1956
2017-09-10    1733
2017-09-17    1976
2017-09-24    1839
2017-10-01    1059
Freq: W-SUN, Length: 300, dtype: int64
```

4. We now have the weekly crime count as a Series with the new index incrementing one week at a time. There are a few things that happen by default that are very important to understand. Sunday is chosen as the last day of the week and is also the date used to label each element in the resulting Series. For instance, the first index value January 8, 2012 is a Sunday. There were 877 crimes committed during that week ending on the 8th. The week of Monday, January 9th to Sunday, January 15th recorded 1,071 crimes. Let's do some sanity checks and ensure that our resampling is doing this:

```
>>> len(crime_sort.loc[:'2012-1-8'])
877
>>> len(crime_sort.loc['2012-1-9':'2012-1-15'])
1071
```

5. Let's choose a different day to end the week besides Sunday with an anchored offset:

```
>>> (crime_sort
...       .resample('W-THU')
...       .size()
... )
REPORTED_DATE
2012-01-05     462
2012-01-12    1116
2012-01-19     924
2012-01-26    1061
2012-02-02     926
```

```
            . . .
2017-09-07    1803
2017-09-14    1866
2017-09-21    1926
2017-09-28    1720
2017-10-05      28
Freq: W-THU, Length: 301, dtype: int64
```

6. Nearly all the functionality of `.resample` may be reproduced by the `.groupby` method. The only difference is that you must pass the offset into a `pd.Grouper` object:

```
>>> weekly_crimes = (crime_sort
...        .groupby(pd.Grouper(freq='W'))
...        .size()
... )
>>> weekly_crimes
REPORTED_DATE
2012-01-08     877
2012-01-15    1071
2012-01-22     991
2012-01-29     988
2012-02-05     888
              . . .
2017-09-03    1956
2017-09-10    1733
2017-09-17    1976
2017-09-24    1839
2017-10-01    1059
Freq: W-SUN, Length: 300, dtype: int64
```

How it works...

The `.resample` method, by default, works implicitly with a `DatetimeIndex`, which is why we set it to `REPORTED_DATE` in *step 1*. In *step 2*, we created an intermediate object that helps us understand how to form groups within the data. The first parameter to `.resample` is the rule determining how the Timestamps in the index will be grouped. In this instance, we use the offset alias `W` to form groups one week in length ending on Sunday. The default ending day is Sunday, but may be changed with an *anchored offset* by appending a dash and the first three letters of a day of the week.

Once we have formed groups with `.resample`, we must chain a method to take action on each of them. In *step 3*, we use the `.size` method to count the number of crimes per week. You might be wondering what are all the possible attributes and methods available to use after calling `.resample`. The following examines the `.resample` object and outputs them:

```
>>> r = crime_sort.resample('W')
>>> [attr for attr in dir(r) if attr[0].islower()]
['agg', 'aggregate', 'apply', 'asfreq', 'ax', 'backfill', 'bfill',
'count',
'ffill', 'fillna', 'first', 'get_group', 'groups', 'indices',
'interpolate', 'last', 'max', 'mean', 'median', 'min', 'ndim', 'ngroups',
'nunique', 'obj', 'ohlc', 'pad', 'plot', 'prod', 'sem', 'size', 'std',
'sum', 'transform', 'var']
```

Step 4 verifies the accuracy of the count from *step 3* by slicing the data by week and counting the number of rows. The `.resample` method is not necessary to group by Timestamp as the functionality is available from the `.groupby` method itself. However, you must pass an instance of `pd.Grouper` to the `groupby` method using the `freq` parameter for the offset, as done in *step 6*.

There's more...

It is possible to use `.resample` even when the index does not contain a Timestamp. You can use the `on` parameter to select the column with Timestamps that will be used to form groups:

```
>>> crime = pd.read_hdf('data/crime.h5', 'crime')
>>> weekly_crimes2 = crime.resample('W', on='REPORTED_DATE').size()
>>> weekly_crimes2.equals(weekly_crimes)
True
```

This is also possible using groupby with `pd.Grouper` by selecting the Timestamp column with the `key` parameter:

```
>>> weekly_crimes_gby2 = (crime
...      .groupby(pd.Grouper(key='REPORTED_DATE', freq='W'))
...      .size()
... )
>>> weekly_crimes2.equals(weekly_crimes)
True
```

We can also produce a line plot of all the crimes in Denver (including traffic accidents) by calling the `.plot` method on our Series of weekly crimes:

```
>>> import matplotlib.pyplot as plt
>>> fig, ax = plt.subplots(figsize=(16, 4))
>>> weekly_crimes.plot(title='All Denver Crimes', ax=ax)
>>> fig.savefig('c12-crimes.png', dpi=300)
```

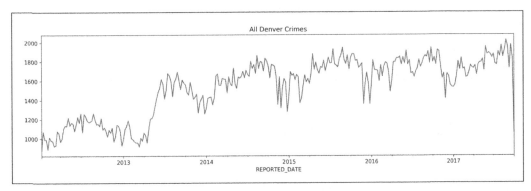

Weekly crime plot

Aggregating weekly crime and traffic accidents separately

The Denver crime dataset has all crime and traffic accidents together in one table, and separates them through the binary columns: IS_CRIME and IS_TRAFFIC. The .resample method allows you to group by a period of time and aggregate specific columns separately.

In this recipe, we will use the .resample method to group by each quarter of the year and then sum up the number of crimes and traffic accidents separately.

How to do it...

1. Read in the crime hdf5 dataset, set the index as REPORTED_DATE, and then sort it to increase performance for the rest of the recipe:

```
>>> crime = (pd.read_hdf('data/crime.h5', 'crime')
...       .set_index('REPORTED_DATE')
...       .sort_index()
... )
```

2. Use the .resample method to group by each quarter of the year and then sum the IS_CRIME and IS_TRAFFIC columns for each group:

```
>>> (crime
```

```
...        .resample('Q')
...        [['IS_CRIME', 'IS_TRAFFIC']]
...        .sum()
... )
```

	IS_CRIME	IS_TRAFFIC
REPORTED_DATE		
2012-03-31	7882	4726
2012-06-30	9641	5255
2012-09-30	10566	5003
2012-12-31	9197	4802
2013-03-31	8730	4442
...	...	...
2016-09-30	17427	6199
2016-12-31	15984	6094
2017-03-31	16426	5587
2017-06-30	17486	6148
2017-09-30	17990	6101

3. Notice that the dates all appear as the last day of the quarter. This is because the offset alias, Q, represents the end of the quarter. Let's use the offset alias QS to represent the start of the quarter:

```
>>> (crime
...        .resample('QS')
...        [['IS_CRIME', 'IS_TRAFFIC']]
...        .sum()
... )
```

	IS_CRIME	IS_TRAFFIC
REPORTED_DATE		
2012-01-01	7882	4726
2012-04-01	9641	5255
2012-07-01	10566	5003
2012-10-01	9197	4802
2013-01-01	8730	4442
...	...	...
2016-07-01	17427	6199
2016-10-01	15984	6094
2017-01-01	16426	5587

2017-04-01	17486	6148
2017-07-01	17990	6101

4. Let's verify these results by checking whether the second quarter of data is correct:

```
>>> (crime
...      .loc['2012-4-1':'2012-6-30', ['IS_CRIME', 'IS_TRAFFIC']]
...      .sum()
... )
IS_CRIME     9641
IS_TRAFFIC   5255
dtype: int64
```

5. It is possible to replicate this operation using the .groupby method:

```
>>> (crime
...      .groupby(pd.Grouper(freq='Q'))
...      [['IS_CRIME', 'IS_TRAFFIC']]
...      .sum()
... )
```

	IS_CRIME	IS_TRAFFIC
REPORTED_DATE		
2012-03-31	7882	4726
2012-06-30	9641	5255
2012-09-30	10566	5003
2012-12-31	9197	4802
2013-03-31	8730	4442
...	...	...
2016-09-30	17427	6199
2016-12-31	15984	6094
2017-03-31	16426	5587
2017-06-30	17486	6148
2017-09-30	17990	6101

6. Let's make a plot to visualize the trends in crime and traffic accidents over time:

```
>>> fig, ax = plt.subplots(figsize=(16, 4))
>>> (crime
...      .groupby(pd.Grouper(freq='Q'))
...      [['IS_CRIME', 'IS_TRAFFIC']]
```

```
...         .sum()
...         .plot(color=['black', 'lightgrey'], ax=ax,
...             title='Denver Crimes and Traffic Accidents')
... )
>>> fig.savefig('c12-crimes2.png', dpi=300)
```

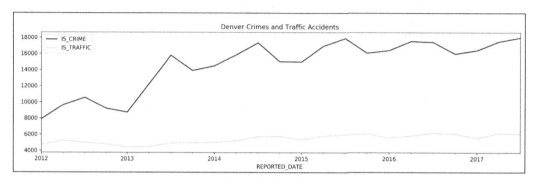

Quarterly crime plot

How it works...

After reading in and preparing our data in *step 1*, we begin grouping and aggregating in *step 2*. Immediately after calling the .resample method, we can continue either by chaining a method or by selecting a group of columns to aggregate. We choose to select the IS_CRIME and IS_TRAFFIC columns to aggregate. If we didn't select just these two, then all of the numeric columns would have been summed with the following outcome:

```
>>> (crime
...         .resample('Q')
...         .sum()
... )
```

	GEO_LON	...	IS_TRAFFIC
REPORTED_DATE		...	
2012-03-31	-1.313006e+06	...	4726
2012-06-30	-1.547274e+06	...	5255
2012-09-30	-1.615835e+06	...	5003
2012-12-31	-1.458177e+06	...	4802
2013-03-31	-1.368931e+06	...	4442
...	...	...	...
2016-09-30	-2.459343e+06	...	6199

2016-12-31	-2.293628e+06	...	6094
2017-03-31	-2.288383e+06	...	5587
2017-06-30	-2.453857e+06	...	6148
2017-09-30	-2.508001e+06	...	6101

By default, the offset alias Q technically uses December 31st as the last day of the year. The span of dates that represent a single quarter are all calculated using this ending date. The aggregated result uses the last day of the quarter as its label. *Step 3* uses the offset alias QS, which, by default, calculates quarters using January 1st as the first day of the year.

Most public businesses report quarterly earnings but they do not all have the same calendar year beginning in January. For instance, if we wanted our quarters to begin March 1st, then we could use QS-MAR to anchor our offset alias:

```
>>> (crime_sort
...      .resample('QS-MAR')
...      [['IS_CRIME', 'IS_TRAFFIC']]
...      .sum()
... )
```

	IS_CRIME	IS_TRAFFIC
REPORTED_DATE		
2011-12-01	5013	3198
2012-03-01	9260	4954
2012-06-01	10524	5190
2012-09-01	9450	4777
2012-12-01	9003	4652
...	...	...
2016-09-01	16932	6202
2016-12-01	15615	5731
2017-03-01	17287	5940
2017-06-01	18545	6246
2017-09-01	5417	1931

As in the preceding recipe, we verify our results via manual slicing in *step 4*. In *step 5* we replicate the result of *step 3* with the .groupby method using pd.Grouper to set our group length. In *step 6*, we call the DataFrame .plot method. By default, a line is plotted for each column of data. The plot clearly shows a sharp increase in reported crimes during the first three quarters of the year. There also appears to be a seasonal component to both crime and traffic, with numbers lower in the cooler months and higher in the warmer months.

There's more...

To get a different visual perspective, we can plot the percentage increase in crime and traffic, instead of the raw count. Let's divide all the data by the first row and plot again:

```
>>> crime_begin = (crime
...        .resample('Q')
...        [['IS_CRIME', 'IS_TRAFFIC']]
...        .sum()
...        .iloc[0]
... )


>>> fig, ax = plt.subplots(figsize=(16, 4))
>>> (crime
...        .resample('Q')
...        [['IS_CRIME', 'IS_TRAFFIC']]
...        .sum()
...        .div(crime_begin)
...        .sub(1)
...        .round(2)
...        .mul(100)
...        .plot.bar(color=['black', 'lightgrey'], ax=ax,
...             title='Denver Crimes and Traffic Accidents % Increase')
... )


>>> fig.autofmt_xdate()
>>> fig.savefig('c12-crimes3.png', dpi=300, bbox_inches='tight')
```

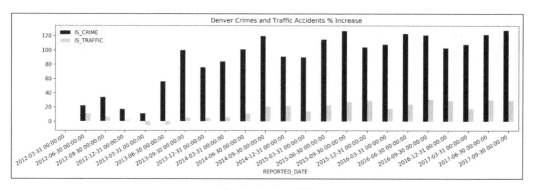

Quarterly crime plot

Measuring crime by weekday and year

Measuring crimes by weekday and by year simultaneously requires the functionality to pull this information from a Timestamp. Thankfully, this functionality is built into any Timestamp column with the `.dt` attribute.

In this recipe, we will use the `.dt` attribute to provide us with both the weekday name and year of each crime as a Series. We count all of the crimes by forming groups using both of these Series. Finally, we adjust the data to consider partial years and population before creating a heatmap of the total amount of crime.

How to do it...

1. Read in the Denver crime hdf5 dataset leaving the `REPORTED_DATE` as a column:

```
>>> crime = pd.read_hdf('data/crime.h5', 'crime')
>>> crime
```

	OFFEN/PE_ID	...	IS_TRAFFIC
0	traffic-accident-dui-duid	...	1
1	vehicular-eluding-no-chase	...	0
2	disturbing-the-peace	...	0
3	curfew	...	0
4	aggravated-assault	...	0
...	...	...	...
460906	burglary-business-by-force	...	0
460907	weapon-unlawful-discharge-of	...	0
460908	traf-habitual-offender	...	0
460909	criminal-mischief-other	...	0
460910	theft-other	...	0

2. All Timestamp columns have a special attribute, `.dt`, which gives access to a variety of extra attributes and methods specifically designed for dates. Let's find the day name of each `REPORTED_DATE` and then count these values:

```
>>> (crime
...     ['REPORTED_DATE']
...     .dt.day_name()
...     .value_counts()
... )
Monday          70024
```

```
Friday          69621
Wednesday       69538
Thursday        69287
Tuesday         68394
Saturday        58834
Sunday          55213
Name: REPORTED_DATE, dtype: int64
```

3. The weekends appear to have substantially less crime and traffic accidents. Let's put this data in correct weekday order and make a horizontal bar plot:

```
>>> days = ['Monday', 'Tuesday', 'Wednesday', 'Thursday',
...              'Friday', 'Saturday', 'Sunday']
>>> title = 'Denver Crimes and Traffic Accidents per Weekday'
>>> fig, ax = plt.subplots(figsize=(6, 4))
>>> (crime
...      ['REPORTED_DATE']
...      .dt.day_name()
...      .value_counts()
...      .reindex(days)
...      .plot.barh(title=title, ax=ax)
... )
>>> fig.savefig('c12-crimes4.png', dpi=300, bbox_inches='tight')
```

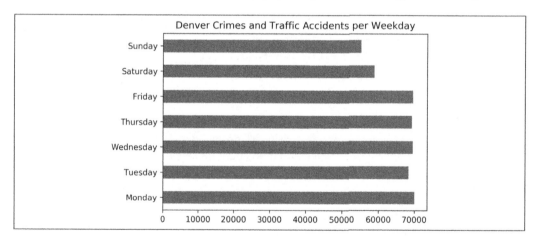

Weekday crime plot

4. We can do a very similar procedure to plot the count by year:

```
>>> title = 'Denver Crimes and Traffic Accidents per Year'
>>> fig, ax = plt.subplots(figsize=(6, 4))
>>> (crime
...     ['REPORTED_DATE']
...     .dt.year
...     .value_counts()
...     .sort_index()
...     .plot.barh(title=title, ax=ax)
... )
>>> fig.savefig('c12-crimes5.png', dpi=300, bbox_inches='tight')
```

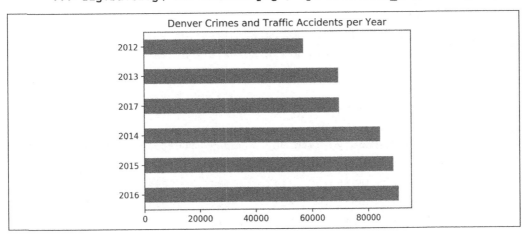

Yearly crime plot

5. We need to group by both weekday and year. One way of doing this is to use these attributes in the `.groupby` method:

```
>>> (crime
...     .groupby([crime['REPORTED_DATE'].dt.year.rename('year'),
...               crime['REPORTED_DATE'].dt.day_name().
rename('day')])
...     .size()
... )
year    day
2012    Friday        8549
        Monday        8786
        Saturday      7442
```

```
        Sunday         7189
        Thursday       8440
                       ...
2017    Saturday       8514
        Sunday         8124
        Thursday      10545
        Tuesday       10628
        Wednesday     10576
Length: 42, dtype: int64
```

6. We have aggregated the data correctly, but the structure is not conducive to make comparisons easily. Let's use the `.unstack` method to get a more readable table:

```
>>> (crime
...      .groupby([crime['REPORTED_DATE'].dt.year.rename('year'),
...               crime['REPORTED_DATE'].dt.day_name().
rename('day')])
...      .size()
...      .unstack('day')
... )
```

day	Friday	Monday	Saturday	Sunday	Thursday	Tuesday
year						
2012	8549	8786	7442	7189	8440	8191
2013	10380	10627	8875	8444	10431	10416
2014	12683	12813	10950	10278	12309	12440
2015	13273	13452	11586	10624	13512	13381
2016	14059	13708	11467	10554	14050	13338
2017	10677	10638	8514	8124	10545	10628

7. We now have a nicer representation that is easier to read but noticeably, the 2017 numbers are incomplete. To help make a fairer comparison, we can make a linear extrapolation to estimate the final number of crimes. Let's first find the last day that we have data for in 2017:

```
>>> criteria = crime['REPORTED_DATE'].dt.year == 2017
>>> crime.loc[criteria, 'REPORTED_DATE'].dt.dayofyear.max()
272
```

8. A naive estimate would be to assume a constant rate of crime throughout the year and multiply all values in the 2017 table by 365/272. However, we can do a little better and look at our historical data and calculate the average percentage of crimes that have taken place through the first 272 days of the year:

```
>>> round(272 / 365, 3)
0.745
>>> crime_pct = (crime
...        ['REPORTED_DATE']
...        .dt.dayofyear.le(272)
...        .groupby(crime.REPORTED_DATE.dt.year)
...        .mean()
...        .mul(100)
...        .round(2)
... )
```

```
>>> crime_pct
REPORTED_DATE
2012      74.84
2013      72.54
2014      75.06
2015      74.81
2016      75.15
2017     100.00
Name: REPORTED_DATE, dtype: float64
```

```
>>> crime_pct.loc[2012:2016].median()
74.84
```

9. It turns out (perhaps coincidentally) that the percentage of crimes that happen during the first 272 days of the year is almost exactly proportional to the percentage of days passed in the year. Let's now update the row for 2017 and change the column order to match the weekday order:

```
>>> def update_2017(df_):
...        df_.loc[2017] = (df_
...            .loc[2017]
...            .div(.748)
...            .astype('int')
...        )
...        return df_
>>> (crime
...        .groupby([crime['REPORTED_DATE'].dt.year.rename('year'),
```

```
...                crime['REPORTED_DATE'].dt.day_name().
rename('day')])
...        .size()
...        .unstack('day')
...        .pipe(update_2017)
...        .reindex(columns=days)
... )
```

day	Monday	Tuesday	Wednesday	...	Friday	Saturday	Sunday
year				...			
2012	8786	8191	8440	...	8549	7442	7189
2013	10627	10416	10354	...	10380	8875	8444
2014	12813	12440	12948	...	12683	10950	10278
2015	13452	13381	13320	...	13273	11586	10624
2016	13708	13338	13900	...	14059	11467	10554
2017	14221	14208	14139	...	14274	11382	10860

10. We could make a bar or line plot, but this is also a good situation for a heatmap, which is in the `seaborn` library:

```
>>> import seaborn as sns
>>> fig, ax = plt.subplots(figsize=(6, 4))
>>> table = (crime
...        .groupby([crime['REPORTED_DATE'].dt.year.rename('year'),
...                crime['REPORTED_DATE'].dt.day_name().
rename('day')])
...        .size()
...        .unstack('day')
...        .pipe(update_2017)
...        .reindex(columns=days)
... )
>>> sns.heatmap(table, cmap='Greys', ax=ax)
>>> fig.savefig('c12-crimes6.png', dpi=300, bbox_inches='tight')
```

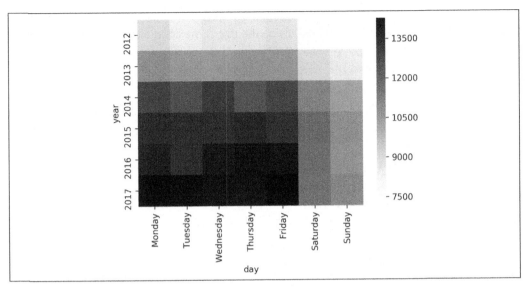

Yearly crime heatmap

11. Crime seems to be rising every year but this data does not account for rising population. Let's read in a table for the Denver population for each year that we have data:

```
>>> denver_pop = pd.read_csv('data/denver_pop.csv',
...      index_col='Year')
>>> denver_pop
       Population
Year
2017     705000
2016     693000
2015     680000
2014     662000
2013     647000
2012     634000
```

12. Many crime metrics are reported as rates per 100,000 residents. Let's divide the population by 100,000 and then divide the raw crime counts by this number to get the crime rate per 100,000 residents:

```
>>> den_100k = denver_pop.div(100_000).squeeze()
>>> normalized = (crime
...         .groupby([crime['REPORTED_DATE'].dt.year.rename('year'),
...                 crime['REPORTED_DATE'].dt.day_name().
rename('day')])
...         .size()
...         .unstack('day')
...         .pipe(update_2017)
...         .reindex(columns=days)
...         .div(den_100k, axis='index')
...         .astype(int)
... )
>>> normalized
```

day	Monday	Tuesday	Wednesday	...	Friday	Saturday	Sunday
2012	1385	1291	1331	...	1348	1173	1133
2013	1642	1609	1600	...	1604	1371	1305
2014	1935	1879	1955	...	1915	1654	1552
2015	1978	1967	1958	...	1951	1703	1562
2016	1978	1924	2005	...	2028	1654	1522
2017	2017	2015	2005	...	2024	1614	1540

13. Once again, we can make a heatmap that, even after adjusting for population increase, looks nearly identical to the first one:

```
>>> import seaborn as sns
>>> fig, ax = plt.subplots(figsize=(6, 4))
>>> sns.heatmap(normalized, cmap='Greys', ax=ax)
>>> fig.savefig('c12-crimes7.png', dpi=300, bbox_inches='tight')
```

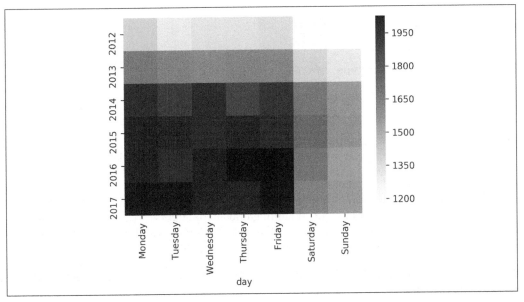

Normalized yearly crime heatmap

How it works...

All DataFrame columns containing Timestamps have access to numerous other attributes and methods with the .dt attribute. In fact, all of these methods and attributes available from the .dt attribute are also available on a Timestamp object.

In *step 2*, we use the .dt attribute (which only works on a Series) to extract the day name and count the occurrences. Before making a plot in *step 3*, we manually rearrange the order of the index with the .reindex method, which, in its most basic use case, accepts a list containing the desired order. This task could have also been accomplished with the .loc indexer like this:

```
>>> (crime
...     ['REPORTED_DATE']
...     .dt.day_name()
...     .value_counts()
...     .loc[days]
... )
Monday       70024
Tuesday      68394
Wednesday    69538
Thursday     69287
```

```
Friday          69621
Saturday        58834
Sunday          55213
Name: REPORTED_DATE, dtype: int64
```

The `.reindex` method is more performant and has many parameters for more diverse situations than `.loc`.

In *step 4*, we do a very similar procedure and retrieve the year using the `.dt` attribute again, and then count the occurrences with the `.value_counts` method. In this instance, we use `.sort_index` over `.reindex`, as years will naturally sort in the desired order.

The goal of the recipe is to group by both weekday and year together, which we do in *step 5*. The `.groupby` method is flexible and can form groups in multiple ways. In this recipe, we pass it two Series derived from the `year` and `weekday` columns. We then chain the `.size` method to it, which returns a single value, the length of each group.

After *step 5*, our Series is long with only a single column of data, which makes it difficult to make comparisons by year and weekday.

To ease the readability, we pivot the weekday level into horizontal column names with `.unstack` in *step 6*. *Step 6* is doing a cross tabulation. Here is another way to do this in pandas:

```
>>> (crime
...       .assign(year=crime.REPORTED_DATE.dt.year,
...               day=crime.REPORTED_DATE.dt.day_name())
...       .pipe(lambda df_: pd.crosstab(df_.year, df_.day))
... )
```

day	Friday	Monday	...	Tuesday	Wednesday
year			...		
2012	8549	8786	...	8191	8440
2013	10380	10627	...	10416	10354
2014	12683	12813	...	12440	12948
2015	13273	13452	...	13381	13320
2016	14059	13708	...	13338	13900
2017	10677	10638	...	10628	10576

In *step 7*, we use Boolean indexing to select only the crimes in 2017 and then use `.dayofyear` from the `.dt` attribute to find the total elapsed days from the beginning of the year. The maximum of this Series should tell us how many days we have data for in 2017.

Step 8 is quite complex. We first create a Boolean Series by testing whether each crime was committed on or before the 272nd day of the year with `crime['REPORTED_DATE'].dt.dayofyear.le(272)`. From here, we again use the `.groupby` method to form groups by the previously calculated year Series and then use the `.mean` method to find the percentage of crimes committed on or before the 272nd day for each year.

The `.loc` attribute selects the entire 2017 row of data in *step 9*. We adjust this row by dividing by the median percentage found in *step 8*.

Lots of crime visualizations are done with heatmaps, and one is done here in *step 10* with the help of the seaborn library. The `cmap` parameter takes a string name of the several dozen available matplotlib colormaps.

In *step 12*, we create a crime rate per 100k residents by dividing by the population of that year. This is another fairly tricky operation. Normally, when you divide one DataFrame by another, they align on their columns and index. However, in this step, there are no columns in common with `denver_pop` so no values will align if we try and divide them. To work around this, we create the `den_100k` Series with the squeeze method. We still can't divide these two objects as, by default, division between a DataFrame and a Series aligns the columns of the DataFrame with the index of the Series, like this:

```
>>> (crime
...       .groupby([crime['REPORTED_DATE'].dt.year.rename('year'),
...                 crime['REPORTED_DATE'].dt.day_name().rename('day')])
...       .size()
...       .unstack('day')
...       .pipe(update_2017)
...       .reindex(columns=days)
... ) / den_100k
          2012   2013   2014   ...   Thursday   Tuesday   Wednesday
year                           ...
2012      NaN    NaN    NaN    ...      NaN        NaN        NaN
2013      NaN    NaN    NaN    ...      NaN        NaN        NaN
2014      NaN    NaN    NaN    ...      NaN        NaN        NaN
2015      NaN    NaN    NaN    ...      NaN        NaN        NaN
2016      NaN    NaN    NaN    ...      NaN        NaN        NaN
2017      NaN    NaN    NaN    ...      NaN        NaN        NaN
```

We need the index of the DataFrame to align with the index of Series, and to do this, we use the `.div` method, which allows us to change the direction of alignment with the `axis` parameter. A heatmap of the adjusted crime rate is plotted in *step 13*.

There's more...

If we wanted to look at specific types of crimes we could do the following:

```
>>> days = ['Monday', 'Tuesday', 'Wednesday', 'Thursday',
...           'Friday', 'Saturday', 'Sunday']
>>> crime_type = 'auto-theft'
>>> normalized = (crime
...       .query('OFFENSE_CATEGORY_ID == @crime_type')
...       .groupby([crime['REPORTED_DATE'].dt.year.rename('year'),
...                 crime['REPORTED_DATE'].dt.day_name().rename('day')])
...       .size()
...       .unstack('day')
...       .pipe(update_2017)
...       .reindex(columns=days)
...       .div(den_100k, axis='index')
...       .astype(int)
... )
>>> normalized
```

day	Monday	Tuesday	Wednesday	...	Friday	Saturday	Sunday
2012	95	72	72	...	71	78	76
2013	85	74	74	...	65	68	67
2014	94	76	72	...	76	67	67
2015	108	102	89	...	92	85	78
2016	119	102	100	...	97	86	85
2017	114	118	111	...	111	91	102

Grouping with anonymous functions with a DatetimeIndex

Using DataFrames with a `DatetimeIndex` opens the door to many new and different operations as seen with several recipes in this chapter.

In this recipe, we will show the versatility of using the `.groupby` method for DataFrames that have a `DatetimeIndex`.

How to do it...

1. Read in the Denver crime hdf5 file, place the `REPORTED_DATE` column in the index, and sort it:

```
>>> crime = (pd.read_hdf('data/crime.h5', 'crime')
...     .set_index('REPORTED_DATE')
...     .sort_index()
... )
```

2. The `DatetimeIndex` has many of the same attributes and methods as a pandas `Timestamp`. Let's take a look at some that they have in common:

```
>>> common_attrs = (set(dir(crime.index)) &
...     set(dir(pd.Timestamp)))
>>> [attr for attr in common_attrs if attr[0] != '_']
['tz_convert', 'is_month_start', 'nanosecond', 'day_name',
'microsecond', 'quarter', 'time', 'tzinfo', 'week', 'year',
'to_period', 'freqstr', 'dayofyear', 'is_year_end', 'weekday_
name', 'month_name', 'minute', 'hour', 'dayofweek', 'second',
'max', 'min', 'to_numpy', 'tz_localize', 'is_quarter_end', 'to_
julian_date', 'strftime', 'day', 'days_in_month', 'weekofyear',
'date', 'daysinmonth', 'month', 'weekday', 'is_year_start', 'is_
month_end', 'ceil', 'timetz', 'freq', 'tz', 'is_quarter_start',
'floor', 'normalize', 'resolution', 'is_leap_year', 'round', 'to_
pydatetime']
```

3. We can then use the `.index` to find weekday names, similarly to what was done in *step 2* of the preceding recipe:

```
>>> crime.index.day_name().value_counts()
Monday       70024
Friday       69621
Wednesday    69538
Thursday     69287
Tuesday      68394
Saturday     58834
Sunday       55213
Name: REPORTED_DATE, dtype: int64
```

4. The `.groupby` method can accept a function as an argument. This function will be passed the `.index` and the return value is used to form groups. Let's see this in action by grouping with a function that turns the `.index` into a weekday name and then counts the number of crimes and traffic accidents separately:

```
>>> (crime
```

```
...          .groupby(lambda idx: idx.day_name())
...          [['IS_CRIME', 'IS_TRAFFIC']]
...          .sum()
... )
              IS_CRIME    IS_TRAFFIC
Friday           48833         20814
Monday           52158         17895
Saturday         43363         15516
Sunday           42315         12968
Thursday         49470         19845
Tuesday          49658         18755
Wednesday        50054         19508
```

5. You can use a list of functions to group by both the hour of day and year, and then reshape the table to make it more readable:

```
>>> funcs = [lambda idx: idx.round('2h').hour, lambda idx: idx.year]
>>> (crime
...        .groupby(funcs)
...        [['IS_CRIME', 'IS_TRAFFIC']]
...        .sum()
...        .unstack()
... )
```

	IS_CRIME			...	IS_TRAFFIC		
	2012	2013	2014	...	2015	2016	2017
0	2422	4040	5649	...	1136	980	782
2	1888	3214	4245	...	773	718	537
4	1472	2181	2956	...	471	464	313
6	1067	1365	1750	...	494	593	462
8	2998	3445	3727	...	2331	2372	1828
..	...	...	...	...	...	...	...
14	4266	5698	6708	...	2840	2763	1990
16	4113	5889	7351	...	3160	3527	2784
18	3660	5094	6586	...	3412	3608	2718
20	3521	4895	6130	...	2071	2184	1491
22	3078	4318	5496	...	1671	1472	1072

6. If you are using Jupyter, you can add `.style.highlight_ max(color='lightgrey')` to bring attention to the largest value in each column:

```
>>> funcs = [lambda idx: idx.round('2h').hour, lambda idx: idx.
year]
>>> (crime
...        .groupby(funcs)
...        [['IS_CRIME', 'IS_TRAFFIC']]
...        .sum()
...        .unstack()
...        .style.highlight_max(color='lightgrey')
... )
```

	IS_CRIME						IS_TRAFFIC					
	2012	2013	2014	2015	2016	2017	2012	2013	2014	2015	2016	2017
0	2422	4040	5649	5649	5377	3811	919	792	978	1136	980	782
2	1888	3214	4245	4050	4091	3041	718	652	779	773	718	537
4	1472	2181	2956	2959	3044	2255	399	378	424	471	464	313
6	1067	1365	1750	2167	2108	1567	411	399	479	494	593	462
8	2998	3445	3727	4161	4488	3251	1957	1955	2210	2331	2372	1828
10	4305	5035	5658	6205	6218	4993	1979	1901	2139	2320	2303	1873
12	4496	5524	6434	6841	7226	5463	2200	2138	2379	2631	2760	1986
14	4266	5698	6708	7218	6896	5396	2241	2245	2630	2840	2763	1990
16	4113	5889	7351	7643	7926	6338	2714	2562	3002	3160	3527	2784
18	3660	5094	6586	7015	7407	6157	3118	2704	3217	3412	3608	2718
20	3521	4895	6130	6360	6963	5272	1787	1806	1994	2071	2184	1491
22	3078	4318	5496	5626	5637	4358	1343	1330	1532	1671	1472	1072

Popular crime hours

How it works...

In *step 1*, we read in our data and placed a Timestamp column into the index to create a `DatetimeIndex`. In *step 2*, we see that a `DatetimeIndex` has lots of the same functionality that a single Timestamp object has. In *step 3*, we use these extra features of the `DatetimeIndex` to extract the day name.

In *step 4*, we take advantage of the `.groupby` method to accept a function that is passed the DatetimeIndex. The `idx` in the anonymous function is the `DatetimeIndex`, and we use it to retrieve the day name. It is possible to pass `.groupby` a list of any number of custom functions, as done in *step 5*. Here, the first function uses the `.round DatetimeIndex` method to round each value to the nearest second hour. The second function returns the `.year` attribute. After the grouping and aggregating, we `.unstack` the years as columns. We then highlight the maximum value of each column. Crime is reported most often between 3 and 5 P.M. Most traffic accidents occur between 5 P.M. and 7 P.M.

Grouping by a Timestamp and another column

The `.resample` method is unable to group by anything other than periods of time. The `.groupby` method, however, has the ability to group by both periods of time and other columns.

In this recipe, we will show two very similar but different approaches to group by Timestamps and another column.

How to do it...

1. Read in the employee dataset, and create a `DatetimeIndex` with the HIRE_DATE column:

```
>>> employee = pd.read_csv('data/employee.csv',
...      parse_dates=['JOB_DATE', 'HIRE_DATE'],
...      index_col='HIRE_DATE')
>>> employee
```

	UNIQUE_ID	...	JOB_DATE
HIRE_DATE		...	
2006-06-12	0	...	2012-10-13
2000-07-19	1	...	2010-09-18
2015-02-03	2	...	2015-02-03
1982-02-08	3	...	1991-05-25
1989-06-19	4	...	1994-10-22
...	...	...	...
2014-06-09	1995	...	2015-06-09
2003-09-02	1996	...	2013-10-06
2014-10-13	1997	...	2015-10-13
2009-01-20	1998	...	2011-07-02
2009-01-12	1999	...	2010-07-12

2. Let's first do a grouping by just gender, and find the average salary for each:

```
>>> (employee
...      .groupby('GENDER')
...      ['BASE_SALARY']
...      .mean()
...      .round(-2)
... )
GENDER
Female    52200.0
Male      57400.0
Name: BASE_SALARY, dtype: float64
```

3. Let's find the average salary based on hire date, and group everyone into 10-year buckets:

```
>>> (employee
...      .resample('10AS')
...      ['BASE_SALARY']
...      .mean()
...      .round(-2)
... )
HIRE_DATE
1958-01-01     81200.0
1968-01-01    106500.0
1978-01-01     69600.0
1988-01-01     62300.0
1998-01-01     58200.0
2008-01-01     47200.0
Freq: 10AS-JAN, Name: BASE_SALARY, dtype: float64
```

4. If we wanted to group by both gender and a ten-year time span, we can call `.resample` after calling `.groupby`:

```
>>> (employee
...      .groupby('GENDER')
...      .resample('10AS')
...      ['BASE_SALARY']
...      .mean()
...      .round(-2)
```

```
    ... )
    GENDER   HIRE_DATE
    Female   1975-01-01      51600.0
             1985-01-01      57600.0
             1995-01-01      55500.0
             2005-01-01      51700.0
             2015-01-01      38600.0
                                ...
    Male     1968-01-01     106500.0
             1978-01-01      72300.0
             1988-01-01      64600.0
             1998-01-01      59700.0
             2008-01-01      47200.0
    Name: BASE_SALARY, Length: 11, dtype: float64
```

5. Now, this does what we set out to do, but we run into a slight issue whenever we want
    to compare female to male salaries. Let's `.unstack` the gender level and see what
    happens:

```
>>> (employee
...     .groupby('GENDER')
...     .resample('10AS')
...     ['BASE_SALARY']
...     .mean()
...     .round(-2)
...     .unstack('GENDER')
... )
GENDER       Female       Male
HIRE_DATE
1958-0...       NaN    81200.0
1968-0...       NaN   106500.0
1975-0...   51600.0        NaN
1978-0...       NaN    72300.0
1985-0...   57600.0        NaN
...             ...        ...
1995-0...   55500.0        NaN
1998-0...       NaN    59700.0
2005-0...   51700.0        NaN
```

```
2008-0...      NaN    47200.0
2015-0...   38600.0      NaN
```

6. The 10-year periods for males and females do not begin on the same date. This happened because the data was first grouped by gender and then, within each gender, more groups were formed based on hire dates. Let's verify that the first hired male was in 1958 and the first hired female was in 1975:

```
>>> employee[employee['GENDER'] == 'Male'].index.min()
Timestamp('1958-12-29 00:00:00')
>>> employee[employee['GENDER'] == 'Female'].index.min()
Timestamp('1975-06-09 00:00:00')
```

7. To resolve this issue, we must group the date together with the gender, and this is only possible with the `.groupby` method:

```
>>> (employee
...      .groupby(['GENDER', pd.Grouper(freq='10AS')])
...      ['BASE_SALARY']
...      .mean()
...      .round(-2)
... )
GENDER   HIRE_DATE
Female   1968-01-01          NaN
         1978-01-01      57100.0
         1988-01-01      57100.0
         1998-01-01      54700.0
         2008-01-01      47300.0
                            ...
Male     1968-01-01     106500.0
         1978-01-01      72300.0
         1988-01-01      64600.0
         1998-01-01      59700.0
         2008-01-01      47200.0
Name: BASE_SALARY, Length: 11, dtype: float64
```

8. Now we can `.unstack` the gender and get our rows aligned perfectly:

```
>>> (employee
...      .groupby(['GENDER', pd.Grouper(freq='10AS')])
...      ['BASE_SALARY']
...      .mean()
```

```
...        .round(-2)
...        .unstack('GENDER')
... )
GENDER      Female      Male
HIRE_DATE
1958-0...      NaN    81200.0
1968-0...      NaN   106500.0
1978-0...  57100.0    72300.0
1988-0...  57100.0    64600.0
1998-0...  54700.0    59700.0
2008-0...  47300.0    47200.0
```

How it works...

The `read_csv` function in *step 1* allows to both convert columns into Timestamps and put them in the index at the same time creating a `DatetimeIndex`. *Step 2* does a `.groupby` operation with a single grouping column, `gender`. *Step 3* uses the `.resample` method with the offset alias `10AS` to form groups in 10-year increments of time. The `A` is the alias for year, and the `S` informs us that the beginning of the period is used as the label. For instance, the data for the label 1988-01-01 spans that date until December 31, 1997.

In *step 4*, for each gender, male and female, completely different starting dates for the 10-year periods are calculated based on the earliest hired employee. *Step 5* shows how this causes misalignment when we try to compare salaries of females to males. They don't have the same 10-year periods. *Step 6* verifies that the year of the earliest hired employee for each gender matches the output from *step 4*.

To alleviate this issue, we must group both the gender and Timestamp together. The `.resample` method is only capable of grouping by a single column of Timestamps. We can only complete this operation with the `.groupby` method. With `pd.Grouper`, we can replicate the functionality of `.resample`. We pass the offset alias to the `freq` parameter and then place the object in a list with all the other columns that we wish to group, as done in *step 7*.

As both males and females now have the same starting dates for the 10-year period, the reshaped data in *step 8* will align for each gender making comparisons much easier. It appears that male salaries tend to be higher given a longer length of employment, though both genders have the same average salary with under ten years of employment.

There's more...

From an outsider's perspective, it would not be obvious that the rows from the output in *step 8* represented 10-year intervals. One way to improve the index labels would be to show the beginning and end of each time interval. We can achieve this by concatenating the current index year with 9 added to itself:

```
>>> sal_final = (employee
...        .groupby(['GENDER', pd.Grouper(freq='10AS')])
...        ['BASE_SALARY']
...        .mean()
...        .round(-2)
...        .unstack('GENDER')
... )
>>> years = sal_final.index.year
>>> years_right = years + 9
>>> sal_final.index = years.astype(str) + '-' + years_right.astype(str)
>>> sal_final
```

GENDER	Female	Male
HIRE_DATE		
1958-1967	NaN	81200.0
1968-1977	NaN	106500.0
1978-1987	57100.0	72300.0
1988-1997	57100.0	64600.0
1998-2007	54700.0	59700.0
2008-2017	47300.0	47200.0

There is a completely different way to do this recipe. We can use the `cut` function to create equal-width intervals based on the year that each employee was hired and form groups from it:

```
>>> cuts = pd.cut(employee.index.year, bins=5, precision=0)
>>> cuts.categories.values
IntervalArray([(1958.0, 1970.0], (1970.0, 1981.0], (1981.0, 1993.0],
(1993.0, 2004.0], (2004.0, 2016.0]],
closed='right',
dtype='interval[float64]')


>>> (employee
```

```
...        .groupby([cuts, 'GENDER'])
...        ['BASE_SALARY']
...        .mean()
...        .unstack('GENDER')
...        .round(-2)
... )
GENDER             Female      Male
(1958.0, 1970.0]      NaN   85400.0
(1970.0, 1981.0]  54400.0   72700.0
(1981.0, 1993.0]  55700.0   69300.0
(1993.0, 2004.0]  56500.0   62300.0
(2004.0, 2016.0]  49100.0   49800.0
```

13

Visualization with Matplotlib, Pandas, and Seaborn

Introduction

Visualization is a critical component in exploratory data analysis, as well as presentations and applications. During exploratory data analysis, you are usually working alone or in small groups and need to create plots quickly to help you better understand your data. It can help you identify outliers and missing data, or it can spark other questions of interest that will lead to further analysis and more visualizations. This type of visualization is usually not done with the end user in mind. It is strictly to help you better your current understanding. The plots do not have to be perfect.

When preparing visualizations for a report or application, a different approach must be used. You should pay attention to small details. Also, you usually will have to narrow down all possible visualizations to only the select few that best represent your data. Good data visualizations have the viewer enjoying the experience of extracting information. Almost like movies that make viewers get lost in them, good visualizations will have lots of information that really sparks interest.

The primary data visualization library in Python is matplotlib, a project begun in the early 2000s, that was built to mimic the plotting capabilities from Matlab. Matplotlib is enormously capable of plotting most things you can imagine, and it gives its users tremendous power to control every aspect of the plotting surface.

That said, it is not the friendliest library for beginners to grasp. Thankfully, pandas makes visualizing data very easy for us and usually plots what we want with a single call to the plot method. pandas does no plotting on its own. It internally calls matplotlib functions to create the plots.

Seaborn is also a visualization library that wraps matplotlib and does not do any actual plotting itself. Seaborn makes beautiful plots and has many types of plots that are not available from matplotlib or pandas. Seaborn works with tidy (long) data, while pandas works best with aggregated (wide) data. Seaborn also accepts pandas DataFrame objects in its plotting functions.

Although it is possible to create plots without ever running any matplotlib code, from time to time, it will be necessary to use it to tweak finer plot details manually. For this reason, the first two recipes will cover some basics of matplotlib that will come in handy if you need to use it. Other than the first two recipes, all plotting examples will use pandas or seaborn.

Visualization in Python does not have to rely on matplotlib. Bokeh is quickly becoming a very popular interactive visualization library targeted for the web. It is completely independent of matplotlib, and it's capable of producing entire applications. There are other plotting libraries as well and future versions of pandas will probably have the capability to use plotting engines other than matplotlib.

Getting started with matplotlib

For many data scientists, the vast majority of their plotting commands will use pandas or seaborn, both rely on matplotlib to do the plotting. However, neither pandas nor seaborn offers a complete replacement for matplotlib, and occasionally you will need to use matplotlib. For this reason, this recipe will offer a short introduction to the most crucial aspects of matplotlib.

One thing to be aware if you are a Jupyter user. You will want to include the:

```
>>> %matplotlib inline
```

directive in your notebook. This tells matplotlib to render plots in the notebook.

Let's begin our introduction with a look at the anatomy of a matplotlib plot in the following figure:

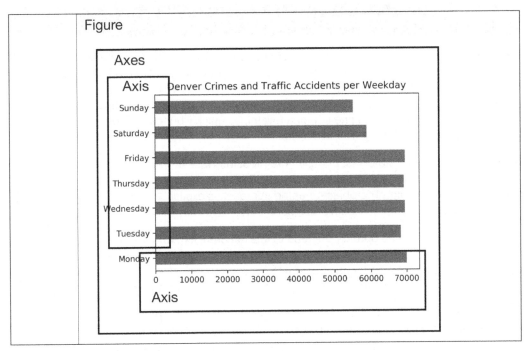

Matplotlib hierarchy

Matplotlib uses a hierarchy of objects to display all of its plotting items in the output. This hierarchy is key to understanding everything about matplotlib. Note that these terms are referring to matplotlib and not pandas objects with the same (perhaps confusing) name. The Figure and Axes objects are the two main components of the hierarchy. The Figure object is at the top of the hierarchy. It is the container for everything that will be plotted. Contained within the Figure is one or more Axes object(s). The Axes is the primary object that you will interact with when using matplotlib and can be thought of as the plotting surface. The Axes contains an x-axis, a y-axis, points, lines, markers, labels, legends, and any other useful item that is plotted.

A distinction needs to be made between an Axes and an axis. They are completely separate objects. An Axes object, using matplotlib terminology, is not the plural of axis but instead, as mentioned earlier, the object that creates and controls most of the useful plotting elements. An axis refers to the x or y (or even z) axis of a plot.

All of these useful plotting elements created by an Axes object are called artists. Even the Figure and the Axes objects themselves are artists. This distinction for artists won't be critical to this recipe but will be useful when doing more advanced matplotlib plotting and especially when reading through the documentation.

Object-oriented guide to matplotlib

Matplotlib provides two distinct interfaces for users. The stateful interface makes all of its calls with the `pyplot` module. This interface is called stateful because matplotlib keeps track internally of the current state of the plotting environment. Whenever a plot is created in the stateful interface, matplotlib finds the current figure or current axes and makes changes to it. This approach is fine to plot a few things quickly but can become unwieldy when dealing with multiple figures and axes.

Matplotlib also offers a stateless, or object-oriented, interface in which you explicitly use variables that reference specific plotting objects. Each variable can then be used to change some property of the plot. The object-oriented approach is explicit, and you are always aware of exactly what object is being modified.

Unfortunately, having both options can lead to lots of confusion, and matplotlib has a reputation for being difficult to learn. The documentation has examples using both approaches. In practice, I find it most useful to combine them. I use the `subplots` function from `pyplot` to create a figure and axes, and then use the methods on those objects.

If you are new to matplotlib, you might not know how to recognize the difference between each approach. With the stateful interface, all commands are functions called on the `pyplot` module, which is usually aliased `plt`. Making a line plot and adding some labels to each axis would look like this:

```
>>> import matplotlib.pyplot as plt
>>> x = [-3, 5, 7]
>>> y = [10, 2, 5]
>>> fig = plt.figure(figsize=(15,3))
>>> plt.plot(x, y)
>>> plt.xlim(0, 10)
>>> plt.ylim(-3, 8)
>>> plt.xlabel('X Axis')
>>> plt.ylabel('Y axis')
>>> plt.title('Line Plot')
>>> plt.suptitle('Figure Title', size=20, y=1.03)
>>> fig.savefig('c13-fig1.png', dpi=300, bbox_inches='tight')
```

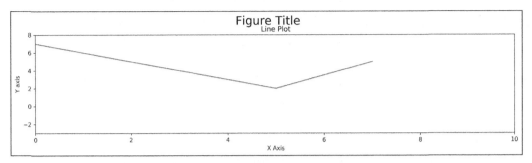

Basic plot using Matlab-like interface

The object-oriented approach is shown as follows:

```
>>> from matplotlib.figure import Figure
>>> from matplotlib.backends.backend_agg import FigureCanvasAgg as
FigureCanvas
>>> from IPython.core.display import display
>>> fig = Figure(figsize=(15, 3))
>>> FigureCanvas(fig)
>>> ax = fig.add_subplot(111)
>>> ax.plot(x, y)
>>> ax.set_xlim(0, 10)
>>> ax.set_ylim(-3, 8)
>>> ax.set_xlabel('X axis')
>>> ax.set_ylabel('Y axis')
>>> ax.set_title('Line Plot')
>>> fig.suptitle('Figure Title', size=20, y=1.03)
>>> display(fig)
>>> fig.savefig('c13-fig2.png', dpi=300, bbox_inches='tight')
```

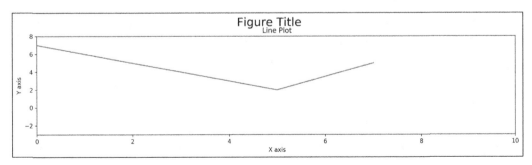

Basic plot created with object oriented interface

In practice, I combine the two approaches and my code would look like this:

```
>>> fig, ax = plt.subplots(figsize=(15,3))
>>> ax.plot(x, y)
>>> ax.set(xlim=(0, 10), ylim=(-3, 8),
...       xlabel='X axis', ylabel='Y axis',
...       title='Line Plot')
>>> fig.suptitle('Figure Title', size=20, y=1.03)
>>> fig.savefig('c13-fig3.png', dpi=300, bbox_inches='tight')
```

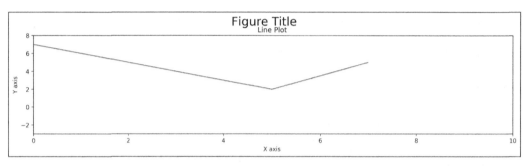

Basic plot created using call to Matlab interface to create figure and axes, then using method calls

In this example, we use only two objects, the Figure, and Axes, but in general, plots can have many hundreds of objects; each one can be used to make modifications in an extremely finely-tuned manner, not easily doable with the stateful interface. In this chapter, we build an empty plot and modify several of its basic properties using the object-oriented interface.

How to do it...

1. To get started with matplotlib using the object-oriented approach, you will need to import the `pyplot` module and alias `plt`:

   ```
   >>> import matplotlib.pyplot as plt
   ```

2. Typically, when using the object-oriented approach, we will create a Figure and one or more Axes objects. Let's use the `subplots` function to create a figure with a single axes:

   ```
   >>> fig, ax = plt.subplots(nrows=1, ncols=1)
   >>> fig.savefig('c13-step2.png', dpi=300)
   ```

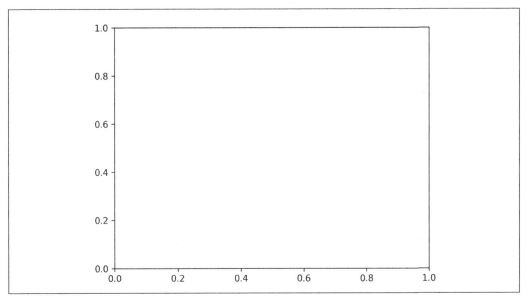

Plot of a figure

3. The `subplots` function returns a two-item tuple object containing the Figure and one or more Axes objects (here it is just one), which is unpacked into the variables `fig` and `ax`. From here on out, we will use these objects by calling methods in a normal object-oriented approach:

```
>>> type(fig)
matplotlib.figure.Figure
>>> type(ax)
matplotlib.axes._subplots.AxesSubplot
```

4. Although you will be calling more axes than figure methods, you might still need to interact with the figure. Let's find the size of the figure and then enlarge it:

```
>>> fig.get_size_inches()
array([ 6.,   4.])
>>> fig.set_size_inches(14, 4)
>>> fig.savefig('c13-step4.png', dpi=300)
>>> fig
```

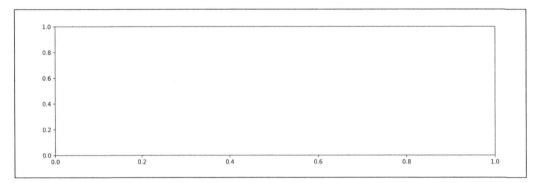

Changing figure size

5. Before we start plotting, let's examine the `matplotlib` hierarchy. You can collect all the axes of the figure with the `.axes` attribute:

```
>>> fig.axes
[<matplotlib.axes._subplots.AxesSubplot at 0x112705ba8>]
```

6. The previous command returns a list of all the Axes objects. However, we already have our Axes object stored in the `ax` variable. Let's verify that they are the same object:

```
>>> fig.axes[0] is ax
True
```

7. To help differentiate the Figure from the Axes, we can give each one a unique facecolor. Matplotlib accepts a variety of different input types for color. Approximately 140 HTML colors are supported by their string name (see this list: http://bit.ly/2y52Ut0). You may also use a string containing a float from zero to one to represent shades of gray:

```
>>> fig.set_facecolor('.7')
>>> ax.set_facecolor('.5')
>>> fig.savefig('c13-step7.png', dpi=300, facecolor='.7')
>>> fig
```

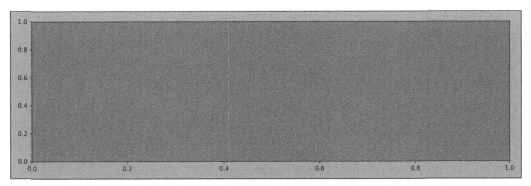

Setting the face color

8. Now that we have differentiated between the Figure and the Axes, let's take a look at all of the immediate children of the Axes with the `.get_children` method:

```
>>> ax_children = ax.get_children()
>>> ax_children
[<matplotlib.spines.Spine at 0x11145b358>,
 <matplotlib.spines.Spine at 0x11145b0f0>,
 <matplotlib.spines.Spine at 0x11145ae80>,
 <matplotlib.spines.Spine at 0x11145ac50>,
 <matplotlib.axis.XAxis at 0x11145aa90>,
 <matplotlib.axis.YAxis at 0x110fa8d30>,
 ...]
```

9. Most plots have four spines and two axis objects. The spines represent the data boundaries and are the four physical lines that you see bordering the darker gray rectangle (the axes). The *x* and *y* axis objects contain more plotting objects such as the ticks and their labels and the label of the entire axis. We can select the spines from the result of the `.get_children` method, but it is easier to access them with the `.spines` attribute:

```
>>> spines = ax.spines
>>> spines
OrderedDict([('left', <matplotlib.spines.Spine at 0x11279e320>),
             ('right', <matplotlib.spines.Spine at 0x11279e0b8>),
             ('bottom', <matplotlib.spines.Spine at 0x11279e048>),
             ('top', <matplotlib.spines.Spine at 0x1127eb5c0>)])
```

10. The spines are contained in an ordered dictionary. Let's select the *left* spine and change its position and width so that it is more prominent and also make the *bottom* spine invisible:

```
>>> spine_left = spines['left']
>>> spine_left.set_position(('outward', -100))
>>> spine_left.set_linewidth(5)
>>> spine_bottom = spines['bottom']
>>> spine_bottom.set_visible(False)
>>> fig.savefig('c13-step10.png', dpi=300, facecolor='.7')
>>> fig
```

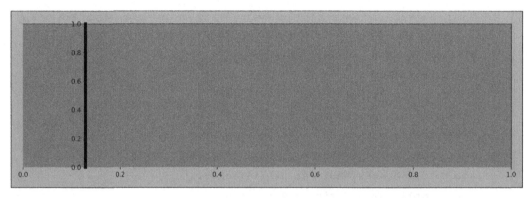

Plot with spines moved or removed

11. Now, let's focus on the axis objects. We can access each axis through the `.xaxis` and `.yaxis` attributes. Some axis properties are also available with the Axes object. In this step, we change some properties of each axis in both manners:

```
>>> ax.xaxis.grid(True, which='major', linewidth=2,
...     color='black', linestyle='--')
>>> ax.xaxis.set_ticks([.2, .4, .55, .93])
>>> ax.xaxis.set_label_text('X Axis', family='Verdana',
...     fontsize=15)
>>> ax.set_ylabel('Y Axis', family='Gotham', fontsize=20)
>>> ax.set_yticks([.1, .9])
>>> ax.set_yticklabels(['point 1', 'point 9'], rotation=45)
>>> fig.savefig('c13-step11.png', dpi=300, facecolor='.7')
```

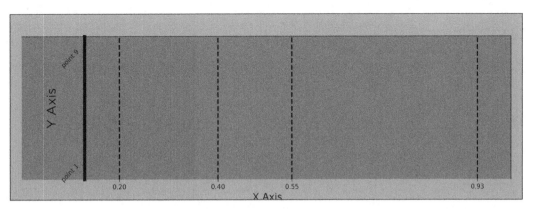

Plot with labels

How it works...

One of the crucial ideas to grasp with the object-oriented approach is that each plotting element has both getter and setter methods. The getter methods all begin with get_. For instance, ax.get_yscale() retrieves the type of scale that the y-axis is plotted with as a string (default is linear), while ax.get_xticklabels() retrieves a list of matplotlib text objects that each have their own getter and setter methods. Setter methods modify a specific property or an entire group of objects. A lot of matplotlib boils down to latching onto a specific plotting element and then examining and modifying it via the getter and setter methods.

The easiest way to start using matplotlib is with the pyplot module, which is commonly aliased plt, as done in *step 1*. *Step 2* shows one method to initiate the object-oriented approach. The plt.subplots function creates a single Figure, along with a grid of Axes objects. The first two parameters, nrows and ncols, define a uniform grid of Axes objects. For example, plt.subplots(2,4) creates eight total Axes objects of the same size inside one Figure.

The plt.subplots returns a tuple. The first element is the Figure, and the second element is the Axes object. This tuple gets unpacked as two variables, fig and ax. If you are not accustomed to tuple unpacking, it may help to see *step 2* written like this:

```
>>> plot_objects = plt.subplots(nrows=1, ncols=1)
>>> type(plot_objects)
tuple
>>> fig = plot_objects[0]
>>> ax = plot_objects[1]
>>> fig.savefig('c13-1-works1.png', dpi=300)
```

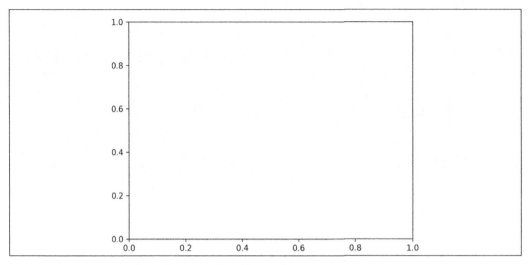

Blot with a single axes

If you create more than one Axes with `plt.subplots`, then the second item in the tuple is a NumPy array containing all the Axes. Let's demonstrate that here:

```
>>> fig, axs = plt.subplots(2, 4)
>>> fig.savefig('c13-1-works2.png', dpi=300)
```

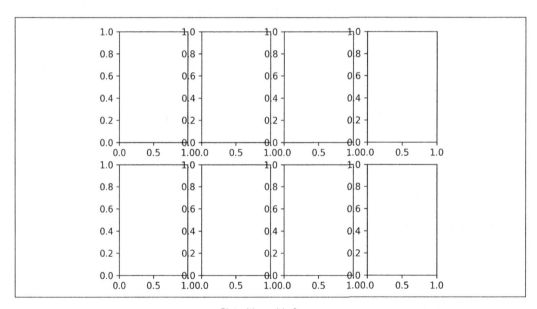

Plot with a grid of axes

The `axs` variable is a NumPy array containing a Figure as its first element and a NumPy array as its second:

```
>>> axs
array([[<matplotlib.axes._subplots.AxesSubplot object at 0x126820668>,
        <matplotlib.axes._subplots.AxesSubplot object at 0x126844ba8>,
        <matplotlib.axes._subplots.AxesSubplot object at 0x126ad1160>,
        <matplotlib.axes._subplots.AxesSubplot object at 0x126afa6d8>],
       [<matplotlib.axes._subplots.AxesSubplot object at 0x126b21c50>,
        <matplotlib.axes._subplots.AxesSubplot object at 0x126b52208>,
        <matplotlib.axes._subplots.AxesSubplot object at 0x11f695588>,
        <matplotlib.axes._subplots.AxesSubplot object at 0x11f6b3b38>]],
      dtype=object)
```

Step 3 verifies that we indeed have Figure and Axes objects referenced by the appropriate variables. In *step 4*, we come across the first example of getter and setter methods. Matplotlib defaults all figures to 6 inches in width by 4 inches in height, which is not the actual size of it on the screen, but would be the exact size if you saved the Figure to a file (with a dpi of 100 pixels per inch).

Step 5 shows that, in addition to the getter method, you can sometimes access another plotting object by its attribute. Often, there exist both an attribute and a getter method to retrieve the same object. For instance, look at these examples:

```
>>> ax = axs[0][0]
>>> fig.axes == fig.get_axes()
True
>>> ax.xaxis == ax.get_xaxis()
True
>>> ax.yaxis == ax.get_yaxis()
True
```

Many artists have a `.facecolor` property that can be set to cover the entire surface one particular color, as in *step 7*. In *step 8*, the `.get_children` method can be used to get a better understanding of the object hierarchy. A list of all the objects directly below the axes is returned. It is possible to select all of the objects from this list and start using the setter methods to modify properties, but this isn't customary. We usually collect our objects from the attributes or getter methods.

Often, when retrieving a plotting object, they will be returned in a container like a list or a dictionary. This is what happens when collecting the spines in *step 9*. You will have to select the individual objects from their respective containers to use the getter or setter methods on them, as done in *step 10*. It is also common to use a for loop to iterate through each of them one at a time.

Step 11 adds grid lines in a peculiar way. We would expect there to be a `.get_grid` and `.set_grid` method, but instead, there is just a `.grid` method, which accepts a Boolean as the first argument to turn on and off the grid lines. Each axis has both major and minor ticks, though by default the minor ticks are turned off. The `which` parameter is used to select which type of tick has a grid line.

Notice that the first three lines of *step 11* select the `.xaxis` attribute and call methods from it, while the last three lines call equivalent methods from the Axes object itself. This second set of methods is a convenience provided by matplotlib to save a few keystrokes. Normally, most objects can only set their own properties, not those of their children. Many of the axis-level properties are not able to be set from the Axes, but in this step, some are. Either method is acceptable.

When adding the grid lines with the first line in *step 11*, we set the properties `.linewidth`, `.color`, and `.linestyle`. These are all properties of a matplotlib line, formally a `Line2D` object. The `.set_ticks` method accepts a sequence of floats and draws tick marks for only those locations. Using an empty list will completely remove all ticks.

Each axis may be labeled with some text, for which matplotlib uses a `Text` object. Only a few of all the available text properties are changed. The `.set_yticklabels` Axes method takes in a list of strings to use as the labels for each of the ticks. You may set any number of text properties along with it.

There's more...

To help find all the possible properties of each of your plotting objects, make a call to the `.properties` method, which displays all of them as a dictionary. Let's see a curated list of the properties of an axis object:

```
>>> ax.xaxis.properties()
{'alpha': None,
'gridlines': <a list of 4 Line2D gridline objects>,
'label': Text(0.5,22.2,'X Axis'),
'label_position': 'bottom',
'label_text': 'X Axis',
'tick_padding': 3.5,
'tick_space': 26,
'ticklabels': <a list of 4 Text major ticklabel objects>,
'ticklocs': array([ 0.2 , 0.4 , 0.55, 0.93]),
'ticks_position': 'bottom',
'visible': True}
```

Visualizing data with matplotlib

Matplotlib has a few dozen plotting methods that make nearly any kind of plot imaginable. Line, bar, histogram, scatter, box, violin, contour, pie, and many more plots are available as methods on the Axes object. It was only in version 1.5 (released in 2015) that matplotlib began accepting data from pandas DataFrames. Before this, data had to be passed to it from NumPy arrays or Python lists.

In this section, we will plot the annual snow levels for the Alta ski resort. The plots in this example were inspired by Trud Antzee (@Antzee_) who created similar plots of snow levels in Norway.

How to do it...

1. Now that we know how to create axes and change their attributes, let's start visualizing data. We will read snowfall data from the Alta ski resort in Utah and visualize how much snow fell in each season:

```
>>> import pandas as pd
>>> import numpy as np
>>> alta = pd.read_csv('data/alta-noaa-1980-2019.csv')
>>> alta
```

	STATION	NAME	LATITUDE	...	WT05	WT06	WT11
0	USC00420072	ALTA, UT US	40.5905	...	NaN	NaN	NaN
1	USC00420072	ALTA, UT US	40.5905	...	NaN	NaN	NaN
2	USC00420072	ALTA, UT US	40.5905	...	NaN	NaN	NaN
3	USC00420072	ALTA, UT US	40.5905	...	NaN	NaN	NaN
4	USC00420072	ALTA, UT US	40.5905	...	NaN	NaN	NaN
...	...	...	...	...	...	...	...
14155	USC00420072	ALTA, UT US	40.5905	...	NaN	NaN	NaN
14156	USC00420072	ALTA, UT US	40.5905	...	NaN	NaN	NaN
14157	USC00420072	ALTA, UT US	40.5905	...	NaN	NaN	NaN
14158	USC00420072	ALTA, UT US	40.5905	...	NaN	NaN	NaN
14159	USC00420072	ALTA, UT US	40.5905	...	NaN	NaN	NaN

2. Get the data for the 2018-2019 season:

```
>>> data = (alta
...        .assign(DATE=pd.to_datetime(alta.DATE))
...        .set_index('DATE')
...        .loc['2018-09':'2019-08']
```

```
...        .SNWD
... )
>>> data
DATE
2018-09-01     0.0
2018-09-02     0.0
2018-09-03     0.0
2018-09-04     0.0
2018-09-05     0.0

                ...
2019-08-27     0.0
2019-08-28     0.0
2019-08-29     0.0
2019-08-30     0.0
2019-08-31     0.0
Name: SNWD, Length: 364, dtype: float64
```

3. Use matplotlib to visualize this data. We could use the default plot, but we will adjust the look of this plot. (Note that we need to specify `facecolor` when calling `.savefig` or the exported image will have a white facecolor):

```
>>> blue = '#99ddee'
>>> white = '#ffffff'
>>> fig, ax = plt.subplots(figsize=(12,4),
...        linewidth=5, facecolor=blue)
>>> ax.set_facecolor(blue)
>>> ax.spines['top'].set_visible(False)
>>> ax.spines['right'].set_visible(False)
>>> ax.spines['bottom'].set_visible(False)
>>> ax.spines['left'].set_visible(False)
>>> ax.tick_params(axis='x', colors=white)
>>> ax.tick_params(axis='y', colors=white)
>>> ax.set_ylabel('Snow Depth (in)', color=white)
>>> ax.set_title('2009-2010', color=white, fontweight='bold')
>>> ax.fill_between(data.index, data, color=white)
>>> fig.savefig('c13-alta1.png', dpi=300, facecolor=blue)
```

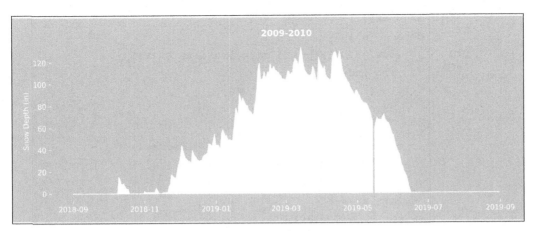

Alta snow level plot for 2009-2010 season

4. Any number of plots may be put on a single figure. Let's refactor to a `plot_year` function and plot many years:

```
>>> import matplotlib.dates as mdt
>>> blue = '#99ddee'
>>> white = '#ffffff'

>>> def plot_year(ax, data, years):
...     ax.set_facecolor(blue)
...     ax.spines['top'].set_visible(False)
...     ax.spines['right'].set_visible(False)
...     ax.spines['bottom'].set_visible(False)
...     ax.spines['left'].set_visible(False)
...     ax.tick_params(axis='x', colors=white)
...     ax.tick_params(axis='y', colors=white)
...     ax.set_ylabel('Snow Depth (in)', color=white)
...     ax.set_title(years, color=white, fontweight='bold')
...     ax.fill_between(data.index, data, color=white)

>>> years = range(2009, 2019)
>>> fig, axs = plt.subplots(ncols=2, nrows=int(len(years)/2),
...     figsize=(16, 10), linewidth=5, facecolor=blue)
>>> axs = axs.flatten()
>>> max_val = None
>>> max_data = None
>>> max_ax = None
>>> for i,y in enumerate(years):
```

```
...         ax = axs[i]
...         data = (alta
...             .assign(DATE=pd.to_datetime(alta.DATE))
...             .set_index('DATE')
...             .loc[f'{y}-09':f'{y+1}-08']
...             .SNWD
...         )
...         if max_val is None or max_val < data.max():
...             max_val = data.max()
...             max_data = data
...             max_ax = ax
...         ax.set_ylim(0, 180)
...         years = f'{y}-{y+1}'
...         plot_year(ax, data, years)
>>> max_ax.annotate(f'Max Snow {max_val}',
...     xy=(mdt.date2num(max_data.idxmax()), max_val),
...     color=white)

>>> fig.suptitle('Alta Snowfall', color=white, fontweight='bold')
>>> fig.tight_layout(rect=[0, 0.03, 1, 0.95])
>>> fig.savefig('c13-alta2.png', dpi=300, facecolor=blue)
```

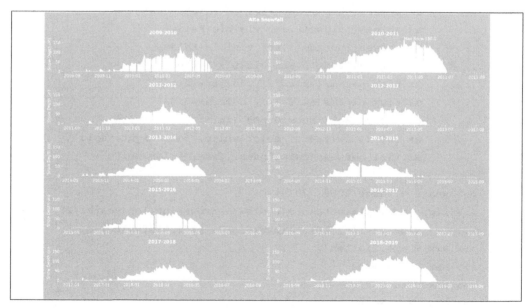

Alta snow level plot for many seasons

How it works...

We load the NOAA data in *step 1*. In *step 2*, we use various pandas tricks to convert the DATE column from a string into a date. Then we set the index to the DATE column so we can slice off a year-long period starting from September. Finally, we pull out the SNWD (the snow depth) column to get a pandas Series.

In *step 3*, we pull out all of the stops. We use the subplots function to create a figure and an axes. We set the facecolor of both the axes and the figure to a light blue color. We also remove the spines and set the label colors to white. Finally, we use the .fill_between plot function to create a plot that is filled in. This plot (inspired by Trud) shows something that I like to emphasize with matplotlib. In matplotlib, you can change almost any aspect of the plot. Using Jupyter in combination with matplotlib allows you to try out tweaks to plots.

In *step 4*, we refactor *step 3* into a function and then plot a decade of plots in a grid. While we are looping over the year data, we also keep track of the maximum value. This allows us to annotate the axis that had the maximum show depth with the .annotate method.

There's more...

When I'm teaching visualization, I always mention that our brains are not optimized for looking at tables of data. However, visualizing said data can give us insights into the data. In this case, it is clear that there is data that is missing, hence the gaps in the plots. In this case, I'm going to clean up the gaps using the .interpolate method:

```
>>> years = range(2009, 2019)
>>> fig, axs = plt.subplots(ncols=2, nrows=int(len(years)/2),
...      figsize=(16, 10), linewidth=5, facecolor=blue)
>>> axs = axs.flatten()
>>> max_val = None
>>> max_data = None
>>> max_ax = None
>>> for i,y in enumerate(years):
...      ax = axs[i]
...      data = (alta.assign(DATE=pd.to_datetime(alta.DATE))
...          .set_index('DATE')
...          .loc[f'{y}-09':f'{y+1}-08']
...          .SNWD
...          .interpolate()
...      )
...      if max_val is None or max_val < data.max():
```

```
...              max_val = data.max()
...              max_data = data
...              max_ax = ax
...          ax.set_ylim(0, 180)
...          years = f'{y}-{y+1}'
...          plot_year(ax, data, years)
>>> max_ax.annotate(f'Max Snow {max_val}',
...      xy=(mdt.date2num(max_data.idxmax()), max_val),
...      color=white)


>>> fig.suptitle('Alta Snowfall', color=white, fontweight='bold')
>>> fig.tight_layout(rect=[0, 0.03, 1, 0.95])
>>> fig.savefig('c13-alta3.png', dpi=300, facecolor=blue)
```

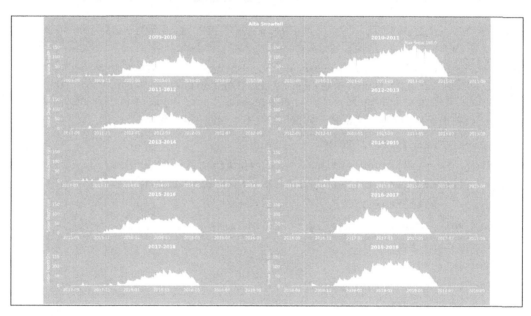

Alta plot plot

Even this plot still has issues. Let's dig in a little more. It looks like there are points during the winter season when the snow level drops off too much. Let's use some pandas to find where the absolute differences between subsequent entries is greater than some value, say 50:

```
>>> (alta
...      .assign(DATE=pd.to_datetime(alta.DATE))
...      .set_index('DATE')
```

```
...        .SNWD
...        .to_frame()
...        .assign(next=lambda df_:df_.SNWD.shift(-1),
...                snwd_diff=lambda df_:df_.next-df_.SNWD)
...        .pipe(lambda df_: df_[df_.snwd_diff.abs() > 50])
... )
           SNWD   next   snwd_diff
DATE
1989-11-27 60.0    0.0     -60.0
2007-02-28 87.0    9.0     -78.0
2008-05-22 62.0    0.0     -62.0
2008-05-23  0.0   66.0      66.0
2009-01-16 76.0    0.0     -76.0
...         ...    ...       ...
2011-05-18  0.0  136.0     136.0
2012-02-09 58.0    0.0     -58.0
2012-02-10  0.0   56.0      56.0
2013-03-01 75.0    0.0     -75.0
2013-03-02  0.0   78.0      78.0
```

It looks like the data has some issues. There are spots when the data goes to zero (actually 0 and not `np.nan`) during the middle of the season. Let's make a `fix_gaps` function that we can use with the `.pipe` method to clean them up:

```
>>> def fix_gaps(ser, threshold=50):
...     'Replace values where the shift is > threshold with nan'
...     mask = (ser
...         .to_frame()
...         .assign(next=lambda df_:df_.SNWD.shift(-1),
...                 snwd_diff=lambda df_:df_.next-df_.SNWD)
...         .pipe(lambda df_: df_.snwd_diff.abs() > threshold)
...     )
...     return ser.where(~mask, np.nan)

>>> years = range(2009, 2019)
>>> fig, axs = plt.subplots(ncols=2, nrows=int(len(years)/2),
...     figsize=(16, 10), linewidth=5, facecolor=blue)
>>> axs = axs.flatten()
```

```
>>> max_val = None
>>> max_data = None
>>> max_ax = None
>>> for i,y in enumerate(years):
...     ax = axs[i]
...     data = (alta.assign(DATE=pd.to_datetime(alta.DATE))
...         .set_index('DATE')
...         .loc[f'{y}-09':f'{y+1}-08']
...         .SNWD
...         .pipe(fix_gaps)
...         .interpolate()
...     )
...     if max_val is None or max_val < data.max():
...         max_val = data.max()
...         max_data = data
...         max_ax = ax
...     ax.set_ylim(0, 180)
...     years = f'{y}-{y+1}'
...     plot_year(ax, data, years)
>>> max_ax.annotate(f'Max Snow {max_val}',
...     xy=(mdt.date2num(max_data.idxmax()), max_val),
...     color=white)

>>> fig.suptitle('Alta Snowfall', color=white, fontweight='bold')
>>> fig.tight_layout(rect=[0, 0.03, 1, 0.95])
>>> fig.savefig('c13-alta4.png', dpi=300, facecolor=blue)
```

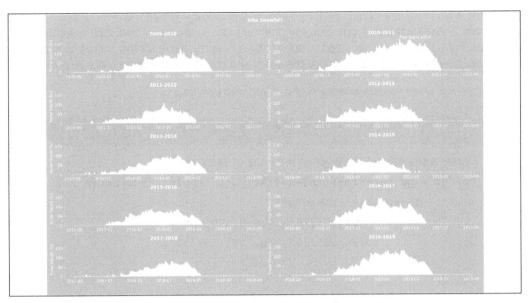

Alta plot

Plotting basics with pandas

pandas makes plotting quite easy by automating much of the procedure for you. Plotting is handled internally by matplotlib and is publicly accessed through the DataFrame or Series .plot attribute (which also acts as a method, but we will use the attribute for plotting). When you create a plot in pandas, you will be returned a matplotlib Axes or Figure. You can then use the full power of matplotlib to tweak this plot to your heart's delight.

pandas is only able to produce a small subset of the plots available with matplotlib, such as line, bar, box, and scatter plots, along with **kernel density estimates** (**KDEs**), and histograms. I find that pandas makes it so easy to plot, that I generally prefer the pandas interface, as it is usually just a single line of code.

One of the keys to understanding plotting in pandas is to know where the x and y-axis come from. The default plot, a line plot, will plot the index in the x-axis and each column in the y-axis. For a scatter plot, we need to specify the columns to use for the x and y-axis. A histogram, boxplot, and KDE plot ignore the index and plot the distribution for each column.

This section will show various examples of plotting with pandas.

How to do it...

1. Create a small DataFrame with a meaningful index:

```
>>> df = pd.DataFrame(index=['Atiya', 'Abbas', 'Cornelia',
...       'Stephanie', 'Monte'],
...     data={'Apples':[20, 10, 40, 20, 50],
...             'Oranges':[35, 40, 25, 19, 33]})
```

```
>>> df
            Apples    Oranges
Atiya           20         35
Abbas           10         40
Cornelia        40         25
Stephanie       20         19
Monte           50         33
```

2. Bar plots use the index as the labels for the x-axis and the column values as the bar heights. Use the `.plot` attribute with the `.bar` method:

```
>>> color = ['.2', '.7']
>>> ax = df.plot.bar(color=color, figsize=(16,4))
>>> ax.get_figure().savefig('c13-pdemo-bar1.png')
```

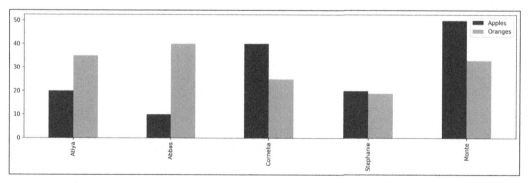

pandas bar plot

3. A KDE plot ignores the index and uses the column names along the x-axis and uses the column values to calculate a probability density along the y values:

```
>>> ax = df.plot.kde(color=color, figsize=(16,4))
>>> ax.get_figure().savefig('c13-pdemo-kde1.png')
```

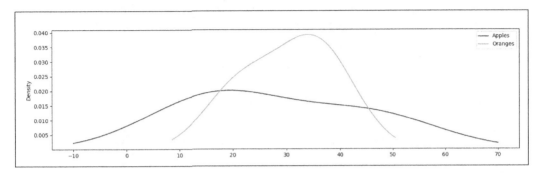

pandas KDE plot

4. Let's plot a line plot, scatter plot, and a bar plot in a single figure. The scatter plot is the only one that requires you to specify columns for the x and y values. If you wish to use the index for a scatter plot, you will have to use the .reset_index method to make it a column. The other two plots use the index for the x-axis and make a new set of lines or bars for every single numeric column:

```
>>> fig, (ax1, ax2, ax3) = plt.subplots(1, 3, figsize=(16,4))
>>> fig.suptitle('Two Variable Plots', size=20, y=1.02)
>>> df.plot.line(ax=ax1, title='Line plot')
>>> df.plot.scatter(x='Apples', y='Oranges',
...      ax=ax2, title='Scatterplot')
>>> df.plot.bar(color=color, ax=ax3, title='Bar plot')
>>> fig.savefig('c13-pdemo-scat.png')
```

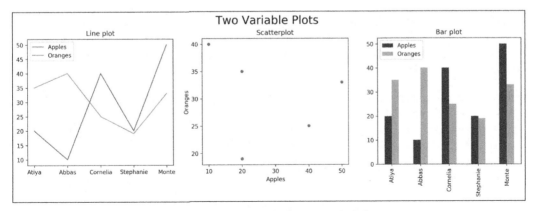

Using pandas to plot multiple charts on a single figure

5. Let's put a KDE, boxplot, and histogram in the same figure as well. These plots are used to visualize the distribution of a column:

```
>>> fig, (ax1, ax2, ax3) = plt.subplots(1, 3, figsize=(16,4))
>>> fig.suptitle('One Variable Plots', size=20, y=1.02)
>>> df.plot.kde(color=color, ax=ax1, title='KDE plot')
>>> df.plot.box(ax=ax2, title='Boxplot')
>>> df.plot.hist(color=color, ax=ax3, title='Histogram')
>>> fig.savefig('c13-pdemo-kde2.png')
```

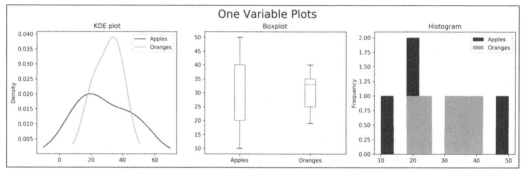

Using pandas to plot a KDE, boxplot, and histogram

How it works...

Step 1 creates a small sample DataFrame that will help us illustrate the differences between two and one-variable plotting with pandas. By default, pandas will use each numeric column of the DataFrame to make a new set of bars, lines, KDEs, boxplots, or histograms and use the index as the x values when it is a two-variable plot. One of the exceptions is the scatter plot, which must be explicitly given a single column for the x and y values.

The pandas .plot attribute has various plotting methods with a large number of parameters that allow you to customize the result to your liking. For instance, you can set the figure size, turn the gridlines on and off, set the range of the x and y-axis, color the plot, rotate the tick marks, and much more.

You can also use any of the arguments available to the specific matplotlib plotting method. The extra arguments will be collected by the **kwds parameter from the plot method and correctly passed to the underlying matplotlib function. For example, in *step 2*, we create a bar plot. This means that we can use all of the parameters available in the matplotlib bar function as well as the ones available in the pandas plotting method.

In *step 3*, we create a single-variable KDE plot, which creates a density estimate for each numeric column in the DataFrame. *Step 4* places all the two-variable plots in the same figure. Likewise, *step 5* places all the one-variable plots together.

Each of *steps 4* and *5* creates a figure with three Axes objects. The code `plt.subplots(1, 3)` creates a figure with three Axes spread over a single row and three columns. It returns a two-item tuple consisting of the figure and a one-dimensional NumPy array containing the Axes. The first item of the tuple is unpacked into the variable `fig`. The second item of the tuple is unpacked into three more variables, one for each Axes. The pandas plotting methods come with an `ax` parameter, allowing us to place the result of the plot into a specific Axes in the figure.

There's more...

With the exception of the scatter plot, none of the plots specified the columns to be used. pandas defaulted to plotting every numeric column, as well as the index in the case of two-variable plots. You can, of course, specify the exact columns that you would like to use for each `x` or `y` value:

```
>>> fig, (ax1, ax2, ax3) = plt.subplots(1, 3, figsize=(16,4))
>>> df.sort_values('Apples').plot.line(x='Apples', y='Oranges',
...         ax=ax1)
>>> df.plot.bar(x='Apples', y='Oranges', ax=ax2)
>>> df.plot.kde(x='Apples', ax=ax3)
>>> fig.savefig('c13-pdemo-kde3.png')
```

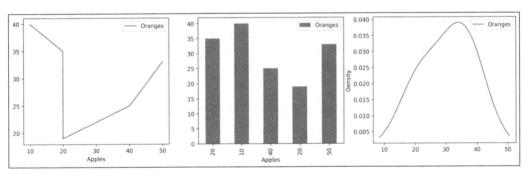

pandas KDE plot

Visualizing the flights dataset

Exploratory data analysis can be guided by visualizations, and pandas provides a great interface for quickly and effortlessly creating them. One strategy when looking at a new dataset is to create some univariate plots. These include bar charts for categorical data (usually strings) and histograms, boxplots, or KDEs for continuous data (always numeric).

In this recipe, we do some basic exploratory data analysis on the flights dataset by creating univariate and multivariate plots with pandas.

How to do it...

1. Read in the flights dataset:

```
>>> flights = pd.read_csv('data/flights.csv')
>>> flights
        MONTH  DAY  WEEKDAY  ...  ARR_DELAY  DIVERTED  CANCELLED
0           1    1        4  ...       65.0         0          0
1           1    1        4  ...      -13.0         0          0
2           1    1        4  ...       35.0         0          0
3           1    1        4  ...       -7.0         0          0
4           1    1        4  ...       39.0         0          0
...       ...  ...      ...  ...        ...       ...        ...
58487      12   31        4  ...      -19.0         0          0
58488      12   31        4  ...        4.0         0          0
58489      12   31        4  ...       -5.0         0          0
58490      12   31        4  ...       34.0         0          0
58491      12   31        4  ...       -1.0         0          0
```

2. Before we start plotting, let's calculate the number of diverted, canceled, delayed, and ontime flights. We already have binary columns for DIVERTED and CANCELLED. Flights are considered delayed whenever they arrive 15 minutes or more later than scheduled. Let's create two new binary columns to track delayed and on-time arrivals:

```
>>> cols = ['DIVERTED', 'CANCELLED', 'DELAYED']
>>> (flights
...      .assign(DELAYED=flights['ARR_DELAY'].ge(15).astype(int),
...              ON_TIME=lambda df_:1 - df_[cols].any(axis=1))
...      .select_dtypes(int)
...      .sum()
... )
MONTH        363858
DAY          918447
WEEKDAY      229690
SCHED_DEP  81186009
DIST       51057671
SCHED_ARR  90627495
DIVERTED        137
CANCELLED       881
```

```
DELAYED          11685
ON_TIME          45789
dtype: int64
```

3. Let's now make several plots on the same figure for both categorical and continuous columns:

```
>>> fig, ax_array = plt.subplots(2, 3, figsize=(18,8))
>>> (ax1, ax2, ax3), (ax4, ax5, ax6) = ax_array
>>> fig.suptitle('2015 US Flights - Univariate Summary', size=20)
>>> ac = flights['AIRLINE'].value_counts()
>>> ac.plot.barh(ax=ax1, title='Airline')
>>> (flights
...      ['ORG_AIR']
...      .value_counts()
...      .plot.bar(ax=ax2, rot=0, title='Origin City')
... )
>>> (flights
...      ['DEST_AIR']
...      .value_counts()
...      .head(10)
...      .plot.bar(ax=ax3, rot=0, title='Destination City')
... )
>>> (flights
...      .assign(DELAYED=flights['ARR_DELAY'].ge(15).astype(int),
...              ON_TIME=lambda df_:1 - df_[cols].any(axis=1))
...      [['DIVERTED', 'CANCELLED', 'DELAYED', 'ON_TIME']]
...      .sum()
...      .plot.bar(ax=ax4, rot=0,
...          log=True, title='Flight Status')
... )
>>> flights['DIST'].plot.kde(ax=ax5, xlim=(0, 3000),
...      title='Distance KDE')
>>> flights['ARR_DELAY'].plot.hist(ax=ax6,
...      title='Arrival Delay',
...      range=(0,200)
... )
>>> fig.savefig('c13-uni1.png')
```

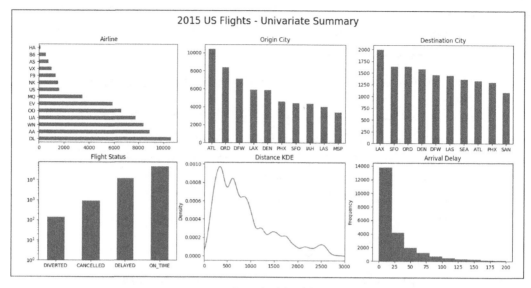

pandas univariate plots

4. This is not an exhaustive look at all the univariate statistics but gives us a good amount of detail on some of the variables. Before we move on to multivariate plots, let's plot the number of flights per week. This is the right situation to use a time series plot with the dates on the *x*-axis. Unfortunately, we don't have pandas Timestamps in any of the columns, but we do have the month and day. The `to_datetime` function has a nifty trick that identifies column names that match Timestamp components. For instance, if you have a DataFrame with exactly three columns titled *year*, *month*, and *day*, then passing this DataFrame to the `to_datetime` function will return a sequence of Timestamps. To prepare our current DataFrame, we need to add a column for the year and use the scheduled departure time to get the hour and minute:

```
>>> df_date = (flights
...      [['MONTH', 'DAY']]
...      .assign(YEAR=2015,
...              HOUR=flights['SCHED_DEP'] // 100,
...              MINUTE=flights['SCHED_DEP'] % 100)
... )
>>> df_date
    MONTH   DAY   YEAR   HOUR   MINUTE
0       1     1   2015     16       25
```

1	1	1	2015	8	23
2	1	1	2015	13	5
3	1	1	2015	15	55
4	1	1	2015	17	20
...	...	...	...	...	...
58487	12	31	2015	5	15
58488	12	31	2015	19	10
58489	12	31	2015	18	46
58490	12	31	2015	5	25
58491	12	31	2015	8	59

5. Then, almost by magic, we can turn this DataFrame into a proper Series of Timestamps with the `to_datetime` function:

```
>>> flight_dep = pd.to_datetime(df_date)
>>> flight_dep
0        2015-01-01 16:25:00
1        2015-01-01 08:23:00
2        2015-01-01 13:05:00
3        2015-01-01 15:55:00
4        2015-01-01 17:20:00
                ...
58487    2015-12-31 05:15:00
58488    2015-12-31 19:10:00
58489    2015-12-31 18:46:00
58490    2015-12-31 05:25:00
58491    2015-12-31 08:59:00
Length: 58492, dtype: datetime64[ns]
```

6. Let's use this result as our new index and then find the count of flights per week with the `.resample` method:

```
>>> flights.index = flight_dep
>>> fc = flights.resample('W').size()
>>> fc.plot.line(figsize=(12,3), title='Flights per Week',
grid=True)
>>> fig.savefig('c13-ts1.png')
```

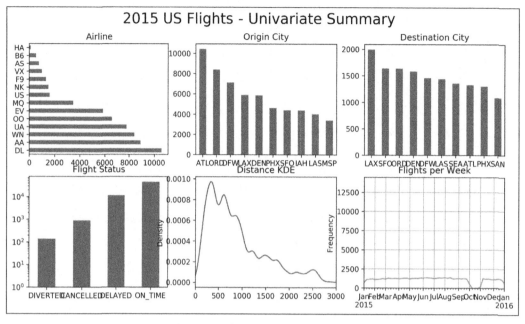

pandas timeseries plot

7. This plot is quite revealing. It appears that we have no data for the month of October. Due to this missing data, it's quite difficult to analyze any trend visually, if one exists. The first and last weeks are also lower than normal, likely because there isn't a full week of data for them. Let's make any week of data with fewer than 600 flights missing. Then, we can use the interpolate method to fill in this missing data:

```
>>> def interp_lt_n(df_, n=600):
...     return (df_
...         .where(df_ > n)
...         .interpolate(limit_direction='both')
... )
>>> fig, ax = plt.subplots(figsize=(16,4))
>>> data = (flights
...     .resample('W')
...     .size()
... )
>>> (data
...     .pipe(interp_lt_n)
...     .iloc[1:-1]
...     .plot.line(color='black', ax=ax)
... )
```

```
>>> mask = data<600
>>> (data
...        .pipe(interp_lt_n)
...        [mask]
...        .plot.line(color='.8', linewidth=10)
... )
>>> ax.annotate(xy=(.8, .55), xytext=(.8, .77),
...             xycoords='axes fraction', s='missing data',
...             ha='center', size=20, arrowprops=dict())
>>> ax.set_title('Flights per Week (Interpolated Missing Data)')
>>> fig.savefig('c13-ts2.png')
```

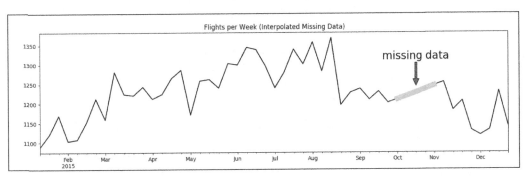

pandas timeseries plot

8. Let's change directions and focus on multivariable plotting. Let's find the 10 airports that:

    ❑ Have the longest average distance traveled for inbound flights
    ❑ Have a minimum of 100 total flights

```
>>> fig, ax = plt.subplots(figsize=(16,4))
>>> (flights
...        .groupby('DEST_AIR')
...        ['DIST']
...        .agg(['mean', 'count'])
...        .query('count > 100')
...        .sort_values('mean')
...        .tail(10)
...        .plot.bar(y='mean', rot=0, legend=False, ax=ax,
...             title='Average Distance per Destination')
... )
>>> fig.savefig('c13-bar1.png')
```

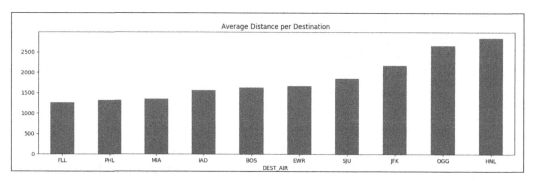

pandas bar plot

9. It's no surprise that the top two destination airports are in Hawaii. Now let's analyze two variables at the same time by making a scatter plot between distance and airtime for all flights under 2,000 miles:

```
>>> fig, ax = plt.subplots(figsize=(8,6))
>>> (flights
...      .reset_index(drop=True)
...      [['DIST', 'AIR_TIME']]
...      .query('DIST <= 2000')
...      .dropna()
...      .plot.scatter(x='DIST', y='AIR_TIME', ax=ax, alpha=.1,
s=1)
... )
>>> fig.savefig('c13-scat1.png')
```

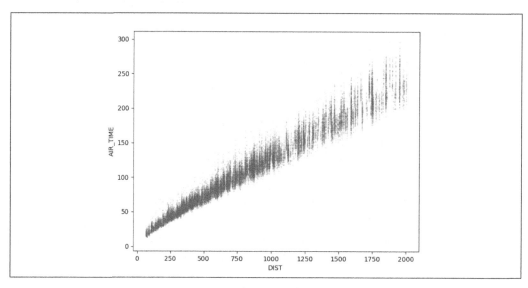

pandas scatter plot

10. As expected, a tight linear relationship exists between distance and airtime, though the variance seems to increase as the number of miles increases. Let's look at the correlation:

```
flights[['DIST', 'AIR_TIME']].corr()
```

11. Back to the plot. There are a few flights that are quite far outside the trendline. Let's try and identify them. A linear regression model may be used to formally identify them, but as pandas doesn't support linear regression, we will take a more manual approach. Let's use the `cut` function to place the flight distances into one of eight groups:

```
>>> (flights
...      .reset_index(drop=True)
...      [['DIST', 'AIR_TIME']]
...      .query('DIST <= 2000')
...      .dropna()
...      .pipe(lambda df_:pd.cut(df_.DIST,
...           bins=range(0, 2001, 250)))
...      .value_counts()
...      .sort_index()
... )
(0, 250]         6529
(250, 500]      12631
(500, 750]      11506
(750, 1000]      8832
(1000, 1250]     5071
(1250, 1500]     3198
(1500, 1750]     3885
(1750, 2000]     1815
Name: DIST, dtype: int64
```

12. We will assume that all flights within each group should have similar flight times, and thus calculate for each flight the number of standard deviations that the flight time deviates from the mean of that group:

```
>>> zscore = lambda x: (x - x.mean()) / x.std()
>>> short = (flights
...      [['DIST', 'AIR_TIME']]
...      .query('DIST <= 2000')
...      .dropna()
...      .reset_index(drop=True)
```

```
...        .assign(BIN=lambda df_:pd.cut(df_.DIST,
...            bins=range(0, 2001, 250)))
... )

>>> scores = (short
...        .groupby('BIN')
...        ['AIR_TIME']
...        .transform(zscore)
... )

>>> (short.assign(SCORE=scores))
        DIST  AIR_TIME            BIN     SCORE
0        590      94.0     (500, 750]  0.490966
1       1452     154.0   (1250, 1500] -1.267551
2        641      85.0     (500, 750] -0.296749
3       1192     126.0   (1000, 1250] -1.211020
4       1363     166.0   (1250, 1500] -0.521999
...      ...      ...            ...       ...
53462   1464     166.0   (1250, 1500] -0.521999
53463    414      71.0     (250, 500]  1.376879
53464    262      46.0     (250, 500] -1.255719
53465    907     124.0    (750, 1000]  0.495005
53466    522      73.0     (500, 750] -1.347036
```

13. We now need a way to discover the outliers. A box plot provides a visual for detecting outliers (beyond 1.5 times the inner quartile range). To create a boxplot for each bin, we need the bin names in the column names. We can use the `.pivot` method to do this:

```
>>> fig, ax = plt.subplots(figsize=(10,6))
>>> (short.assign(SCORE=scores)
...        .pivot(columns='BIN')
...        ['SCORE']
...        .plot.box(ax=ax)
... )
>>> ax.set_title('Z-Scores for Distance Groups')
>>> fig.savefig('c13-box2.png')
```

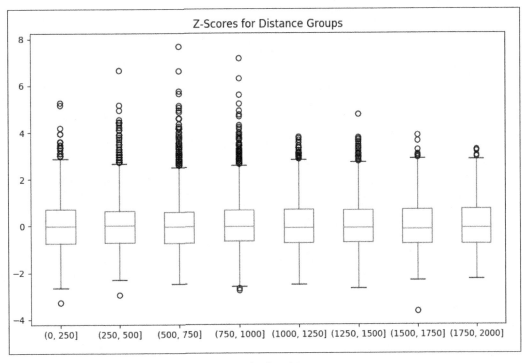

pandas box plot

14. Let's examine the points that are greater than six standard deviations away from the mean. Because we reset the index in the flights DataFrame in *step 9*, we can use it to identify each unique row in the flights DataFrame. Let's create a separate DataFrame with just the outliers:

```
>>> mask = (short
...         .assign(SCORE=scores)
...         .pipe(lambda df_:df_.SCORE.abs() >6)
... )

>>> outliers = (flights
...         [['DIST', 'AIR_TIME']]
...         .query('DIST <= 2000')
...         .dropna()
...         .reset_index(drop=True)
...         [mask]
...         .assign(PLOT_NUM=lambda df_:range(1, len(df_)+1))
... )
```

```
>>> outliers
        DIST  AIR_TIME  PLOT_NUM
14972   373     121.0         1
22507   907     199.0         2
40768   643     176.0         3
50141   651     164.0         4
52699   802     210.0         5
```

15. We can use this table to identify the outliers on the plot from *step 9*. pandas also
    provides a way to attach tables to the bottom of the graph if we use the `tables`
    parameter:

```
>>> fig, ax = plt.subplots(figsize=(8,6))
>>> (short
...       .assign(SCORE=scores)
...       .plot.scatter(x='DIST', y='AIR_TIME',
...                     alpha=.1, s=1, ax=ax,
...                     table=outliers)
... )
>>> outliers.plot.scatter(x='DIST', y='AIR_TIME',
...       s=25, ax=ax, grid=True)
>>> outs = outliers[['AIR_TIME', 'DIST', 'PLOT_NUM']]
>>> for t, d, n in outs.itertuples(index=False):
...       ax.text(d + 5, t + 5, str(n))
>>> plt.setp(ax.get_xticklabels(), y=.1)
>>> plt.setp(ax.get_xticklines(), visible=False)
>>> ax.set_xlabel('')
>>> ax.set_title('Flight Time vs Distance with Outliers')
>>> fig.savefig('c13-scat3.png', dpi=300, bbox_inches='tight')
```

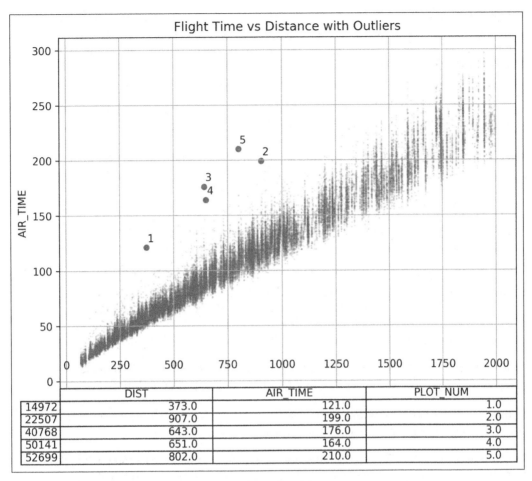

	DIST	AIR_TIME	PLOT_NUM
14972	373.0	121.0	1.0
22507	907.0	199.0	2.0
40768	643.0	176.0	3.0
50141	651.0	164.0	4.0
52699	802.0	210.0	5.0

pandas scatter plot

How it works...

After reading in our data in *step 1* and calculating columns for delayed and on-time flights, we are ready to begin making univariate plots. The call to the `subplots` function in *step 3* creates a 2 x 3 grid of equal-sized Axes. We unpack each Axes into its own variable to reference it. Each of the calls to the plotting methods references the specific Axes in the figure with the `ax` parameter. The `.value_counts` method is used to create the three Series that form the plots in the top row. The `rot` parameter rotates the tick labels to the given angle.

The plot in the bottom left-hand corner uses a logarithmic scale for the *y*-axis, as the number of on-time flights is about two orders of magnitude greater than the number of canceled flights. Without the log scale, the left two bars would be difficult to see. By default, KDE plots may result in positive areas for impossible values, such as negative miles in the plot on the bottom row. For this reason, we limit the range of the x values with the `xlim` parameter.

The histogram created in the bottom right-hand corner on arrival delays was passed the range parameter. This is not part of the method signature of the pandas `.plot.hist` method. Instead, this parameter gets collected by the `**kwds` argument and then passed along to the matplotlib `hist` function. Using `xlim` as done in the previous plot would not work in this case. The plot would be cropped without recalculating the new bin widths for just that portion of the graph. The `range` parameter, however, both limits the *x*-axis and calculates the bin widths for just that range.

Step 4 creates a special extra DataFrame to hold columns with only datetime components so that we can instantly turn each row into a Timestamp with the `to_datetime` function in *step 5*.

In *step 6* we use the `.resample` method. This method uses the index to form groups based on the date offset alias passed. We return the number of flights per week (`W`) as a Series and then call the `.plot.line` method on it, which formats the index as the *x*-axis. A glaring hole for the month of October appears.

To fill this hole, we use the `.where` method to set only values less than 600 to missing in *step 7*. We then fill in the missing data through linear interpolation. By default, the `.interpolate` method only interpolates in a forward direction, so any missing values at the start of the DataFrame will remain. By setting the `limit_direction` parameter to `both`, we ensure that there are no missing values.

The new data is plotted. To show the missing data more clearly, we select the points that were missing from the original and make a line plot on the same Axes on top of the previous line. Typically, when we annotate the plot, we can use the data coordinates, but in this instance, it isn't obvious what the coordinates of the *x*-axis are. To use the Axes coordinate system (the one that ranges from (0,0), to (1,1)), the `xycoords` parameter is set to `axes fraction`. This new plot now excludes the erroneous data and it makes it is much easier to spot a trend. The summer months have much more air traffic than any other time of the year.

In *step 8*, we use a long chain of methods to group by each destination airport and apply two functions, `mean` and `count`, to the `DIST` column. The `.query` method works well in a method for simple filtering. We have two columns in our DataFrame when we get to the `.plot.bar` method, which, by default, would make a bar plot for each column. We are not interested in the `count` column and therefore select only the `mean` column to form the bars. Also, when plotting with a DataFrame, each column name appears in the legend. This would put the word mean in the legend, which would not be useful, so we remove it by setting the `legend` parameter to `False`.

Step 9 starts to look at the relationship between distance traveled and flight airtime. Due to the huge number of points, we shrink their size with the s parameter. We also use the `alpha` parameter to reveal overlapping points.

We see a correlation and quantify that value in *step 10*.

To find the flights that took much longer on average to reach their destination, we group each flight into 250-mile chunks in *step 11* and find the number of standard deviations from their group mean in *step 12*.

In *step 13*, a new box plot is created in the same Axes for every unique value of the BIN.

In *step 14*, the current DataFrame, short, contains the information we need to find the slowest flights, but it does not possess all of the original data that we might want to investigate further. Because we reset the index of short in *step 12*, we can use it to identify the same row from the original. We also give each of the outlier rows a unique integer, PLOT_NUM, to identify it later on when plotting.

In *step 15*, we begin with the same scatter plot as in *step 9* but use the `table` parameter to append the outlier table to the bottom of the plot. We then plot our outliers as a scatter plot on top and ensure that their points are larger to identify them easily. The `.itertuples` method loops through each DataFrame row and returns its values as a tuple. We unpack the corresponding x and y values for our plot and label it with the number we assigned to it.

As the table is placed underneath of the plot, it interferes with the plotting objects on the x-axis. We move the tick labels to the inside of the axis and remove the tick lines and axis label. This table provides information about outlying events.

Stacking area charts to discover emerging trends

Stacked area charts are great visualizations to discover emerging trends, especially in the marketplace. It is a common choice to show the percentage of the market share for things such as internet browsers, cell phones, or vehicles.

In this recipe, we will use data gathered from the popular website meetup.com. Using a stacked area chart, we will show membership distribution between five data science-related meetup groups.

How to do it...

1. Read in the meetup dataset, convert the join_date column into a Timestamp, and set it as the index:

```
>>> meetup = pd.read_csv('data/meetup_groups.csv',
```

```
...         parse_dates=['join_date'],
...         index_col='join_date')
>>> meetup
                                        group  ... country
                                               ...
join_date
2016-11-18 02:41:29      houston machine learning  ...      us
2017-05-09 14:16:37      houston machine learning  ...      us
2016-12-30 02:34:16      houston machine learning  ...      us
2016-07-18 00:48:17      houston machine learning  ...      us
2017-05-25 12:58:16      houston machine learning  ...      us
...                                          ...  ...     ...
2017-10-07 18:05:24   houston data visualization  ...      us
2017-06-24 14:06:26   houston data visualization  ...      us
2015-10-05 17:08:40   houston data visualization  ...      us
2016-11-04 22:36:24   houston data visualization  ...      us
2016-08-02 17:47:29   houston data visualization  ...      us
```

2. Let's get the number of people who joined each group each week:

```
>>> (meetup
...         .groupby([pd.Grouper(freq='W'), 'group'])
...         .size()
... )
join_date     group
2010-11-07    houstonr                       5
2010-11-14    houstonr                      11
2010-11-21    houstonr                       2
2010-12-05    houstonr                       1
2011-01-16    houstonr                       2
                                            ..
2017-10-15    houston data science          14
              houston data visualization    13
              houston energy data science    9
              houston machine learning      11
              houstonr                       2
Length: 763, dtype: int64
```

3. Unstack the group level so that each meetup group has its own column of data:

```
>>> (meetup
...       .groupby([pd.Grouper(freq='W'), 'group'])
...       .size()
...       .unstack('group', fill_value=0)
... )
```

group	houston data science	...	houstonr
join_date		...	
2010-11-07	0	...	5
2010-11-14	0	...	11
2010-11-21	0	...	2
2010-12-05	0	...	1
2011-01-16	0	...	2
...	...	...	...
2017-09-17	16	...	0
2017-09-24	19	...	7
2017-10-01	20	...	1
2017-10-08	22	...	2
2017-10-15	14	...	2

4. This data represents the number of members who joined that particular week. Let's take the cumulative sum of each column to get the grand total number of members:

```
>>> (meetup
...       .groupby([pd.Grouper(freq='W'), 'group'])
...       .size()
...       .unstack('group', fill_value=0)
...       .cumsum()
... )
```

group	houston data science	...	houstonr
join_date		...	
2010-11-07	0	...	5
2010-11-14	0	...	16
2010-11-21	0	...	18
2010-12-05	0	...	19
2011-01-16	0	...	21
...	...	...	...
2017-09-17	2105	...	1056

2017-09-24	2124	...	1063
2017-10-01	2144	...	1064
2017-10-08	2166	...	1066
2017-10-15	2180	...	1068

5. Many stacked area charts use the percentage of the total so that each row always adds up to 1. Let's divide each row by the row total to find the relative number:

```
>>> (meetup
...      .groupby([pd.Grouper(freq='W'), 'group'])
...      .size()
...      .unstack('group', fill_value=0)
...      .cumsum()
...      .pipe(lambda df_: df_.div(
...           df_.sum(axis='columns'), axis='index'))
... )
group          houston data science  ...  houstonr
join_date                             ...
2010-11-07               0.000000     ...  1.000000
2010-11-14               0.000000     ...  1.000000
2010-11-21               0.000000     ...  1.000000
2010-12-05               0.000000     ...  1.000000
2011-01-16               0.000000     ...  1.000000
...                           ...     ...       ...
2017-09-17               0.282058     ...  0.141498
2017-09-24               0.282409     ...  0.141338
2017-10-01               0.283074     ...  0.140481
2017-10-08               0.284177     ...  0.139858
2017-10-15               0.284187     ...  0.139226
```

6. We can now create our stacked area plot, which will continually accumulate the columns, one on top of the other:

```
>>> fig, ax = plt.subplots(figsize=(18,6))
>>> (meetup
...      .groupby([pd.Grouper(freq='W'), 'group'])
...      .size()
...      .unstack('group', fill_value=0)
...      .cumsum()
```

```
...        .pipe(lambda df_: df_.div(
...            df_.sum(axis='columns'), axis='index'))
...        .plot.area(ax=ax,
...            cmap='Greys', xlim=('2013-6', None),
...            ylim=(0, 1), legend=False)
... )
>>> ax.figure.suptitle('Houston Meetup Groups', size=25)
>>> ax.set_xlabel('')
>>> ax.yaxis.tick_right()
>>> kwargs = {'xycoords':'axes fraction', 'size':15}
>>> ax.annotate(xy=(.1, .7), s='R Users',
...     color='w', **kwargs)
>>> ax.annotate(xy=(.25, .16), s='Data Visualization',
...     color='k', **kwargs)
>>> ax.annotate(xy=(.5, .55), s='Energy Data Science',
...     color='k', **kwargs)
>>> ax.annotate(xy=(.83, .07), s='Data Science',
...     color='k', **kwargs)
>>> ax.annotate(xy=(.86, .78), s='Machine Learning',
...     color='w', **kwargs)
>>> fig.savefig('c13-stacked1.png')
```

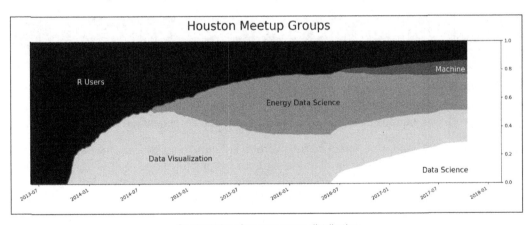

Stacked plot of meetup group distribution

How it works...

Our goal is to determine the distribution of members among the five largest data science meetup groups in Houston over time. To do this, we need to find the total membership at every point in time since each group began.

In *step 2*, we group by each week (offset alias `W`) and meetup group and return the number of sign-ups for that week with the `.size` method.

The resulting Series is not suitable to make plots with pandas. Each meetup group needs its own column, so we reshape the group index level as columns. We set the option `fill_value` to zero so that groups with no memberships during a particular week will not have missing values.

We are in need of the total number of members each week. The `.cumsum` method in *step 4* provides this for us. We could create our stacked area plot after this step, which would be a nice way to visualize the raw total membership.

In *step 5*, we find the distribution of each group as a fraction of the total members in all groups by dividing each value by its row total. By default, pandas automatically aligns objects by their columns, so we cannot use the division operator. Instead, we must use the `.div` method and use the `axis` parameter with a value of `index`.

The data is now ready for a stacked area plot, which we create in *step 6*. Notice that pandas allows you to set the axis limits with a datetime string. This will not work if done in matplotlib using the `ax.set_xlim` method. The starting date for the plot is moved up a couple years because the Houston R Users group began much earlier than any of the other groups.

Understanding the differences between seaborn and pandas

The seaborn library is a popular Python library for creating visualizations. Like pandas, it does not do any actual plotting itself and is a wrapper around matplotlib. Seaborn plotting functions work with pandas DataFrames to create aesthetically pleasing visualizations.

While seaborn and pandas both reduce the overhead of matplotlib, the way they approach data is completely different. Nearly all of the seaborn plotting functions require tidy (or long) data.

Processing tidy data during data analysis often creates aggregated or wide data. This data, in wide format, is what pandas uses to make its plots.

In this recipe, we will build similar plots with both seaborn and pandas to show the types of data (tidy versus wide) that they accept.

How to do it...

1. Read in the employee dataset:

    ```
    >>> employee = pd.read_csv('data/employee.csv',
    ...       parse_dates=['HIRE_DATE', 'JOB_DATE'])
    >>> employee
            UNIQUE_ID POSITION_TITLE   DEPARTMENT   ...  \
    0               0 ASSISTAN...      Municipa...  ...
    1               1 LIBRARY ...         Library   ...
    2               2 POLICE O...      Houston ...  ...
    3               3 ENGINEER...      Houston ...  ...
    4               4 ELECTRICIAN      General ...  ...
    ...           ...        ...             ...   ...
    1995         1995 POLICE O...      Houston ...  ...
    1996         1996 COMMUNIC...      Houston ...  ...
    1997         1997 POLICE O...      Houston ...  ...
    1998         1998 POLICE O...      Houston ...  ...
    1999         1999 FIRE FIG...      Houston ...  ...

    [2000 rows x 10 columns]
    ```

2. Import the seaborn library, and alias it as `sns`:

    ```
    >>> import seaborn as sns
    ```

3. Let's make a bar chart of the count of each department with seaborn:

    ```
    >>> fig, ax = plt.subplots(figsize=(8, 6))
    >>> sns.countplot(y='DEPARTMENT', data=employee, ax=ax)
    >>> fig.savefig('c13-sns1.png', dpi=300, bbox_inches='tight')
    ```

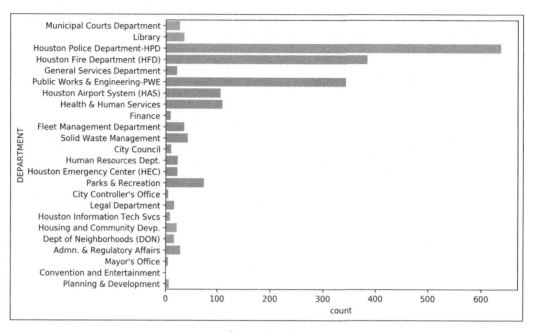

Seaborn bar plot

4. To reproduce this plot with pandas, we will need to aggregate the data beforehand:

```
>>> fig, ax = plt.subplots(figsize=(8, 6))
>>> (employee
...     ['DEPARTMENT']
...     .value_counts()
...     .plot.barh(ax=ax)
... )
>>> fig.savefig('c13-sns2.png', dpi=300, bbox_inches='tight')
```

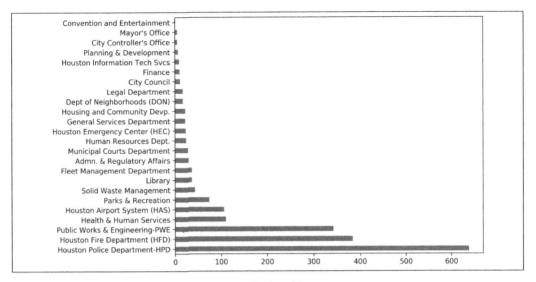

pandas bar plot

5. Now, let's find the average salary for each race with seaborn:

```
>>> fig, ax = plt.subplots(figsize=(8, 6))
>>> sns.barplot(y='RACE', x='BASE_SALARY', data=employee, ax=ax)
>>> fig.savefig('c13-sns3.png', dpi=300, bbox_inches='tight')
```

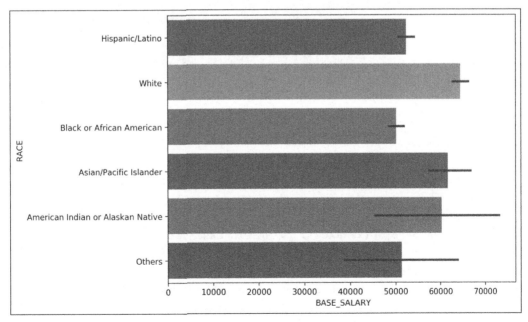

Seaborn bar plot

6. To replicate this with pandas, we will need to group by RACE first:

```
>>> fig, ax = plt.subplots(figsize=(8, 6))
>>> (employee
...      .groupby('RACE', sort=False)
...      ['BASE_SALARY']
...      .mean()
...      .plot.barh(rot=0, width=.8, ax=ax)
... )
>>> ax.set_xlabel('Mean Salary')
>>> fig.savefig('c13-sns4.png', dpi=300, bbox_inches='tight')
```

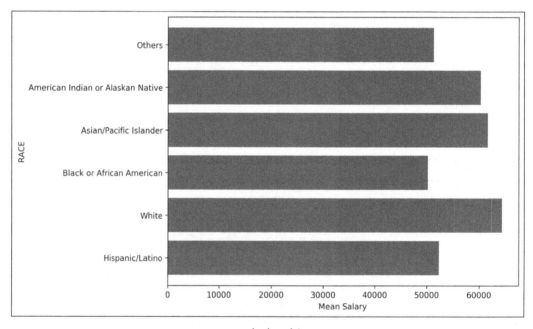

pandas bar plot

7. Seaborn also has the ability to distinguish groups within the data through a third variable, hue, in most of its plotting functions. Let's find the mean salary by RACE and GENDER:

```
>>> fig, ax = plt.subplots(figsize=(18, 6))
>>> sns.barplot(x='RACE', y='BASE_SALARY', hue='GENDER',
...      ax=ax, data=employee, palette='Greys',
...      order=['Hispanic/Latino',
...             'Black or African American',
...             'American Indian or Alaskan Native',
...             'Asian/Pacific Islander', 'Others',
```

```
...                'White'])
>>> fig.savefig('c13-sns5.png', dpi=300, bbox_inches='tight')
```

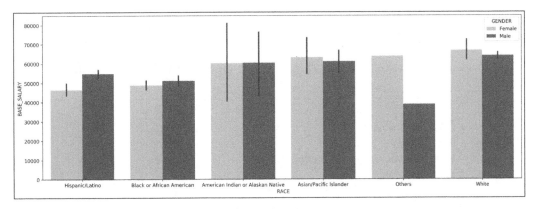

Seaborn bar plot

8. With pandas, we will have to group by both RACE and GENDER and then unstack the genders as column names:

```
>>> fig, ax = plt.subplots(figsize=(18, 6))
>>> (employee
...      .groupby(['RACE', 'GENDER'], sort=False)
...      ['BASE_SALARY']
...      .mean()
...      .unstack('GENDER')
...      .sort_values('Female')
...      .plot.bar(rot=0, ax=ax,
...          width=.8, cmap='viridis')
... )
>>> fig.savefig('c13-sns6.png', dpi=300, bbox_inches='tight')
```

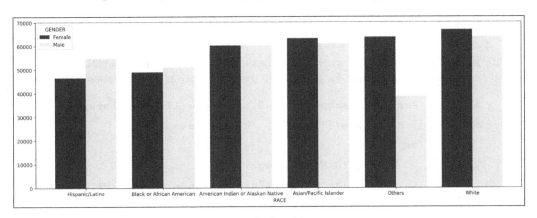

pandas bar plot

9. A box plot is another plot that both seaborn and pandas have in common. Let's create a box plot of salary by RACE and GENDER with seaborn:

```
>>> fig, ax = plt.subplots(figsize=(8, 6))
>>> sns.boxplot(x='GENDER', y='BASE_SALARY', data=employee,
...             hue='RACE', palette='Greys', ax=ax)
>>> fig.savefig('c13-sns7.png', dpi=300, bbox_inches='tight')
```

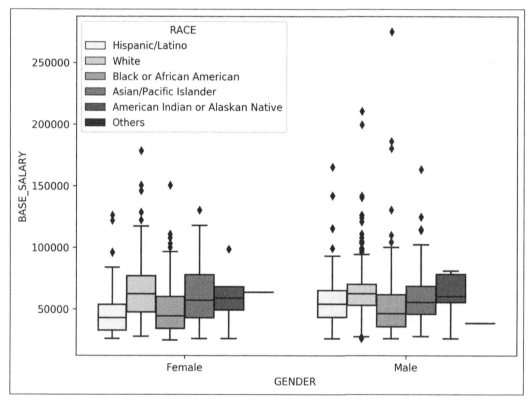

Seaborn box plot

10. pandas is not easily able to produce an exact replication for this box plot. It can create two separate Axes for gender and then make box plots of salaries by race:

```
>>> fig, axs = plt.subplots(1, 2, figsize=(12, 6), sharey=True)
>>> for g, ax in zip(['Female', 'Male'], axs):
...     (employee
...         .query('GENDER == @g')
...         .assign(RACE=lambda df_:df_.RACE.fillna('NA'))
...         .pivot(columns='RACE')
```

```
...            ['BASE_SALARY']
...            .plot.box(ax=ax, rot=30)
...         )
...       ax.set_title(g + ' Salary')
...       ax.set_xlabel('')
>>> fig.savefig('c13-sns8.png', bbox_inches='tight')
```

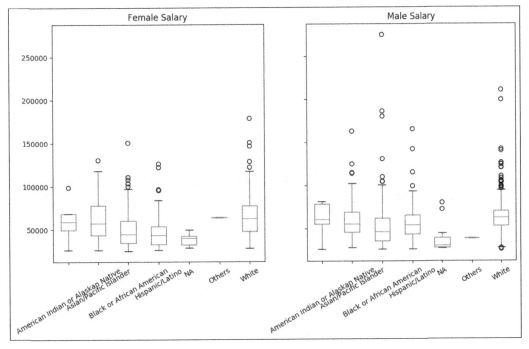

pandas box plot

How it works...

Importing seaborn in *step 2* changes many of the default properties of matplotlib. There are about 300 default plotting parameters that can be accessed within the dictionary-like object `plt.rcParams`. To restore the matplotlib defaults, call the `plt.rcdefaults` function with no arguments.

The style of pandas plots will also be affected when importing seaborn. Our employee dataset meets the requirements for tidy data and thus makes it perfect to use for nearly all seaborn's plotting functions.

Seaborn will do all the aggregation; you just need to supply your DataFrame to the data parameter and refer to the columns with their string names. For instance, in *step 3*, the `countplot` function effortlessly counts each occurrence of a `DEPARTMENT` to create a bar chart. Most seaborn plotting functions have x and y parameters. We could have made a vertical bar plot by switching the values for x and y. pandas forces you to do a bit more work to get the same plot. In *step 4*, we must precalculate the height of the bins using the `.value_counts` method.

Seaborn is able to do more complex aggregations, as seen in *steps 5* and *7*, with the `barplot` function. The `hue` parameter further splits each of the groups on the x-axis. pandas is capable of nearly replicating these plots by grouping by the x and hue variables in *steps 6* and *8*.

Box plots are available in both seaborn and pandas and can be plotted with tidy data without any aggregation. Even though no aggregation is necessary, seaborn still has the upper hand, as it can split data neatly into separate groups using the `hue` parameter. pandas cannot easily replicate this function from seaborn, as seen in *step 10*. Each group needs to be split with the `.query` method and plotted on its own Axes.

Multivariate analysis with seaborn Grids

Seaborn has the ability to *facet* multiple plots in a grid. Certain functions in seaborn do not work at the matplotlib axis level, but rather at the figure level. These include `catplot`, `lmplot`, `pairplot`, `jointplot`, and `clustermap`.

The `figure` or `grid` functions, for the most part, use the `axes` functions to build the grid. The final objects returned from the `grid` functions are of grid type, of which there are four different kinds. Advanced use cases necessitate the use of grid types, but the vast majority of the time, you will call the underlying `grid` functions to produce the actual Grid and not the constructor itself.

In this recipe, we will examine the relationship between years of experience and salary by gender and race. We will begin by creating a regression plot with a seaborn Axes function and then add more dimensions to the plot with `grid` functions.

How to do it...

1. Read in the employee dataset, and create a column for years of experience:

```
>>> emp = pd.read_csv('data/employee.csv',
...      parse_dates=['HIRE_DATE', 'JOB_DATE'])
>>> def yrs_exp(df_):
...      days_hired = pd.to_datetime('12-1-2016') - df_.HIRE_DATE
...      return days_hired.dt.days / 365.25

>>> emp = (emp
...      .assign(YEARS_EXPERIENCE=yrs_exp)
... )

>>> emp[['HIRE_DATE', 'YEARS_EXPERIENCE']]
      HIRE_DATE  YEARS_EXPERIENCE
0    2006-06-12      10.472494
1    2000-07-19      16.369946
2    2015-02-03       1.826184
3    1982-02-08      34.812488
4    1989-06-19      27.452994
...         ...            ...
1995 2014-06-09       2.480544
1996 2003-09-02      13.248732
1997 2014-10-13       2.135567
1998 2009-01-20       7.863269
1999 2009-01-12       7.885172
```

2. Let's create a scatter plot with a fitted regression line to represent the relationship between years of experience and salary:

```
>>> fig, ax = plt.subplots(figsize=(8, 6))
>>> sns.regplot(x='YEARS_EXPERIENCE', y='BASE_SALARY',
...     data=emp, ax=ax)
>>> fig.savefig('c13-scat4.png', dpi=300, bbox_inches='tight')
```

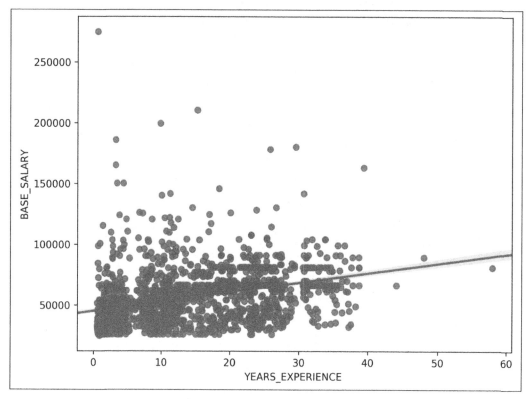

Seaborn scatter plot

3. The `regplot` function cannot plot multiple regression lines for different columns. Let's use the `lmplot` function to plot a seaborn `grid` that adds regression lines for males and females:

```
>>> grid = sns.lmplot(x='YEARS_EXPERIENCE', y='BASE_SALARY',
...     hue='GENDER', palette='Greys',
...     scatter_kws={'s':10}, data=emp)
>>> grid.fig.set_size_inches(8, 6)
>>> grid.fig.savefig('c13-scat5.png', dpi=300, bbox_
inches='tight')
```

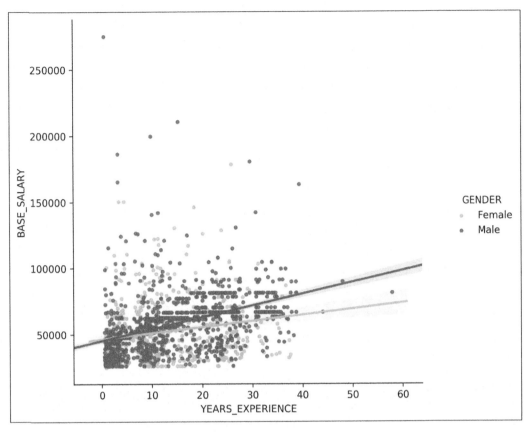

Seaborn scatter plot

4. The real power of the seaborn `grid` functions is their ability to add more Axes based on another variable. The `lmplot` function has the `col` and `row` parameters available to divide the data further into different groups. For instance, we can create a separate plot for each unique race in the dataset and still fit the regression lines by gender:

```
>>> grid = sns.lmplot(x='YEARS_EXPERIENCE', y='BASE_SALARY',
...                    hue='GENDER', col='RACE', col_wrap=3,
...                    palette='Greys', sharex=False,
...                    line_kws = {'linewidth':5},
...                    data=emp)
>>> grid.set(ylim=(20000, 120000))
>>> grid.fig.savefig('c13-scat6.png', dpi=300, bbox_
inches='tight')
```

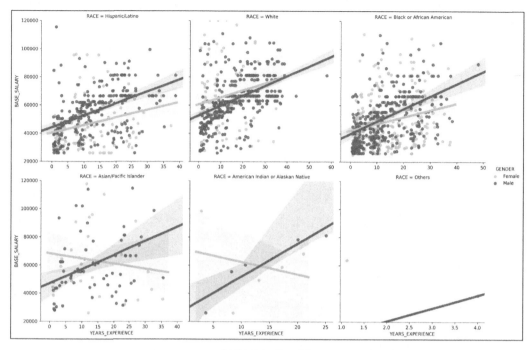

Seaborn scatter plot

How it works...

In *step 1*, we create another continuous variable by using pandas date functionality. This data was collected from the city of Houston on December 1, 2016. We use this date to determine how long each employee has worked for the city. When we subtract dates, as done in the second line of code, we are returned a `Timedelta` object whose largest unit is days. We divided the days of this result by 365.25 to calculate the years of experience.

Step 2 uses the `regplot` function to create a scatter plot with the estimated regression line. It returns a matplotlib `Axes`, which we use to change the size of the figure. To create two separate regression lines for each gender, we must use the `lmplot` function, which returns a seaborn `FacetGrid`. This function has a `hue` parameter, which overlays a new regression line of distinct color for each unique value of that column.

The seaborn `FacetGrid` is essentially a wrapper around the matplotlib `Figure`, with a few convenience methods to alter its elements. You can access the underlying matplotlib `Figure` with their `.fig` attribute. *Step 4* shows a common use-case for seaborn functions that return `FacetGrids`, which is to create multiple plots based on a third or even fourth variable. We set the `col` parameter to `RACE`. Six regression plots are created for each of the six unique races in the `RACE` column. Normally, this would return a grid consisting of one row and six columns, but we use the `col_wrap` parameter to wrap the row after three columns.

There are other parameters to control aspects of the `Grid`. It is possible to use parameters from the underlying `line` and `scatter` plot functions from matplotlib. To do so, set the `scatter_kws` or the `line_kws` parameters to a dictionary that has the matplotlib parameter as a key paired with the value.

There's more...

We can do a similar type of analysis when we have categorical features. First, let's reduce the number of levels in the categorical variables RACE and DEPARTMENT to the top two and three most common, respectively:

```
>>> deps = emp['DEPARTMENT'].value_counts().index[:2]
>>> races = emp['RACE'].value_counts().index[:3]
>>> is_dep = emp['DEPARTMENT'].isin(deps)
>>> is_race = emp['RACE'].isin(races)
>>> emp2 = (emp
...        [is_dep & is_race]
...        .assign(DEPARTMENT=lambda df_:
...                df_['DEPARTMENT'].str.extract('(HPD|HFD)',
...                                              expand=True))
... )

>>> emp2.shape
(968, 11)

>>> emp2['DEPARTMENT'].value_counts()
HPD    591
HFD    377
Name: DEPARTMENT, dtype: int64

>>> emp2['RACE'].value_counts()
White                        478
Hispanic/Latino              250
Black or African American    240
Name: RACE, dtype: int64
```

Let's use one of the simpler Axes-level functions, such as `violinplot` to view the distribution of years of experience by gender:

```
>>> common_depts = (emp
...        .groupby('DEPARTMENT')
...        .filter(lambda group: len(group) > 50)
... )

>>> fig, ax = plt.subplots(figsize=(8, 6))
>>> sns.violinplot(x='YEARS_EXPERIENCE', y='GENDER',
...        data=common_depts)
>>> fig.savefig('c13-viol.png', dpi=300, bbox_inches='tight')
```

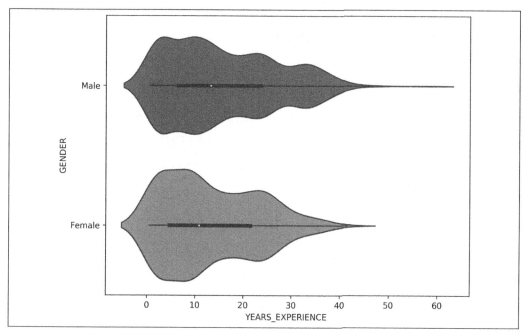

Seaborn violin plot

We can then use the `catplot` to add a violin plot for each unique combination of department and race with the `col` and `row` parameters:

```
>>> grid = sns.catplot(x='YEARS_EXPERIENCE', y='GENDER',
...                    col='RACE', row='DEPARTMENT',
...                    height=3, aspect=2,
...                    data=emp2, kind='violin')
>>> grid.fig.savefig('c13-vio2.png', dpi=300, bbox_inches='tight')
```

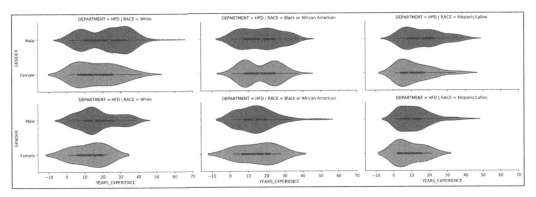

Seaborn violin plot

Uncovering Simpson's Paradox in the diamonds dataset with seaborn

It is unfortunately quite easy to report erroneous results when doing data analysis. *Simpson's Paradox* is one of the more common phenomena that can appear. It occurs when one group shows a higher result than another group, when all the data is aggregated, but it shows the opposite when the data is subdivided into different segments. For instance, let's say we have two students, *A* and *B*, who have each been given a test with 100 questions on it. Student *A* answers 50% of the questions correct, while Student *B* gets 80% correct. This obviously suggests Student *B* has greater aptitude:

Student	Raw Score	Percent Correct
A	50/100	50
B	80/100	80

Let's say that the two tests were very different. Student *A*'s test consisted of 95 problems that were difficult and only five that were easy. Student *B* was given a test with the exact opposite ratio:

Student	Difficult	Easy	Difficult Percent	Easy Percent	Percent
A	45/95	5/5	47	100	50
B	2/5	78/95	40	82	80

This paints a completely different picture. Student A now has a higher percentage of both the difficult and easy problems but has a much lower percentage as a whole. This is a quintessential example of Simpson's Paradox. The aggregated whole shows the opposite of each individual segment.

In this recipe, we will first reach a perplexing result that appears to suggest that higher quality diamonds are worth less than lower quality ones. We uncover Simpson's Paradox by taking more finely grained glimpses into the data that suggest the opposite is true.

How to do it...

1. Read in the diamonds dataset:

```
>>> dia = pd.read_csv('data/diamonds.csv')
>>> dia
```

	carat	cut	color	...	x	y	z
0	0.23	Ideal	E	...	3.95	3.98	2.43
1	0.21	Premium	E	...	3.89	3.84	2.31
2	0.23	Good	E	...	4.05	4.07	2.31
3	0.29	Premium	I	...	4.20	4.23	2.63
4	0.31	Good	J	...	4.34	4.35	2.75
...	...	...	...	...	...	...	...
53935	0.72	Ideal	D	...	5.75	5.76	3.50
53936	0.72	Good	D	...	5.69	5.75	3.61
53937	0.70	Very Good	D	...	5.66	5.68	3.56
53938	0.86	Premium	H	...	6.15	6.12	3.74
53939	0.75	Ideal	D	...	5.83	5.87	3.64

2. Before we begin analysis, let's change the cut, color, and clarity columns into ordered categorical variables:

```
>>> cut_cats = ['Fair', 'Good', 'Very Good', 'Premium', 'Ideal']
>>> color_cats = ['J', 'I', 'H', 'G', 'F', 'E', 'D']
>>> clarity_cats = ['I1', 'SI2', 'SI1', 'VS2',
...                 'VS1', 'VVS2', 'VVS1', 'IF']
>>> dia2 = (dia
...         .assign(cut=pd.Categorical(dia['cut'],
...                     categories=cut_cats,
...                     ordered=True),
...             color=pd.Categorical(dia['color'],
...                     categories=color_cats,
...                     ordered=True),
...             clarity=pd.Categorical(dia['clarity'],
...                     categories=clarity_cats,
```

```
...                    ordered=True))
... )
```

```
>>> dia2
       carat        cut color  ...      x     y     z
0       0.23      Ideal     E  ...   3.95  3.98  2.43
1       0.21    Premium     E  ...   3.89  3.84  2.31
2       0.23       Good     E  ...   4.05  4.07  2.31
3       0.29    Premium     I  ...   4.20  4.23  2.63
4       0.31       Good     J  ...   4.34  4.35  2.75
...      ...        ...   ...  ...    ...   ...   ...
53935   0.72      Ideal     D  ...   5.75  5.76  3.50
53936   0.72       Good     D  ...   5.69  5.75  3.61
53937   0.70  Very Good     D  ...   5.66  5.68  3.56
53938   0.86    Premium     H  ...   6.15  6.12  3.74
53939   0.75      Ideal     D  ...   5.83  5.87  3.64
```

3. Seaborn uses category orders for its plots. Let's make a bar plot of the mean price for each level of the `cut`, `color`, and `clarity` columns:

```
>>> import seaborn as sns
>>> fig, (ax1, ax2, ax3) = plt.subplots(1, 3, figsize=(14,4))
>>> sns.barplot(x='color', y='price', data=dia2, ax=ax1)
>>> sns.barplot(x='cut', y='price', data=dia2, ax=ax2)
>>> sns.barplot(x='clarity', y='price', data=dia2, ax=ax3)
>>> fig.suptitle('Price Decreasing with Increasing Quality?')
>>> fig.savefig('c13-bar4.png', dpi=300, bbox_inches='tight')
```

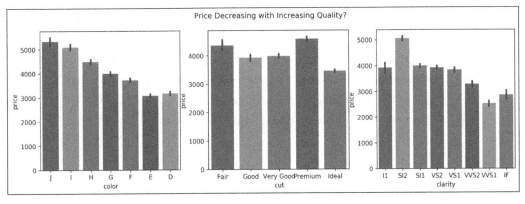

Seaborn bar plot

4. There seems to be a decreasing trend for color and price. The highest quality cut and clarity levels also have low prices. How can this be? Let's dig a little deeper and plot the price for each diamond color again, but make a new plot for each level of the `clarity` column:

```
>>> grid = sns.catplot(x='color', y='price', col='clarity',
...        col_wrap=4, data=dia2, kind='bar')
>>> grid.fig.savefig('c13-bar5.png', dpi=300, bbox_inches='tight')
```

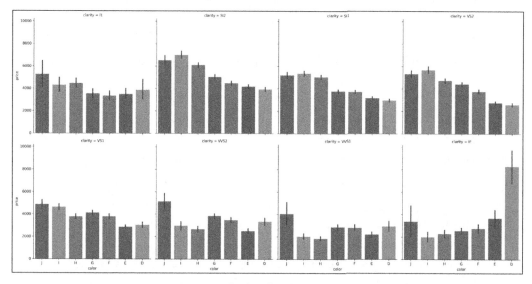

Seaborn bar plot

5. This plot is a little more revealing. Although price appears to decrease as the quality of color increases, it does not do so when clarity is at its highest level. There is a substantial increase in price. We have yet to look at just the price of the diamond without paying any attention to its size. Let's recreate the plot from *step 3* but use the carat size in place of price:

```
>>> fig, (ax1, ax2, ax3) = plt.subplots(1, 3, figsize=(14,4))
>>> sns.barplot(x='color', y='carat', data=dia2, ax=ax1)
>>> sns.barplot(x='cut', y='carat', data=dia2, ax=ax2)
>>> sns.barplot(x='clarity', y='carat', data=dia2, ax=ax3)
>>> fig.suptitle('Diamond size decreases with quality')
>>> fig.savefig('c13-bar6.png', dpi=300, bbox_inches='tight')
```

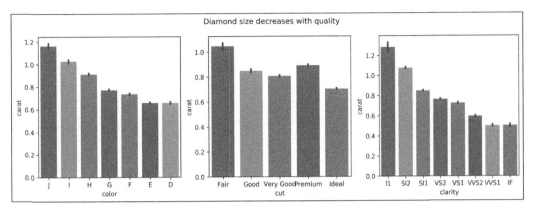

Seaborn bar plot

6. Now our story is starting to make a bit more sense. Higher quality diamonds appear to be smaller in size, which intuitively makes sense. Let's create a new variable that segments the carat values into five distinct sections, and then create a point plot. The plot that follows reveals that higher quality diamonds do, in fact, cost more money when they are segmented based on size:

```
>>> dia2 = (dia2
...        .assign(carat_category=pd.qcut(dia2.carat, 5))
... )


>>> from matplotlib.cm import Greys
>>> greys = Greys(np.arange(50,250,40))
>>> grid = sns.catplot(x='clarity', y='price', data=dia2,
...     hue='carat_category', col='color',
...     col_wrap=4, kind='point', palette=greys)
>>> grid.fig.suptitle('Diamond price by size, color and clarity',
...     y=1.02, size=20)
>>> grid.fig.savefig('c13-bar7.png', dpi=300, bbox_inches='tight')
```

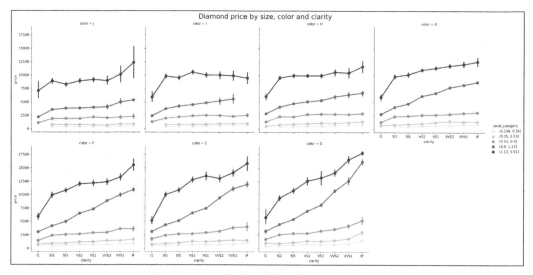

Seaborn point plot

How it works...

In this recipe, it is important to create categorical columns, as they are allowed to be ordered. Seaborn uses this ordering to place the labels on the plot. *Steps 3* and *4* show what appears to be a downward trend for increasing diamond quality. This is where Simpson's paradox takes center stage. This aggregated result of the whole is being confounded by other variables not yet examined.

The key to uncovering this paradox is to focus on carat size. *Step 5* reveals to us that carat size is also decreasing with increasing quality. To account for this fact, we cut the diamond size into five equally-sized bins with the qcut function. By default, this function cuts the variable into discrete categories based on the given quantiles. By passing it an integer, as was done in this step, it creates equally-spaced quantiles. You also have the option of passing it a sequence of explicit non-regular quantiles.

With this new variable, we can make a plot of the mean price per diamond size per group, as done in *step 6*. The point plot in seaborn creates a line plot connecting the means of each category. The vertical bar at each point is the standard deviation for that group. This plot confirms that diamonds do indeed become more expensive as their quality increases, as long as we hold the carat size as the constant.

There's more...

The bar plots in *steps 3* and *5* could have been created with the more advanced seaborn
`PairGrid` constructor, which can plot a bivariate relationship. Using a `PairGrid` is a
two-step process. The first step is to call the constructor and alert it to which variables will
be x and which will be y. The second step calls the `.map` method to apply a plot to all of the
combinations of x and y columns:

```
>>> g = sns.PairGrid(dia2, height=5,
...      x_vars=["color", "cut", "clarity"],
...      y_vars=["price"])
>>> g.map(sns.barplot)
>>> g.fig.suptitle('Replication of Step 3 with PairGrid', y=1.02)
>>> g.fig.savefig('c13-bar8.png', dpi=300, bbox_inches='tight')
```

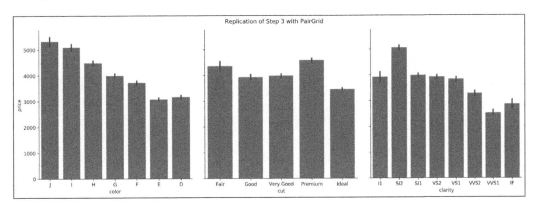

Seaborn bar plot

14

Debugging and Testing Pandas

Code to transform data

In this chapter, we will look at some code that analyzes survey data that Kaggle did in 2018. The survey queried Kaggle users about socio-economic information.

This section will present the survey data along with some code to analyze it. The subtitle for this data is "the most comprehensive dataset available on the state of machine learning and data science". Let's dig into this data and see what it has. The data was originally available at `https://www.kaggle.com/kaggle/kaggle-survey-2018`.

How to do it...

1. Load the data into a DataFrame:

```
>>> import pandas as pd
>>> import numpy as np
>>> import zipfile
>>> url = 'data/kaggle-survey-2018.zip'

>>> with zipfile.ZipFile(url) as z:
...     print(z.namelist())
...     kag = pd.read_csv(z.open('multipleChoiceResponses.csv'))
```

```
...         df = kag.iloc[1:]
['multipleChoiceResponses.csv', 'freeFormResponses.csv',
'SurveySchema.csv']
```

2. Look at the data and data types:

```
>>> df.T
```

	1	2	3	...	23857
Time from...	710	434	718	...	370
Q1	Female	Male	Female	...	Male
Q1_OTHER_...	-1	-1	-1	...	-1
Q2	45-49	30-34	30-34	...	22-24
Q3	United S...	Indonesia	United S...	...	Turkey
...	...	...	...	...	...
Q50_Part_5	NaN	NaN	NaN	...	NaN
Q50_Part_6	NaN	NaN	NaN	...	NaN
Q50_Part_7	NaN	NaN	NaN	...	NaN
Q50_Part_8	NaN	NaN	NaN	...	NaN
Q50_OTHER...	-1	-1	-1	...	-1

```
>>> df.dtypes
Time from Start to Finish (seconds)      object
Q1                                       object
Q1_OTHER_TEXT                            object
Q2                                       object
Q3                                       object
                                         ...
Q50_Part_5                               object
Q50_Part_6                               object
Q50_Part_7                               object
Q50_Part_8                               object
Q50_OTHER_TEXT                           object
Length: 395, dtype: object
```

3. It turns out that most of the survey data was selecting from options of responses. We see that the type of all of the columns is `object`. We could go through our standard process of exploring these values using the `.value_counts` method:

```
>>> df.Q1.value_counts(dropna=False)
Male                    19430
```

```
Female                        4010
Prefer not to say              340
Prefer to self-describe         79
Name: Q1, dtype: int64
```

4. To make a long story short, I pull out each column of interest as a Series. I filtered most of the values to a limited number of values. I used the Series `.rename` method to give the column a better name. Some of the values, such as the Q2, Q8, and Q9, have range answers. In the case of age (Q2), you have values like *55-59* and *60-69*. I use the `.str.slice` method to pull out the first two characters, and convert the type from string to integer.

For the education column (Q4), I convert the values to ordinal numbers. Finally, after I have converted many columns I'm working with to numbers and cleaned up some of the others, I put all of the Series back in a DataFrame with `pd.concat`.

I put all of this code into a function, `tweak_kag`:

```
>>> def tweak_kag(df):
...         na_mask = df.Q9.isna()
...         hide_mask = df.Q9.str.startswith('I do not').fillna(False)
...         df = df[~na_mask & ~hide_mask]
...
...         q1 = (df.Q1
...            .replace({'Prefer not to say': 'Another',
...                      'Prefer to self-describe': 'Another'})
...            .rename('Gender')
...         )
...         q2 = df.Q2.str.slice(0,2).astype(int).rename('Age')
...         def limit_countries(val):
...             if val in  {'United States of America', 'India',
'China'}:
...                 return val
...             return 'Another'
...         q3 = df.Q3.apply(limit_countries).rename('Country')
...
...         q4 = (df.Q4
...            .replace({'Master's degree': 18,
...            'Bachelor's degree': 16,
...            'Doctoral degree': 20,
...            'Some college/university study without earning a
```

```
      bachelor's degree': 13,
...          'Professional degree': 19,
...          'I prefer not to answer': None,
...          'No formal education past high school': 12})
...          .fillna(11)
...          .rename('Edu')
...          )
...
...      def only_cs_stat_val(val):
...          if val not in {'cs', 'eng', 'stat'}:
...              return 'another'
...          return val
...
...      q5 = (df.Q5
...              .replace({
...                  'Computer science (software engineering,
etc.)': 'cs',
...                  'Engineering (non-computer focused)': 'eng',
...                  'Mathematics or statistics': 'stat'})
...              .apply(only_cs_stat_val)
...              .rename('Studies'))
...      def limit_occupation(val):
...          if val in {'Student', 'Data Scientist', 'Software
Engineer', 'Not employed',
...                      'Data Engineer'}:
...              return val
...          return 'Another'
...
...      q6 = df.Q6.apply(limit_occupation).rename('Occupation')
...
...      q8 = (df.Q8
...          .str.replace('+', '')
...          .str.split('-', expand=True)
...          .iloc[:,0]
...          .fillna(-1)
...          .astype(int)
```

```
...          .rename('Experience')
...      )
...
...      q9 = (df.Q9
...          .str.replace('+','')
...          .str.replace(',','')
...          .str.replace('500000', '500')
...          .str.replace('I do not wish to disclose my approximate
yearly compensation','')
...          .str.split('-', expand=True)
...          .iloc[:,0]
...          .astype(int)
...          .mul(1000)
...          .rename('Salary'))
...      return pd.concat([q1, q2, q3, q4, q5, q6, q8, q9], axis=1)


>>> tweak_kag(df)
        Gender   Age       Country   ...    Occupation Experience
2         Male    30       Another   ...       Another          5
3       Female    30    United S...   ...    Data Sci...         0
5         Male    22         India   ...       Another          0
7         Male    35       Another   ...       Another         10
8         Male    18         India   ...       Another          0
...        ...   ...           ...   ...           ...        ...
23844     Male    30       Another   ...    Software...        10
23845     Male    22       Another   ...       Student          0
23854     Male    30       Another   ...       Another          5
23855     Male    45       Another   ...       Another          5
23857     Male    22       Another   ...    Software...         0


>>> tweak_kag(df).dtypes
Gender        object
Age            int64
Country       object
Edu          float64
Studies       object
```

```
Occupation      object
Experience       int64
Salary           int64
dtype: object
```

How it works...

The survey data is rich with information, but it's a little hard to analyze it because all of the columns come in as objects. Our `tweak_kag` function filters out respondents who did not provide salary information. We also convert a few of the columns (`Age`, `Edu`, `Experience`, and `Salary`) to numeric values for easier quantification. The remaining categorical columns are pruned down to lower cardinality.

Cleaning up our data makes it easier to analyze. For example, we can easily group by country and correlate salary and experience:

```
>>> kag = tweak_kag(df)
>>> (kag
...      .groupby('Country')
...      .apply(lambda g: g.Salary.corr(g.Experience))
... )
Country
Another                   0.289827
China                     0.252974
India                     0.167335
United States of America  0.354125
dtype: float64
```

Apply performance

The `.apply` method on a Series and DataFrame is one of the slowest operations in pandas. In this recipe, we will explore the speed of it and see if we can debug what is going on.

How to do it...

1. Let's time how long one use of the `.apply` method takes using the `%%timeit` cell magic in Jupiter. This is the code from the `tweak_kag` function that limits the cardinality of the country column (Q3):

```
>>> %%timeit
>>> def limit_countries(val):
...         if val in  {'United States of America', 'India',
'China'}:
...             return val
...         return 'Another'

>>> q3 = df.Q3.apply(limit_countries).rename('Country')
6.42 ms ± 1.22 ms per loop (mean ± std. dev. of 7 runs, 100 loops
each)
```

2. Let's look at using the `.replace` method instead of `.apply` and see if that improves performance:

```
>>> %%timeit
>>> other_values = df.Q3.value_counts().iloc[3:].index
>>> q3_2 = df.Q3.replace(other_values, 'Another')
27.7 ms ± 535 µs per loop (mean ± std. dev. of 7 runs, 10 loops
each)
```

3. Woah! That was slower than the `.apply` method! Let's try again. If we recreate this code using the `.isin` method combined with `.where`, it runs over twice as fast as `.apply`:

```
>>> %%timeit
>>> values = {'United States of America', 'India', 'China'}
>>> q3_3 = df.Q3.where(df.Q3.isin(values), 'Another')
3.39 ms ± 570 µs per loop (mean ± std. dev. of 7 runs, 100 loops
each)
```

4. Finally, let's try the `np.where` function. This is not part of pandas, but pandas often works with NumPy functions:

```
>>> %%timeit
>>> values = {'United States of America', 'India', 'China'}
>>> q3_4 = pd.Series(np.where(df.Q3.isin(values), df.Q3,
'Another'),
...         index=df.index)
2.75 ms ± 345 µs per loop (mean ± std. dev. of 7 runs, 100 loops
each)
```

5. Let's check if the results are the same:

```
>>> q3.equals(q3_2)
True
```

```
>>> q3.equals(q3_3)
True
>>> q3.equals(q3_4)
True
```

How it works...

This recipe benchmarked the `.apply`, `.replace`, and `.where` methods. Of those three, the `.where` method was the quickest. Finally, it showed the NumPy `where` function, which is even faster than pandas. However, if we use the NumPy function, we need to convert the result back into a series (and give it the same index as the original DataFrame).

There's more...

The documentation for the `.apply` method states that if you pass in a NumPy function, it will run a fast path and pass the whole series to the function. However, if you pass in a Python function, that function will be called for each value in the Series. This can be confusing because the method behaves differently depending on the parameter that is passed into it.

If you find yourself in a situation where you are passing in a function to `.apply` (or have done a groupby operation and are calling `.agg`, `.transform`, or some other method that takes a function as a parameter) and cannot remember what arguments will be passed into the function, you can use the following code to help. (Of course, you can also look at the documentation or even look at the code for `.apply`):

```
>>> def limit_countries(val):
...         if val in  {'United States of America', 'India', 'China'}:
...             return val
...         return 'Another'

>>> q3 = df.Q3.apply(limit_countries).rename('Country')

>>> def debug(something):
...     # what is something? A cell, series, dataframe?
...     print(type(something), something)
...     1/0

>>> q3.apply(debug)
<class 'str'> United States of America
```

```
Traceback (most recent call last)

...

ZeroDivisionError: division by zero
```

The output shows that a string (a scalar value from the series q3) was passed into the debug function.

If you do not want to throw an exception, you can set a global variable to hold the parameter passed into the function:

```
>>> the_item = None
>>> def debug(something):
...      global the_item
...      the_item = something
...      return something

>>> _ = q3.apply(debug)

>>> the_item
'Another'
```

One thing to keep in mind is that the function we pass into the .apply method is called once per item in the Series. Operating on single items is a slow path, and we should try to avoid it if possible. The next recipe will show another option for speeding calls to .apply.

Improving apply performance with Dask, Pandarell, Swifter, and more

Sometimes .apply is convenient. Various libraries enable parallelizing such operations. There are various mechanisms to do this. The easiest is to try and leverage *vectorization*. Math operations are vectorized in pandas, if you add a number (say 5) to a numerical series, pandas will not add 5 to each value. Rather it will leverage a feature of modern CPUs to do the operation one time.

If you cannot vectorize, as is the case with our limit_countries function, you have other options. This section will show a few of them.

Note that you will need to install these libraries as they are not included with pandas.

The examples show limiting values in the country column from the survey data to a few values.

How to do it...

1. Import and initialize the Pandarallel library. This library tries to parallelize pandas operations across all available CPUs. Note that this library runs fine on Linux and Mac. Because of the shared memory technique it leverages, it will not work on Windows unless Python is being executed with the Windows Subsystem for Linux:

```
>>> from pandarallel import pandarallel
>>> pandarallel.initialize()
```

2. This library augments the DataFrame to add some extra methods. Use the .parallel_apply method:

```
>>> def limit_countries(val):
...         if val in  {'United States of America', 'India',
'China'}:
...                 return val
...         return 'Another'


>>> %%timeit
>>> res_p = df.Q3.parallel_apply(limit_countries).
rename('Country')
133 ms ± 11.1 ms per loop (mean ± std. dev. of 7 runs, 10 loops
each)
```

3. Let's try another library. Import the swifter library:

```
>>> import swifter
```

4. This library also augments the DataFrame to add a .swifter accessor. Use the swifter library:

```
>>> %%timeit
>>> res_s = df.Q3.swifter.apply(limit_countries).rename('Country')
187 ms ± 31.4 ms per loop (mean ± std. dev. of 7 runs, 10 loops
each)
```

5. Import the Dask library:

```
>>> import dask
```

6. Use the Dask .map_partitions function:

```
>>> %%timeit
>>> res_d = (dask.dataframe.from_pandas(
...         df, npartitions=4)
...     .map_partitions(lambda df: df.Q3.apply(limit_countries))
```

```
...        .rename('Countries')
... )
29.1 s ± 1.75 s per loop (mean ± std. dev. of 7 runs, 1 loop each)
```

7. Use `np.vectorize`:

```
>>> np_fn = np.vectorize(limit_countries)

>>> %%timeit
>>> res_v = df.Q3.apply(np_fn).rename('Country')
643 ms ± 86.8 ms per loop (mean ± std. dev. of 7 runs, 1 loop
each)
```

8. Import `numba` and decorate the function with the `jit` decorator:

```
>>> from numba import jit
>>> @jit
... def limit_countries2(val):
...        if val in  ['United States of America', 'India',
'China']:
...                return val
...        return 'Another'
```

9. Use the decorated `numba` function:

```
>>> %%timeit
>>> res_n = df.Q3.apply(limit_countries2).rename('Country')
158 ms ± 16.1 ms per loop (mean ± std. dev. of 7 runs, 10 loops
each)
```

How it works...

Note that there is overhead to parallelizing code. In the examples above, all of the code ran faster in serial with normal pandas code. There is a crossover point where the overhead penalty makes sense. The examples for the Pandarallel library use at least a million samples. Our dataset is much smaller than that, so the vanilla `.apply` method is faster in our case.

In *step 1* and *2* we use the Pandarallel library. This library leverages the `multiprocessing` library from the standard library to try and run computations in parallel. When you initialize the library, you can specify an `nb_workers` parameter that indicates how many CPUs to use (by default it will use all of the CPUs). The example shows how to use the `.parallel_apply` method which is analogous to the `.apply` method in pandas. This library also works with groupby objects and series objects.

Step 3 and *4* show use of the `swifter` library. This library adds a `.swifter` attribute to a DataFrame and series. This library takes a different approach to speeding up code. It will try to see if the operation can be vectorized. Otherwise, it will see how long pandas will take (by running on a small sample), it then determines whether to leverage the Dask library, or to just stick with pandas. Again, the logic to even determine which path to use has overhead, so blindly using this library might not lead to the most efficient code.

The Swifter website has a notebook where they performed comparisons of Swifter, `np.vectorize`, Dask, and pandas. It has extensive benchmarking on different types of functions. For what it calls *non-vectorized functions* (which our `limit_countries` is as it has normal Python logic), it isn't until you get to almost a million rows that the vanilla pandas `.apply` method starts to lose out.

In *step 5* and *6* the Dask library is presented. Note that there is a bit of overhead loading the data and leveraging the parallelization afforded by the library. Many users of Dask forgo pandas completely and just use Dask, as it implements similar functionality but allows processing to scale out to big data (and running on a cluster).

Next, we try the `vectorize` function from NumPy in *step 7*. It creates a NumPy `ufunc` (a universal function that operates on NumPy arrays) from an arbitrary Python function. It tries to leverage NumPy broadcasting rules. In this case, there is no performance increase by using it.

Step 8 and *9* demonstrate using the Numba library. We leverage the `jit` decorator to create a new function `limit_countries2`. This decorator converts the Python function into native code. Again, this function is not amenable to speed increases from this decorator.

Many of the options illustrated here may provide a performance boost with larger datasets. In our case, blindly applying them would slow down the code.

Inspecting code

The Jupyter environment has an extension that allows you to quickly pull up the documentation or the source code for a class, method, or function. I strongly encourage you to get used to using these. If you can stay in the Jupyter environment to answer questions that may come up, you will increase your productivity.

In this section, we will show how to look at the source code for the `.apply` method. It is easiest to look at the documentation for a DataFrame or series method directly on the DataFrame or series object, respectively. Throughout this book, we have heavily recommended chaining operations on pandas objects. Sadly Jupyter (and any other editor environment) is not able to perform code completion or look up documentation on the intermediate object returned from a chained method call. Hence the recommendation to perform the lookup directly on a method that is not chained.

How to do it...

1. Load the survey data:

```
>>> import zipfile
>>> url = 'data/kaggle-survey-2018.zip'

>>> with zipfile.ZipFile(url) as z:
...     kag = pd.read_csv(z.open('multipleChoiceResponses.csv'))
...     df = kag.iloc[1:]
```

2. Let's look up the documentation for .apply using the Jupyter ? extension. (We could also hit *Shift + Tab* four times to get this in Jupyter):

```
>>> df.Q3.apply?
Signature: df.Q3.apply(func, convert_dtype=True, args=(), **kwds)
Docstring:
Invoke function on values of Series.


Can be ufunc (a NumPy function that applies to the entire Series)
or a Python function that only works on single values.


Parameters
----------
func : function
    Python function or NumPy ufunc to apply.
convert_dtype : bool, default True
    Try to find better dtype for elementwise function results. If
    False, leave as dtype=object.
args : tuple
    Positional arguments passed to func after the series value.
**kwds
    Additional keyword arguments passed to func.


Returns
-------
Series or DataFrame
    If func returns a Series object the result will be a
DataFrame.
```

```
See Also
--------
Series.map: For element-wise operations.
Series.agg: Only perform aggregating type operations.
Series.transform: Only perform transforming type operations.


Examples
--------


    ...


File:       ~/.env/364/lib/python3.6/site-packages/pandas/core/
series.py
Type:       method
```

3. Let's look at the source code by using ??. (There is no *Shift + Tab* keyboard shortcut to get the code):

```
>>> df.Q3.apply??
Signature: df.Q3.apply(func, convert_dtype=True, args=(), **kwds)
Source:
    def apply(self, func, convert_dtype=True, args=(), **kwds):


        ...


        if len(self) == 0:
            return self._constructor(dtype=self.dtype, index=self.
index).__finalize__(
                self
            )


        # dispatch to agg
        if isinstance(func, (list, dict)):
            return self.aggregate(func, *args, **kwds)


        # if we are a string, try to dispatch
        if isinstance(func, str):
```

```
            return self._try_aggregate_string_function(func,
*args, **kwds)


        # handle ufuncs and lambdas
        if kwds or args and not isinstance(func, np.ufunc):

            def f(x):
                return func(x, *args, **kwds)

        else:
            f = func

        with np.errstate(all="ignore"):
            if isinstance(f, np.ufunc):
                return f(self)

            # row-wise access
            if is_extension_type(self.dtype):
                mapped = self._values.map(f)
            else:
                values = self.astype(object).values
                mapped = lib.map_infer(values, f, convert=convert_
dtype)

        if len(mapped) and isinstance(mapped[0], Series):
            # GH 25959 use pd.array instead of tolist
            # so extension arrays can be used
            return self._constructor_expanddim(pd.array(mapped),
index=self.index)
        else:
            return self._constructor(mapped, index=self.index).__
finalize__(self)
File:      ~/.env/364/lib/python3.6/site-packages/pandas/core/
series.py
Type:      method
```

4. We can see that this method tries to figure out the appropriate code to call. If those all fail, eventually it calculates the `mapped` variable. Let's try and figure out what `lib.map_infer` does:

```
>>> import pandas.core.series
>>> pandas.core.series.lib
<module 'pandas._libs.lib' from '.env/364/lib/python3.6/site-
packages/pandas/_libs/lib.cpython-36m-darwin.so'>

>>> pandas.core.series.lib.map_infer??
Docstring:
Substitute for np.vectorize with pandas-friendly dtype inference

Parameters
----------
arr : ndarray
f : function

Returns
-------
mapped : ndarray
Type:        builtin_function_or_method
```

How it works...

Jupyter has the ability to inspect both the docstrings and the source code for Python objects. The standard Python REPL can leverage the built-in `help` function to view a docstring, but it cannot display the source code.

Jupyter, however has some tricks up its sleeves. If you tack on a single question mark (?) following a function or method, it will show the documentation for that code. Note that this is not valid Python syntax, it is a feature of Jupyter. If you add on two question marks (??), then Jupyter will display the source code of the function or method.

This recipe showed tracing through the source code to see how the `.apply` method in pandas works under the covers.

We can see a shortcut in *step 3* if there are no results. We can also see how string functions (that is, passing in the string literal `mean`) work. The `getattr` function pulls off the corresponding method from the DataFrame.

Next, the code checks if it is dealing with a NumPy function. Eventually, it will call the function if it is an instance of `np.ufunc`, or it will call the `.map` method on the underlying `._values` attribute, or it will call `lib.map_infer`.

In *step 4*, we tried to inspect `lib.map_infer` but saw that it was an `so` file (`pyd` on Windows). This is a compiled file that is usually the result of writing Python in C or using Cython. Jupyter cannot show us the source of compiled files.

There's more...

When you view the source code for a function or method, Jupyter will display the file that it belongs to at the bottom of pane. If I really need to dig into the source code, I will open that in an editor outside of Jupyter. Then I can browse through that code and any corresponding code with my editor (most editors have better code navigation capabilities than Jupyter).

Debugging in Jupyter

The previous recipes have shown how to understand pandas code and inspect it from Jupyter. In this section, we will look at using the **IPython debugger** (**ipdb**) in Jupyter.

In this section, I will create a function that throws an error when I try to use it with the series `.apply` method. I will use ipdb to debug it.

How to do it...

1. Load the survey data:

```
>>> import zipfile
>>> url = 'data/kaggle-survey-2018.zip'

>>> with zipfile.ZipFile(url) as z:
...     kag = pd.read_csv(z.open('multipleChoiceResponses.csv'))
...     df = kag.iloc[1:]
```

2. Try and run a function to add one to a series:

```
>>> def add1(x):
...     return x + 1

>>> df.Q3.apply(add1)
------------------------------------------------------------------
```

```
- - - - - - - - -
TypeError                                        Traceback (most recent
call last)
<ipython-input-9-6ce28d2fea57> in <module>
      2     return x + 1
      3
----> 4 df.Q3.apply(add1)


~/.env/364/lib/python3.6/site-packages/pandas/core/series.py in
apply(self, func, convert_dtype, args, **kwds)
   4043             else:
   4044                 values = self.astype(object).values
-> 4045                 mapped = lib.map_infer(values, f,
convert=convert_dtype)
   4046
   4047         if len(mapped) and isinstance(mapped[0], Series):


pandas/_libs/lib.pyx in pandas._libs.lib.map_infer()


<ipython-input-9-6ce28d2fea57> in add1(x)
      1 def add1(x):
----> 2     return x + 1
      3
      4 df.Q3.apply(add1)


TypeError: must be str, not int
```

3. Use the `%debug` cell magic immediately following an exception to drop into a debug window. (This might seem a little backward because you call this after you have run a cell with an exception). This will open the debugger to the point where the exception was thrown.

    You can use the debugger commands to navigate through the stack. Hitting *U* key will pop the stack to the function that called the current line. You can inspect objects using the print command (`p`):

```
<ipython-input-9-6ce28d2fea57> in add1(x)
      1 def add1(x):
----> 2     return x + 1
      3
      4 df.Q3.apply(add1)

TypeError: must be str, not int
```

```
In [*]:  %debug
```
```
> <ipython-input-9-6ce28d2fea57>(2)add1()
      1 def add1(x):
----> 2     return x + 1
      3
      4 df.Q3.apply(add1)

ipdb> p x
'United States of America'
ipdb> u
> /Users/matt/.env/364/lib/python3.6/site-packages/pandas/core/series.py(4045)apply()
   4043             else:
   4044                 values = self.astype(object).values
-> 4045                 mapped = lib.map_infer(values, f, convert=convert_dtype)
   4046
   4047             if len(mapped) and isinstance(mapped[0], Series):

ipdb> p self
1          United S...
2           Indonesia
3          United S...
4          United S...
5               India
           ...
23855          France
23856          Turkey
23857          Turkey
23858       United K...
23859           Spain
Name: Q3, Length: 23859, dtype: object

ipdb>
```

Jupyter debugging

4. If you want to step into code without requiring that an exception be thrown, you can use the `set_trace` function from the IPython debugger. This will drop you into the debugger immediately following that line:

```
>>> from IPython.core.debugger import set_trace
```

```
>>> def add1(x):
...     set_trace()
...     return x + 1
```

```
>>> df.Q3.apply(add1)
```

```
from IPython.core.debugger import set_trace

def add1(x):
    set_trace()
    return x + 1

df.Q3.apply(add1)
```

```
> <ipython-input-11-cb997d0cb281>(5)add1()
      3 def add1(x):
      4     set_trace()
----> 5     return x + 1
      6
      7 df.Q3.apply(add1)

ipdb>
```

Jupyter debugging

How it works...

Jupyter (which is derived from IPython) ships with the IPython debugger. This replicates the functionality of the pdb module in the standard library, but with niceties such as syntax highlighting. (It also has tab completion, but this does not work in Jupyter, only in the IPython console).

There's more...

If you are unfamiliar with using the debugger, here is a lifejacket for you: The command h will print out all of the commands that you can run from the debugger:

```
ipdb> h

Documented commands (type help <topic>):
========================================
EOF     cl         disable  interact  next   psource  rv       unt
a       clear      display  j         p      q        s        until
alias   commands   down     jump      pdef   quit     source   up
args    condition  enable   l         pdoc   r        step     w
b       cont       exit     list      pfile  restart  tbreak   whatis
```

break	continue	h	ll	pinfo	return	u		where
bt	d	help	longlist	pinfo2	retval	unalias		
c	debug	ignore	n	pp	run	undisplay		

The most common commands that I use are s, n, l, u, d, and c. If you want to know what s does, then type:

```
ipdb> h s
s(tep)
```

```
        Execute the current line, stop at the first possible occasion
        (either in a function that is called or in the current
        function).
```

This tells the debugger to print the `help` (h) documentation for `step` (s). Because we are usually coding in small steps in Jupyter, a debugger is often overkill. But knowing how to use it can come in handy, especially if you want to jump into pandas source code and understand what is going on.

Managing data integrity with Great Expectations

Great Expectations is a third-party tool that allows you to capture and define the properties of a dataset. You can save these properties and then use them to validate future data to ensure data integrity. This can be very useful when building machine learning models, as new categorical data values and numeric outliers tend to cause a model to perform poorly or error out.

In this section, we will look at the Kaggle dataset and make an expectation suite to test and validate the data.

How to do it...

1. Read the data using the `tweak_kag` function previously defined:

   ```
   >>> kag = tweak_kag(df)
   ```

2. Use the Great Expectations `from_pandas` function to read in a Great Expectations DataFrame (a subclass of DataFrame with some extra methods):

   ```
   >>> import great_expectations as ge
   >>> kag_ge = ge.from_pandas(kag)
   ```

3. Examine the extra methods on the DataFrame:

```
>>> sorted([x for x in set(dir(kag_ge)) - set(dir(kag))
...     if not x.startswith('_')])
['autoinspect',
'batch_fingerprint',
'batch_id',
'batch_kwargs',
'column_aggregate_expectation',
'column_map_expectation',
'column_pair_map_expectation',
'discard_failing_expectations',
'edit_expectation_suite',
'expect_column_bootstrapped_ks_test_p_value_to_be_greater_than',
'expect_column_chisquare_test_p_value_to_be_greater_than',
'expect_column_distinct_values_to_be_in_set',
'expect_column_distinct_values_to_contain_set',
'expect_column_distinct_values_to_equal_set',
'expect_column_kl_divergence_to_be_less_than',
'expect_column_max_to_be_between',
'expect_column_mean_to_be_between',
'expect_column_median_to_be_between',
'expect_column_min_to_be_between',
'expect_column_most_common_value_to_be_in_set',
'expect_column_pair_values_A_to_be_greater_than_B',
'expect_column_pair_values_to_be_equal',
'expect_column_pair_values_to_be_in_set',
'expect_column_parameterized_distribution_ks_test_p_value_to_be_
greater_than',
'expect_column_proportion_of_unique_values_to_be_between',
'expect_column_quantile_values_to_be_between',
'expect_column_stdev_to_be_between',
'expect_column_sum_to_be_between',
'expect_column_to_exist',
'expect_column_unique_value_count_to_be_between',
'expect_column_value_lengths_to_be_between',
'expect_column_value_lengths_to_equal',
```

```
'expect_column_values_to_be_between',

'expect_column_values_to_be_dateutil_parseable',

'expect_column_values_to_be_decreasing',

'expect_column_values_to_be_in_set',

'expect_column_values_to_be_in_type_list',

'expect_column_values_to_be_increasing',

'expect_column_values_to_be_json_parseable',

'expect_column_values_to_be_null',

'expect_column_values_to_be_of_type',

'expect_column_values_to_be_unique',

'expect_column_values_to_match_json_schema',

'expect_column_values_to_match_regex',

'expect_column_values_to_match_regex_list',

'expect_column_values_to_match_strftime_format',

'expect_column_values_to_not_be_in_set',
'expect_column_values_to_not_be_null',

'expect_column_values_to_not_match_regex','expect_column_values_
to_not_match_regex_list',

'expect_multicolumn_values_to_be_unique',

'expect_table_column_count_to_be_between',

'expect_table_column_count_to_equal',

'expect_table_columns_to_match_ordered_list',

'expect_table_row_count_to_be_between',

'expect_table_row_count_to_equal',

'expectation',

'find_expectation_indexes',

'find_expectations',

'from_dataset',

'get_column_count',

'get_column_count_in_range',

'get_column_hist',

'get_column_max',

'get_column_mean',

'get_column_median',

'get_column_min',

'get_column_modes',
```

```
'get_column_nonnull_count',
'get_column_partition',
'get_column_quantiles',
'get_column_stdev',
'get_column_sum',
'get_column_unique_count',
'get_column_value_counts',
'get_config_value',
'get_data_asset_name',
'get_default_expectation_arguments',
'get_evaluation_parameter',
'get_expectation_suite',
'get_expectation_suite_name',
'get_expectations_config',
'get_row_count',
'get_table_columns',
'hashable_getters',
'multicolumn_map_expectation',
'profile',
'remove_expectation',
'save_expectation_suite',
'save_expectation_suite_name',
'set_config_value',
'set_data_asset_name',
'set_default_expectation_argument',
'set_evaluation_parameter',
'test_column_aggregate_expectation_function',
'test_column_map_expectation_function',
'test_expectation_function',
'validate']
```

4. Great Expectations has expectations for table shape, missing values, types, ranges, strings, dates, aggregate functions, column pairs, distributions, and file properties. Let's use some of them. As we do, the library will track the expectations we use. We can later save these as a *suite* of expectations:

```
>>> kag_ge.expect_column_to_exist('Salary')
{'success': True}
```

```
>>> kag_ge.expect_column_mean_to_be_between(
...     'Salary', min_value=10_000, max_value=100_000)
{'success': True,
'result': {'observed_value': 43869.66102793441,
'element_count': 15429,
'missing_count': 0,
'missing_percent': 0.0}}


>>> kag_ge.expect_column_values_to_be_between(
...     'Salary', min_value=0, max_value=500_000)
{'success': True,
'result': {'element_count': 15429,
'missing_count': 0,
'missing_percent': 0.0,
'unexpected_count': 0,
'unexpected_percent': 0.0,
'unexpected_percent_nonmissing': 0.0,
'partial_unexpected_list': []}}


>>> kag_ge.expect_column_values_to_not_be_null('Salary')
{'success': True,
'result': {'element_count': 15429,
'unexpected_count': 0,
'unexpected_percent': 0.0,
'partial_unexpected_list': []}}


>>> kag_ge.expect_column_values_to_match_regex(
...     'Country', r'America|India|Another|China')
{'success': True,
'result': {'element_count': 15429,
'missing_count': 0,
'missing_percent': 0.0,
'unexpected_count': 0,
'unexpected_percent': 0.0,
'unexpected_percent_nonmissing': 0.0,
```

```
                'partial_unexpected_list': []}}


>>> kag_ge.expect_column_values_to_be_of_type(
...     'Salary', type_='int')
{'success': True, 'result': {'observed_value': 'int64'}}
```

5. Save the expectations to a file. Great Expectations uses JSON to specify them:

    ```
    >>> kag_ge.save_expectation_suite('kaggle_expectations.json')
    ```

    The file should look like this:

    ```json
    {
      "data_asset_name": null,
      "expectation_suite_name": "default",
      "meta": {
        "great_expectations.__version__": "0.8.6"
      },
      "expectations": [
        {
          "expectation_type": "expect_column_to_exist",
          "kwargs": {
            "column": "Salary"
          }
        },
        {
          "expectation_type": "expect_column_mean_to_be_between",
          "kwargs": {
            "column": "Salary",
            "min_value": 10000,
            "max_value": 100000
          }
        },
        {
          "expectation_type": "expect_column_values_to_be_between",
          "kwargs": {
            "column": "Salary",
            "min_value": 0,
            "max_value": 500000
    ```

```
          }
        },
        {
          "expectation_type": "expect_column_values_to_not_be_null",
          "kwargs": {
            "column": "Salary"
          }
        },
        {
          "expectation_type": "expect_column_values_to_match_regex",
          "kwargs": {
            "column": "Country",
            "regex": "America|India|Another|China"
          }
        },
        {
          "expectation_type": "expect_column_values_to_be_of_type",
          "kwargs": {
            "column": "Salary",
            "type_": "int"
          }
        }
      ],
      "data_asset_type": "Dataset"
    }
```

6. Use the suite to evaluate data found in a CSV file. We will persist our Kaggle data to a CSV file and test that to make sure it still passes:

```
>>> kag_ge.to_csv('kag.csv')
>>> import json
>>> ge.validate(ge.read_csv('kag.csv'),
...       expectation_suite=json.load(
...           open('kaggle_expectations.json')))
{'results': [{'success': True,
    'expectation_config': {'expectation_type': 'expect_column_to_
exist',
      'kwargs': {'column': 'Salary'}},
```

```
              'exception_info': {'raised_exception': False,
               'exception_message': None,
               'exception_traceback': None}},
            {'success': True,
             'result': {'observed_value': 43869.66102793441,
              'element_count': 15429,
              'missing_count': 0,
              'missing_percent': 0.0},
             'expectation_config': {'expectation_type': 'expect_column_mean_
        to_be_between',
              'kwargs': {'column': 'Salary', 'min_value': 10000, 'max_
        value': 100000}},
              'exception_info': {'raised_exception': False,
               'exception_message': None,
               'exception_traceback': None}},
            {'success': True,
             'result': {'element_count': 15429,
              'missing_count': 0,
              'missing_percent': 0.0,
              'unexpected_count': 0,
              'unexpected_percent': 0.0,
              'unexpected_percent_nonmissing': 0.0,
              'partial_unexpected_list': []},
             'expectation_config': {'expectation_type': 'expect_column_
        values_to_be_between',
              'kwargs': {'column': 'Salary', 'min_value': 0, 'max_value':
        500000}},
              'exception_info': {'raised_exception': False,
               'exception_message': None,
               'exception_traceback': None}},
            {'success': True,
             'result': {'element_count': 15429,
              'unexpected_count': 0,
              'unexpected_percent': 0.0,
              'partial_unexpected_list': []},
             'expectation_config': {'expectation_type': 'expect_column_
        values_to_not_be_null',
```

```
              'kwargs': {'column': 'Salary'}},
         'exception_info': {'raised_exception': False,
          'exception_message': None,
          'exception_traceback': None}},
       {'success': True,
        'result': {'observed_value': 'int64'},
        'expectation_config': {'expectation_type': 'expect_column_
   values_to_be_of_type',
          'kwargs': {'column': 'Salary', 'type_': 'int'}},
        'exception_info': {'raised_exception': False,
          'exception_message': None,
          'exception_traceback': None}},
       {'success': True,
        'result': {'element_count': 15429,
          'missing_count': 0,
          'missing_percent': 0.0,
          'unexpected_count': 0,
          'unexpected_percent': 0.0,
          'unexpected_percent_nonmissing': 0.0,
          'partial_unexpected_list': []},
        'expectation_config': {'expectation_type': 'expect_column_
   values_to_match_regex',
          'kwargs': {'column': 'Country', 'regex': 'America|India|Anothe
   r|China'}},
        'exception_info': {'raised_exception': False,
          'exception_message': None,
          'exception_traceback': None}}],
    'success': True,
    'statistics': {'evaluated_expectations': 6,
     'successful_expectations': 6,
     'unsuccessful_expectations': 0,
     'success_percent': 100.0},
    'meta': {'great_expectations.__version__': '0.8.6',
     'data_asset_name': None,
     'expectation_suite_name': 'default',
     'run_id': '2020-01-08T214957.098199Z'}}
```

How it works...

The Great Expectations library extends a pandas DataFrame. You can use it to validate raw data, or data that you have used pandas to tweak. In our example, we showed how to create expectations for a DataFrame.

There are numerous built-in expectations that are listed in *step 3*. You can leverage those, or build a custom expectation if you desire. The result of validating the data is a JSON object with entries for "success". You can integrate these into a test suite to ensure that your data processing pipeline will work with new data.

Using pytest with pandas

In this section, we will show how to test your pandas code. We do this by testing the artifacts. We will use the third-party library, `pytest`, to do this testing.

For this recipe, we will not be using Jupyter, but rather the command line.

How to do it...

1. Create a project data layout. The `pytest` library supports projects laid out in a couple different styles. We will create a folder structure that looks like this:

```
kag-demo-pytest/
├── data
|   └── kaggle-survey-2018.zip
├── kag.py
└── test
    └── test_kag.py
```

The `kag.py` file has code to load the raw data and code to tweak it. It looks like this:

```python
import pandas as pd

import zipfile


def load_raw(zip_fname):
    with zipfile.ZipFile(zip_fname) as z:
        kag = pd.read_csv(z.open('multipleChoiceResponses.csv'))
        df = kag.iloc[1:]
```

```
        return df


def tweak_kag(df):
    na_mask = df.Q9.isna()
    hide_mask = df.Q9.str.startswith('I do not').fillna(False)
    df = df[~na_mask & ~hide_mask]

    q1 = (df.Q1
      .replace({'Prefer not to say': 'Another',
                'Prefer to self-describe': 'Another'})
      .rename('Gender')
    )
    q2 = df.Q2.str.slice(0,2).astype(int).rename('Age')
    def limit_countries(val):
        if val in  {'United States of America', 'India', 'China'}:
            return val
        return 'Another'
    q3 = df.Q3.apply(limit_countries).rename('Country')

    q4 = (df.Q4
      .replace({'Master\'s degree': 18,
      'Bachelor\'s degree': 16,
      'Doctoral degree': 20,
      'Some college/university study without earning a bachelor's
degree': 13,
      'Professional degree': 19,
      'I prefer not to answer': None,
      'No formal education past high school': 12})
      .fillna(11)
      .rename('Edu')
    )

    def only_cs_stat_val(val):
        if val not in {'cs', 'eng', 'stat'}:
            return 'another'
```

```
            return val


    q5 = (df.Q5
            .replace({
                'Computer science (software engineering, etc.)':
'cs',
                'Engineering (non-computer focused)': 'eng',
                'Mathematics or statistics': 'stat'})
            .apply(only_cs_stat_val)
            .rename('Studies'))
    def limit_occupation(val):
        if val in {'Student', 'Data Scientist', 'Software
Engineer', 'Not employed',
                    'Data Engineer'}:
            return val
        return 'Another'


    q6 = df.Q6.apply(limit_occupation).rename('Occupation')


    q8 = (df.Q8
      .str.replace('+', '')
      .str.split('-', expand=True)
      .iloc[:,0]
      .fillna(-1)
      .astype(int)
      .rename('Experience')
    )


    q9 = (df.Q9
      .str.replace('+','')
      .str.replace(',','')
      .str.replace('500000', '500')
      .str.replace('I do not wish to disclose my approximate yearly
compensation','')
      .str.split('-', expand=True)
      .iloc[:,0]
      .astype(int)
```

```
    .mul(1000)
     .rename('Salary'))
    return pd.concat([q1, q2, q3, q4, q5, q6, q8, q9], axis=1)
```

The `test_kag.py` file looks like this:

```
import pytest


import kag



@pytest.fixture(scope='session')
def df():
    df = kag.load_raw('data/kaggle-survey-2018.zip')
    return kag.tweak_kag(df)



def test_salary_mean(df):
    assert 10_000 < df.Salary.mean() < 100_000


def test_salary_between(df):
    assert df.Salary.min() >= 0
    assert df.Salary.max() <= 500_000


def test_salary_not_null(df):
    assert not df.Salary.isna().any()


def test_country_values(df):
    assert set(df.Country.unique()) == {'Another', 'United States
of America', 'India', 'China'}


def test_salary_dtype(df):
    assert df.Salary.dtype == int
```

2. Run the tests from the `kag-demo` directory. If you installed the `pytest` library, you will have a pytest executable. If you try to run that command you will get an error:

```
(env)$ pytest
=================== test session starts ===================
platform darwin -- Python 3.6.4, pytest-3.10.1, py-1.7.0,
```

```
pluggy-0.8.0
rootdir: /Users/matt/pandas-cookbook/kag-demo, inifile:
plugins: asyncio-0.10.0
collected 0 items / 1 errors


========================= ERRORS =========================
_____ ERROR collecting test/test_kag.py _____
ImportError while importing test module '/Users/matt/pandas-
cookbook/kag

demo/test/test_kag.py'.
Hint: make sure your test modules/packages have valid Python
names.
Traceback:
test/test_kag.py:3: in <module>
    import kag
E   ModuleNotFoundError: No module named 'kag'
!!!!!!!! Interrupted: 1 errors during collection !!!!!!!!
================ 1 error in 0.15 seconds ================
```

This error is because pytest wants to use installed code to run the tests. Because I
have not used `pip` (or another mechanism) to install `kag.py`, pytest complains that
it cannot find the module in locations where code is installed.

3. A workaround to help pytest find the `kag.py` file is to invoke pytest as a module. Run
    this command instead:

```
$ python -m pytest
=========================== test session starts
===========================
platform darwin -- Python 3.6.4, pytest-3.10.1, py-1.7.0,
pluggy-0.8.0
rootdir: /Users/matt/pandas-cookbook/kag-demo, inifile:
collected 5 items


test/test_kag.py .....
[100%]


=================== 5 passed, 1 warnings in 3.51 seconds
===================
```

Invoking pytest in this manner adds the current directory to the `PYTHONPATH` and
now the import for the `kag` module succeeds.

How it works...

Complete coverage of using the `pytest` library is beyond the scope of this book. However, the `test_kag.py` file contains tests specified so that pytest understands them. Any function name that begins with `test_` will be recognized as a test. The parameter to these test functions, `df`, is called a *fixture*.

Near the top of the file, I specified a function named `df` that was decorated with `@pytest.fixture(scope='session')`. This function will be called once when the test session begins. Any test function with the parameter named `df` will get the output of this function. The scope is specified as a *session* scope, so that the data is only loaded once (for the entire test session). If we did not specify the scope, the fixture scope would be at the function-level (the default). With function-level scope, the fixture would be executed once for every test function that uses it as a parameter, which makes the tests run in 12 seconds (instead of three on my machine).

There's more...

You can run Great Expectations test from pytest too. Add the following function to `test_kag.py` (You will need to update the path to the expectation suite):

```
def test_ge(df):
    import json
    import great_expectations as ge
    res = ge.validate(ge.from_pandas(df),
        expectation_suite=json.load(open('kaggle_expectations.json')))
    failures = []
    for exp in res['results']:
        if not exp['success']:
            failures.append(json.dumps(exp, indent=2))
    if failures:
        assert False, '\n'.join(failures)
    else:
        assert True
```

Generating tests with Hypothesis

The Hypothesis library is a third-party library for generating tests, or performing *property-based testing*. You create a *strategy* (an object that generates samples of data) and then run your code against the generated output of the strategy. You want to test an *invariant*, or something about your data that you presume to always hold true.

Again, there could be a book written solely about this type of testing, but in this section we will show an example of using the library.

We will show how to generate Kaggle survey data, then using that generated survey data, we will run it against the `tweak_kag` function and validate that the function will work on new data.

We will leverage the testing code found in the previous section. The Hypothesis library works with pytest, so we can use the same layout.

How to do it...

1. Create a project data layout. If you had the code from the previous section, add a `test_hypot.py` file and a `conftest.py` file:

kag-demo-hypo/

```
├── data
│   └── kaggle-survey-2018.zip
├── kag.py
└── test
    ├── conftest.py
    ├── test_hypot.py
    └── test_kag.py
```

2. We will put shared fixtures into `conftest.py`. This file is a special file that pytest looks for when trying to find fixtures. We do not need to import it, but any fixture defined in there can be used by the other test files.

   Move the fixture code from `test_kag.py` to `conftest.py` so that it has the following code. We will also do a little refactoring to create a `raw_` function that is not a fixture that we can call outside of tests:

```python
import pytest


import kag


@pytest.fixture(scope='session')
def raw():
    return raw_()


def raw_():
    return kag.load_raw('data/kaggle-survey-2018.zip')
```

```
@pytest.fixture(scope='session')
def df(raw):
    return kag.tweak_kag(raw)
```

Put the following code in `test_hypot.py`:

```
from hypothesis import given, strategies
from hypothesis.extra.pandas import column, data_frames


from conftest import raw_


import kag


def hypot_df_generator():
    df = raw_()
    cols = []
    for col in ['Q1', 'Q2', 'Q3', 'Q4', 'Q5', 'Q6', 'Q8', 'Q9']:
        cols.append(column(col, elements=strategies.sampled_
from(df[col].unique())))
    return data_frames(columns=cols)



@given(hypot_df_generator())
def test_countries(gen_df):
    if gen_df.shape[0] == 0:
        return
    kag_ = kag.tweak_kag(gen_df)
    assert len(kag_.Country.unique()) <= 4
```

The function `hypot_df_generator` constructs a Hypothesis search strategy. The search strategy can generate data of different types. We can manually create these strategies. In this case, I'm using the existing CSV file to populate the different values that are possible for the columns that I am interested in.

The function `test_countries` is a pytest test that is decorated with the `@ given(hypot_df_generator())` decorator. The decoration will pass a `gen_df` object into the test function. This object will be a DataFrame that complies with the specifications that the search strategy has. We can now test our invariants against that DataFrame. In this case, we will run the `tweak_kag` function and ensure that the number of unique countries in the `Country` column is less than or equal to four.

3. Go to the `kag_demo` directory and run the test. Here is a command to run only the `test_countries` test:

```
$ python -m pytest -k test_countries
```

The output looks like this:

```
======================= test session starts =======================
platform darwin -- Python 3.6.4, pytest-5.3.2, py-1.7.0,
pluggy-0.13.1
rootdir: /Users/matt/kag-demo
plugins: asyncio-0.10.0, hypothesis-5.1.2
collected 6 items / 5 deselected / 1 selected


test/test_hypot.py F                                        [100%]


============================ FAILURES ============================
_____ test_countries _____


    @given(hypot_df_generator())
>   def test_countries(gen_df):


test/test_hypot.py:19:
- - - - - - - - - - - - - - - - - - - - - - - - - - - - - - - -
test/test_hypot.py:23: in test_countries
    kag_ = kag.tweak_kag(gen_df)
kag.py:63: in tweak_kag
    q8 = (df.Q8
/Users/matt/.env/364/lib/python3.6/site-packages/pandas/core/
generic.py:5175: in
__getattr__
    return object.__getattribute__(self, name)
/Users/matt/.env/364/lib/python3.6/site-packages/pandas/core/
accessor.py:175: in
__get__
    accessor_obj = self._accessor(obj)
/Users/matt/.env/364/lib/python3.6/site-packages/pandas/core/
strings.py:1917: in __init__
    self._inferred_dtype = self._validate(data)
- - - - - - - - - - - - - - - - - - - - - - - - - - - - - - - -
```

```
data = Series([], Name: Q8, dtype: float64)


    @staticmethod
    def _validate(data):
        """

        Auxiliary function for StringMethods, infers and checks
dtype of data.
        This is a "first line of defence" at the creation of the
StringMethods-
        object (see _make_accessor), and just checks that the
dtype is in the
        *union* of the allowed types over all string methods
below; this
        restriction is then refined on a per-method basis using
the decorator
        @forbid_nonstring_types (more info in the corresponding
docstring).


        This really should exclude all series/index with any non-
string values,
        but that isn't practical for performance reasons until we
have a str
        dtype (GH 9343 / 13877)


        Parameters
        ----------
        data : The content of the Series


        Returns
        -------
        dtype : inferred dtype of data
        """
        if isinstance(data, ABCMultiIndex):
            raise AttributeError(
                "Can only use .str accessor with Index, " "not
MultiIndex"
            )
```

```
            # see _libs/lib.pyx for list of inferred types
        allowed_types = ["string", "empty", "bytes", "mixed",
"mixed-integer"]


        values = getattr(data, "values", data)  # Series / Index
        values = getattr(values, "categories", values)  #
categorical / normal


        try:
            inferred_dtype = lib.infer_dtype(values, skipna=True)
        except ValueError:
            # GH#27571 mostly occurs with ExtensionArray
            inferred_dtype = None


        if inferred_dtype not in allowed_types:
>           raise AttributeError("Can only use .str accessor with
string " "values!")
E           AttributeError: Can only use .str accessor with string
values!


/Users/matt/.env/364/lib/python3.6/site-packages/pandas/core/
strings.py:1967: AttributeError
----------------------- Hypothesis --------------------------
Falsifying example: test_countries(
    gen_df=        Q1     Q2                          Q3  ...
Q6  Q8   Q9
    0  Female  45-49  United States of America  ...  Consultant
NaN NaN

    [1 rows x 8 columns],
)
========== 1 failed, 5 deselected, 1 warning in 2.23s ===========
```

There is a lot of noise in the output, but if you scan through it you will find that it is complaining about the code that processes the column Q8. The reason for this is that it generated a single row with a NaN entry for Q8. If we run `tweak_kag` with this DataFrame, pandas infers that the Q8 column has a float type and errors out when trying to use the `.str` accessor.

Is this a bug? It's hard to give a definitive answer on that. But this shows that if our raw data has only missing values then our code will not work.

How it works...

The Hypothesis library tries to generate a span of data that conforms to a specification. You can use this generated data to test that invariants hold. In our case, we saw that the survey data had missing data. When we generated a DataFrame with a single row of missing data, our `tweak_kag` function did not work. The `.str` accessor only works if there is at least one string value in a column, and our column only had missing data (a float value).

We could address these issues and continue to test other invariants. This illustrates another point that comes up when programming. We get caught in the forest and only see specific trees. Sometimes we need to take a step back and look at things from a different perspective. Using Hypothesis is one way to do this.

Other Books You May Enjoy

If you enjoyed this book, you may be interested in these other books by Packt:

Artificial Intelligence with Python – Second Edition

Alberto Artasanchez, Prateek Joshi

ISBN: 978-1-83921-953-5

- Understand what artificial intelligence, machine learning, and data science are
- Explore the most common artificial intelligence use cases
- Learn how to build a machine learning pipeline
- Assimilate the basics of feature selection and feature engineering
- Identify the differences between supervised and unsupervised learning
- Discover the most recent advances and tools offered for AI development in the cloud
- Develop automatic speech recognition systems and chatbots
- Apply AI algorithms to time series data

Mastering Machine Learning Algorithms - Second Edition

Giuseppe Bonaccorso

ISBN: 978-1-83882-029-9

- Understand the characteristics of a machine learning algorithm
- Implement algorithms from supervised, semi-supervised, unsupervised, and RL domains
- Learn how regression works in time-series analysis and risk prediction
- Create, model, and train complex probabilistic models
- Cluster high-dimensional data and evaluate model accuracy
- Discover how artificial neural networks work – train, optimize, and validate them
- Work with autoencoders, Hebbian networks, and GANs

Leave a review - let other readers know what you think

Please share your thoughts on this book with others by leaving a review on the site that you bought it from. If you purchased the book from Amazon, please leave us an honest review on this book's Amazon page. This is vital so that other potential readers can see and use your unbiased opinion to make purchasing decisions, we can understand what our customers think about our products, and our authors can see your feedback on the title that they have worked with Packt to create. It will only take a few minutes of your time, but is valuable to other potential customers, our authors, and Packt. Thank you!

Leave a review - let other readers know what you think

Index